Shared Experiences
In
Human
Communication

Shared Experiences

In

Human

Communication

Edited by

STEWART L. TUBBS
and
ROBERT M. CARTER

General Motors Institute

HAYDEN BOOK COMPANY, INC.
Rochelle Park, New Jersey

To
Gail, Brian and Kelly
Phyllis, Kathy, Rick, Chris and John

Library of Congress Cataloging in Publication Data

Main entry under title:

Shared experiences in human communication.

   Includes bibliographies and index.
   1. Communication—Social aspects—Addresses, essays,
lectures.   2. Communication—Psychological aspects—
Addresses, essays, lectures.   3. Nonverbal communication
—Addresses, essays, lectures.   I. Tubbs, Stewart L.,
1943–   II. Carter, Robert M.
HM258.S414   301.14   77-15031
ISBN   0-8104-6089-0

1	2	3	4	5	6	7	8	9	PRINTING
78	79	80	81	82	83	84	85		YEAR

PREFACE

One of the frustrating things about writing a textbook is that authors often have to interpret and synthesize the ideas of hundreds of other authors for the student reader. On the other hand, one of the real thrills of editing a book of readings is being able to select some of the best writings of some of the best authors and *share* them with you in the original. Since selections contained in this book represent the *experiences* and insights of some of the best minds in our discipline, we decided to entitle the book *Shared Experiences*.

We used three criteria in choosing these selections. First, we wanted to share some classics which have withstood the test of time and still prove valuable. Second, we strongly preferred selections which were interesting, provocative and dealt with traditional communication topics in a novel way. Third, we required selections which represented the broad range of topics frequently included in a human communication course. The selections included herein meet one or more of those criteria.

We begin with two introductory essays written originally for this book. Chapter One consists of four selections on the process of human communication which offer you different but complementary theoretical viewpoints for analyzing communication events. Theoretical articles are by nature a bit heavy, but from Chapter Two on, you should find relatively smooth sailing. Chapters Two and Three contain selections dealing with verbal and nonverbal portions of communication, respectively.

Chapters Four through Eight examine the different contexts of communication namely, two-person, small group, public speaking, organizational and mass communication. We hope you have as much fun reading and discussing these selections as we have had choosing them, and that after reading this book, you will have a much greater appreciation and awareness of the complexity of this subject matter.

S.L.T.
R.M.C.

Flint, Michigan

CONTENTS

Shared Experiences
In
Human
Communication

I

Stewart L. Tubbs

A PSYCHOLOGICAL VIEW OF HUMAN COMMUNICATION

Let us examine a typical day for Cindy Coed. She arises in the morning and exchanges a few words with her roommate. That morning she attends a class in which the professor lectures. At lunch she meets with a group of friends to discuss the upcoming weekend events. Later she visits one of her professors to discuss the university's requirements for graduation in her major field. In the evening she watches the news on television before reading some homework for the next day's classes.

Cindy has just experienced five contexts of human communication. Her exchange with her roommate was *two-person* or dyadic communication. At lunch she engaged in *group communication*. In class she was the recipient of *public communication*. When discussing university graduation requirements with her prof she was involved in *organizational communication*. And when she watched TV and read her textbooks she was a participant in *mass communication*.

Most of us encounter these communication contexts on a daily basis. Two things typically result from this frequent experience. First, we become falsely confident that we know a great deal about communication. Second, we are sometimes confused, disappointed, frustrated, or angered by communication events which do not turn out to our satisfaction.

In this book we will be examining each of these five communication contexts in greater depth. But before looking at each context individually, let us identify some common elements which bind these contexts together.

A WORD ABOUT DEFINITIONS

Before proceeding further, we would like briefly to address the problem of definitions. Although you might think it a relatively simple task to define the word *communication,* Dance and Larson (1976) list 126 definitions which were taken from the literature. Although this is a very impressive list, it is only a representative list. The list is not exhaustive. Our point is that a great deal of attention can be paid to defining very meticulously a lot of technical terms related to topics in this book. However, for the purpose of this book, we prefer a rather brief treatment and we hope that as you read on, you will become more sophisticated with the terminology as you see it used by different authors.

We think a good definition is offered by Reusch and Bateson (1951):

. . . the concept of communication would include all those processes by which people influence one another. . . . This definition is based upon the premise that all actions and events have communicative aspects, as soon as they are perceived by a human being; it implies, furthermore, that such perception changes the information which an individual possesses and therefore influences him.

The most important element of this definition is that which identifies *all* actions and events as potentially communicative. This point will become more and more apparent throughout the book. In order to more thoroughly understand the pervasive influence of communication let us examine four communication axioms or laws which seem to be operating.

Axiom 1: You cannot not communicate

Suppose you decide that you do not want to communicate anything to anyone for a day. How would you do it? You would probably withdraw as much as possible—thus not talking to anyone. What if you were supposed to meet someone that day? What would your absence communicate? Perhaps that you were ill, or unreliable, or thoughtless for not phoning to tell them that you wouldn't be there. Obviously, we do not have to say anything—yet a message will be conveyed.

What about the situation in which you ask someone to go to a movie with you and they repeatedly say that they would really like to go but they can't because they have other plans. Sooner or later, in spite of their words, we "get the message" that they probably aren't interested.

Communication involves not only the verbal message (i.e., the person's words), but the nonverbal message as well. The lack of any contact when a person is supposed to meet with us nonverbally communicates something negative. The failure to go with us to the movie nonverbally communicates the message of disinterest. These examples illustrate what Keltner (1970) calls "mixed messages" where the verbal and nonverbal messages contradict one another.

No matter how hard we try, whether we say anything or not, it is impossible to not communicate. Watzlawick et al. (1967) show how this principle can manifest itself in the most extreme form, namely, the schizophrenic. They state that:

> . . . the schizophrenic tries *not to communicate*. But since even nonsense, silence, withdrawal, immobility (postural silence), or any other form of denial is itself a communication the schizophrenic is faced with the impossible task of denying that he is communicating at the same time denying that his denial is a communication.

This illustration leads us to a related issue—namely intentional versus unintentional communication. A good deal of our daily communication is consciously motivated. For example, if we want to impress a special person, we go out and buy a flattering item of clothing. However, we have all learned from the toothpaste and mouthwash commercials that the item of clothing may be communicating the intended positive message, while our bad breath or unsightly teeth are communicating a less desirable message unintentionally. Unintentional communication is certainly one of the most frustrating for the sender, for without some corrective feedback, we remain puzzled as to why the new clothing didn't get us the date, when in fact the clothing was not the issue at all. When we look at the combinations of verbal, nonverbal, intentional and unintentional communicative cues, a four cell matrix appears as in Figure 1.

Given all the possibilities for communicating with these four combinations of cues, we begin to see the validity of the axiom "you cannot not communicate."

	Intentional	Unintentional
Verbal	Verbal Intentional	Verbal Unintentional
Nonverbal	Nonverbal Intentional	Nonverbal Unintentional

Axiom 2: Communication involves both content and relationship aspects

Suppose we ask someone at a dinner table to pass us the salt. The *content* of this message is as it appears. However, in addition to this message, there is a message which has to do with the *relationship* between the two people involved. For comparison let us look at these ways of communicating basically the same content, but with three different relationship messages.

1. Pass the salt.
2. Pass the salt please.
3. Honey, would you pass the salt?

We believe that the first request is relatively lacking in relationship cues. However, request 2 adds a please which signals an element of politeness and possibly respect for the other person. The third request suggests a warmer, more intimate relationship than in the first two requests. As you can see, the content aspect of the message is the same in all three requests, while the relationship aspect differs. In fact, Reusch and Bateson (1951) observed that " . . . every courtesy term between persons, every inflection of voice denoting respect or contempt, condescension or dependency, is a statement about the relationship between the two persons."

Giffin and Patton (1971) offer an interesting point which helps illustrate the content and relationship aspects of communication. They state that nonverbal communication ultimately defines an interpersonal relationship.

. . . While language can be used to communicate almost anything, nonverbal behavior is rather limited in range. It is usually used to communicate feelings, likings and preferences and to reinforce or contradict the feelings that are communicated verbally. It may add a new dimension to the verbal message as when a salesman describes his product to a client and simultaneously conveys, nonverbally, the impression that he likes the client.

The relationship aspect of communication is critical in determining the ultimate effectiveness of the communication event. For example, if a boss and employee have a trusting relationship, the employee will be more likely to tell the boss when something goes wrong. However, if they have a hostile relationship, the employee will cover up his mistakes and distort communication to keep from possibly hurting himself. As Mellinger (1956) puts it, ". . . a primary goal of a distrusted person becomes the reduction of one's own anxiety, rather than the accurate transmission of ideas."

Watzlawick, et.al. (1967) clarify this point even further when they state that:

> . . . relationships are only rarely defined deliberately or with full awareness. In fact, it seems that the more spontaneous and "healthy" a relationship, the more the relationship aspect of communication recedes into the background. Conversely, "sick" relationships are characterized by a constant struggle about the nature of the relationship, with the content aspect of communication becoming less and less important.

Axiom 3: Communication may be either confirming or disconfirming

Growing out of earlier work by Reusch (1957, 1961) and Watzlawick et al. (1967), Sieburg and Larson (1971) have begun developing a theory around the confirming/disconfirming aspects of communication. They define these concepts in the following way: ". . . confirmation, as used in an interpersonal sense, refers to any behavior that causes another person to value himself more. Its opposite, disconfirmation, refers to any behavior that causes another person to value himself less."

The confirmation/disconfirmation literature has expanded within recent years. Dance and Larson (1972), Sieburg (1973, 1974, 1975), Cissna (1976), Dance and Larson (1976). While the basic thrust of the theory remains the same, i.e., that communication with others is potentially confirming or disconfirming, the specifics of the theory have been continually refined.

The latest work in this area, Dance and Larson (1976), divides communication patterns into four types:

(1) explicit rejection
(2) implicit rejection (both are disconfirming)
(3) explicit acceptance
(4) implicit acceptance (both are confirming)

Explicit rejection involves either a negative evaluation or an overt dismissal of the person or his message. For example:

A. "I can't understand how they can just sit on their duffs and not do anything about it. Time is running out."
B. "Yeah, well I don't see you doing anything about it."

Implicit rejection involves four more subtle types of disconfirmation.

1. Interruptions—when a speaker cuts you off in mid-sentence.
2. Imperviousness—when a speaker ignores what you say as if you had never said it.
3. Irrelevant response—when the speaker starts off on a totally unrelated topic in response to your initial comment.
4. Tangential response—when a person gives some acknowledgment to your initial comment, but immediately launches off on a new irrelevant topic.

Explicit acceptance involves a positive evaluation of either the person or his communication content. For example:

A. "So I just told him straight out that he wasn't going to pull that kind of stuff with me."
B. "That took balls."

Implicit acceptance involves either a direct acknowledgment of a person's remark, an attempt to clarify their remark by asking for more information, or an expression of positive feeling. For example:

A. "What I meant to say was that I've known him for a long time and I've never seen him do anything like that."
B. "Oh, well now I understand."

The importance of confirmation/disconfirmation literature lies in the specific identification of communication patterns which seem to help or hinder communication effectiveness in most any situation. Cissna (1976) in summarized studies in widely differing situations involving counselors-juvenile delinquents, spouses, fathers-sons, and supervisors-subordinates, found that the only factor which appeared in all these studies was the confirmation/disconfirmation factor. This evidence leads to the claim that this factor may be the most pervasive dimension in human communication.

Axiom 4: Communication can range from therapeutic to pathological

It is easy to see how axioms 1-3 can lead one to the conclusion that communication is related to a person's mental health. Communication which establishes and maintains a confirming set of relationships for a person can add substantially to that person's healthy outlook on life.

On the other hand, a long history of disconfirming communication and hostile relationships can and does cause severe damage to a person's mental health.

To be more specific, by a mentally healthy person we mean one who exhibits some of the following characteristics which have been identified by Levinson et al. (1962).

1. *They treat others as individuals.* They are sensitive to individual differences among people and are able to establish good relationships with others despite these differences.
2. *They are flexible under stress.* Stress includes both internal and external environmental pressures which threaten to disrupt the organized way in which a person customarily behaves.
3. *They obtain gratification from a wide variety of sources.* These include people, tasks, ideas, interests, and values.
4. *They accept their own capacities and limitations.* They have a realistic self-concept, neither overvaluing or undervaluing their potentialities.
5. *They are active and productive.* They use their capacities in the interest of their own self-fulfillment and in the service of others. This differs from a neurotically driven need to achieve.

Given these characteristics, the question becomes, "What situations bring about such mentally healthy characteristics?" Reusch (1961) refers to these situations as involving *therapeutic communication.* He states,

. . . a child can be therapeutic for the mother and a boss can be therapeutic for his employee; therapy is done all day long by many people who do not know that they act as therapists, and many people benefit from such experiences without knowing it. Therapeutic communication is not a method invented by physicians to combat illness; it is simply something that occurs spontaneously everywhere in daily life, and the physician is challenged to make these naturally occurring events happen more frequently.

Barnlund (1968) differentiates between therapeutic and destructive communication in the following way,

. . . Interpersonal communications are destructive when they leave participants more vulnerable than before to the strains of future interactions; they are neutral when they add information but do not affect underlying values or attitudes; they are regarded as therapeutic when they provoke personal insight or reorientation, and when they enable persons to participate in more satisfying ways in future social encounters.

Tubbs and Baird (1976) summarize the literature in identifying eight factors which are conducive to healthy relationships. These are:

1. demonstrate a willingness to become involved with another;
2. communicate a sincere warm regard for one another;
3. demonstrate the capacity and desire to listen;
4. develop empathy for the other person's feelings and point of view;
5. exhibit tolerance, permissiveness, and supportiveness for the other person's individuality, even though it might be different;
6. develop an appropriate level of openness in revealing genuine feelings;
7. demonstrate a willingness to trust one another;
8. accept partial responsibility for misunderstandings and seek to correct them.

At the opposite end of the continuum we find communication patterns which are so disturbed as to warrant the label *pathological.* People who manifest these behaviors have themselves been the recipient of unhealthy communication during their developmental years. In other words, pathological communication to some extent caused their mental illness, and is also the symptom they manifest as their reaction.

Pathological communication is often described as *inappropriate.* Reusch (1957) describes the phenomenon this way,

. . . Either it does not fit the circumstance or it is irrelevant and is not matched to the initial statement. The reply may be exaggerated, as in the case of the person who explodes or is visibly upset when asked a polite question; or it may be overwhelming, as it is to a child who asks for a utensil and is immediately given a whole battery of implements.

A more severe form of inappropriateness occurs with the person suffering from a form of neurosis called *hysteria.* A person may develop hysterical blindness or paralysis for which there is no physical cause. In other words, the malady is psychologically induced. The person is trying to communicate in a very crude nonverbal way that he wants attention and needs help. The same is often true of the person who repeatedly attempts suicide. Sexual secondary impotence and frigidity are other types of nonverbal messages indicating psychological disturbances. For lack of a better term, these communication attempts may be called *protocommunication* (prototypes of communication). They are crude substitutes for the real thing, just as a prototype is a relatively simplified version of a real machine.

Undoubtedly the most severe forms of pathological communication occur among psychotics. Catatonics sit or stand in statue-like poses in a perpetual state of withdrawal. Hebephrenic schizophrenics make up their own language so that no one else can understand their "word salad" form of speech. Manic-depressives rant and rave and bang their heads against the walls only to change into periods of deep depression and melancholia. The paranoid will suffer from delusions of grandeur and imagine that he is Christ or Napoleon and that everyone is plotting to kill him because of their jealousy. Finally, the schizophrenics who imagine they hear voices and who may also have visual hallucinations use these methods to withdraw from normal contact with other human beings since previous contacts have been too painful to continue. It is easy to see that communication does indeed range all the way from therapeutic to pathological.

OVERVIEW OF THE TEXT

The text is organized into eight major chapters. There is an introduction with two original essays, one outlining some fundamental concepts of human communication and the other describing a method for analyzing human communication events—namely transactional analysis.

Chapter 1 contains articles which elaborate on some basic issues in human communication.

Chapter 2 focuses on the verbal cues which we mentioned briefly in this essay.

Chapter 3 deals with the highly provocative topic of nonverbal communication.

The second half of the book examines five different communication contexts.

Chapter 4 examines the two-person or dyadic context.

Chapter 5 focuses on communication within the small group.

Chapter 6 discusses the public communication context.

Chapter 7 is devoted to organizational communication.

Chapter 8 concludes with a discussion of mass communication.

REFERENCES

Barker, Larry L. and Robert J. Kibler (eds.). *Speech Communication Behavior: Perspectives and Principles.* Englewood Cliffs, N.J.: Prentice-Hall, 1971.

Barnlund, Dean C. *Interpersonal Communication: Survey and Studies.* Boston: Houghton Mifflin, 1968.

Cissna, Kenneth. "Interpersonal Confirmation: A Review of Current Theory and Research." A paper presented at the annual convention of the Central States Speech Association, Chicago, April, 1976.

Dance, Frank E. X. and Carl E. Larson. *Speech Communication: Concepts and Behavior.* New York: Holt, Rinehart and Winston, 1972.

Dance, Frank E. X. and Carl E. Larson. *The Functions of Human Communication: A Theoretical Approach.* New York: Holt, Rinehart and Winston, 1976.

Giffin, Kim and Bobby R. Patton. *Fundamentals of Interpersonal Communication.* New York: Harper and Row, 1971.

Keltner, John. *Interpersonal Speech Communication.* Belmont, Cal.: Wadsworth, 1970.

Levinson, H. C. et al. *Men, Management and Mental Health.* Cambridge, Mass.: Harvard University Press, 1962.

Mellinger, Glen D. "Interpersonal Trust as a Factor in Communication," *Journal of Abnormal and Social Psychology, 52,* 1956, p. 304.

Reusch, Jurgen and Gregory Bateson. *Communication: The Social Matrix of Psychiatry.* New York: Norton, 1951.

Reusch, Jurgen. *Disturbed Communication: The Clinical Assessment of Normal and Pathological Communicative Behavior.* New York: Norton, 1957.

Reusch, Jurgen. *Therapeutic Communication.* New York: Norton, 1961.

Sieburg, Evelyn and Carl E. Larson. "Dimensions of Interpersonal Response." A paper presented at the annual convention of the International Communication Association, Phoenix, April, 1971.

Sieburg, Evelyn. "Interpersonal Confirmation: Conceptualization and Measurement." A paper presented at the annual convention of the International Communication Association, Montreal, April, 1973.

Sieburg, Evelyn. "Confirming and Disconfirming Communication in an Organizational Context," *Personnel Women, 18,* 1974, 4-11.

Sieburg, Evelyn. *Interpersonal Confirmation: A Paradigm for Conceptualization and Measurement.* San Diego: United States International University, 1975.

Tubbs, Stewart L. and Sylvia Moss. *Human Communication* (2nd Ed.). New York: Random House, 1977.

Tubbs, Stewart L. and John W. Baird. *The Open Person: Self-Disclosure and Personal Growth.* Columbus, Ohio: Merrill, 1976.

Watzlawick, Paul, Janet Helmich Beavin, and Dan D. Jackson. *Pragmatics of Human Communication: A Study of Interaction Patterns, Pathologies, and Paradoxes.* New York: Norton, 1967.

Watzlawick, Paul, John Weakland, and Richard Fisch. *Change: Principles of Problem Formation and Problem Resolution.* New York: Norton, 1974.

Weaver, Carl H. and Warren L. Strausbaugh. *Fundamentals of Speech Communication.* New York: American Book Company, 1964.

II
Robert M. Carter

A TRANSACTIONAL ANALYSIS VIEW OF HUMAN COMMUNICATION

We can explore the field of communication by many avenues, one being Transactional Analysis. In this section we first define Transactional Analysis (TA) and later look at how each of this reader's remaining chapters appear in a "TA" frame of reference: fundamentals, verbal, nonverbal, two-person, small group, public, organizational, and mass communication.

I. DEFINITION

The TA model gives a way to "take a picture" of ourselves, of others, and of some human systems as well. All of this results in a psychological "glimpse" at "innards." Unlike a conventional photo, the picture may reveal deeper elements, even different from an X-ray view. Rather than show skin, hair, bone or fiber, a "TA camera" focuses on ego states labeled the Parent (P), Adult (A), and Child (C), always capitalized and usually represented as three vertical circles with edges touching. Eric Berne[1] created TA.

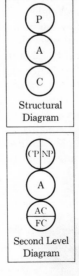

Structural
Diagram

Second Level
Diagram

---

[1] A practicing psychoanalyst, Berne adapted much of his original basic TA theory from Sigmund Freud's work. In contrast with Freud's construct of the superego, ego, and id, in which only the ego functions at the conscious level, Berne's concept of the Parent, Adult, and Child suggests that all three states can function at the level of consciousness.

A. Ego States

To understand ego states, think of energy flow—inside Tom Student's brain and body. Suppose Tom feels judgmental about rainy weather, a political personality, or a pal who has "bugged" him. His judgmental attitude's energy flows from his Parent ego state, actually from his Critical Parent state (CP).

At other times, Tom may caress and care for another person, maybe a youngster, thus activating another phase of his Parent ego state—his Nurturing Parent (NP).

Parent ego state does not refer to his dad and mom (separate people); it means instead a portion of his individual total self. Tom's conscience "resides" here along with his fathering or parenting needs. Together, his CP and NP form his Parent consisting of a sort of recording, similar to a cassette tape recording, storing everything he saw or heard the big people doing when he was a tiny person, from birth to age five.

A lot of the time, Tom functions very differently, much as a computer responding to the data of the outside world, making note of such information as:

A healthy human body averages a temperature of about 37 degrees Celsius or 99 degrees Fahrenheit.
The month of January has 31 days.

Such observations originate in Tom's Adult (A). The Adult has no capacity for feeling as it can deal only with measurable information. It developed approximately during the time Tom was 10 months and 12 years of age. He thinks with the Adult.

At still other times, Tom will respond differently to what happens. Sometimes he has a long face and sighs or clenches his teeth and scowls, or laughs heartily, thus experiencing feelings and discovering his Child (C) ego state. If Tom's feeling comes spontaneously "straight from the gut," we call it Tom's Free Child (FC) or Natural Child state.

On the other hand, if Tom only appears to have certain feelings in order somehow to please other people, we say that his Adapted Child (AC) has the focus of his energy.

The Child ego state stores up everything Tom felt about what happened to him between birth and roughly six years of age. Such "recorded" feelings may have no words attached to them, only sensations of one of your possible feelings: fear, sadness, anger, or joy.

B. Life Positions

When life runs smoothly for Candy Scholar, she feels "OK," gets on well within herself and with others, too. She does not commence huge tasks which she can never accomplish, nor hold a load of guilt inside because of past errors. She also enjoys associating with Tom and other people, feeling warm just having them around.

At other times, she weakens herself by dwelling on fears and guilt, she feels "not OK." Either she itches to get away from others so she can "suffer in silence," or she temporarily makes life miserable for those close by with direct or subtle insults.

TA life positions follow.

I'm OK, you're OK.
I'm not OK, you're OK.
I'm OK, you're not OK.
I'm not OK, you're not OK.

According to this theory, we all emerged from our mothers' wombs without significant previous programming; however, by age five or six, we made a decision about which life position to take. Eric Berne estimates that the overwhelming majority of us chose "I'm not OK, you're OK," and that very few took "I'm OK, you're OK." Thus the "both OK" view becomes the goal of serious students of TA.

The "I'm OK, you're not OK" position apparently belongs to *some* evangelists (God and I versus you and the devil), and the "I'm not OK, you're not OK" position describes another small percentage, mainly criminals and psychopaths, who see no hope for anybody.

Candy feels all four of these ways for fleeting moments, but this theory concerns where she "finds herself" most of the time. Sometimes she "puts on a happy face," but somehow feels sad at the same time.

Another way to look at life positions involves winning and losing. If a person wins in life, she experiences more "OKness" than "notOKness." The opposite applies to the loser. Of course Candy, just as each of us, needs to define "winning" to match personal values.

C. Strokes

If Tom says genuinely to a friend, "You're great, and I really enjoy you," he has given an unconditional positive stroke to that person. Since Tom does this with words, it becomes a "verbal" stroke.

A gentle touch (physical stroke) at the right moment may do as much or more. Think of a mother caressing her baby, a father embracing his son, or two lovers holding hands. Such unconditional positive strokes happen infrequently compared with the other three kinds of strokes, listed in order from most beneficial to most destructive.

Unconditional Positive (unlimited, total encouragement)
Conditional Positive (a pat on the back, with reservations)
Conditional Negative (a put down, with reservations)
Unconditional Negative (unlimited, total put down)

In giving a conditional positive stroke, Tom selects out one item for praise, thus suggesting that other items fall short of praiseworthy:

"You did a good job of pitching in the third inning." (only the third?)
"Your shirt looks clean." (what of trousers?)

Conditional negative strokes focus on one behavior supposedly to "help" the hearer:

"You're three days behind your schedule."
"That speech you gave had no conclusion."

Unconditional negative strokes have a decidedly destructive effect:

"You're a failure and always have been."
"You stink."

Notice both comments suggest "all the time"; "You stink ALL THE TIME."

Do you see how only a few unconditional negative strokes from both mother and father can make a little person decide, "I'm not OK"?

D. Transactions

A transaction means an everyday human interaction usually explained with ego state models. Tom and Candy talk together. He asks "What time is it?" (Arrow 1) She answers "It's three o'clock." (Arrow 2) These two remarks, the question and reply, make up a "complementary transaction." The second one completes the exchange intended by the first. Tom learns the correct time from Candy.

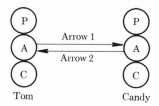

Other complementary transactions include these.

> *Tom:* "Are you ready to catch the bus?" (Arrow 1)
> *Candy:* "Sure. Let's go." (Arrow 2)
> *Tom:* "I'm going to relax." (Arrow 1)
> *Candy:* "I'm going to relax." (Arrow 2)

TA COMMUNICATION PRINCIPLE NUMBER 1: As long as the arrows remain parallel, communication can continue indefinitely.

So far, the examples of transactions involve only the Adult ego states, but this principle applies with other states as well.

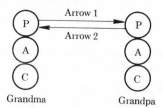

> *Candy's Grandma:* "Isn't it terrible
> what tiny swimming suits people wear
> now?"
> (Arrow 1)
> *Candy's Grandpa:* "Yes! positively indecent."
> (Arrow 2)

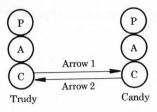

Trudy   Candy

Trudy: "Wow! This sunlight
          makes the whole world pretty."
          (Arrow 1)
Candy: "Yeah! And it feels
          warm, too."
          (Arrow 2)

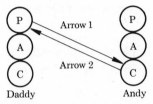

Daddy   Andy

Tom's dad: "I love you, Andy."
          (Arrow 1)
Tom's three-year-old brother Andy:
          "I love you, too, Daddy."
          (Arrow 2)

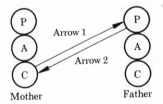

Mother   Father

Candy's mother: "This thunderstorm
          scares me."
          (Arrow 1)
Candy's father: "I'll hold you so
          you won't be so scared."
          (Arrow 2)

Unfortunately, not all transactions go smoothly and complement each other as these do. Consider the next one:

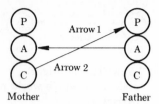

Candy's mother: "This thunderstorm
        scares me."
        (Arrow 1)
Candy's father: "Be sensible. We
        are inside a dry house."
        (Arrow 2)

The first TA principle of communication holds here. The arrows are not parallel, therefore communication as Candy's mother intended it has to stop.

TA COMMUNICATION PRINCIPLE NUMBER 2: If one arrow crosses another, or if more than two ego states enter the transaction, communication changes direction.

Another example of crossed arrows follows:

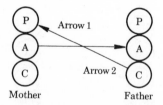

Tom's mother: "Where did you put
        the car keys?"
        (Arrow 1)
Tom's dad: "Wouldn't you like to
        know?"
        (Arrow 2)

Since Mom's original intention, learning the whereabouts of the keys, has been frustrated, she has to initiate communication in a different direction. She may switch to her Critical Parent state and shout, "Now you tell me where those keys are right now!" (not modeled). Or, she may switch and respond to her hubby's Free Child remark with her own Free Child by saying nothing but instead tickling him playfully and laughing (not modeled). Either way, communication changes direction.

Berne labels situations with crossed arrows "crossed transactions" because one arrow does cross another. Most such transactions produce TA games. In addition, "ulterior transactions," exchanges with both social (apparent) and psychological (hidden) levels, produce TA games.

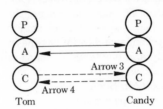

Tom   Candy

Social Level—
> *Tom:* "Will you come over to see my new apartment's decoration?"
> (Arrow 1)

Candy: "Yes. Apartment decor really interests me."
> (Arrow 2)

Psychological Level—
> *Tom:* Will you fool around?"
> (Arrow 3)

Candy: "Sure, I'll fool around."
> (Arrow 4)

TA COMMUNICATION PRINCIPLE NUMBER 3: What really happens if a transaction goes on at the psychological level?

Berne maintains that those who engage in crossed or ulterior transactions, although often unaware of their behavior, really play TA games with others. He identifies many games in the book *Games People Play.* Karpman notes that repetitive game patterns produce rackets which many use, consciously or not, to sustain feelings of anger or sadness most of the time.

Favorite games (identified by Woollams, Brown, and Huige) to maintain oneself in mad or sad rackets follow:

ANGER RACKET GAMES	SADNESS RACKET GAMES
If it weren't for you	Kick me
See what you made me do	Poor me
NIGYSOB (Now I've got you, you son of a bitch)	Stupid me

The anger games are played from a persecutor's position, and the sadness racket games from a victim's position. Consult the bibliography at the end of this section for further details on these sources.

E. Time Structuring

Between birth and death, we human beings control how we spend our time to a great extent. We use time six ways arranged here in order from the least to greatest risk.

1. Withdrawal—Sometimes Candy wants nobody around her, so she goes off somewhere by herself. Other times, when in a group, she temporarily withdraws into her own thoughts, as in a classroom during a boring lecture. She spends several hours a week in this way. Do you?
2. Rituals—Tom passes a friend in the corridor and says "Hi." His friend replies "Hi." After 50 such exchanges, the two have established a ritual behavior. Tom's worship in his church involves more elaborate rituals. Actually Tom spends a lot of time in ritual behavior. Do you?
3. Pastimes—Candy and her female friends often discuss new clothing styles and recipes while Tom and his male friends rap about car problems and football. Such behavior involves no real closeness or risk. Do you do some pastiming?
4. Activities—Almost everyone, including Tom and Candy, spend considerable time in activities such as working or practicing hobbies. Although more risky than pastiming, activities usually involve no intimacy. Do you engage in many activities?
5. Games and Rackets—People "collect" payoffs of bad feelings (sadness, anger, or fear) from games and rackets. Usually involving only two persons, games do involve greater risk than pastimes or activities. Even Candy and Tom sometimes play TA games. Do you?
6. Intimacy—If Candy and Tom have some time alone together, and neither structures the time in any of the five ways listed above on this list, they probably achieve true game-free intimacy. Then they really value one another's friendship. They may not touch each other at all, or they may. But each shares with the other actual unguarded statements about thoughts and feelings on life in general, fears, joys, and anything else they want to. Each listens carefully and makes no judgmental remark. Many people wish they had more time for true intimacy.

F. Scripts

Still another TA concept suggests that each person has a life plan to be lived out always based on the original life-position decision (I'm OK, etc.).

Type 1—Winner's Script
Type 2—Loser's Script
Type 3—Banal Script

A winner enjoys life most of the time, taking pleasure in eating good food, visiting companions, and working at a rewarding task. Many happy, successful people follow such a script.

A loser feels out of tune with most of the world's people, seeing life as a veil of tears or one long grind with little or no enjoyment. Some end up in mental hospitals, some in prisons with bars, but the vast majority in prisons created from their own imaginings. Ever hear of a "born loser"?

A banal script fits the person who plods sluggishly through life, somehow existing from one meal to the next, one day to another, and so on, ad nauseam. Certain housewives with small children fit this script as well as some business persons moving robot-like to and from the office, the car, and the bed.

Both Candy and Tom have winners' scripts.

II. TA AND COMMUNICATION FUNDAMENTALS

Both TA and the communicating of ideas appear very simple on the surface but entail great complexity. A glance at the TA transaction models and the three TA communication principles suggests much in common with the communication axioms covered in the previous section of this book.

Communication theory proclaims that the message sent does not always match the message received. TA theory supports this and adds that not only the receiver but also the sender of a message may have almost no understanding of the message he or she sends because of lack of awareness of which ego state the energy comes from.

III. TA AND VERBAL COMMUNICATION

Ulterior transactions usually involve spoken words used to insure misunderstanding or produce "hard feelings." However, an absence of games means parallel, complementary transactions and honest exchanges of straight messages.

If Professor Sly uses hard-to-understand words in lectures, he really wants to make the students feel stupid, but he may not admit it, even to himself. His need for parenting has most of his energy.

IV. TA AND NONVERBAL COMMUNICATION

Nonverbal cues provide one of the surest indicators of ego states. A pointing index finger, furrowed brow and shaking head signal Critical Parent.

Outstretched arms and a gentle smile say Nurturing Parent.

A thoughtful alert facial expression with upright posture indicate Adult.

Spontaneous, unpredictable movements with a happy expression radiate Free Child.

And finally, a sad pout and hunched shoulders telegraph Adapted Child.

In ulterior transactions, the social level message moves by verbal means, but the actual (psychological) message, moves by nonverbal signals. Such strokes may mean more than verbal ones. Can you think of any instances where this was true for you?

V. TA AND TWO-PERSON COMMUNICATION

Nearly all of this TA material falls within the two-person model of interaction. You noticed how circle models involved two people. Review the transactions between Candy, Tom, and their relatives and friends to see this clearly.

VI. TA AND SMALL-GROUP COMMUNICATION

Many authoritarian leaders remain in the Parent ego state most of the time. Leaders who allow group members to participate meaningfully in decision making stay in the Adult a lot of the time. And those designated as leaders who really do not perform the functions of leadership, but merely "play at it," operate mainly in the Child state.

Group members often structure large blocks of time in pastiming rather than seriously on tasks.

VII. TA AND PUBLIC COMMUNICATION

Imagine that as Candy sits in a lecture room, Professor Nora Dripp speaking up front holds her body rigidly upright so that she must look downward at the students' eyes. Dripp may have a need to parent students, and her gaze makes them feel put down or not OK.

That same class hour finds Tom in a different classroom listening intently as Professor Ann Warmz stands comfortably conversing up front with head inclined naturally so that her eyes line up with the eyes of the students. Tom feels at ease and OK.

Later in the day, Tom experiences confusion when smiling lecturer Al Chamelio says to the class, "Now this assignment has great importance." Tom wonders, "Shall I believe his smile, suggesting fun and play or his somewhat serious words"? He probably believes the nonverbal message over the verbal one.

VIII. TA AND ORGANIZATIONAL COMMUNICATION

Tom's dad works for a Mr. Boss Bemis whom he really likes and respects. Bemis does a good job of managing the people in a business office because he can "read" employees' ego states accurately and respond appropriately to them.

Bemis knows, for example, that Mary Secretary usually stays in her Adapted Child ego state; therefore, he parents her gently, never taking advantage of her weakness.

He realizes that Sam, Tom's dad, a dependable supervisor, prides himself on accuracy and attention to detail. As a result, Bemis works with Sam on an Adult to Adult basis.

Bemis also sees that Oliver Preach enjoys parenting younger employees, showing them how to perform difficult tasks. In exchanges with Oliver, Bemis always listens to some sage advice (seldom acting on it) before dealing with business matters.

Some organizations have losers' scripts just as people do. They may do well for a decade and fail, possibly because the top operating officer subconsciously hires people who will allow the business to falter.

You may know of some paternalistic organizations having presidents who treat all employees as their children. Such an executive may give employees very minimal responsibility so that he or she can "look after them." His or her Nurturing Parent state has control.

Corporations in existence for 50, 100 or more years doubtless have winners' scripts.

IX. TA AND MASS COMMUNICATION

Editor Rigid of the *Daily Trombone* allows only political statements harmonious with his view of government to appear in his newspaper. He parents his readers, "protecting" them from undesirable messages. On a national scale, Editor Rigid becomes Pravda, the news-control agency for the USSR.

Consider the variety of TV commercials targeted on you. Some attempt to parent (Ma tells daughter to use Blah soap). Others aim at your Free Child spontaneity (Fly to Fun Island). Very few offer adult messages.

Remember, TA offers only one way to view the field of communication. Be aware that many others exist.

BIBLIOGRAPHY

Berne, Eric. *Games People Play,* New York: Grove Press, 1964.

Ernst, Ken. *Games Students Play and What to Do About Them,* Millbrae, California: Celestial Arts, 1972.

Goldhaber, Gerald M. and Goldhaber, Marylynn B. *Transactional Analysis; Principles and Applications,* Boston: Allyn and Bacon, 1976.

Harris, Thomas A. *I'm OK—You're OK,* New York: Avon Books, 1973.

James, Muriel. *The OK Boss,* Reading, Massachusetts: Addison-Wesley, 1975.

James, Muriel and Jongeward, Dorothy. *The People Book; TA for Students,* Menlo Park, California: Addison-Wesley, 1975.

Jongeward, Dorothy and Contributors. *Everybody Wins; TA Applied to Organizations,* Reading, Massachusetts: Addison-Wesley, 1973.

Meininger, Jut. *Success Through TA,* New York: Grosset and Dunlap, 1973.

Novey, Theodore B. *Making Life Work; TA and Management,* Sacramento, California: Jalmar Press, 1973.

Woollams, Stanley, Brown, Michael, and Huige, Kristyn. *TA in Brief,* Ann Arbor, Michigan: Huron Valley Institute, 1975.

FUNDAMENTAL CONCEPTS OF HUMAN COMMUNICATION 1

In the first article Johnson makes a persuasive case in favor of learning to improve human communication skills. He focuses on interpersonal skills which will help us in our daily communication activities. He also outlines a five-step process for learning a new communication skill.

In the second and third articles the authors discuss some basic but profound issues related to communication theory. Barnlund talks about a meaning-centered philosophy of communication. That is, a philosophy which emphasizes the importance of creating meanings in the mind of a receiver which are consistent with those we intended to send. Note specifically his point that communication is irreversible and unrepeatable. Try to think of situations in your experience in which this has been true. Westley and MacLean focus their discussion of communication around a conceptual model. Although communication models are a dime a dozen, this one has stood the test of time. Also their discussion is particularly relevant since they discuss communication across contexts which range from face to face to mass as we do throughout this book.

Gibb's article on defensive communication is one of the best available on the subject. This article extends the idea that communication involves both content and relationship aspects. It also offers specific evidence on how to be confirming (supportive climate) as opposed to disconfirming (defensive climate). As Gibb points out, the applications of these concepts are numerous.

David W. Johnson

THE IMPORTANCE OF INTERPERSONAL SKILLS

One of the most distinctive aspects of being alive is the potential for joy, fun, excitement, caring, warmth, and personal fulfillment in your relationships with other people. Making new friends, deepening ongoing relationships, even falling in love, depend upon your interpersonal skills. Much of human society and human action seems based upon the liking people have for each other. The words which name degrees of interpersonal attraction, such as *like, love, dislike,* and *hate,* are among the most frequently used words in the English language. Because man is a social animal, most of his happiness and fulfillment rests upon his ability to relate effectively to other humans. In addition, the foundations of all civilizations rest upon man's ability to cooperate with other humans and to coordinate his actions with theirs. We are dependent upon other people for much of our personal happiness and fulfillment, and we must work effectively with other people in order to engage in our vocations and avocations competently. There is no way to overemphasize the importance of interpersonal skills in our lives.

What makes us human is the way in which we interact with other people. To the extent that our relationships reflect concern, friendship, love, caring, helping, kindness, and responsiveness we are becoming more human. To the extent that our relationships reflect the opposite of such qualities as these we are becoming more inhuman. It is the cruelty to and the destruction of other people that we label inhumane; it is the positive involvement with other people which we label humane.

Effective interpersonal skills do not just happen, nor do they appear magically; they are learned. The purpose of this essay is to help you increase your skills in initiating, developing, and maintaining effective, fulfilling relationships with other people. For those of us whose work requires a great deal of interaction with other people (such as teachers, counselors, supervisors, social workers), the ability to relate to other individuals in productive and meaningful ways is a necessity. For those of us who feel that our growth and development as a person depend upon the quality of our personal friendships, the skills involved in creating such relationships are a necessity. This book is aimed at helping you to increase your interpersonal skills whether in order to improve your job performance or to find greater satisfaction in your friendships. Increasing those skills will also lead to an increasing capacity to be human.

SELF-ACTUALIZATION

The rapid technological change we have been experiencing for the past several decades has resulted in rapid cultural change within our society.

David W. Johnson, *Reaching Out: Interpersonal Effectiveness and Self-Actualization,* © 1972, pp. 1-7. Reprinted by permission of Prentice-Hall, Inc., Englewood Cliffs, New Jersey.

Our culture seems to be changing from an emphasis on achievement to an emphasis upon self-actualization, from self-control to self-expression, from independence to interdependence, from endurance of stress to a capacity for joy, from full employment to full lives. The values of our society seem to be changing from an achievement-oriented, puritanical emphasis to a self-actualizing emphasis on the development of personal resources and the experiencing of joy and a sense of fulfillment in one's life. Mobility has become a hallmark of our society; the people we know and love today may be hundreds of miles away tomorrow. Several times in our lives we may be faced with beginning new relationships with a group of people whom we don't know. The ability to develop relationships which actualize our personal resources and in which we experience joy and a sense of fulfillment is becoming more and more crucial. The ability to initiate and terminate relationships is becoming more and more of a necessity.

Many psychologists believe that there is a drive for an organism to actualize its potentialities, that is, a drive towards self-actualization. Whether or not there is such a drive, it is apparent that self-actualization is an increasingly important concern for many people. Self-actualization consists primarily of being *time-competent,* that is, of having the ability to tie the past and the future to the present in meaningful continuity while fully living in the present. The self-actualized person appears to be less burdened by guilts, regrets, and resentments from the past than is the nonself-actualizing person, and his aspirations are tied meaningfully to present working goals.

Self-actualization is also dependent upon being autonomous. In order to understand autonomy it is necessary to differentiate between inner and other directedness. The *inner-directed person* adopted early in life a small number of values and principles which he rigidly adheres to no matter what the situation in which he finds himself is like. The *other-directed person* receives guidance and direction from the people he relates to; his behavior conforms rigidly to whatever is necessary to gain the approval of other people. The *autonomous person* is liberated from rigid adherence to parental values or to social presures and expectancies. He flexibly applies his values and principles in order to behave in ways appropriate to the situations he is in.

The time-competence and the autonomy of the self-actualizing person are related in the sense that a person who lives primarily in the present relies more upon his own support and expressiveness than does a person living primarily in the past or in the future. To live fully in the present means that you must be autonomous of both rigid inner values and excessive needs to conform to social prescriptions to obtain approval from other people.

Self-actualization is achieved through relating to other people in time-competent and autonomous ways. A person's interpersonal skills are the foundation for his self-actualization. Whether we are aged 6, 16, or 60, the level of our interpersonal skills largely determines how effective and happy we are. In the following section the specific skills involved in creating self-actualizing relationships will be discussed.

INTERPERSONAL SKILLS

To initiate, develop, and maintain effective and fulfilling relationships certain basic skills must be present. These skills generally fall into four areas: (1) knowing and trusting each other, (2) accurately and unambiguously understanding each other, (3) influencing and helping each other, and (4) constructively resolving problems and conflicts in your relationship.

The first area of skill development involves self-disclosure, self-awareness, self-acceptance, and trust. There must be a high level of trust between you and the other person in order for you to get to know each other. Getting to know each other involves disclosing how you are reacting to and feeling about what is presently taking place. Such openness depends upon your self-awareness and your self-acceptance; if you are unaware of your feelings and reactions you cannot communicate them to another person and if you cannot accept your feelings and reactions you will try to hide them.

The second area of skill development focuses upon being able to communicate your ideas and feelings accurately and unambiguously. Especially important is the communication of warmth and liking. Unless you feel the other person likes you and he feels that you like him, a relationship will not grow.

When a friend asks you for help, what is the best way to respond? When someone you know is going through a personal or family crisis and needs your support, what is the best way to express your concern? The third area of skill development concerns mutual support and influence in the relationship. Responding in helpful ways to another person's problems and concerns, communicating acceptance and support, constructively confronting a friend, using reinforcement and modeling to influence another person's behavior are all important relationship skills.

Finally, learning how to resolve problems and conflicts in ways that bring you and the other person closer together and facilitate the growth and development of the relationship is vitally important to maintaining a relationship.

THE APPLICATION OF BEHAVIORAL SCIENCE RESEARCH TO INTERPERSONAL SKILLS

Relating to other individuals in effective and productive ways is a vital need of modern society. We have at our disposal a vast amount of behavioral science research on interpersonal dynamics. Yet this knowledge has not been translated into a form useful to individuals who wish to apply it to increase their interpersonal skills. This essay aims to fill the gap between the findings of research on interpersonal interaction and the application of this knowledge to the development of interpersonal skills.

To make this essay as readable as possible, however, a minimum of footnote references to research and theory are included. This does not mean that there is no empirical support for the behaviors recommended. The basic skills which determine a person's interpersonal effectiveness have been identified from the results of the author's research (Johnson, 1966, 1967, 1971a, 1971b, 1971c; Johnson and Dustin, 1970; Johnson and Lewicki, 1969), from the results of the research on effective therapeutic relationships (for example, Truax and Carkhuff, 1967; Bierman, 1969; Strupp and Bergin, 1969), and from the results of the social psychological research on interpersonal relationships (see Johnson, 1970, 1972; Watson and Johnson, 1972).

Any individual concerned with increasing his interpersonal skills, and any practitioners who work with other people, will find this essay helpful. It is not a review of the theory and research for scholars. It translates the findings of theory and research on interpersonal relations into a program for developing the skills necessary for forming effective and fulfilling relationships with other people. Any individual, from a teenager to an elderly person, will be able to comprehend easily the material in this essay.

CO-ORIENTATION

In building a relationship two individuals must be co-oriented; that is, they must operate under the same norms and adhere to the same values. The co-orientation does not have to be perfect; rewarding relationships are quite common between individuals from different cultures and different backgrounds. But in order to develop a relationship you must agree upon the norms and values which will determine your behavior in your relationship.

Norms refer to common expectations about the behavior appropriate for you and the other person in the relationship. Whether you ask each other to do favors, how personal your discussions are, what types of things you can a relationship depend to a large extent upon the values the two individuals agree to adhere to in the relationship. The skills emphasized in this essay will set norms about expected behavior in a relationship (that is, you should self-disclose, build trust, be supportive and accepting, try to help each other, and so on), and they are based upon a set of humanistic values (that is, you should assume responsibility for your ideas and feelings, strive towards self-actualization, engage in cooperative interaction, and have the capacity for intimate and personal relationships). Using the skills presented in your interaction with other people will promote norms which facilitate the development of effective and fulfilling relationships.

Often the establishment of mutual norms and values concerning how you and the other person are going to relate is more important than the actual technical interpersonal skills the two of you have. The mutual commitment to face differences and conflicts and resolve them constructively, for example, may be more important in facilitating the growth of the relationship than the actual technical skill you have for resolving conflicts constructively. Or the mutual commitment to be self-disclosing and genuine with each other may be more important in creating intimacy and comradeship than the actual skill with which you disclose your feelings and reactions. In this essay the emphasis is placed upon developing your interpersonal skills. It should be remembered, however, that whenever you apply the skills discussed in this essay you are also promoting a set of norms and values for your relationships. The mutual adoption of these norms and values may be more important in facilitating the development of effective and fulfilling relationships than the actual skill with which you apply the skills.

LEARNING NEW INTERPERSONAL SKILLS

There is a five-step process for learning a new skill:

1. Becoming aware of the need for and uses of a new skill.
2. Identifying the behaviors involved in the new skill.
3. Practicing the behaviors.
4. Receiving feedback concerning how well you are performing the behaviors.
5. Integrating the behaviors into your behavioral repertoire.

While you practice the behaviors involved in the skills discussed, you may at first feel self-conscious and awkward. Practicing the behaviors may sometimes seem more like role-playing than genuine behavior. Do not let this stand in the way of increasing your interpersonal skills. It is through role-playing that most new skills are developed. If you keep practicing the behaviors, the self-consciousness and awkwardness will pass and you will become quite comfortable in using your increased skills.

A mechanical process is involved in specifying the behaviors that constitute a skill and in practicing them. While you engage in the exercises, you may at times feel the process is somewhat mechanical and unreal. But this is true of every kind of skill development. Learning how to play the piano, for example, also involves the mechanical practice of specific behaviors that seem unreal compared to the performance of a beautiful piano concerto. It is when you apply your new skills to real situations that they will gain the fire and life that may sometimes be lacking from practicing the exercises.

GROUP SUPPORT

In learning any new skills the approval of a group is a powerful source of motivation and support. Readers of this book may find it most rewarding to go through the exercises as part of a group. The group should consciously try to give approval to those members who are seriously trying to increase their interpersonal skills. The more a person practices and develops these skills the more group approval he should receive. By the same token, if a group supports member's attempts to experiment with new behavior and take risks in trying out their new skills, everyone's progress will be enhanced. There are few influences upon our behavior more powerful than the support and approval of a group of friends. Using the group influence to facilitate our learning is one of the most constructive ways of ensuring the development of our interpersonal skills.

Dean C. Barnlund

TOWARD A MEANING-CENTERED PHILOSOPHY OF COMMUNICATION[1]

A philosophy of training is essential in determining the aim, fixing the boundaries and evaluating the methods of any field. Yet formulating such a philosophy is an uncommon, formidable and sensitive venture. Uncommon, because in the daily round of classes, research projects, student conferences and faculty meetings, few teachers have the time or the perspective to canvass their purposes. Formidable, because to evolve such a philosophy is an immense undertaking requiring one to question the nature of our discipline, the legitimate boundaries of our scholarship and the character of our actions as teachers. Sensitive, because at every point one is forced to expose assumptions and motives that are only vaguely known or admitted even in the most mature human being. Each step in such an evaluation touches a raw nerve ending somewhere in that complex called the human ego. Yet this sort of periodic re-evaluation is absolutely essential. Loyalty to a discipline does not lie in an unquestioning acceptance of the status quo; it requires a continuous and vigorous testing of the postulates and practices of any field.

In attempting to phrase a more acceptable philosophy of communication training, I have been guided by a simple, but germinal, idea that can be succinctly stated. It is that a sound philosophy of training is implicit in a sound philosophy of communication. Whatever pedagogical decisions must be made —concerning the proper scope of the curriculum, the legitimacy of certain kinds of research, or the spirit and temper of student-teacher relations—they turn ultimately, if sometimes obscurely, on the nature and goals of successful communication. One cannot have a superficial, or narrow, or opportunistic concept of communication and be a thorough and responsible teacher of that same subject.

The question, therefore, of our role as scholar-teacher (and both the ordering and linking of those terms is deliberate) involves us in a circuitous, but essential, return to the communication process itself. Like the modern architect, one begins by discovering the "nature of his material." To be acceptable, a philosophy of communication should fulfill the following criteria:

(1) It should provide a satisfactory explanation of the aim of communication

Dean Barnlund, "Toward A Meaning-Centered Philosophy of Communication," *Journal of Communication,* Vol. 12, no. 4 (1962), pp. 197-211. Permission to reprint granted by *Journal of Communication.*
[1]This paper was presented originally at the SAA Convention in New York in 1961 under the title "A Philosophy of Communication Training."

(2) It should provide a technically adequate description of the process of communication

(3) It should provide a moral standard that will protect and promote the healthiest communicative behavior. Once this process is defined and its nature exposed, the way should be clear for facing the practical decisions involved in giving effective instruction.

AIM OF COMMUNICATION

We begin by asking why men communicate? What human need does it, or should it, satisfy? While there is almost universal agreement that communication is tied to the manipulation of symbols, there is widespread disagreement as to what constitutes effectiveness in this endeavor. A brief review of some abortive explanations of communication is essential because, in spite of repeated criticism, these conceptions continue to influence current training in speech.

One of these theories is that the aim of communication is to transmit information. Success hinges on mastery of the facts, effective arrangement of materials and strength of expression. It is a message-centered philosophy of communication. And it is largely amoral. Critical standards for determining the effectiveness of communication, as in the critical evaluation of literature, are internal; they are found within the message itself. When a writer or speaker or critic asks, "Was it well said?" he is usually viewing communication as a mode of expression. The training in communication that follows from this premise and perspective is destined to be truncated and unrealistic. Talk is not a guarantee of communication. Facts and ideas are not shared because they are articulated loudly or even well. Messages do not influence automatically because of being broadcast on the mass media. The inadequacy of this approach lies in its neglect of the listener as terminus of the communicative act, in its failure to provide an explanation of how meaning arises through communication and in its disregard for all but public and continuous discourse.

A second theory is that the aim of communication is to transfer ideas from one person to another. Here the listener is admitted as part of the communicative situation. The focus, however, in research and training, is upon the message formulator. Effectiveness in communication is thought to turn not only on the content and phrasing of the message, but on the intelligence and credibility of the source. Relatively little attention is paid to the listener other than to note that messages should be adapted to his interests. It ends by becoming a speaker-centered philosophy. Communicative events are explained largely in terms of the experiential milieu that shaped the mind of the speaker and find expression in his messages.

As an explanation of communication it, too, fails in several important respects. First, the listener tends to be regarded as a passive object, rather than an active force in communication. Unfortunately, it is not that simple to deposit ideas in another mind. Teachers of great intelligence and high purpose often find their lessons disregarded or misapplied. Messages flowing through an industrial complex are not received undistorted like images in a hall of mirrors. Second, this approach also fails to provide a satisfactory theory of meaning, and of how messages from highly credible sources can provoke so many and such contradictory meanings. Finally, it is too parochial. It neglects man's communication with himself—an area that is fast becoming one of the most vital in communication research—and it fails to account for the fact that communication is as often a matter of hiding or protecting what is in men's minds as it is a matter of revealing their thoughts and intentions.

Neither of these schools of thought, of course, omits the constituent elements in communication altogether. It is, rather, a question of emphasis. Questions of emphasis, however, are not irrelevant or inconsequential in establishing a productive orientation for a discipline. The pedagogical consequences of both of these approaches is to place a disproportionate emphasis (in research, courses and textbooks) on the source and message elements in communication. Both schools of thought tend, also, to minimize or overlook completely, the interactive and dynamic nature of the communicative process. Communication, as I conceive it, is a word that describes the process of creating a meaning. Two words in this sentence are critical. They are "create" and "meaning." Messages may be generated from the outside—by a speaker, a television screen, a scolding parent—but meanings are generated from within. This position parallels that of Berlo when he writes, "Communication does not consist of the transmission of meaning. Meanings are not transmitted, nor transferable. Only messages are transmittable, and meanings are not in the message, they are in the message-user."[2] Communication is man's attempt to cope with his experience, his current mood, his emerging needs. For every person it is a unique act of creation involving dissimilar materials. But it is, within broad limits, assumed to be predictable or there could be no theory of communication.

The second, and more troublesome word, is "meaning." Meaning is not apparent in the ordinary flow of sensation. We are born into and inhabit a world without "meaning." That life becomes intelligible to us—full of beauty or ugliness, hope or despair—is because it is assigned that significance by the experiencing being. As Karl Britton put it, "A world without minds is a world without structure, without relations, without facts."[3] Sensations do not come to us, sorted and labeled, as if we were visitors in a vast, but ordered, museum. Each of us, instead, is his own curator. We learn to look with a selective eye, to classify, to assign significance.

Communication arises out of the need to reduce uncertainty, to act effectively, to defend or strengthen the ego. On some occasions words are used to ward off anxiety. On other occasions they are means of evolving more deeply satisfying ways of expressing ourselves. *The aim of communication is to increase the number and consistency of our meanings within the limits set by patterns of evaluation that have proven successful in the past, our emerging needs and drives, and the demands of the physical and social setting of the moment.* Communication ceases when meanings are adequate; it is initiated as soon as new meanings are required. However, since man is a homeostatic, rather than static, organism, it is impossible for him to discover any permanently satisfying way of relating all his needs; each temporary adjustment is both relieving and disturbing, leading to successively novel ways of relating himself to his environment.

[2]David Berlo, *The Process of Communication* (New York: Holt, Rinehart, Winston, 1960), p. 175.
[3]Karl Britton, *Communication: A Philosophical Study of Language* (New York: Harcourt, Brace, 1939), p. 206.

To say that communication occurs whenever meaning is assigned to internal or external stimuli is to enlarge greatly the span of our discipline. Communication, in this sense, may occur while a man waits alone outside a hospital operating room, or watches the New York skyline disappear at dusk. It can take place in the privacy of his study as he introspects about some internal doubt, or contemplates the fading images of a frightening dream. When man discovers meaning in nature, or in insight in his own reflections, he is a communication system unto himself. Festinger refers to this as "consummatory communication." The creation of meanings, however, also goes on in countless social situations where men talk with those who share or dispute their purposes. Messages are exchanged in the hope of altering the attitudes or actions of those around us. This can be characterized as "instrumental communication," as long as we remember that these two purposes are not mutually exclusive.

What I am describing is a meaning-centered philosophy of communication. It admits that meaning in the sender, and the words of the messages are important, but regards as most critical the state of mind, the assumptive world and the needs of the listener or observer. The impact of any message from "See me after class" to "What's good for General Motors is good for the country" is determined by the physical, personal and social context, the most critical ingredient of which is the mind of the interpreter. Communication, so defined, does not require a speaker, a message, or a listener, in the restricted sense in which these terms are used in the field of speech. All may be combined in a single person, and often are.

A theory that leaves out man's communication with himself, his communication with the world about him and a large proportion of his interactions with his fellowman, is not a theory of communication at all, but a theory of speechmaking. Indeed, it seems applicable to speechmaking only in the most formal and restricted sense of that word. There is little in the traditional view of speech that is helpful in the analysis of conversation, interviewing, conflict negotiations, or in the diagnosis of the whole span of communicative disorders and breakdowns that are receiving so much attention currently. Upon so limited a view of communication it is unlikely that there can develop theories of sufficient scope and stature to command the respect of other disciplines or of the larger public that ultimately decides our role in the solution of man's problems. The field of speech seems to be fast approaching what the airlines call a "checkpoint" where one loses the freedom to choose between alternative flight plans, between a limited interest in speechmaking and a broad concern with the total communicative behavior of man. By defining communication operationally, by examining a wider range of communicative acts, the way might be prepared for making the startling theoretical advances that have, so far, not characterized our field.

THE COMMUNICATION PROCESS

A satisfactory philosophy should also provide a starting point for the technical analysis of communication. One way of accomplishing this is to ask what characteristics would have to be built into a scientific model that would represent, at the same time and equally well, the entire spectrum from intrapersonal to mass communication. It should not be a model that is mechanically or structurally faithful, but one that is symbolically and functionally similar.

Space is too limited here to more than suggest a few of the principles that would have to be reflected in such a model.

Communication is not a thing, it is a process. Sender, message and receiver do not remain constant throughout an act of communication. To treat these as static entities, as they often are in our research, is questionable when applied to the most extreme form of continuous discourse, is misleading when used to analyze the episodic verbal exchanges that characterize face-to-face communication, and is totally useless in probing man's communication with himself. Changes in any of these forces, and few forces remain constant very long, reverberate throughout the entire system. Students of communication are not dissecting a cadaver, but are probing the pulsing evolution of meaning in a living organism.

Communication is not linear, it is circular. There are many situations in life where a simple, linear, causal analysis is useful. One thing leads to another. A, then B, then C. I push over the first domino and the rest, in turn, topple over. But this sort of thinking is not very helpful, though quite appealing in its simplicity, in studying communication. There is not first a sender, then a message and finally an interpreter. There is, instead, what Henderson calls "mutual dependence" or what I have termed "interdependent functionalism." The words "sender" and "receiver" no longer name the elements in a communicative act, but indicate the point of view of the critic at the moment.

Communication is complex. Someone once said that whenever there is communication there are at least six "people" involved: The person you think yourself to be; the man your partner thinks you are; the person you believe your partner thinks you are; plus the three equivalent "persons" at the other end of the circuit. If, with as few as four constants, mathematicians must cope with approximately fifty possible relations, then we, in studying communication, where an even greater number of variables is concerned, ought to expound with considerable humility. In this age of Freudian and non-Freudian analysts, of information theory specialists, of structural linguists, and so on, we are just beginning to unravel the mysteries of this terribly involved, and therefore fascinating, puzzle.

Communication is irreversible and unrepeatable. The distinction being suggested here is between systems that are deterministic and mechanical, and those that are spontaneous and evolutionary. One can start a motor, beat a rug, or return a book. But you cannot start a man thinking, beat your son, or return a compliment with the same consequences. The words of a teacher, even when faithfully repeated, do not produce the same effect, but may lead to new insight, increased tension, or complete boredom. A moment of indifference or interest, a disarming or tangential remark, leave indelible traces.

Communication involves the total personality. Despite all efforts to divide body and mind, reason and emotion, thought and action, meanings continue to be generated by the whole organism. This is not to say that some messages do not produce greater or lesser dissonance, or shallower or deeper effects on the personality; it is only to hold that eventually every fact, conclusion, guilt, or enthusiasm must somehow be accommodated by the entire personality. The deeper the involvement produced by any communication, the sooner and more pervasive its effects upon behavior.

Research or instruction that disregards these characteristics of the communicative act would appear both unsound and of dubious value.

THE MORAL DIMENSION

The perennial and legitimate concern with ethics in the field of speech arises out of the inherent moral aspect of every interpersonal communication. As was noted earlier, the aim of communication is to transform chaotic sense impressions into some sort of coherent, intelligible and useful relationship. When men do this privately, either in confronting nature or in assessing their own impulses, they are free to invent whatever meaning they can. But when men encounter each other, a moral issue invades every exchange because the manipulation of symbols always involves a purpose that is external to, and in some degree manipulative of, the interpreter of the message. The complexity of communication makes it difficult to know in advance, and with certainty, the impact of any bundle of words upon the receiver of them. The irreversibility of communication means that whatever meaning is provoked by a message cannot be annulled. A teacher may erase a blackboard, a colleague apologize, or an employer change his mind, but there is no way of erasing the effect of a threatening ultimatum, a bitter remark, or a crushing personal evaluation.

Meaning, in my opinion, is a private preserve and trespassers always run a risk. To speak of personal integrity at all is to acknowledge this. Any exchange of words is an invasion of the privacy of the listener which is aimed at preventing, restricting, or stimulating the cultivation of meaning. Briefly, three types of interference may be distinguished. First, there are messages whose intent is to coerce. Meaning is controlled by choosing symbols that so threaten the interpreter that he becomes incapable of, and blind to, alternative meanings; second, there are messages of an exploitative sort in which words are arranged to filter the information, narrow the choices, obscure the consequences, so that only one meaning becomes attractive or appropriate; third, there is facilitative communication in which words are used to inform, to enlarge perspective, to deepen sensitivity, to remove external threat, to encourage independence of meaning. The values of the listener are, in the first case, ignored, in the second, subverted, in the third respected. While some qualification of this principle is needed, it appears that only facilitative communication is entirely consistent with the protection and improvement of man's symbolic experience. Unless a teacher is aware of these possibilities and appreciates the differences in these kinds of communication, it is unlikely that he will communicate responsibly in the classroom.

IMPLICATIONS FOR PREPARATION

The outline of any philosophy must be expressed in abstract terminology. For that reason some will see little in this philosophy that is inconsistent with current practice in the field of speech. If so, my meaning has been less than clear. Once one accepts that communication is a study of meaning, and of all of the symbols and circumstances that give rise to meaning, he assumes new and formidable responsibilities as a scholar. Once he agrees that communication is a complicated, irreversible process, and accepts the moral obligation that inheres in such a conception, he embraces a new role as a teacher. Lest the practical consequences of endorsing such a philosophy go unexamined, let me attempt to translate the foregoing abstractions into more concrete form. What habits of preparation, what research interests, what sort of curriculum and what instructional methods, follow from a commitment to a "meaning-centered philosophy of communication"?

All instruction begins with the discovery of knowledge, in this case with knowledge about communication. And the vast bulk of current information about communication is to be found not in the literature of our field but in the experimental investigations and theoretical systems of men in other disciplines. For this reason it would be difficult to imagine anyone committed to a meaning-centered philosophy of communication who was not already conversant with, or wanted to become conversant with, the men and works listed in the brief "Sampler in Communication" that follows. Each of these works is concerned at a sophisticated level with some aspect of meaning.*

Sampler in Communication

Allport, F. *Theories of Perception and the Concept of Structure.* (New York: Wiley, 1955).

Anschen, R. *Language: An Enquiry into its Meaning and Function.* (New York: Harper, 1957).

Berlo, D. *The Process of Communication.* (New York: Holt, Rinehart, Winston, 1960).

Brown, R. *Words and Things.* (Glencoe, Ill.: The Free Press, 1958).

Burke, K. *A Philosophy of Literary Form.* (Baton Rouge: Louisiana State University Press, 1941).

Festinger, L. *A Theory of Cognitive Dissonance* (Evanston, Ill.: Row, Peterson, 1957).

Fromm, E. *The Forgotten Language.* (New York: Rinehart, 1952).

Hovland, C., Janis, I., and Kelly, H. *Communication and Persuasion.* (New Haven, Conn.: Yale University Press, 1953).

Langer, S. *Philosophy in a New Key.* (New York: Mentor Books, New American Library, 1948).

Osgood, C., Suci, G., and Tannenbaum, P. *The Measurement of Meaning.* (Urbana, Ill.: University of Illinois Press, 1957).

Rogers, C. *Client-Centered Therapy.* (New York: Houghton Mifflin, 1951).

Ruesch, J. *Communication: The Social Matrix of Psychiatry.* (New York: Norton, 1951).

Ruesch, J. and Kess, W. *Nonverbal Communication.* (Berkeley: University of California Press, 1956).

Wheelwright, P. *The Burning Fountain.* (Bloomington, Ind.: Indiana University Press, 1956).

Wiener, N. *The Human Use of Human Beings.* (New York: Anchor Books, Doubleday, 1950).

The breadth of this list, stretching from perception theory to symbolic processes, from cybernetics to psychotherapy, from literary criticism to cultural anthropology, matches the breadth of viewpoint intended in the phrase a "meaning-centered philosophy of communication." It is what George Miller seemed to have in mind when he wrote as preface to the first text in communi-

---

* This is not intended to be a definitive bibliography, only a suggestive sampling of sources. Substitutes could easily be made in every division of this bibliography. For example, in psychotherapy one could as easily recommend Ruesch's *Disturbed Communication* or Hoch and Zubin's *Psychopathology of Communication;* in cybernetics there is Walter's *The Living Brain* and Latil's *Machines That Think;* in literary criticism I. A. Richard's *Principles of Literary Criticism* or Burke's *Grammar of Motives;* in perception theory, Blake and Ramsey's *Perception: An Approach to Personality* and Beardslee and Wertheimer's *Readings in Perception;* in nonverbal communication one could recommend Hall's *The Silent Language* or Birdwhistell's *Introduction to Kinesics;* in semantics, Hayakawa's *Language in Thought and Action,* Korzybski's *Science and Sanity,* or Weinberg's *Levels of Knowing and Existence.* The purpose of the "Sampler" is only to indicate the broad scope of germinal studies of communicative behavior.

cation theory, "When one tries to assemble the facts about this important social event . . . the data come from all the fields of science."[4]

RESEARCH IMPLICATIONS

Preparation for offering training in communication, however, cannot depend upon sponging on the discoveries of others; it must, if our field is to survive, be advanced by empirical studies and theoretical constructs of our own. Tenure in the academic community is rightly contingent upon respect for the original contributions of a discipline. And, in this respect, it would be difficult to deny our theoretical sterility during the past forty years. A large part of the fault seems to lie in the truncated view we hold of human communication. Medicine would scarcely have obtained recognition if it had limited itself to a study of the human arm. Sociology would be unknown today if it had never gone beyond the classification of criminals. Most of us would find unacceptable a psychology of man based on studies of hypnotism. Yet in our exclusive, or nearly exclusive, interest in formal public address we seem to be attempting the impossible—to build an overall theory of communication based upon a significant, but altogether too restricted, sample of human speech.[5]

What is needed is a broadening of perspective as to what constitutes legitimate research in communication, combined with an intensification of our efforts as research workers. There is no reason why the public platform should monopolize our attention. There is a whole universe of communication currently being neglected that could, and should be, studied. Whenever men work out new meanings, or defend old meanings, whether it involves parent and child, worker and boss, or client and therapist, the student of communication should be there. Sound training in communication is dependent upon the availability of respectable theories and objective data and these will be most valid when they are based on the whole span of human communication. The laboratory and library legitimize instruction.

CURRICULAR IMPLICATIONS

The lopsidedness of current work in speech is also evident in the hierarchy of courses offered to students. College catalogues show an almost exclusive concern with the formal aspects of communication. There are courses in public speaking, advanced public speaking, public debate, forms of public address, history of public address and so on. Here and there is a course in propaganda, in semantics, in business communication. But the curricular monolith we have designed adds to the impression that the rostrum is the only setting where communication among men matters.

The acceptance of a broader conception of our responsibilities should lead to a better balance in the curriculum in communication. Much of what

---

[4]George A. Miller, *Language and Communication* (New York: McGraw-Hill, 1951), p. v.
[5]This is dramatically underscored whenever copies of *Speech Monographs* and the *Journal of Abnormal and Social Psychology* arrive in the same mail. Seldom does the former carry more than one title of empirical research in communication broadly conceived. Yet the last four issues of the *Journal of Abnormal and Social Psychology,* whose contributors are supposedly unqualified and uninterested in speech, carry between eight and ten titles on various aspects of communication in each issue.

exists would remain. But there would be a shift in emphasis in some offerings, and a compensating development of new work in areas currently neglected. There is no reason, if scholarship supports it, why there should not be courses in interpersonal communication, in conflict resolution, in decision-making, in organizational communication, in psycholinguistics, in societal communication, in network theory and so on. These can all be accommodated within a department of speech as long as the unifying focus of the curriculum is the problem of meaning and the control of it through symbols.

While the magnitude of a discipline of communication may seem frightening to envision, it does not seem any more so than the conception of psychology as the study of human behavior, or sociology as the study of social institutions, or anthropology as the study of cultures. Indeed, to build a significant discipline seems hopeless unless it encompasses a sufficiently broad cross-section of human activity to give it substance and scope.

If there is objection to this conception of communication because the lines separating our interests from those of psychology and sociology would be blurred and overlapping, they would appear to be no less blurred and overlapping than those already separating the behavioral sciences from each other. If students of communication will need to know their psychology, political science and history, it should also be true that a substantial discipline of communication will require students in other fields to be equally familiar with our contributions. If a distinguishing and unifying theme is required for the field of speech let it be our interest in language and how the manipulation of symbols alters human behavior, human institutions and cultural patterns.[6]

PEDAGOGICAL IMPLICATIONS

We come, finally, to the question of instruction. As in any problem of communication, meaning is a response to tensions in the nervous system of the communicant. This tension may be triggered externally for students through lectures, films, demonstrations, or any other directive teaching technique. Or it may be generated from within by providing a facilitative setting which permits subconscious feelings of inadequacy, ineffectiveness, or inconsistency, to be admitted. As long as this tension is productive rather than reductive, that is, as long as it is disturbing without becoming unmanageable, it creates an opportunity for the evolution of new discriminations and meanings.

The resulting tension may be resolved, and learning accomplished, at a number of different psychological levels. Indexing of these types of learning, or *communication,* may clarify their differences. Learning$_1$ consists of acquiring new facts, new information, new terms. This is the simplest type of communication and probably involves the least disturbance to the receiver, for considerable information can be accommodated without altering the existing personality structure. When facts are discrepant with the student's world view, they are denied or distorted to protect past meanings. Learning$_2$ involves changes in outward behavior. The student acquires new skills which are largely the product of conforming to the directives of a coach or teacher. Recent studies suggest that this type of role-taking is likely to alter the personality in some ways, not all of which are desirable. Learning$_3$ occurs when the student discovers and adopts new attitudes toward communication. He begins to ques-

---

[6]The broad conception of communication urged here is also the most promising basis for stopping, or even reversing, the continuing fractionalization of departments of speech.

tion his own assumptions and values, develops insight into his own motives and assumes more responsibility for his own behavior. Learning₄ operates at all the preceding levels. The total personality of the student is involved—his knowledge, his attitudes, his actions. Teaching of this type aims at helping the student to become more conscious of his reasons for communicating and how these are linked to larger philosophical issues. It assists him in becoming increasingly aware of the complicated nature of communication, and its variety of uses and settings. It acquaints him with the multitude of technical means consequences. But while it sensitizes and informs him it should, in my opinion, leave the student free to evolve his own style and standards of communicating.

Alfred North Whitehead once said that any discipline deserving a place in the curriculum must have a philosophy, a method and a technique. The statement is undoubtedly true, but somewhat incomplete if philosophy, method and technique exist as isolated units of instruction. Too often what results is that the technical and moral aspects remain separate, lacking any vital connection in the classroom, and more importantly, in the personality of the student. The result is schizophrenic communication. Men learn to blot out all but technical considerations when communicating in a coercive or prejudicial way, but turn around and attack someone else's communication on moral grounds when it proves technically superior to their own. It is this sort of inconsistency that fosters pathological communication and pathological personalities.

Integrative instruction in communication encourages the student to work out better meanings concerning his own communication with himself and his fellowmen. By "better" I refer to meanings that permit more consistency in his personality between what he assumes, what he sees, and what he does. By "better" I refer to meanings that will increase his openness, curiosity and flexibility. By "better" I refer to meanings that will make him more independent, and more confident of his own judgment.

Lest the point of view presented here be interpreted as a paragon of philosophical virtue, the best possible theory in this best of all possible worlds, let me suggest some of the real obstacles and difficulties that stand in opposition to it. First there is the risk, in embracing the whole gamut of human communication, of tackling too much so that it cannot possibly be brought under control. There is a risk, too, of finding so much complexity that we shall have to return to the view that communication is an art that defies scientific analysis. The problems in making such an all-out attack on so broad a field are great; a conscientious teacher of speech already runs the risk of spending so much time in allied literature there is no time for original investigation of his own specialty. The view of training presented here is, also, an exceedingly moralistic one which, of itself, makes an academic discipline suspect these days. But science and morality must be conjoined when evidence indicates that the warping of communication is one of the most important factors in personality distortion.[7] These, and other objections, must be raised before taking this philosophy seriously.

---

[7] Others in the behavioral sciences are belatedly reaching the same conclusion. The most penetrating and persuasive statement of the argument for linking psychological science with human values is to be found in Sigmund Koch's article, "Psychological Science versus the Science-Humanism Antinomy: Intimations of a Significant Science of Man," in the *American Psychologist,* October, 1961.

Writing in the final pages of his last book, John Dewey made the remark that "As philosophers, our disagreements with one another as to conclusions are trivial in comparison with our disagreements as to problems; to see the same problem another sees, in the same perspective and at the same angle—that amounts to something. Agreement as to conclusions is in comparison perfunctory."[8] The hope is not that all will share my conclusions—for few may—but that all will admit the problem facing our discipline, and see it from somewhat the same angle. That, indeed, would be something.

---

[8] John Dewey and Arthur Bentley, *Knowing and the Known* (Beacon Press, 1949), p. 314.

Bruce H. Westley and Malcolm S. MacLean, Jr.

A CONCEPTUAL MODEL FOR COMMUNICATIONS RESEARCH

Communications research and theory have blossomed from a variety of disciplinary sources in recent years. People probing the communications area have here focused on theoretical issues and there on "practical" concerns. Thus, one finds today a jungle of unrelated concepts and systems of concepts on the one hand and a mass of undigested, often sterile empirical data on the other.

In this paper, we are trying to develop a single communications model which may help to order existing findings. It also may provide a system of concepts which will evoke new and interrelated research directions, compose old theoretical and disciplinary differences, and in general bring some order out of a chaotic situation. Clearly, we do not propose here a full-blown theory of mass communications, but rather a paradigm or model as a preliminary orientation to a theoretical system.

Can a simple, parsimonious model be built capable of drawing together many of the existing approaches to mass communications without serious loss in utility?

FROM FACE-TO-FACE TO MASS

First, let us look at a simple act of communication. Person A transmits something about an object X to person B. Newcomb has found this simple model of interpersonal communications useful in the study of roles and norms. He says that, when A communicates to B about X (other things being equal), systematic changes in the condition of the system can be predicted. For example, if B likes A (or, at least, does not dislike him), B's perception of X will be more similar to A's after than before the communicative act.

This model frees one from the limitations of either the personality or social systems as such. Can it serve as a guide to both face-to-face and mass communications? Need the extension from the simple communicative act destroy its system character?

Two basic distinctions between face-to-face and mass communications are suggested: Face-to-face communication involves more sense modalities. It also provides immediate "feedback"—that is, information from B back to A about the change condition of B. In other words, more senses (and kinds of stimuli) can come into play in the person-person act than in any other situation. Thus, B has a "cross-modality" check. He can clear impressions he gets through one sense with those he gets through another. And A has the advantage of learning B's response almost immediately—for instance, "message received."

Bruce H. Westley and Malcolm S. MacLean, Jr. "A Conceptual Model for Communications Research," *Journalism Quarterly*, Vol. 34 (1957), pp. 31-38. Reprinted by permission of Association for Education in Journalism.

Mass communications, then, differ from face-to-face communications to the extent that (a) the number of modalities tends to be minimized and (b) "orientative" feedback is minimized or delayed.

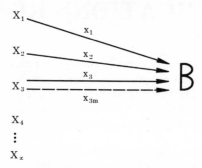

FIG. 1-1. *Objects of orientation (X_1 . . . X_∞) in the sensory field of the receiver (B) are transmitted directly to him in abstracted form (X_1 . . . X_3) after a process of selection from among all Xs, such selection being based at least in part on the needs and problems of B. Some or all are transmitted in more than one sense (X_{3m}, for example).*

Now for a look at X, which may be taken as an "object of orientation." From the standpoint of B, the world consists of a confusion of X's. And these Xs may include As. B has within his sensory field an infinity of potential Xs. He has learned that in order to maximize satisfactions and solve security problems he must orient toward Xs selectively. But the mature B, Newcomb emphasizes, does not orient toward X alone, but tends, in the presence of an A, to orient simultaneously toward both A and X. This means that he comes to orient toward an X not alone on the basis of its intrinsic capacity to provide satisfactions and help solve problems but also with respect to the relationship between A and X. This also means that A and X relate systematically to B.

Let us assume that an X is any object (or event) that has characteristics capable of being transmitted in some abstracted form. Let us assume further that a system has a need for transmissible messages as a means of orienting itself in its environment and as a means of securing problem solutions and need satisfactions. The significant things is that Xs have stimulus characteristics that can be responded to in the absence of an A.

For instance, B looks out his window and sees flames in the house of his neighbor. This event as surely transmits information to him as would the shouts of his neighbor *about* the fire.

With respect to the As and Xs in his own immediate sensory field, B is capable of receiving and acting upon information thus transmitted to him and must do so if he is to maintain an adequate orientation to his immediate environment. But what of As and Xs relevant to such orientation but lying outside his immediate reach? If these are to impinge on him, there is need for another role, which we will call C.

C is conceived of as one who can (a) select the abstractions of object X appropriate to B's need satisfactions or problem solutions (b) transform them into some form of symbol containing meanings shared with B, and finally (c) transmit such symbols by means of some channel or medium to B.

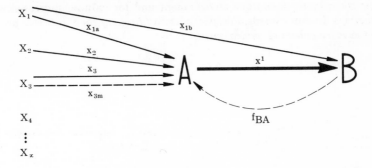

FIG. 1-2. *The same Xs are selected and abstracted by communicator (A) and transmitted as a message (X') to B, who may or may not have part or all of the Xs in his own sensory field (X₁b). Either purposively or nonpurposively B transmits feedback (fBA) to A.*

The added element *C* will be recognized as the "gatekeeper" of Lewin as adapted to mass communications by White. It is also recognizable as the "encoder" suggested by Bush as an adaptation of the encoding process in information theory.

It may be asked why *C* would choose *X*s "appropriate" to the requirements of *B*. The answer would appear to be that the *C* role can survive only to the extent that this is true. For *B* is still a selector among the offerings of various *C*s and this means that *C*s are in effect competitors for the attention of *B*s (and for that matter competitors with *A*s and *X*s in *B*'s immediate field). *C*s therefore survive as *C*s to the extent that they satisfy needs for *B*s. And *B*s, on the basis of the most obvious propositions of learning theory, will tend to return to those *C*s which have provided past need satisfactions and problem solutions.

C, then, is capable of serving as an agent for *B* in selecting and transmitting information about an *X* (or an *A-X* relationship). He does so by means of symbols expressing shared meanings about *X*s through channels that provide connection between *X* and *B*. And he does so in circumstances where such a connection is otherwise impossible for *B*. Thus *B* has a basis for increas-

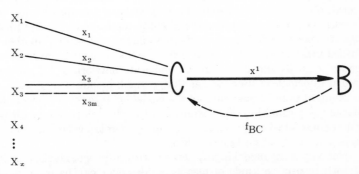

FIG. 1-3. *What Xs B receives may be owing to selected abstractions transmitted by a non-purposive encoder (C), acting for B and thus extending B's environment. C's selections are necessarily based in part on feedback (fBC) from B.*

ing his security in the larger environment and for gaining increased need satisfactions. In other words, *the effect of the addition of the C role is to provide B with a more extended environment.*

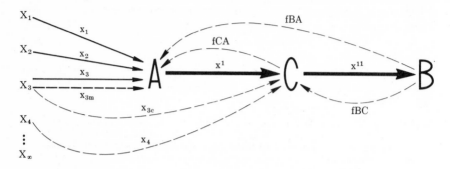

FIG. 1-4. *The messages C transmits to B (X") represent his selections from both messages to him from A's (X') and C's selections and abstractions from Xs in his own sensory field (X₃c, X₄), which may or may not be Xs in A's field. Feedback not only moves from B to A (fʙᴀ) and from B to C (fʙc) but also from C to A (fcᴀ). Clearly, in the mass communication situation, a large number of Cs receive from a very large number of As and transmit to a vastly larger number of Bs, who simultaneously receive from other Cs.*

For Newcomb, A and B can only be persons. While we have tended to imply persons in these roles, it should now be made clear that we do not intend to confine the model to the level of the individual personality. The role of B, for instance, may be that of a person, or a primary group, or a total social system.

In stating that any "system" has need for transmissible messages as a means of orienting itself in its environment, it is meant that this statement be applied to a person, a primary group, or even a social system. Any of these levels can be plugged into the role of B. At the personality level, B can be the housewife, too busy to rush around the neighborhood in order to observe the details of her surroundings; in such a case the C function can be attributed to the neighborhood gossip, and transmits a limited portion of all possible messages supplying the information needs of B. At something like the primary group level, one can think of the relatively isolated frontier colony, which posted sentinels as Cs to observe and report the condition of the environment by means of a special code such as a rifle shot and greeted eagerly another kind of C, the information-bearing circuit rider. At the social system level, a national state requires and maintains an elaborate network of Cs performing such special information functions as that of the diplomatic service.

It might even be possible that the model holds for even "lower" levels than that of the personality. For instance, at the physiological level, it would appear that homeostasis requires some sort of "transmission" of "information" with respect to states of parts of the body.

Not only is the model highly general with respect to levels, it is highly general with respect to kinds of messages. Messages can be seen as either *purposive* or *non-purposive.* Other models have tended to obscure one or the other.

"PURPOSIVE" OR "NON-PURPOSIVE"?

A purpose message is one A originates for the purpose of modifying B's perception of an X. A non-purposive message is one which is transmitted to B directly or by means of a C and in the absence of any communicator's intent to influence him. The absence of a communicator's intent to influence B transforms his act into an X. When a person says something he hopes will reach another person's ears, he is an A; but if he says it without such intent and it nevertheless is transmitted to B, his act must be conceived of as an X, the selection and transmission having been performed by a C. The reasons we consider this distinction to be crucial for mass communications theory will be discussed below.

Messages are transmitted in codes (symbol systems). But this model is by no means limited to the most obvious ones—linguistic systems. In fact, as Newcomb has already emphasized, the crucial characteristic is the shared meanings associated with symbols. Such symbols can take virtually any form, so long as and to the extent that there exist shared meanings and that they are transmissible. Such shared meanings surrounding symbols can be either *affective* or *cognitive*. Language has both affective and cognitive elements. Poetry, for instance, emphasizes the former. This emphasis is, of course, characteristic of all the arts. For instance, modern artist A in communicating with a series of Bs casts his message in a symbol system which is shared, even though with only a few of them; those Bs who share it or part of it will attain satisfaction from the communication of an affective state; those who cannot decode the message but attempt to do so will probably be frustrated in the attempt and express hostility toward the message, or the communicator, or conceivably even the gatekeeper.

The example above leads into further illustration of how the model deals with "special public." The are illustrated by the immense segment of the media consisting of trade publications, scholarly journals, hobby and craft media, house organs, and the like. These are often defined out of the area of mass communications, usually on the grounds of audience size; and this in spite of the fact that some of these special interest publications media shade off from the specificity of the *Turkey Grower's Gazette* to attain circulations in the millions. The fact would seem to be that these with the generality of *Holiday,* suggesting that decisions as to what is "mass" and what is not mass must necessarily be arbitrary.

The present model requires no such distinction. Our Bs vary in the degree to which they share common problems. Common problems imply the necessity of attaining communication with common Xs. Media serving to bring such Xs to such Bs arise out of the perceptions by Cs of the existence of just such a need. Special symbol systems are developed to maximize transmission.

It will be noted that we have consistently referred to both "need satisfactions" and "problem solution." These concepts relate directly to the "immediate" and "delayed" rewards of Schramm which seem to us to be provocative and potentially fruitful. Building on the two-factor learning theory of Mowrer, Schramm proposed a "reader reward" basis for characterizing the content of news stories. The correspondence is, of course, between his "immediate reward" and our "need satisfactions" and between his "delayed reward" and our "problem solutions."

FEEDBACK

Another concept crucial to the model is that of "feedback." In the first place it should be clear from the foregoing that it is feedback that assures the system character of the *ABX* (or *ABCX*) relationship. If *A* is to utilize his experience in influencing *B*, he must have information about any changes in the condition of *B* attributable to his communications. *C* is equally concerned with effects on *B* if he is to make realistic adjustments in his role as *B*'s "agent." Such *A*s as advertisers facilitate feedback by means of elaborate market research; public relations men obtain feedback by means of public-opinion polls and other devices for determining the effects of their messages. Such *C*s as newspaper publishers sponsor readership surveys and, more recently, reader motivation studies to estimate and predict reader response. Radio's concern with "fan mail" and popularity ratings is well known.

Although feedback originates with *B* under most circumstances, it need not be assumed that *B* is necessarily trying to communicate back to *C* or *A*. When he does try to do so, we may think of this as *purposive* feedback. This is the case when an angry reader writes a letter "straightening out" the editor on some favorite issue. But there are also many ways *B* can feed back without intending to. These we will call *non-purposive* feedback. When a television fan decides to try a well-advertised detergent, his purchase becomes part of the date of a market survey, even though he may not have intended to let the sponsor know he had won a convert.

OTHER MODELS

In the final analysis the worth of such a model as this lies in its heuristic value. In view of the fact that several other models already exist in this field, it is reasonable to ask why another is necessary. A brief look at some others may be in order.

Perhaps the most pervasive of existing "models" is that of Lasswell: "*Who says what* through *what channels* to *whom* with *what effect.*" The difficulty here is that the model seems to demand the presence of a communicator —the *who*—and to imply that his communication is a purposive one. It is no accident that our model has included the non-purposive case, transmitting *X*s to *B*s by the way of *C*s in the total absence of *A*s. The fortuitous origination of a great deal of the news material transmitted in all media seems to demand a place in the model. There is also an unidirectional implication in the Lasswellian formulation that ignores feedback phenomena.

The information theory-cybernetics paradigm has excited some interesting theoretical contributions but would appear to have certain drawbacks. It, too, appears to require the presence of a communicator, although not necessarily a purposive one. In addition it poses all the problems of a "borrowed" model. Taylor's use of the redundancy concept would appear to be an example of an exact mapping from mass communications phenomena to an element in the model. But such precise correspondences appear to be rare, and mappings become contrived and tenuous. The model strains common knowledge, for instance, in assuming perfect correspondence of symbol systems encoded and decoded.

SUMMARY

A conceptual model of the total communication process has been presented in the belief that such a model will prove useful in ordering existing data in mass communications research, point to areas of strength and weakness in our knowledge, and stimulate further efforts. The model is intended to be sufficiently general to treat all kinds of human communication from two-person face-to-face interaction to international and intercultural communications. It assumes that a minimum number of roles and processes are needed in any general theory of communications and attempts to isolate and tentatively define them. It must not be viewed as a theory but as a preliminary step to the construction of a general theory.

The principal elements in the model are these:

As. (Advocacy roles)

This is what is usually meant by "the communicator"—a personality or social system engaged in selecting and transmitting messages *purposively*.

Bs. (Behavioral system roles)

This is usually meant by "the receiver," "the public," etc.—a personality or social system requiring and using communications about the condition of its environment for the satisfaction of its needs and solution of its problems.

Cs. (Channel roles)

Often confounded with *A*s, *C*s serve as the agents of *B*s in selecting and transmitting non-purposively the information *B*s require, especially when the information is beyond the immediate reach of *B*.

X.

The totality of objects and events "out there." X^1 is these objects and events as abstracted into transmissible form: "*messages*" about *X*s and *A-X* relationships (such as "opinions").

Channels

The means by which *X*s are moved by way of *A*s and/or *C*s to *B*s. Channels include "gates" manned by *C*s who in various ways alter messages.

Encoding

The process by which *A*s and *C*s transform *X*s into X^1s. *Decoding* is the process by which *B*s interiorize messages.

Feedback

The means by which *A*s and *C*s obtain information about the effects of messages on *B*s.

Jack R. Gibb

DEFENSIVE COMMUNICATION

One way to understand communication is to view it as a people process rather than as a language process. If one is to make fundamental improvement in communication, he must make changes in interpersonal relationships. One possible type of alteration—and the one with which this paper is concerned— is that of reducing the degree of defensiveness.

DEFINITION AND SIGNIFICANCE

Defensive behavior is defined as that behavior which occurs when an individual perceives threat or anticipates threat in the group. The person who behaves defensively, even though he also gives some attention to the common task, devotes an appreciable portion of his energy to defending himself. Besides talking about the topic, he thinks about how he appears to others, how he may be seen more favorably, how he may win, dominate, impress, or escape punishment, and/or how he may avoid or mitigate a perceived or an anticipated attack.

Such inner feelings and outward acts tend to create similarly defensive postures in others; and, if unchecked, the ensuing circular response becomes increasingly destructive. Defensive behavior, in short, engenders defensive listening, and this in turn produces postural, facial, and verbal cues which raise the defense level of the original communicator.

Defense arousal prevents the listener from concentrating upon the message. Not only do defensive communicators send off multiple value, motive, and affect cues, but also defensive recipients distort what they receive. As a person becomes more and more defensive, he becomes less and less able to perceive accurately the motives, the values, and the emotions of the sender. The writer's analyses of tape-recorded discussions revealed that increases in defensive behavior were correlated positively with losses in efficiency in communication.[1] Specifically, distortions became greater when defensive states existed in the groups.

The converse, moreover, also is true. The more "supportive" or defense reductive the climate, the less the receiver reads into the communication distorted loadings which arise from projections of his own anxieties, motives, and concerns. As defenses are reduced, the receivers become better able to concentrate upon the structure, the content, and the cognitive meanings of the message.

Jack R. Gibb, "Defensive Communication," *Journal Of Communication,* Vol. 11, No. 3 (1961), pp. 141-148. Reprinted by permission.
[1] J. R. Gibb, "Defense Level and Influence Potential in Small Groups," in L. Petrullo and B. M. Bass (eds.), *Leadership and Interpersonal Behavior* (New York: Holt, Rinehart and Winston, Inc., 1961), pp. 66-81.

CATEGORIES OF DEFENSIVE AND SUPPORTIVE COMMUNICATION

In working over an eight-year period with recordings of discussions occurring in varied settings, the writer developed the six pairs of defensive and supportive categories presented in Table I. Behavior which a listener perceives as possessing any of the characteristics listed in the left-hand column arouses defensiveness, whereas that which he interprets as having any of the qualities designated as supportive reduces defensive feelings. The degree to which these reactions occur depends upon the personal level of defensiveness and upon the general climate in the group at the time.[2]

Evaluation and Description

Speech or other behavior which appears evaluative increases defensiveness. If by expression, manner of speech, tone of voice, or verbal content the sender seems to be evaluating or judging the listener, then the receiver goes on guard. Of course, other factors may inhibit the reaction. If the listener thought that the speaker regarded him as an equal and was being open and spontaneous, for example, the evaluativeness in a message would be neutralized and perhaps not even perceived. This same principle applies equally to the other five categories of potentially defense-producing climates. The six sets are interactive.

Because our attitudes toward other persons are frequently, and often necessarily, evaluative expressions which the defensive person will regard as nonjudgmental are hard to frame. Even the simplest question usually conveys the answer that the sender wishes or implies the response that would fit into his value system. A mother, for example, immediately following an earth tremor that shook the house, sought for her small son with the question: "Bobby, where are you?" The timid and plaintive "Mommy, I didn't do it" indicated how Bobby's chronic mild defensiveness predisposed him to react with a projection of his own guilt and in the context of his chronic assumption that questions are full of accusation.

Anyone who has attempted to train professionals to use information-seeking speech with neutral affect appreciates how difficult it is to teach a person to say even the simple "who did that?" without being seen as accusing. Speech is so frequently judgmental that there is a reality base for the defensive interpretations which are so common.

When insecure, group members are particularly likely to place blame, to see others as fitting into categories of good or bad, to make moral judgments of their colleagues, and to question the value, motive, and affect loadings of the speech which they hear. Since value loadings imply a judgment of others, a belief that the standards of the speaker differ from his own causes the listener to become defensive.

Descriptive speech, in contrast to that which is evaluative, tends to arouse a minimum of uneasiness. Speech acts which the listener perceives as

---

[2]J. R. Gibb, "Sociopsychological Processes of Group Instruction," in N. B. Henry (ed.), *The Dynamics of Instructional Groups* (fifty-ninth yearbook of the National Society for the Study of Education, Part II, 1960), pp. 115-135.

genuine requests for information or as material with neutral loadings is descriptive. Specifically, presentations of feelings, events, perceptions, or processes which do not ask or imply that the receiver change behavior or attitude are minimally defense producing. The difficulty in avoiding overtone is illustrated by the problems of news reporters in writing stories about unions, communists, Negroes, and religious activities without tipping off the "party" line of the newspaper. One can often tell from the opening words in a news article which side the newspaper's editorial policy favors.

Control and Problem Orientation

Speech which is used to control the listener evokes resistance. In most of our social intercourse someone is trying to do something to someone else— to change an attitude, to influence behavior, or to restrict the field of activity. The degree to which attempts to control produce defensiveness depends upon the openness of the effort, for a suspicion that hidden motives exist heightens resistance. For this reason, attempts of nondirective therapists and progressive educators to refrain from imposing a set of values, a point of view, or a problem solution upon the receivers meet with many barriers. Since the norm is control, noncontrollers must earn the perceptions that their efforts have no hidden motives. A bombardment of persuasive "messages" in the fields of politics, education, special causes, advertising, religion, medicine, industrial relations, and guidance has bred cynical and paranoidal responses in listeners.

TABLE I

Categories of Behavior Characteristics of Supportive and Defensive Climates in Small Groups

Defensive Climates	*Supportive Climates*
1. Evaluation	1. Description
2. Control	2. Problem orientation
3. Strategy	3. Spontaneity
4. Neutrality	4. Empathy
5. Superiority	5. Equality
6. Certainty	6. Provisionalism

Implicit in all attempts to alter another person is the assumption by the change agent that the person to be altered is inadequate. That the speaker secretly views the listener as ignorant, unable to make his own decisions, uninformed, immature, unwise, or possessed of wrong or inadequate attitudes is a subconscious perception which gives the latter a valid base for defensive reactions.

Methods of control are many and varied. Legalistic insistence on detail, restrictive regulations and policies, conformity norms, and all laws are among the methods. Gestures, facial expressions, other forms of nonverbal communication, and even such simple acts as holding a door open in a particular manner are means of imposing one's will upon another and hence are potential sources of resistance.

Problem orientation, on the other hand, is the antithesis of persuasion. When the sender communicates a desire to collaborate in defining a mutual problem and in seeking its solution, he tends to create the same problem orientation in the listener; and, of greater importance, he implies that he has no predetermined solution, attitude, or method to impose. Such behavior is permissive in that it allows the receiver to set his own goals, make his own decisions, and evaluate his own progressor to share with the sender in doing so. The exact methods of attaining permissiveness are not known, but they must involve a constellation of cues and they certainly go beyond mere verbal assurances that the communicator has no hidden desires to exercise control.

Strategy and Spontaneity

When the sender is perceived as engaged in a stratagem involving ambiguous and multiple motivations, the receiver becomes defensive. No one wishes to be a guinea pig, a role player, or an impressed actor, and no one likes to be the victim of some hidden motivation. That which is concealed, also, may appear larger than it really is with the degree of defensiveness of the listener determining the perceived size of the suppressed element. The intense reaction of the reading audience to the material in the Hidden Persuaders indicates the prevalence of defensive reactions to multiple motivations behind strategy. Group members who are seen as "taking a role," as feigning emotion, as toying with their colleagues, as withholding information, or as having special sources of data are especially resented. One participant once complained that another was "using a listening technique" on him!

A large part of the adverse reaction to much of the so-called human relations training is a feeling against what are perceived as gimmicks and tricks to fool or to "involve" people, to make a person think he is making his own decision, or to make the listener feel that the sender is genuinely interested in him as a person. Particularly violent reactions occur when it appears that someone is trying to make a stratagem appear spontaneous. One person has reported a boss who incurred resentment by habitually using the gimmick of "spontaneously" looking at his watch and saying, "My gosh, look at the time —I must run to an appointment." The belief was that the boss would create less irritation by honestly asking to be excused.

Similarly, the deliberate assumption of guilelessness and natural simplicity is especially resented. Monitoring the tapes of feedback and evaluation sessions in training groups indicates the surprising extent to which members perceive the strategies of their colleagues. This perceptual clarity may be quite shocking to the strategist, who usually feels that he has cleverly hidden the motivational aura around the "gimmick."

This aversion to deceit may account for one's resistance to politicians who are suspected of behind-the-scenes planning to get his vote, to psychologists whose listening apparently is motivated by more than the manifest or content-level interest in his behavior, or to the sophisticated, smooth, or clever person whose "oneupmanship" is marked with guile. In training groups the role-flexible person frequently is resented because his changes in behavior are perceived as strategic maneuvers.

In contrast, behavior which appears to be spontaneous and free of deception is defense reductive. If the communicator is seen as having a clean id, as having uncomplicated motivations, as being straightforward and honest, and as behaving spontaneously in response to the situation, he is likely to arouse minimal defense.

Neutrality and Empathy

When neutrality in speech appears to the listener to indicate a lack of concern for his welfare, he becomes defensive. Group members usually desire to be perceived as valued persons, as individuals of speech worth, and as objects of concern and affection. The clinical, detached, person-is-an-object-of-study attitude on the part of many psychologist-trainers is resented by group members. Speech with low affect that communicates little warmth or caring is in such contrast with the affect laden speech in social situations that it sometimes communicates rejection.

Communication that conveys empathy for the feelings and respect for the worth of the listener, however, is particularly supportive and defense reductive. Reassurance results when a message indicates that the speaker identifies himself with the listener's problems, shares his feelings, and accepts his emotional reactions at face value. Abortive efforts to deny the legitimacy of the receiver's emotions by assuring the receiver that he need not feel bad, that he should not feel rejected or that he is overly anxious, though often intended as support giving, may impress the listener as lack of acceptance. The combination of understanding and empathizing with the other person's emotions with no accompanying effort to change him apparently is supportive at a high level.

The importance of gestural behavioral cues in communicating empathy should be mentioned. Apparently spontaneous facial and bodily evidences of concern are often interpreted as especially valid evidence of deep-level acceptance.

Superiority and Equality

When a person communicates to another that he feels superior in position, power, wealth, intellectual ability, physical characteristics, or other ways, he arouses defensiveness. Here, as with the other sources of disturbance, whatever arouses feelings of inadequacy causes the listener to center upon the affect loading of the statement rather than upon the cognitive elements. The receiver then reacts by not hearing the message, by forgetting it, by competing with the sender, or by becoming jealous of him.

The person who is perceived as feeling superior communicates that he is not willing to enter into a shared problem-solving relationship, that he probably does not desire feedback, that he does not require help, and/or that he will be likely to try to reduce the power, the status, or the worth of the receiver.

Many ways exist for creating the atmosphere that the sender feels himself equal to the listener. Defenses are reduced when one perceives the sender as being willing to enter into participative planning with mutual trust and respect. Differences in talent, ability, worth, appearance, status, and power often exist, but the low defense communicator seems to attach little importance to these distinctions.

Certainty and Provisionalism

The effects of dogmatism in producing defensiveness are well known. Those who seem to know the answers, to require no additional data, and to regard themselves as teachers rather than as co-workers tend to put others on guard. Moreover, in the writer's experiment, listeners often perceived manifest expressions of certainty as connoting inward feelings of inferiority. They saw the dogmatic individual as needing to be right, as wanting to win an argument rather than solve a problem, and as seeing his ideas as truths to be defended. This kind of behavior often was associated with acts which others regarded as attempts to exercise control. People who were right seemed to have low tolerance for members who were "wrong"—i.e., who did not agree with the sender.

One reduces the defensiveness of the listener when he communicates that he is willing to experiment with his own behavior, attitudes, and ideas. The person who appears to be taking provisional attitudes, to be investigating issues rather than taking sides on them, to be problem solving rather than debating, and to be willing to experiment and explore tends to communicate that the listener may have some control over the shared quest or the investigation of the ideas. If a person is genuinely searching for information and data, he does not resent help or company along the way.

CONCLUSION

The implications of the above material for the parent, the teacher, the manager, the administrator, or the therapist are fairly obvious. Arousing defensiveness interferes with communication and thus makes it difficult—and sometimes impossible—for anyone to convey ideas clearly and to move effectively toward the solution of therapeutic, educational, or managerial problems.

VERBAL COMMUNICATION 2

If you write some word symbols or speak some vocal word symbols, you present a verbal message to somebody else. If you function as an average North American doing this, you find that sometimes the intended receiver of your word-symbol message understands what you intend at once, but that at other times, he, she, or they somehow miss your meaning, possibly adding some different interpretation. Haney deals delightfully with this problem in "Bypassing," the first selection.

One way to think of a communication act relates it to an electrical circuit which may get shorted out. Albrecht explains this in the second one "Five Ways to Short Circuit Your Communication."

Third, even profanity has come under the magnifying glass of the forbidden-language sleuth as demonstrated in "A Multivariate Investigation of Profane Language" by Mabry.

Making suggestions about word meanings to those students desiring to write more successful messages, Vik presents "Bridging the Communication Gap," the last article in the chapter.

William V. Haney

BYPASSING

DEFINITION

Belden, West and Bartell[1] was a medium-sized brokerage firm with approximately 95 employees. The accounting department had 17 employees, of whom three were middle-aged women who operated the bookkeeping machines. With the average volume of business, all three were normally finished with their posting about one hour before the usual quitting time.

On February 21st one of the bookkeepers, Elizabeth Morley, phoned in to say she was ill and would be unable to report for duty. The other two pitched in and completed about 75 percent of the absent woman's posting before the normal quitting time. The supervisor then approached one of the bookkeepers, Jane Dover, and said: "Elizabeth just called and said she'll be absent again tomorrow, so the balance of her work [25 percent of her normal work load] will have to be completed the first thing in the morning."

Miss Dover, a very conscientious and somewhat unassertive woman, said nothing. The following morning the supervisor found that Miss Dover had worked until 8:30 P.M. the previous evening to complete Miss Morley's posting. The supervisor had intended that she and the other bookkeeper continue with the remainder of Miss Morley's work in the morning before starting on their own posting.

A motorist was driving on the Merritt Parkway outside New York City when his engine stalled. He quickly determined that his battery was dead and managed to stop another driver, a woman. She consented to push his car to get it started.

"My car has an automatic transmission," he explained to her, "so you'll have to get up to 30 to 35 miles per hour to get me started."

The woman smiled sweetly and walked back to her car. The motorist climbed into his own car and waited for her to line up her car behind his. He waited—and waited. Finally, he turned around to see what was wrong.

There was the woman—coming at his car at 30 to 35 miles per hour! The damage to his car amounted to $300!

In each of the preceding instances there was talking and there was listening. There were people "sending" messages and other people "receiving" them. But somehow the communication went awry. The speaker didn't "get through"—the listener didn't "get *him.*" The listener presumably heard the same words that the speaker said, but the communicators seem to have *talked past* one another.

This communication phenomenon is called *bypassing*. The figure diagrams the *bypassing* between Sipert and his foreman.

It is evident that the foreman had one meaning for "better clean up around here" and Sipert had another. Their meanings *bypassed* one another

Reprinted with permission from William V. Haney, "Bypassing," *Communication and Organizational Behavior* (Homewood, Illinois: Richard D. Irwin, Inc., 1973.) pp. 245-282.
[1] All names have been disguised.

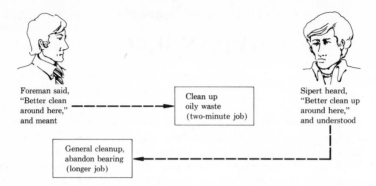

without meeting. *Bypassing,* then, is the name for the miscommunication pattern which occurs when the *sender* (speaker, writer, and so on) and the *receiver* (listener, reader, and so forth) *miss each other with their meanings.*

Same word—different things

Before going on, it should be noted that the three *bypassing* illustrations took the form of some persons "sending" and others "receiving" the *same words* but attributing *different meanings* to them. Miss Dover, for example, heard the *same words* her supervisor had said but interpreted them quite differently from what he had intended. This is a very common type of *bypassing,* but it has an equally prevalent counterpart.

Different words—same thing

Bypassing may occur just as readily when people are using *different words* to represent the *same thing.* I once witnessed with thinly disguised amusement a heated and fruitless argument between my 12-year-old nephew and a Massachusetts soda fountain clerk, only a year or two older. Jimmy, born and reared in Illinois, was visiting the East Coast for the first time.

The conversation went something like this:

JIMMY: Do you have pop?
CLERK: What?
JIMMY: Pop.
CLERK: I don't know what you're talking about.
JIMMY (scornfully): You never heard of pop?
CLERK: No, and neither did you!
JIMMY: Listen, it's that stuff that comes in a bottle—you shake it up and it fizzes out!
CLERK: Oh! You mean a soda!
JIMMY: No! I don't want a soda! (A "soda" where Jimmy lives is made with ice cream, flavoring, and soda water.)
CLERK: Well, then, what *do* you want?
JIMMY: Never mind! You wouldn't have it anyway!

At this point I partially reconciled the two antagonists by suggesting that they were both talking about the same thing. Jimmy, incidentally, finally got his "pop," "soda," "tonic," "minerals," "soft drink," or whatever it is called in your part of the country.

Both types of *bypassing* (same word—different things and different words—same thing) have a common basis, of course. Both involve people missing one another's meanings, and their consequences are equally worthy of consideration.

SOME CONSEQUENCES

Bypassing may occur under such a variety of circumstances that it may be helpful to suggest something of the range of its consequences.

The range of consequences

Bypassing is certainly one of the most prevalent and potentially costly and dangerous patterns of miscommunication in organizations or virtually anywhere else. But bypassing isn't always serious, hazardous, or even important. Much of the time its effects are inconsequential. And at other times its results may be amusing or even hilarious. In fact, much of our humor is based on bypassing. Permit me to make the point with a personal story. It happened on my first day of college teaching years ago. Mustering as much dignity as possible for a neophyte, I walked into the classroom and announced that I was going to seat the class alphabetically. I explained that I had difficulty in associating names with faces, and in seating them alphabetically, "I will get to know you by your seats." You may be quite sure the class bypassed me!

But I was not to have the only red face that day, for 20 minutes later a young, innocent freshman miss rose to describe her initial campus impressions. She said she was particularly fond of the serenades—when the fraternity boys would come as a group to sing beneath the girls' dormitory windows. "We girls love it so," she emphasized, "we wish the boys could stay all night!"

Unfortunately, not all bypassings end so delightfully (at least from the audience's point of view). Bypassings occurring every day in industry, in government, and in homes, result in enormous wastes of time, money, effort, and tempers. History is full of examples of bypassing which have led to catastrophes. There is even disturbing evidence to suggest that a bypassing on a word in the Japanese response to the World War II Potsdam ultimatum may have led to the dropping of the atomic bombs on Japan and Russia's declaration of war on Japan—events which have had irrevocable effect upon world affairs.[2]

Immediate consequences

Before we leave this cursory review of bypassing we should note that the *immediate* effects of this breakdown in communication generally fall into one or the other of two broad classifications.

Apparent agreement. Most of the bypassing illustrations we have been considering have had *apparent agreement* as their immediate consequences. That is, the initial result of the bypassing was such that those involved felt they were in harmony with one another. Sipert and his foreman. Miss Dover and her supervisor, and the stalled motorist and the woman driver, for example, believed that they had had an adequate understanding. The bypassing, however,

---

[2] William J. Coughlin, "Was It the Deadliest Error of Our Time?" *Harper's Magazine*, March 1953, pp. 31-40.

concealed an *actual disagreement* (i.e., the people involved differed on meanings).

It is acting on the false assurance of agreement which so frequently leads us into trouble.

Jeannie, 9, called to her mother upstairs: "Mom, may I fix the Easter eggs?" "Yes, dear," mother called back, "just put three dozen eggs into the kettle and be sure to cook them for at least 15 minutes."

Jeannie placed the eggs in the largest kettle she could find and filled it with cold water. Then she set the kettle on the stove and turned on the gas.

After 15 minutes of eager clock watching, Jeannie removed the eggs from the water (which had not yet begun to boil) and set them on the table.

While she was preparing the Easter egg dyes, her brother Tom, 14, walked into the kitchen and picked up an egg. "Are you sure you cooked these long enough?," he asked. "Sure. Exactly 15 minutes, just like Mom said." "Well, okay—say, want to see what a hard head I have?" And with that Tom cracked a very uncooked egg on his head!

Apparent disagreement. But bypassing which conceals *actual agreement* by manifesting *apparent disagreement* can also be disconcerting.

Major Gregory Klimov, for two years an official of the Soviet Military Administration in Occupied Berlin and who later fled to the West, recounts the first meeting of the Allied Control Commission, Economic Directorate. After routine matters had been settled, the head of the American delegation proposed that the first item on the agenda should be: "The working out of basic policy for the economic demilitarization of Germany."

And this futile battle over the awkward word *policy* was the beginning of the first of many long and similar arguments around the conference table.

Whether the immediate consequence of bypassing is an *apparent agreement* or an *apparent disagreement,* the subsequent effect *can* be unpleasant, unproductive, and even fatal. Let us now look into some of the contributing factors of this often troublesome pattern of miscommunication.

THE UNDERLYING MECHANISM

To cope with harmful bypassing we must examine its underlying *mechanism.* Just what happens when people bypass? What kind of thought process occurs which leads to such dangerous and costly miscommunication?

Let us return to the Sipert-foreman incident. They bypassed one another, i.e., missed each other with their meanings. But *why?* Let us presume that neither *intended* to miscommunicate. Certainly the foreman did not use any "big," foreign, or unfamiliar words. Why, then, did the communication go askew?

Suppose we asked Sipert and the foreman what they thought went wrong in their communication. Their responses might follow this pattern:

Sipert: I was sure I knew what the boss meant. I never thought he was talking about cleaning up the waste.

Foreman: I was certain Sipert would understand what I was driving at. It never occurred to me that he would put a different interpretation on my remark.

"I was sure . . . I never thought . . . "; "I was certain . . . It never occurred to me . . . " These men are revealing the key assumption underlying their behavior—the assumption that *"words mean the same to the other fellow as they do to me."*

That is an enormously pervasive assumption. Most of us act on this assumption much of the time—and usually the assumption proves correct. That is, more often than not people *do* interpret our words as we intend—and usually we decode their words appropriately as well. But consistent success sometimes leads to overconfidence and complacency—the ideal attitudes for bypassing.

There are at least two additional reasons for the epidemic prevalence of the assumption. First, it is a highly *enticing* notion. We *want* to feel we are understanding and being understood by the other fellow. Second, the assumption supports our basic egocentrism as evidenced by this passage from Lewis Carroll's *Through the Looking Glass:*

> Humpty-Dumpty said: "There's glory for you." "I don't know what you mean by 'glory,' " Alice said. Humpty-Dumpty smiled contemptuously. "Of course you don't till I tell you. I meant, 'There's a nice knock-down argument for you.' " "But 'glory' doesn't mean a 'nice knock-down argument,' " Alice objected. "When I use a word," Humpty-Dumpty said in a rather scornful tone, "it means just what I choose it to mean, neither more nor less."

Few of us are as frank as Humpty, although we are frequently as arrogant. We would not call it "arrogance" (unless we were talking about the other fellow) because we are largely unaware of the prevailing egocentrism which so frequently accompanies our use of words. If a person were to resolve to watch scrupulously his own language use during a 24-hour period, he would almost certainly catch himself talking or listening (writing or reading) dozens of times with the Humpty-Dumpty attitude. He would find himself assuming, "I *knew* what the other person understood or meant simply because that was the way I used or would have used the words."

It is understandable why so much communicating occurs under the influence of such an assumption. But the stark fact remains: The assumption is *not unfailingly valid*—and we have already suggested the scope of consequences of acting unconsciously upon the assumption when it is false.

Digging more deeply we find that the assumption is supported by two pernicious fallacies. One is that words are used in only one way ("the way *I* am using them")—that *words have mono-usage*. The other is that *words have meanings*. I shall attack each of these fallacies for they lie at the foundation of bypassing.

The fallacy that words have mono-usage

The first of the fallacies underlying bypassing is the assumption of mono-usage. The notion that words are used for one and only one meaning is so patently ridiculous that it hardly appears necessary to refute it. Yet so much of our communication seems based on this misconception that I must comment on it.

To begin, let me ask a question: How many words are used in only one way? Excepting certain technological terms, virtually all of our common words (so far as I have been able to determine) are used in more than one way. That is, the words we usually use in our day-to-day communications almost invariably have multi-usage. In fact, for the 500 most commonly used words in our language there is an aggregate of over 14,000 dictionary definitions! Take the word *fast,* for instance:

> A person is *fast* when he can run rapidly.
> But he is also *fast* when he is tied down and cannot run at all.
> And colors are *fast* when they do not run.
> One is *fast* when he moves in suspect company.
> But this is not quite the same thing as playing *fast* and loose.
> A racetrack is *fast* when it is in good running condition.
> A friend is *fast* when he is loyal.
> A watch is *fast* when it is ahead of time.
> To be *fast* asleep is to be deep in sleep.
> To be *fast* by is to be near.
> To *fast* is to refrain from eating.
> A *fast* may be a period of noneating—or a ship's mooring line.
> Photographic film is *fast* when it is *sensitive* (to light).
> But bacteria are *fast* when they are *insensitive* (to antiseptics).

And note the versatility of *call* in this gripping narrative:

> Jim *called* on Joe to *call* him out for *calling* him up at midnight and *calling* him down, but their wives *called* in friends who got the fight *called* off.[3]

If one recognizes the prevalence of *multi-usage* in our language, he will anticipate that words can readily be understood differently by different people.

Neologisms. The prevalence of multi-usage in a language is directly related to the extent of the *neologizing* which occurs in that language. When something new appears—an invention, a novel event, a new relationship or combination, and so on—how does it become named? Basically, there are two neological tacks: (1) Invent a new word (word coinage) or (2) use an old word in a different way (usage coinage).

1) **Word Coinage.** The coining of words is a fascinating art. Manufacturers sometimes pay handsome rewards to those who contrive new names which most aptly and appealingly represent their products. Especially impressive are the fabricated labels for the miracle ingredients of some products. Somehow the term suggests a mystique of power, romance, or virtue which even the Federal Trade Commission finds difficult to refute.

A special kind of word coinage is the acronym such as:

RADAR: *R*adio *D*etecting *A*nd *R*anging
SCUBA: *S*elf *C*ontained *U*nderwater *B*reathing *A*pparatus
LASER: *L*ight *A*mplification by *S*timulated *E*mission of *R*adiation
LEM: *L*unar *E*xcursion *M*odule
SNAFU: (The ubiquitous term from World War II) *S*ituation *N*ormal: *A*ll *F*ouled *U*p.[4]

---

[3]The sentence hardly suggests the multi-usages of *call.* Webster's Unabridged lists 40 different definitions for the word. Other kaleidoscopic words: *turn* (54 definitions), *fall* (50), *touch* (46).
[4]*Approximate* translation.

Verbal Communication 57

Sometimes words are coined by combining words or parts of words: television, phonevision, motel, teen-ager. Or they are nicknames for longer words such as *fan* which is short for *fanatic* and nincompoop which is a telescoped version of *non compos mentis*. Often common nouns spring from the name of the person who innovated, discovered, or was otherwise associated with the referent.

Earl of Sandwich	Jules Léotard
Lord Cardigan	George Pullman
Lord Raglan	James Watt
Earl of Davenport	Count Ferdinand von Zeppelin
Lord Chesterfield	Antoine Sax
Charles C. Boycott	François-René de Chateaubriand
Rudolph Diesel	Vidkun Quisling
Daniel Fahrenheit	Gaston Chevrolet
Colonel Martinet	Joseph I. Guillotine
Nicolas Chauvin	Etienne de Silhouette

And lest the ladies feel neglected: Amelia Bloomer.

Flowers seem especially beholden to individuals for their names. Among their benefactors:

Michel Bégon	Matthias de l'Obel
Georg Camel	Joel Poinsett
Anders Dahl	Caspar Wistar
William Forsythe	Johann Gottfried Zinn
Alexander Garden	

Our language is occasionally enriched by the proper name of a fictional character becoming a genetic word: *babbitt—quixotic—malapropism —mentor—gargantuan—pollyanna—robot—serendipity*.

2) **Usage Coinage.** The kind of neologism which is more germane to bypassing, however, is that which occurs when a new usage is made of an existing word. But briefly in defense, were it not for usage coinage, puns, sad to contemplate, would be impossible. Thus, we would have been deprived of the delightful liberties taken by the suppliers of names for the colors of the '69 Maverick: *Thanks Vermillion, Hulla Blue, Anti-Establish Mint, Last Stand Custard, Freudian Gilt,* and *Original Cinnamon.* Maverick's marketers opted not to use *Come-and-Get-Me Copper, Gang Green,* and *Statutory Grape.*

Highlighting the frequency of usage coinage *Life* recently published a list of words which are now being used in ways which are quite different from (and in addition to) the way(s) they were defined less than a decade ago.[5]

acid	demonstration	militant	silo
AFL	dove	Minuteman	soul
Apollo	drop out	moratorium	split
bag	freak	pad	Dr. Spock
black	grass	panther	stoned
blitz	hangup	pig	straight
bread	hawk	pill	topless
brother	head	pot	transplant

[5] *Life*, January 23, 1970, p. 28.

busing	joint	Pueblo	trip
Camelot	Sen. McCarthy	rap	turn on
camp	mace	rock	Wallace

This "piling on" of usages moved one anonymous bard to express his frustration in verse:

Remember when hippie meant big in the hips,
And a trip involved travel in cars, planes and ships?
When pot was a vessel for cooking things in,
And hooked was what grandmother's rugs may have been?
When fix was a verb that meant mend or repair,
And be-in meant merely existing somewhere?
When neat meant well-organized, tidy and clean,
And grass was a ground cover, normally green?
When groovy meant furrowed with channels and hollows,
And birds were winged creatures, like robins and swallows?
When fuzz was a substance, real fluffy, like lint,
And bread came from bakeries and not from the mint?
When roll meant a bun, and rock was a stone,
And hang-up was something you did with the phone?
It's groovy, man, groovy, but English it's not.
Methinks that our language is going to pot.

The *accumulation* of *usages* occurs incessantly in a living language. And if we consider some of the special kinds of usage accumulation we may be alerted to some of the areas of potential bypassing. Among them: (a) etymological shifts, (b) regionalisms, and (c) technical/common usage.

a) Etymological shifts. A great many of our older words have undergone etymological shifts. That is, they have acquired new usages as they have been passed down through time. Some of the usages drop out after a time, but many remain, and the result is often a formidable accumulation of definitions, all of which are operating presently. The word *mess* is a good example. A Latin term, it originally stood for *something sent.* This usage is still reflected in words such as *message, messenger, mission, missile, missive, missionary, emissary, emission, remission,* and so on. Later *mess* came to represent food *sent* from the kitchen to the dining table; then a quantity of soft food (*mess* of porridge); then a sufficient quantity of a certain kind of food for a dish or meal (*mess* of peas). Still later, *mess* referred to the entire dining situation including the people sitting about the dining table (the soldiers were at *mess*). Finally, *mess* came to denote the various dinnerware, glasses, and dishes with the unfinished food still clinging to them which were piled together in a heap after dinner, and thus represents any general disorganization (what a *mess!*)[6] We even speak of *emotionally* disorganized people in this way. (Is she a *mess!*)

We have a great knack for using old words in new ways. The words listed above are among the thousands of words which have acquired new usages during the last several years. Incidentally, I have found that whether one approves of them or not, it is generally wise to keep abreast of these new usages. Recently, my office was chilly, and I walked into my young secretary's

---

[6] Adapted from "Meanings of 'Mess,'" by Dwight Everett Hawkins, *Word Study* (published by G. & C. Merriam Co., Springfield, Mass.), October 1956.

office to ask: "Are you cool in here?" "Crazy, man!" she responded gleefully.

The rapidity of the etymological shifts is one reason why learning English is so difficult for foreigners. While they may have mastered the grammar and conventional usages (which remain relatively constant), they may have trouble keeping up with the ever-changing idiom. Not long ago a student from India enrolled at Northwestern University. On his first day at the university, an American student generously escorted him about the campus, helpfully pointing out the buildings in which the new student would be having classes, the cafeterias, library, and so on. Finally, they returned to the Indian's dormitory room. When the American had seen that the newcomer was comfortably situated, he left with a cheery, "See you later!" The Indian stayed up until 3 o'clock in the morning, for he did not want to be so impolite as to retire when his new friend had obviously promised to return!

A Thailander enrolled at another midwestern university. He eagerly waited for an opportunity to meet the university's president, a renowned scholar, he was granted an appointment and, with the utmost of humility and solemnity, walked into the president's office. He bowed deeply to the president and said: "I am most honored to meet with you, sir. I know that you are a very wise guy."

And sometimes the tables are turned. Copywriters for General Motors discovered that "Body by Fisher" became "Corpse by Fisher" in Flemish. And one U.S. airline learned after a vigorous advertising campaign that their luxurious "rendezvous lounges" were misconstrued. In Portuguese, "rendezvous" denotes a room hired for assignations.

b) **Regional variations.** Word usages vary, not only from time to time but from geographical region to region. Jimmy in his quest for "pop" learned this the hard way. What is a "sweet roll" in some areas is a "bun" in others and a "danish" in still others. "Evening" in some parts of the South is the period from noon through twilight. In the rest of the country, however, it generally refers to the period from sunset or the evening meal to ordinary bedtime.

The Pennsylvania Dutch present a special communication problem. These good people speak English all right, but often using a Germanic-type grammar. The results are sometimes quite charming:

"Throw Papa down the stairs his hat."
  Girl to her brother chopping wood: "Chonny—come from the woodpile in . . . Mom's on the table still . . . and Pop's et himself already."

But how would you respond to the pleasant chap, standing in front of you in a line at the post office, who asks: "If a body goes quick out and comes right aways back in again, will he be where he was yet?" And no one will be able to convince the American motorist that the English speak "English." While driving in England, a motorist finds that instead of "No Passing" the sign reads "No Overtaking." When the danger zone is passed, you come to "End of Prohibition!" You are told not to "Stop" but "Halt" at highway intersections. If you try to park in a no-parking area, you find a sign "No Waiting."[7]

---

[7]Clyde S. Kilby, "Signs in Great Britain," *Word Study,* December 1955. Copyright 1955 by G. & C. Merriam Co., publishers of the Merriam-Webster Dictionaries.

Small wonder that G. B. Shaw described England and the United States as two great nations separated by the barrier of a common language.

c) **Technical common usage.** Specialists (and almost everyone is a specialist to some degree) tend to develop their own "private language." Salesmen speak of "closure" (the completion of a sale); plumbers of "wiping a joint" (applying molten lead with a pad to join pipes); publishers of "fillers" (short items to fill out columns); television directors of "stretching" (slowing up to consume time); and laundry men of "mangling the wash" (smoothing it by roller pressure). Ordinarily, these specialists use these terms to good effect when communicating with their fellow specialists. Many of these words and phrases, however, are *also* used by the general public, but in quite different ways. Let the technician forget that the outsider is not accustomed to these words in his specialized sense, and the results are likely to be confusing at best.

I learned something of the intricacies of plain English at an early stage in my career. A woman of thirty-five came in one day to tell me that she wanted a baby but that she had been told that she had a certain type of heart-disease which might not interfere with a normal life but would be dangerous if she ever had a baby. From her description I thought at once of mitral stenosis. This condition is characterized by a rather distinctive rumbling murmur near the apex of the heart, and especially by a peculiar vibration felt by the examining finger on the patient's chest. The vibration is known as the "thrill" of mitral stenosis.

When this woman had been undressed and was lying on my table in her white kimono, my stethoscope quickly found the heart-sounds I had expected. Dictating to my nurse, I described them carefully. I put my stethoscope aside and felt intently for the typical vibration which may be found in a small but variable area of the left chest.

I closed my eyes for better concentration, and felt long and carefully for the tremor. I did not find it and with my hand still on the woman's bare breast, lifting it upward and out of the way, I finally turned to the nurse and said: "No thrill."

The patient's black eyes snapped open, and with venom in her voice she said: "Well, isn't that just too bad? Perhaps it's just as well you don't get one. That isn't what I came for."

My nurse almost choked, and my explanation still seems a nightmare of futile words.[8]

Miscommunication is also possible, of course, from specialty to specialty. The dentist's "closure" (the extent to which the upper and lower teeth fit together when the jaw is closed) differs from the salesman's. And the parliamentarian's "closure" (a method for ending debate and securing an immediate vote on a measure) differs from both. Consider the machinist who ordered a tree. "What caliper size do you want?" inquired the nurseryman. "About three or four inches," said the machinist, whose calipers measure *diameters*. The tree man brought a sapling only one inch across, for his calipers measure *circumferences*.

Computers and multi-usage. Because of the multi-usage of English (and many other languages) it is unlikely that computers will replace human trans-

---

[8] Frederic Loomis, M.D., *Consultation Room* (New York: Alfred A. Knopf, Inc., 1939), p. 47.

lators—at least in the near future. The very precision the computer requires of its inputs severely limits its coping with a highly ambiguous natural language.[9] For example, when asked to interpret the sentence, "Time flies like an arrow," a computer gave two answers: "Check the speed of flies as fast as you can," and "Certain flies have a fondness for an arrow."

And when computerized translation *between* natural languages is attempted the problem is compounded. In one test, the computer received in English, "The spirit is willing but the flesh is weak." It is translated into Russian, "The liquor is still good but the meat has gone bad." In an English-Japanese attempt the output was, "Invisible lunatic." The input? "Out of sight, out of mind."

The fallacy that words have meanings

The persistent delusion that words *have* meanings possibly stems from what Irving J. Lee called the "container myth":

> If you think of words as vessels, then you are likely to talk about "the meaning of a word" as if the meaning were *in* the word. Assuming this, it is easy to endow words with characteristics. Just as you may say that one vessel is costlier or more symmetrical than another, you may say that one word is intrinsically more suitable for one purpose than another, or that, in and of itself, a word will have this or that meaning rather than any other. When one takes this view, he seems to say that meaning is to a word as contents are to a container.[10]

He suggested that when one acts upon his unconscious assumption that words *contain* meanings, he is insidiously led to assume that when he talks (or writes) he is handing his listener (or reader) so many *containers* of meanings. If this is the case, the recipient is "bound to get the correct meanings."

Saint Augustine recognized this fallacy almost 15 centuries ago when he argued in his *Christian Instruction* that words do not possess intrinsic meaning. "Rather, they 'have' a meaning because men have agreed upon them."

Words, of course, do not "contain" or "have" meanings. Apart from people using them, words are merely marks on paper, vibrations in the air, raised dots on a Braille card, and so on. Words really do not *mean* at all—only the *users* of words can mean something, with the words they use. This is a sensible enough statement to accept—*intellectually*. Unfortunately, our *behavior* with words very frequently does not abide by it.

But just what *do* words do—or, more precisely, what do people do *with* them? What happens *inside* people as they use words? By way of examining this internal verbal behavior, perhaps you would respond to the three questions below.

---

[9] In fact, artificial languages such as FORTRAN, ALGOL, and COBOL had to be devised to accommodate the computer.

[10] Irving J. Lee, "On a Mechanism of Misunderstanding," *Promoting Growth toward Maturity in Interpreting What Is Read,* ed. Gray, Supplementary Educational Monographs, No. 74 (Chicago: University of Chicago Press, 1951), pp. 86-90. Copyright, 1951, by the University of Chicago.

Question one. In a redwood forest in Northern California stands a huge tree —15 feet in diameter at breast-high level. Clutched to the bark at this level is Super-Squirrel. (Why *Super*-Squirrel will be clear in a moment.) On the opposite side of the tree is a photographer who would like to take Super-Squirrel's picture.

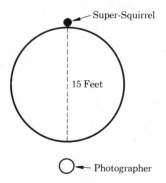

Super-Squirrel

15 Feet

Photographer

Fig. 2–1.

However, when the photographer walks to his right, Super-Squirrel senses the photographer's movement and does the same. When the photographer moves to his left so does Super-Squirrel. No matter how fast or quietly the man moves, Super-Squirrel is a match for him and manages to keep the tree's diameter between them. The photographer decides to back off a mile or two and sneak in from behind, but the uncanny squirrel detects this as well.

A squirrel hunter would suggest throwing a stone or stick to one side of the tree to scare the squirrel around to the other side. And that might work with an ordinary squirrel but this is *Super*-Squirrel! And a *given* in this case is that he keeps the tree's diameter between himself and the photographer at all times.

Another *given:* There is no elevation change such as tree- or mountain-climbing by either Super-Squirrel or the photographer.

The *question:* Can the photographer circle Super-Squirrel?

Question two. Would you pay $25 for a slightly used but fully functioning Zalunk?

Question three. Does $X + 3 = 5$?

I have no way of knowing your answers but I can report the answers given by over 2,000 people including college students, business and government executives, police administrators, military officers, medical personnel, etc., distributed among 67 groups. Their answers were confined to three choices: "Yes," "No," and "I don't know."

TABLE 1

	Yes	No	I don't know
Question one (Super-Squirrel)	59%	39%	2%
Question two (Zalunk)	11%	32%	57%
Question three (X)	5%	2%	93%

Note two aspects about the foregoing figures:

1. The apparent controversy generated by question one in particular. (You might try the Super-Squirrel problem at your next party or coffee break—if you are willing to risk group disintegration!)
2. The rapidly mounting "I don't know" answers and, conversely, the decreasing assurance of answers as we move down through the questions—e.g., 98% positive answers ("yes" or "no") to question one but only 7% to question three.

And yet the three questions share a basic feature. Each contains a key variable and the question cannot be answered "yes" or "no" until that variable is fixed, i.e., defined.

The clearest example is question three. Obviously, the answer is "yes" *if* one fixes the variable X as 2—or "no" if he fixes it as *other than* 2. And perhaps that is why there were so few "yes" or "no" answers. Since the question-asker did not fix the variable for them, people recognized the *active* role they would have to play in fixing it for themselves.

But this was true of the other two questions, too. However, significantly fewer people seemed aware that *they* were the variable-fixers. To say "yes" to the "Zalunk" question, one (unless he were answering facetiously) would presumably have had to fix (define) "Zalunk" as something that was worth $25 to him to own or, at least, to satisfy his curiosity about. To answer "no" would require his defining "Zalunk" as *not* worth $25 to own, etc.

The question with which responders seemed *least* conscious of their roles as variable-fixers was the first. Many steadfastly held that the photographer *could* circle the squirrel and others tenaciously claimed that he could *not*. Put these opposing camps in the same room and observe the decibels rise!

The "yes" responders generally argued that the photographer could walk all the way around the tree. That would cause the squirrel to scamper all the way around it, too, so that the photographer's path would encompass the squirrel's route.

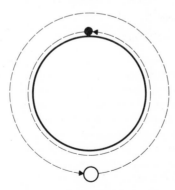

Fig. 2-2.

And *That*, according to the "yes-ers," is "circling the squirrel."

"Hardly," the "no" responders retort. "Circling the squirrel requires that the photographer orbit about the squirrel with the latter as the orbit's axis —or at least pass around the back of the squirrel.

Fig. 2–3.

"Since a given in the case prohibits the photographer from being on the same side of the tree as the squirrel (to say nothing of the photographer's passing *through* the tree!), this cannot occur. Thus, the photographer cannot circle the squirrel."

So *either* answer is "correct" depending upon whose definition we accept.

Now why do people quarrel over silly, petty questions like this—and even sillier and pettier ones? Partly because they *think* they are disputing about *facts*—they are not. They are disagreeing about what *name* they will give to those facts. The issue is not a physical but a semantic one.

The cardinal delusion is their belief that *words* have meaning—apart from the people using them. Words are just so many meaningless variables—like "X" and "Y" and "Zalunk"—until someone fixes the *variable*, i.e., chooses to intend or interpret the words in a particular way.

When one assumes that *words* have meaning, he fails to realize the active role the communicator (sender or receiver) plays as a variable-fixer. The communication problem, then, is *not* that people fix variables (i.e., define words). For we could not communicate otherwise. The problem arises only when (1) the speaker (or writer) fixes a variable one way, (2) the listener (or reader) fixes the variable differently, and (3) each *assumes* the other is or should be fixing it the *same* way.

DELIBERATE BYPASSING

Up to this point we have been presuming that the communicators, regardless of their degree of success or failure, *intended* to understand one another. Clearly, this is not always a warranted assumption. The speaker (or writer) may *desire* to be bypassed. Or the listener (or reader) may just as earnestly contrive to miss meanings. The *motives* of the communicators, therefore, must be considered in any analysis of the factors of a bypassing.

The story is told of the Congressman, running for reelection, who was speaking before a group of constituents. At the conclusion of his prepared talk, a question came from the floor:

"Congressman, you didn't say anything about Social Security. Just how do you feel about Social Security?"

Realizing that his audience was evenly and irreconcilably divided on the issue, he responded with a wink and a knowing smile:

"Don't worry about that subject, my friend—I'm *all right* on that one!" And *everyone* applauded!

And a certain used car dealer used purposeful bypassing to his advantage with this advertisement: "Money cheerfully refunded in 24 hours if not satisfied." Some wishful-thinking buyers were convinced that they were being offered an unlimited guarantee on their purchase and that it would require only a day for the dealer to refund their money. Weeks (or days) later, when some of the second-hand autos began to break down, expectant owners approached the dealer, who retorted: "The advertisement? Oh, that meant I was giving you a one-day guarantee!"

This is akin to the newspaper ad which appeared briefly:

HOW TO AVOID THE DRAFT
LEGALLY AND HONORABLY
SEND $1

For his dollar the customer received one word on a card:

ENLIST

Purposeful bypassing can be used constructively as well. Take the case of a certain labor-management conciliator. The union contract had only a week to run. The union had adamantly refused to discuss terms with management and was preparing to strike. When the conciliator asked union officials why they had refused to bargain, he was told: "Why, we want a *substantial* increase [they told him confidentially that this meant 15 to 20 cents per hour], and we're dead sure management won't go along with us, so why waste time?" Nothing the conciliator could say would persuade them to meet with management. Finally, he turned to the company, where he was told in confidence that it was willing to give 5 or 6 cents. "Would you say this would be a 'substantial increase'?" he asked. "It certainly would be," he was assured. He then returned to the union officials and reported that the company was willing to talk in terms of a "substantial increase." With that, he was able to coax the union's representatives to meet with the company's. With his guidance, the two parties were able to reach a compromise in time to avert a strike that neither side wanted.

Of course, the *receiver* of communication may bypass intentionally just as readily as the *sender*. Our legal system takes this into account by insisting that a law must be obeyed not merely in accord with its *letter* (words) but with its *spirit* (intent). The law recognizes that the *letter* of even the most cautiously written statute may be subject to willful misinterpretation.

Gobbledygook

Before leaving the area of intentional miscommunication we should consider "gobbledygook." This is the smoke-screen kind of communication which, through the use of technical jargon, involved sentences, and polysyllabic words, seem more calculated to obscure than to inform:

In the pursuit of total organizational flexibility and integrated management mobility, one must consider such factors as systematized transitional capability and synchronized logistical programming as well as parallel reciprocal contingencies. Perhaps, however, the most significant factor of all is the basic balanced policy concept. For after all without optional digital and incremental projections the network is by and large merely a functional second or third generation time-phase continuum.

If that has you reeling it has served its purpose. Impressive, sophisticated—but utterly nonsensical. I composed it from the now famous (infamous?) "Systematic Buzz Phrase Projector" which was purportedly originated in the Royal Canadian Air Force. For aid in constructing your own esoteric prolixities and verbose amphibolies here are the raw materials:

Column 1	Column 2	Column 3
0. integrated	0. management	0. options
1. total	1. organizational	1. flexibility
2. systematized	2. monitored	2. capability
3. parallel	3. reciprocal	3. mobility
4. functional	4. digital	4. programming
5. responsive	5. logic	5. concept
6. optical	6. transitional	6. time-phase
7. synchronized	7. incremental	7. projection
8. compatible	8. third-generation	8. hardware
9. balanced	9. policy	9. contingency

Simply think of a three-digit number and select the corresponding "buzz words" from the three columns above. For example, 230 produces "systematized reciprocal options," an expression bound to bring instant respect—and confusion.

Gobbledygook leads not so much to miscommunication as to noncommunication. It is often the refuge of the insecure writer (or speaker). (If you can't say it clearly and simply, to paraphrase Jean Sibelius, you don't understand it.) Unsure of what he means or of the reception of his ideas, he—like the proverbial cuttlefish—evades his enemies by disappearing in a cloud of ink.

But whether bypassing be purposeful or not, the pattern of miscommunication is essentially the same and the corrective measures are applicable in either case.

CORRECTIVES

There is no panacea for curing harmful bypassing, but these time-tested techniques can prevent a great deal of it:

1. Be person-minded, not word-minded.
2. Query and paraphrase.
3. Be approachable.
4. Be sensitive to contexts.

Make these techniques *habitual*. Make them your conditioned response to a communication situation. Consider them as the finely tempered muscles of the athlete. Even after these habits have been established, they must be practiced and strengthened daily.

Be person-minded—not word-minded

The communicator who habitually looks for meanings in the *people* using words, rather than in the *words* themselves, is much less prone to bypass or to be bypassed. He realizes that the important issue in communication is not what the *words* mean, but what the *user* means by them. When an alert communicator talks or writes, he is aware that his listeners or readers may *not* necessarily interpret his words as he means them. When he listens or reads, he is aware that the speaker or writer may have intended the words other than as he is interpreting them at the moment. He recognizes that communication involves *variable-fixing* by the sender—*and* by the receiver.

To keep person-minded in his communications he frequently asks himself:

This is what it means to *me,* but what does it, or will it, mean to *him?*
What would I mean if I were in *his* position?
Does my interpretation of his words coincide with his viewpoint (as I see it)?
Are the sender and receiver fixing the variables the *same way?*

Query and paraphrase

Query the speaker or writer. Some of the best parental advice a child ever receives somehow becomes lost as he grows older. Almost everyone has been told: "If you don't understand the teacher, ask her what she means." But as time goes on, something happens to us. We evidently become too inhibited or proud or embarrassed to ask another person what he means.

A common complaint among my colleagues in college teaching is that students do not ask enough questions in the classroom—the very place where questions should abound![11] It is almost as if we believed that asking a question of a speaker or writer (assuming that circumstances permit) would lead him to doubt our intelligence! Nothing could be farther from the truth. Professors and executives alike indicate that they respect a thoughtful question. To them it indicates interest and a sense of responsibility rather than stupidity.

To be sure, some managers (and teachers) resent questions from subordinates. But more about that later under heading of "approachability."

So, ask questions when:

1. You don't understand or can't make sense out of what you have heard or read.
2. You think there may be a legitimate interpretation other than the one which first occurred to you.
3. You sense something out of alignment—something which doesn't quite mesh with the rest of your knowledge of a situation.

Paraphrase the speaker or writer. Putting a speaker's or writer's communication into your own words and asking him if he will accept your paraphrasing is one of the oldest, simplest, most useful, and most neglected techniques in communication.

I once observed a fascinating series of business meetings in which the technique of paraphrasing was put to a special use. The meetings involved the regular executive conferences of a certain firm, but a new touch had been added. An outsider was engaged to serve as moderator. The requirements were

---

[11]Business executives express much the same concern. "What do you have to do to get people to ask questions?" a vice president of a manufacturing firm asks. "If people would only make *sure* they got it straight, we'd save a hundred thousand dollars a year."

that he be reasonably intelligent, that he have a good memory for spoken communication, and that he develop the knack of paraphrasing the statement of another *without* embellishments, judgments, deletions, or additions of his own.

This is how it worked. The agenda having been set up previously, the meeting began with the moderator in charge. "Gentlemen," he would say, "the meeting is convened. Who would like to begin?" Some of the men raised their hands, and the moderator recognized, say, Executive A, who then made a statement. Then, *before* anyone else was permitted to speak, the moderator *paraphrased* A's remark. A would now either accept the moderator's rephrasing as accurate (in which case the next person would be permitted to speak) or correct it. In the latter case the moderator would then paraphrase A's correction, which A would either accept or correct, and so on, until A accepted the moderator's paraphrasing *without qualification*.

After A and the moderator agreed on A's communication, any other member was permitted to query or paraphrase what had been said if he were still in doubt about A's meaning.

The procedure sounds laborious, and, indeed, it was for the first few meetings. But after a brief period of practice this group of executives was holding conferences (which had been somewhat notorious for their miscommunications) with startling equanimity and progress. This writer has never experienced group discussions with so few instances of bypassing; moreover, many *potential* bypassings were revealed by the moderator's rewordings. An additional benefit, according to the men involved, was that with the moderator's paraphrasings the speaker was assured that at least one other person in the room understood fully what he was trying to say—a very satisfying and previously infrequent experience!

The meetings, it is true, were somewhat longer[12] than usual, but who can estimate the amounts of time and the money, effort, and nervous tension saved thus by the prevention of miscommunications?

The simple techniques of the query and the paraphrase can be potent defenses against bypassing. But discretion must be exercised. Occasionally a person may go to absurd lengths wherein the techniques seem an end in themselves rather than a means toward clarifying communication.

A *Peanuts* cartoons a few years ago made the point aptly. It showed Charlie Brown greeting Linus, who was making a snowman in his backyard. The dialogue went approximately like this:

Charlie: Hi, Linus. Did you have a good Christmas?
Linus: What do you mean: "Did I have a good Christmas?"
Linus: Do you mean did I get a lot of good presents?
Linus: Or do you mean did I have a good time with all my cousins who came to visit?
Linus: Or do you mean was it good in a spiritual sense?
Linus: Or do you mean . . .
Charlie: (Sigh)

---

[12]Frequently, of course, B's reaction to A's statement was delayed by the moderator's interposition.

Be approachable

The responsibilities of the sender. So far we have been discussing the techniques of querying and paraphrasing from the receiver's point of view; that is, how the listener or reader should use them. But communication is a two-way street, with responsibilities at both ends. The sender (speaker, writer) should do his utmost to make querying and paraphrasing possible. He should not only permit it or make himself approachable—he should encourage it, invite it—even, on some occasions, insist on it.

But some people in positions of responsibility are threatened by feedback. They may feel so insecure or poorly versed in their field that they regard a question as a challenge they must ward off. Ironically, the defensiveness of a manager, for example, often leads to even more destructive consequences than those he feared.

For under the best of circumstances most subordinates are somewhat inhibited in dealing with their superiors. Conditioned by past experiences with authority figures and regarding the boss as reward controller, the subordinate tends to be circumspect in communicating upward. So when a manager deliberately—or unwittingly—becomes *unapproachable,* he virtually assures the strangulation of the channel up to him.

To the extent that communicating up to the boss is perceived as dangerous, painful, embarrassing, or unpleasant the upward flow will be curtailed and filtered. The boss just won't get the bad news until it becomes *so bad* it can no longer be concealed from him—then he *really* has a problem!

A superior who thus contributes to an "approachability gap" between himself and his people is doing a disservice to them, to his organization, and particularly to himself.

A useful daily self-examination:

> *Am I approachable?*[13] Do my people[14] really feel free to query, paraphrase, and, in general, communicate up to me? Have I done everything possible to make their channel to me free and clear—and do I *keep* it that way? Do I make an extra effort to be approachable to more timid, reticent people?[15] Am I *genuinely* receptive to feedback and do I continuously communicate my receptivity to others?

Be sensitive to contexts

Verbal context. Suppose I overhear two men talking. However, they are so far away the only word I pick up is "plufe." What under the sun did they mean?! The men are drawing closer and now I hear: "Say, Ralph, could you plufe me a dollar? I'll pay it back tomorrow." Then later: "It was raining last night when

---

[13]Lest a current or aspiring manager absolves himself too readily—"my people really feel free with me"—let him consider the marked discrepancy between the subordinate's perception of his freedom to communicate up to the boss and boss' perception of that freedom. See: Rensis Likert, *New Patterns in Management,* pp. 41-47.

[14]By "my people" I mean the manager's immediate subordinates—those who report directly to him.

[15]This emphasis on receptivity is not intended to retard the development and maturation of employees. The manager must use discretion to assure an open communication channel without inducing excessive dependence on him by his subordinates.

I landed at O'Hare. So the stewardess plufed me an umbrella, to get from the plane to the terminal."

While I may wonder at that strange word, I am now reasonably confident that I understand what they are saying. But why? No one *defined* "plufe." No one said: "This is what I mean by 'plufe' . . . " I guessed at what the men meant by this term from the *verbal context* in which it occurred. Using the surrounding words as clues. I zeroed in from an almost unlimited number of possible interpretations to one—a synonym for "loan."

Verbal context is not limited to the accompanying *words* in a sentence but consists of the neighboring sentences, paragraphs, and so on, as well. If you hold up an object and ask: "What's this?" the appropriate response might be "a shirt," "off-white," "$7.50," or "broadcloth," depending upon whether we had been talking about classifications of garments, colors, prices, or fabrics.

It is the *verbal context,* then, that provides the prime body of clues by which others deduce how we are fixing the variables—and vice versa.

Sometimes, however, we are admonished to *reduce* the verbal context —"boil it down," "be concise," "don't camouflage your meaning with excess verbiage."

Pliny the Elder confessed: "I am writing you at length because I do not have time to write a short letter." And we are reminded that the *Lord's Prayer,* the *Gettysburg Address,* the *Declaration of Independence,* and a recent government directive on cabbage prices required 56, 266, 300, and 26,911 words, respectively. Certainly it is possible to overcommunicate.[16] But an equal if not greater danger lurks in *under*communication which provides such scanty context that bypassing is virtually invited. This memorandum purportedly appeared *briefly* on a federal agency bulletin board a few years ago.

Those department heads who do not have the services of full-time secretaries may take advantage of the stenographers in the secretarial pool.

Somehow that reminds me of Groucho Marx' reply to the airline stewardess who informed him that "You can smoke your cigar if you don't

---

[16]Discretion must be exercised especially by the sender, who must avoid unnecessarily long and repetitious communications, for they can be as confusing as if they were intended to deceive.

Dr. George Russell Harrison, dean of the Massachusetts Institute of Technology, recalled this incident:

"A plumber of foreign extraction wrote the National Bureau of Standards and said he found that hydrochloric acid quickly opened plugged drainage pipes and inquired if that was a good thing to use. A scientist at the bureau replied that 'the efficacy of hydrochloric acid is indisputable, but the corrosive residue is incompatible with metallic permanence.'

"The plumber wrote back thanking the Bureau for telling him that hydrochloric acid was all right. The scientist was disturbed about the misunderstanding and showed the correspondence to his boss—another scientist—who wrote the plumber: 'We cannot assume responsibility for the production of toxic and noxious residue with hydrochloric acid and suggest you use an alternative procedure.'

"The plumber wrote back thanking the Bureau for telling him that hydrochloric works fine. Greatly disturbed, the scientists took their problem to the top boss. He broke with scientific jargon and wrote the plumber: 'Don't use hydrochloric acid. It eats hell out of pipes.' " From "Inside Washington" by the Chicago Sun Washington Bureau, *Chicago Sun,* February 17, 1947, p. 10.

annoy the ladies." "You mean there's a choice?" egerly asked Groucho. "Then I'll annoy the ladies!"

Because of the necessity for conciseness, signs are particularly vulnerable targets for bypassing. Among my "collection":

Sign over a combination gasoline station and diner:

```
EAT HERE AND GET GAS
```

One wonders whether the proprietor was (1) obtuse, (2) banking on others sharing his sense of humor, or (3) issuing a fair warning.

Sign outside a church announcing a forthcoming sermon:

```
DO YOU KNOW
WHAT HELL IS?


Come hear our
new organist.
```

Another church sign:

```
IF YOU'RE TIRED
OF SIN—COME IN
```

Penciled beneath: "If you're not—phone 366-5619."

And finally this sign at a power station in Ireland:

```
TO TOUCH THESE OVERHEAD
CABLES MEANS INSTANT DEATH

Offenders will be prosecuted.
```

Which seems only just for such a shocking offense.

Classified advertisements are another fertile field for inadvertent bypassing. The ad placer, keen on reducing costs, reduces his context:

Apartment for Rent. View takes in
4 counties, 2 bedrooms.

For Sale: 1969 Cadillac hearse.
Body in good condition.

For Sale: Large great dane. Regis-
tered pedigree. Will eat anything.
Especially fond of children.

Wanted: Man to handle dynamite.
Must be prepared to travel unexpectedly.

Even grafitti is susceptible. From Norton Mockridge's compendium of some of the more imaginative washroom wall literature, *The Scrawl of the Wild:*

Written on the wall:

> MY MOTHER MADE
> ME A HOMOSEXUAL

Scribbled beneath it:

"If I buy her the wool, will she make me one, too?"

Returning to the issue of inadvertent bypassing—an answer to the problem of insufficient verbal contexts is, of course, for the sender to provide and/or the receiver to obtain enough related information to determine the intent of the excerpt.

In conclusion, be sensitive to verbal contexts, the surrounding words and sentences which may help to determine the meaning of any word, phrase, or passage. Ask yourself: Is this word, phrase, and so on, taken out of its verbal context? Might I interpret it differently if I knew what went before or after it? Am I giving my receiver sufficient (but not too much) context for him to understand my communication?

Situational context. What lies beyond the context of words and phrases? How does this communication fit into the larger framework of people and happenings? Make a habit of orienting yourself toward the situational context of a situation.

Suppose we reenact the Sipert-foreman case, with one change—Sipert now has a sensitivity about the "bigger picture":

Foreman: Better clean up around here.

Sipert: Okay. (Then moments later after the foreman has left)—Wait a minute! The Boss has me working on this bearing. It's supposed to be a rush-order job. Now he tells me to drop it and clean up my work area. Something is wrong somewhere—I'd better check.

Clearly, if Sipert *had* "checked" (queried or paraphrased), the delay and embarrassment presumably would have been avoided.

SUMMARY

Bypassing occurs when communicators miss one another's meanings. It may take place when they use the same word to mean different things or when they use different words to mean the same thing. The effects of bypassing may range from the trivial and humorous to the serious and even catastrophic. In general, the immediate consequence of a bypassing may be either an apparent agreement on meanings when actually a disagreement exists, or an apparent disagreement when an actual agreement is the case.

Basically a person bypasses because of the assumption, often unconscious, that words mean the same to the other person as they do to him. Underlying this assumption are two insidious fallacies. The first fallacy, that *words have mono-usage,* thrives despite the manifest multi-usage of so many words in our language. The second fallacy is that *words HAVE meanings.* This fallacy obscures the fact that words are not "containers" of meaning but rather they are *variables to be fixed (defined)* by those who use the words in sending and receiving messages. In this sense, bypassing occurs when (1) the sender fixes a variable one way, (2) the receiver fixes it another way, and (3) each assumes the other is fixing the *same* way. *Deliberate* bypassing was acknowledged. It is relatively easy to misunderstand or to be misunderstood, if one intends to do so.

Four commonsense but uncommonly used techniques are effective in curbing bypassing. (1) Be person-minded—not word-minded. (2) Query and paraphrase. (3) Be approachable. (4) Be sensitive to contexts (verbal and situational). To be truly effective, these techniques must become deeply imbedded habits which, in a sense, are on the alert even when we are not.

POSTSCRIPT

If everyone at all times practiced the bypassing prevention techniques, the following probably would never have occurred:

Scene: Floor of the United States Senate

Senator Wayne Morse had been denouncing Mrs. Clare Booth Luce. The chivalrous late Senator Everett Dirksen sprang up and with his voice ringing righteous wrath demanded that Morse "stop beating an old bag of bones."

I don't think I would have wanted us to be deprived of that one!

DISCUSSION QUESTIONS

1. If you were looking for a church to join and you were invited to join a church that professed to be based on communistic beliefs, would you:
   a) Refuse the invitation?
   b) Report the group to the proper authorities?
   c) Take some other action? If so, what?
2. Our Constitution states that "all men are created equal," but evidence clearly indicates that babies are born with great variations in mental and physical capacities. Discuss the apparent discrepancy.
3. During a discussion among friends, someone suggests that "more socialistic concepts should be incorporated into our federal government." Then he turns to you and says: "What do you think?" How would you respond?

4. Doing some research on differing socioeconomic classes you spend a couple of weeks in a tiny and remote village in Appalachia. These people refer to their shoes as "holy bibles." How would you respond to this? Why?

5. Precisely what is entailed in "bypassing"?

6. What unconsciously held, fallacious assumptions contribute to it?

7. Why might people find these assumptions attractive?

8. How can one prevent bypassing in his own communication experiences? As sender? As receiver?

9. How can you help others to avoid bypassing without insulting their intelligence?

10. "Our communication would be just as effective if the large sphere in the sky that shines at night were called 'the sun,' if persons who wear dresses were called 'boys,' and if members of the Republican party were called 'communists.' " How do you respond to this assertion? Why?

11. "Words mean the same to the other fellow as they do to me." Why would communicators make this assumption?

12. The words, "sandwich," "diesel," "bloomers," "magnolia," and "quixotic," have what in common? What was the point of including them in the bypassing chapter?

13. What did G. B. Shaw mean when he defined England and the U.S. as "two great nations separated by the barrier of a common language"? Can you think of analogous situations?

14. What is the principal advantage and limitation of computer languages over natural languages such as English?

15. Give an example of deliberate bypassing. Are there walks of life where deliberate bypassing tends to be practiced? Is deliberate bypassing ever defensible ethically?

16. Discuss the four approaches to minimizing bypassing. Are there limitations to their use?

Karl G. Albrecht

FIVE WAYS TO SHORT-CIRCUIT YOUR COMMUNICATION

Communication is hard work. It takes just as much effort to be a good communicator as it does to be a good planner, administrator, or salesman. Ironically, people who exert effort and intelligence to solve a business problem are often incredibly lazy about communicating. Reacting to the first thought that comes into their minds, they make snap judgments about what the other person means. But just as you can't make snap business decisions, you can't make snap communication decisions. Most communication breakdowns, in fact, are caused by faulty reaction patterns in people who are trying to communicate.

By paying more attention to your own thinking processes, you will be able to eliminate some of these faulty reactions in your day-to-day communication with subordinates, peers, superiors, and friends. In your efforts to improve your ability to think when you communicate, direct your efforts to the following five areas:

Snap reactions

People tend to make snap reactions when they hear someone speak about a subject with which they are familiar. They assume that they have little to gain by listening carefully. The possibility that the speaker has a new fact, idea, or point of view doesn't occur to them.

Snap reactions typify communication between two people in open conflict. Each adversary is so intent on "shooting down" the other that he is no longer alert for new information. As one speaks, the other gets the general gist and then tunes him out in a wild search for a powerful rebuttal. Even when someone does pay attention to what his opponent is saying, it is usually because he is looking for a weak point vulnerable to attack. If either or both would take the trouble to listen unemotionally, they might be able to find an area of consensus—or even find that they're closer to agreement than they had realized.

Snap reactions are also characteristic of those who "fly off the handle" easily. Another term for this kind of behavior is "signal reaction." As the term implies, the person literally responds as though he were a pre-programmed machine, triggered by a signal from someone else. The response is so immediate and so automatic that his thinking processes are simply bypassed. It's almost as though he were helpless to control his own behavior.

The first step in eliminating snap reactions is to begin to be aware of them. Pay attention to the reactions of others and try to spot the mechanism in yourself. Then experiment by putting a small delay into your responses to

---

Reprinted by permission of the publisher from *Supervisory Management,* June 1974, © by AMACOM, a division of American Management Associations.

others. Develop the habit of pausing for a few seconds before you reply, especially when someone has made a particularly provocative remark. This brief pause will allow your higher-level thinking processes to come into play, paving the way for a more mature reaction.

The process of delaying your signal reactions is a useful strategy in all interactions. Learn to delay your evaluation of a person until you have an adequate basis for judgment. Don't snap-react to someone's style of dress, hair, or even overt behavior. Learn to wait and watch for a little while before forming an opinion.

The "allness orientation"

You can never know "all" about anything. Yet many people act and speak as though they could. Try this experiment: The next time you are involved in a casual conversation with a group of people, try to count the number of times you hear such words as *all, always, everybody, every time,* and *never.* These are called "allness" words because they convey an impression of totality. An allness statement is usually symptomatic of allness thinking.

How many times do *you* use these allness words? Ask a friend to count these words in your conversation on some occasion when you are conversing in your usual style. You may be surprised at what he finds.

The trouble with "allness" thinking and "allness" talking? They tend to block the kinds of thought processes that are beneficial to communication. When you refer to "women," "blacks," "hippies," or "today's young people," you are clamping chains on your thought processes. The implied word *all* in these terms prevents you or your listeners from paying attention to the differences among the people about whom you are speaking. These differences may be more important—and more relevant—to you than the similarities.

"Allness" talking is quite common. A man may say to his wife, "You *never* listen to me." A businessman who has been swindled may say, "You can't trust *anyone*." To a certain extent, the suicidal person's thinking may be distorted by this allness orientation. He may feel that "no one loves him" or that there is "no reason to go on living." "*Everything* he does fails." Such a person may elect to blast out his brains rather than re-orient his view of reality.

In everyday communication situations, the allness orientation can have damaging effects, especially when it goes undetected. Make a conscious effort to drop these allness words from your conversation. They are seldom fully justified. Try to pay attention to relative values when you use evaluative terms. Introduce such terms into your conversation as "to me," "from my point of view," "so far as I know," and "up to a point." Make these terms a part of your style of speech. The effect is contagious.

"Either-or" thinking

From the time we are children, we are trained to think and speak in what linguists call "polar terms." We learn such word-pairs as tall/short, black/white, near/far, objective/subjective—literally hundreds of such dualities. We train our own children to think and speak in this way. These so-called polar terms convey a feeling of opposites. A man is described as being either tall or short. But most men are neither tall *nor* short. According to the very definition of those terms, most men are in the middle. The physical world does not always conform to these convenient verbal maps.

QUESTIONS FOR COMMUNICATORS

The next time you must communicate with someone, stop and think. Then respond. The following questions may help you avoid any dangerous and unrealistic reactions. Ask yourself:

1. Have I given this person a chance? Have I paid close attention to everything he has said—or have I tuned him out after a certain point?
2. Do I assume that this person has nothing new to tell me?
3. Is there an area of agreement that I have overlooked?
4. Am I judging this person by what he says—or by what he looks like?
5. Am I reacting to any "allness" statements he has made? Have I made any—without qualifying them?
6. Have I looked for the middle ground in the issue? Or have I taken an "either-or" position?
7. Have I taken too much for granted? Have I checked my assumptions against the facts?
8. How do my inferences check out with the facts?
9. Am I being objective? Or am I going on preconceived notions?

This conditioning process, which we undergo from our early years, causes many people to think in strictly an "either-or" fashion. A subordinate may take an unalterable position that if his supervisor does not give him a pay raise, he will quit. Once he has committed himself to this position, he will have difficulty compromising. In reality, he may be pleased with a transfer to another job with greater long-run potential. But his either-or orientation prevents this kind of compromise.

The art of negotiating calls for the ability to avoid this either-or position. In a compromise situation, neither person is forced to win or lose. Each can consider himself successful if he has achieved his key objectives.

Try to develop the habit of looking for the middle ground when you must make a decision. A problem will seldom force you to choose between two completely opposite alternatives. There is usually room for a number of possible solutions.

In everyday communication situations, try to be alert for either-or thinking and speaking by others, and learn to spot them in yourself. In this way you will be able to avoid many fruitless debate situations. You can also save yourself the exasperation of trying to defend an extreme position that you did not plan to adopt.

Unjustified assumptions

The problem with assumptions is not that we make them, but that we act on them. Assumptions, of course, are necessary to the business of living. Without them, we would not have language, civilization, or scientific advancement. Everyone makes a number of assumptions about the environment and the people in it. But communication breaks down with a jolt when someone makes a high-level assumption without checking the facts.

One of the most frequent examples of faulty assumptions is referred to as "bypassing." In this situation, two people assume that they are communicating on the same wavelength when they are actually talking about two different things. Two friends, for example, agree to meet for lunch. One suggests a certain restaurant, referring to it by its local nickname (the pub, for example). But that nickname is similar to the official name of another restaurant. With other things on their minds, they both assume that they are referring to the same place. The result? They end up eating lunch at separate restaurants.

Communication malfunctions caused by unjustified assumptions are often more serious. One reason, for example, that Confederate General George Pickett ordered 12,000 men into a frontal attack against the heavily armed Union line at Gettysburg was that he assumed J. E. B. Stuart's cavalry unit would strike the line simultaneously from the rear. Unfortunately, Stuart encountered a Union force under the command of General George Custer. The rear attack was stalled and thousands of men were slaughtered. Pickett's plan allowed for no alternative course of action in case his assumption proved unjustified.

In everyday communication situations, be on the alert for assumptions made by other people that can strongly influence their opinions. Also, learn to spot key assumptions that you may make. Particularly in the case of communication with subordinates, don't assume that they have understood when you give them instructions. Or don't assume that a symptom such as absenteeism or poor attitude is actually the problem. Whenever you must communicate with someone else, probe deeply to find out the facts. Don't take mutual understanding for granted.

Inferences

Another common cause of faulty communication is the tendency to confuse inferences with actual observations. Try this experiment: Select a photograph of a typical situation involving a group of people. Hand it to someone you know and ask him to make as many observations as possible about the people and objects in the picture. Write down his statements as he makes them. Then check them against the picture. How many of the observations can be verified by looking at the picture? How many are inferences? Does he, for example, refer to a couple in the photograph as husband and wife—a fact that cannot be verified by simply looking at the picture? How many real observations can be made from the picture?

In the following situation, the supervisor was not able to distinguish fact from inference: When Harry Jones walked out of his office into the main work area where most of the secretaries sat, he noticed that three of the women were standing together, speaking in low whispers. Straining to hear what they were whispering about, he heard one of them saying, "I guess Sheila will be leaving in a few weeks." Always on the lookout for fresh gossip, Harry inferred that Sheila Mandel, his supervisor's secretary, was planning to quit her job. The next time Harry saw his boss, he mentioned casually that he had heard via the grapevine that Sheila was planning to leave. "That's hardly likely," Harry's boss said, "because Sheila's been promoted to office manager. And before she assumes her new responsibilities, she's going to take off for a week's vacation. I don't know where you get your information from—but it doesn't seem too reliable."

Examine your own thinking processes. To what extent do you make inferences and treat them as though they were observations? In everyday situations, learn to spot inference-observation confusion in others—and be alert for it in yourself.

Edward A. Mabry

A MULTIVARIATE INVESTIGATION OF PROFANE LANGUAGE

Profanity and taboo language have demonstrated effects on the assessment of speaker credibility and message impact[1] and show important implications as a rhetorical strategy in many social settings.[2] A less developed though related area of study has been to account for propensities to use various profane or taboo language symbols in the discourse of routine interpersonal transactions.[3] The present study reports on a classification of profane and taboo language derived from factor analytic results of a questionnaire on personal usage.

Previous classifications of profane and taboo language have been based upon psychobiological[4] and derivational[5] criteria for selection and on such specific considerations as categorizing targets of expletive language.[6] Lodle investigated the sociological and psychological motives behind assertion of different types of sexual and excretory argot.[7] He formed three broad categories of taboo words related to their usage properties: *obscene* (fuck, shit, piss, etc), *technical* (copulate, defecate, penis, etc.) and *common usage* ("make love", "go to bed", etc.).[8] Each category classifies taboo sexual and excretory words and phrases on the basis of explicitness and social abrasiveness.

As an example, the word "fuck" has little acceptance in current socially approved discourse, but a less explicitly perceived phrase like, "make

Edward A. Mabry, "A Multivariate Investigation of Profane Language," *Central States Speech Journal*, Vol. 26, No. 1 (Spring 1975), pp. 39-44. Reprinted by Permission.
[1] Charles M. Rossiter, Jr. & Robert Bostrom, "Profanity, Justification and Source Credibility," paper presented at the annual conference of the National Society for the Study of Communication, April, 1969; Robert Bostrom, John R. Baseheart and Charles M. Rossiter, Jr., "The Effects of Three Types of Profane Language in Persuasive Messages," *Journal of Communication,* 23 (1973), 461-475; E. Scott Baudhuin, "Obscene Language and Source Credibility: An Experimental Study," paper presented at the International Communication Association convention, April, 1971.
[2] Dan Rothwell, "Verbal Obscenity: Time for Second Thoughts," *Western Speech,* 35 (1971), 231-242; Robert M. Smith, "Explorations for a Rhetorical Study of Pornography," *Kansas Speech Journal,* 34 (1973), 31-38.
[3] Paul Cameron, "Frequency and Kinds of Words in Various Social Settings, or What the Hell's Going On?" *Pacific Sociological Review,* 12 (1969), 101-104; E. Scott Baudhuin, "Obscene Language and Evaluative Response: An Empirical Study," *Psychological Reports,* 32 (1973), 399-402.
[4] Warren Gorman, "Body Words," *Psychoanalytic Review,* 51 (1964), 15-28.
[5] Rossiter and Bostrom, and Baudhuin.
[6] Arthur Berger, "Swearing and Society," *ETC,* 30 (1973), 283-286.
[7] Steve E. Lodle, Sexual and Excretory Vernacular: A Delineative Examination and Empirical Analysis of the Nature, Scope and Function of Taboo, Inhibitory, Euphemistic and Dysphemistic Communication Paradigms. Unpublished M. A. Thesis, California State University-Long Beach, 1972.
[8] Lodle, pp. 109-114.

love," can be used to stimulate the same images. In some settings, a less veiled terminology for behaviors that carry socially suppressed or taboo interpretations is needed. An argot of technical, explicitly defined terms has developed to fill those needs. These words are most obvious in the medical and health-related professions and in public media.

Previous research has established that different classes of taboo words are differentially evaluated. Rossiter and Bostrom found significant differences in usage and offensiveness rankings between words with religious derivations (hell, Goddamn, Jesus, etc.), excretory derivations (shit, piss, crap, etc.) and sexual derivations (fuck, cock, cunt, etc.).[9] Baudhuin factor analyzed students'

TABLE 1
Rotated Factor Matrix, for Sexual Vernacular Word List

	Factors*				
	I	II	III	IV	V
			Abrasive-		Euphemistic-
Words	Abrasive	Technical	Expletive	Latent	Colloquial
cunt	727	178	153	037	061
cock	711	210	202	015	037
dick	682	123	259	014	145
pussy	680	149	325	058	005
jack-off	672	281	326	084	063
cherry	600	127	008	186	195
balls	597	177	271	021	147
peter	587	257	148	250	065
nuts	554	080	101	194	168
ejaculation	218	762	140	038	177
erection	268	760	053	092	156
semen	180	730	080	208	069
vagina	210	722	003	067	160
testicles	229	691	023	207	086
penis	266	633	108	028	178
masturbation	173	620	322	024	170
bastard	098	124	743	014	081
bitch	074	037	727	066	150
son-of-a-bitch	195	103	696	021	074
ass	147	039	696	064	091
shit	122	071	666	158	234
behind	014	150	020	553	242
bloody	155	101	023	550	260
scuz	257	157	232	486	193
goose	236	087	168	455	005
virgin	043	253	229	168	—628
make-love	171	187	229	137	—603
go to bed	150	231	170	122	—567
% of total variation	30%	10%	5%	3%	2%

* Factor loadings have been rounded off to three decimal places, decimal points deleted and variables reordered; all factorally complex variables have been deleted.

---

[9] Rossiter and Bostrom, p. 6.

semantic differential evaluation ratings for twenty taboo words and found that religous words were slightly positively rated while excretory and sexual words, respectively, were negatively evaluated.[10] The trends in the Baudhuin data is additional substantiation for the Rossiter and Bostrom findings.

Cameron performed a content analysis of verbal behavior used by students, adults at work, and adults at leisure to determine how frequently they used sexual, sacred and excretory profanity. He found that students uttered more sexual profanities than sacred or excretory words, respectively, while both adult samples used sacred profanities more often than sexyal or excretory.[11]

Lodle examined the relationships between sexual and excretory terminology, demographic variables and attitudes toward various sociological constructs in a sample of college students. He concluded that higher rates of verbalizing sexual and excretory terminology were characteristic of politically radical, non-religious males while significantly more restrictiveness was exhibited by politically conservative, strongly religious, middle class females.[12]

With the exceptions of Cameron and Lodle, profanity and taboo language have not been studied to determine whether predilections for use can be used to derive meaningful terminology clusters. Classification of profane and taboo language has proceeded more from impressionistic assumptions about categorization than empirical data. Sexual vernacular in particular may hold a variety of relevant categories that vary according to user and situation. As yet, however, usage-based assessment of terminology intercorrelations has received little attention. The purpose of this study was to generate a factor structure for student ratings of their predispositions to use various sexual and excretory terminology.

METHOD

The subjects were 151 female and 132 male students enrolled in introductory speech communication classes at Bowling Green State University.

Each S was asked to respond to a "sexual vernacular" questionnaire as part of a longer testing period devoted to "attitude measurement." The questionnaire was identical to that devised by Lodle.[13] The form consists of 48 terms each followed by a Likert-type rating scale ranging from "would use this word freely . . . " to "would never use the word . . . " A low score indicates little inhibition associated with using the word list; a high score indicates much inhibition with the word list.

A principle axes factor analysis with a varimax rotation to simple structure was performed on the 283 responses. Squared multiple correlation coefficients were inserted as diagonal elements of the correlation matrix and an eigenvector decision creiterion of 1.00 was used in deriving orthogonal factors for rotation.[14]

---

[10]Baudhuin, 1973, p. 401.

[11]Cameron, p. 103.

[12]Lodle, 1972, pp. 329-330.

[13]Steve E. Lodle, "Sexual Vernacular: An Empirical Analysis of Taboo Communication Behavior," paper presented at the International Communication Convention, April, 1971.

[14]For a more extensive discussion of these methods see R. J. Rummel, *Applied Factor Analysis* (Evanston: Northwestern University Press, 1970).

RESULTS

Factor Analytic Results

Table 1 contains five factors derived from the factor analysis of the questionnaire. The five factors accounted for nearly 50 percent of the total variables in the factor structure and were deleted from subsequent analysis.[15]

Factor I contains words generally classified as "sexual obscenity." Sexual obscenities include those kinds of sexual vernacular socially defined as crude or coarse verbal representations of sexual organs and activities. Words loading highly in Factor I were preponderantly slang representations of sex organs (e.g., cock, pussy, etc.). These kinds of obscenities Lodle discussed as highly "abrasive" in most social contexts.[16] Therefore, this factor was labeled "Abrasive" due to the consistency of words loading in the vector.

Contrasted to those in Factor I, the words loading in Factor II could be described as neutral or technical expressions of sexual processes and sex organs (e.g., ejaculation, vagina, penis, etc.). Since these words in this factor evinced a high degree of homogeneity and all seven words seemed representative of non-slang terminology, Factor II was labeled a "Technical" dimension of the factor structure.

Factor III appeared to contain words similar to those in the first dimension (Abrasive) of the factor structure. Further inspection, however, led to the conclusion that such words are both abrasive and *personally defaming*. These words, singularly or in combinations with other similar words, are commonly used as insults and serve as exclamations in terminal displays of emotion. Cameron noted for example that the words "Bastard" and "Bitch" were used 15 to 25 times more frequently than such words as dick and cunt.[17] These words are abrasive in social conversation except where role expectations permit deviant interpretations (e.g., *"men"* are expected to use certain types of words at times *because* they are men). The factor analytic results suggest that words of a similar type are differentiated on the basis of personal usage. This factor was designated "Abrasive-Expletive" since it contained words that were abrasive and commonly used in oaths and defamation.

With the exception of the word *scuz*, Factor IV contains words that identify body areas, functions and suggestive sexual play. Though intrafactor commonality was low for word concepts in this factor, Factor IV was designated as a "Latent" factor indicating latent sexual overtones surrounding the words listed. A most notable example of this was the word *goose*.

The fifth factor rotated contained words and phrases similar to those discussed by Lodle as "euphemistic" language.[18] These are phrases found acceptable to use in semiguarded but "polite" conversation. Factor V was designated as "Euphemistic-Colloquial" in accordance with similarly expressive phrases clustered in that vector.

---

[15] Factorally complex words deleted are: Boobs, Bosom, Buttocks, Climax, Come, Copulate, Crap, Fornicate, Fuck, Hard-on, Horney, Knocked-up, Laid, Motherfucker, Piss, Prick, Screw, Sexual Intercourse, Tits, Toilet.
[16] Lodle, 1972, p. 107.
[17] Cameron, p. 103.
[18] Lodle, 1972, p. 110.

MANOVA Results

Lodle reported that sex and strength of religious beliefs were highly related to a person's total score for the entire sexual vernacular word list. Secondary analyses were conducted to determine whether these findings held for Ss' use of the five factors obtained in this study. Responses on each of the factors were compared for male and female Ss that had previously indicated whether the strength of their religious beliefs was strong, moderate or low.

These data were submitted to a multivariate analysis of variance (MANOVA) for two-way fixed-effects model with unequal cell frequencies. Wilks' maximum likelihood-ratio statistic, Lambda, which yields an approximation to tabled values of the univariate F statistic, was used for multivariate significance testing.[19] The three highest loading words in each vector were summed and the resulting values used as dependent variables.

Significant multivariate F-ratios were found between male and female ratings (F=13.3945, d.f.=5, 273.; p<.0001), between the three levels of strength of religious belief (F=2.5602; d.f.=10, 546.; p<.005) and for the sex x strength of religious belief interaction (F=2.4233; d.f.=10, 546.; p<.008).

The presence of a significant multivariate interaction made subsequent consideration of main effects of questionable value.[20] Tatsuoka suggests using information from multiple discriminant function analysis to identify variables that maximally differentiate treatment effects as criterion variables.[21] Discriminant function analysis provides an index to the number of uncorrelated dimensions of effects that exist for a set of treatment groups on a set of criterion measures.[22]

Multiple discriminant function analysis of the six treatment groups (cells in the design) disclosed one significant (p<.008) discriminant function accounting for 69 percent of the total variance. The standardized discriminant function coefficients (which indicate the amount each variable contributes to the discriminant function) for the five dependent variables were $-.7052, .0369, -.4114, -.1526, .8140$, respectively. Coefficients for the Abrasive and Euphemistic-Colloquial dimensions were nearly twice as large as those for the other three factors. Due to the amount of their contribution to the significant discriminant function *a posteriori* analysis of the Abrasive and Euphemistic-Colloquial dimensions cell means, Table 2, was conducted using nonorthogonal Scheffé S tests.

A significant difference (p<.05) was found between females rating their religious beliefs as "strong" and all male groups. Trends in the data indicated that similar, though nonsignificant, differences could be found between strongly religious students and more moderate females. No significant differences were found between cell means for the Euphemistic-Colloquial dimension. Inspection of the cell means in Table 2 does show that strongly

---

[19] A discussion of the maximum likelihood ratio criterion as applied to a two-way classification can be found in Maurice M. Tatsuoka, *Multivariate Analysis: Techniques for Educational and Psychological Research* (New York: John Wiley, 1971), Chs. 4 and 7.
[20] The rationale for this position may be found in Roger Kirk, *Experimental Design: Procedures for the Behavioral Sciences* (Belmont, California: Brooks/Cole, 1968), pp. 177-178.
[21] Tatsuoka, pp. 206-207.
[22] *Ibid.*, pp. 162-163.

TABLE 2
Cell Means, for the Five Dependent Variables

| | | Factors | | |
Groups	Abrasive	Technical	Abrasive-Expletive	Latent	Euphemistic-Colloquial
Males					
Strong	8.83	8.76	6.08	7.65	5.77
Moderate	8.71	7.63	6.38	5.96	4.41
Weak	8.06	7.93	5.85	6.94	4.64
Females					
Strong	12.46	9.74	9.91	7.89	5.20
Moderate	10.88	8.41	8.44	6.09	5.18
Weak	10.38	8.22	6.83	4.94	5.22

religious males rated words in that dimension less favorably (higher) than other males *or females.*

DISCUSSION

The five factors, Abrasive, Technical, Abrasive-Expletive, Latent and Euphemistic-Colloquial, derived from the factor analysis of the 48 items on the word list indicate that Ss differentiated profane and taboo words clusters based on their perceptions of how they use such words. The first three factors are, by far, the most important. They account for the most common variance (45%) included the most words (21) and have words loading in their vectors that are relatively homogeneous. The fourth and fifth factors, since they combine to include only five percent of the variance accounted for by all factors, and include only seven words, could be assumed to prove unstable upon replication.

There were some surprises in the factor loading matrix. Words like "fuck" and "motherfucker," previously found to be highly abrasive and used very little in common discourse, could not be classified into any one dimension. Both, for example, were factorally complex variables with almost equally sized loadings in Factors I and III. This does not indicate that some words might have more than one legitimate socially defined classification based upon their use.

The emergence of factors II and V denotes technical non-slang and colloquial terminology lends support to the position advanced by Montague[23] and Lodle[24] that Anglo-Saxon language maintains several lexical references for sexual processes, body areas and other taboo topics. In most cases western societies have developed sets of words that are used to differentiate social occasions and social positions of persons.

According to Goffman, decisions about how to present oneself, what "demeanor" to assume, are crucial in any social setting.[25] The lexical dimension of a person's total response repertoire becomes a reference for his evalua-

---

[23] Ashley Montague, *The Anatomy of Swearing* (New York: Macmillan, 1967).
[24] Lodle, 1972, pp. 106-109.
[25] Irving Goffman, *Interaction Ritual* (New York: Anchor Books, 1967), pp. 77-90.

tion by others in the setting. An ability to adopt suitable language symbols to a situation, therefore, is a vital part of human social behavior. The extent one is limited in his ability to adapt appropriate language restricts his entry into some social groups. Having more than one kind of word class to choose from increases the likelihood of entry into more and varied social settings.

Comparison of the factor analytic outcomes of this study with *a priori* categorizations of profane and taboo language by Bostrom and Rossiter, Cameron and Lodle suggests that usage of sexual and excretory argot differentiates possible lexical choices more than had been assumed. However, since those words referred to as "religious" profanities (e.g., damn, hell, etc.) were not included in this analysis, specific comparison with other studies is untenable.

Multivariate and *a posteriori* analyses between male and female students reporting strong, moderate and weak religious beliefs show that these two variables interact on the Abrasive and Euphemistic-Colloquial dimensions. The results do support the findings by Lodle that female students reporting strong religious beliefs use Abrasive sexual vernacular significantly less than males. It would appear that religious identification has a profound impact on women's use of language. Whether this is a function of socialization patterns coexistent with strong religious identification or socialization patterns within various religious sects is not clear.

Although discriminant function analysis pointed toward Euphemistic-Colloquial language as a contributor to the multivariate interaction, subsequent analysis of cell means did not confirm the influence of this factor. The data did indicate that males evincing strong religious beliefs had higher mean scores (lower use) for Euphemistic-Colloquial word usage than all other groups. Moreover, a comparison of the means for strongly religious males indicates they use all five factors of sexual vernacular less than other males.

On the other hand, there appears to be little empirical support for the assumption that Ss discriminate between sexual and excretory terms. Factor analytic results indicate that use preferences appear to differentiate between words that are purely abrasive, abrasive but usable for insults and ventilating emotions, technical non-slang terminology and those words and phrases that have latent sexual overtones or are euphemisms for sexual behaviors. These results indicate a predisposition to view sexual and excretory words as more complex than previous researchers had assumed.

Usage preferences of the subjects in this study indicate five dimensions of words differentiated on the basis of phenotypical semantic characteristics rather than genotypical social origins. Comparison of male and female subjects reporting varying strengths of religious belief indicates that strongly religious males and females are substantially more reserved in their perceived use of sexual and excretory words than other subjects.

There is a definite need for replication and extension of the study reported here. Specifically, it would be quite desirable to add religious profanities to the word list and obtain a new factor structure for that set of words. Second, analyzing a larger complex of demographic variables would facilitate understanding the differential uses of the factor analytic dimensions by sample groups. Last, investigations of the relationship between actual and reported usage is essential for performing validity checks on the self report instrument and as an end in itself. Hopefully, studying variables associated with profane and taboo language use will provide greater insight into those processes influencing language acquisition and language use.

Gretchen N. Vik

BRIDGING THE COMMUNICATION GAP: HOW APPLIED SEMANTICS CAN HELP STUDENTS OF BUSINESS AND TECHNICAL WRITING

Over the past 25 years communication theory has become big business academically, and it's time for a re-evaluation of why and how such theory can help in teaching writing, particularly in business courses. Some valuable concepts of communication theory seem buried for students under the mass of theorizing about it, whereas the useful concepts ought to be applied rather than merely presented as theory.

One result of the 1959 Gordon and Howell report recommending upgrading of the business curriculum was the addition of communication theory to the old business writing course. To augment the business English, letters, and reports that had always been taught, textbook writers added sections on communication theory and semantics to their texts.

In the years since 1959, books have added descriptions of the theory of communication in various ways. A common analysis of the component parts of the process of communication is:

> *Source:* the creator of an idea, developer or sender of a message.
> *Message:* ideas, content, or subject matter to be communicated.
> *Medium:* spoken or written language, codes, semaphore signals, smoke signals, music, paintings, gestures.
> *Channel:* printed texts, graphic displays, phonographic recording, sheet music, films, radio, television, newspapers, the five senses.
> *Destination:* the receiver or receivers of a message, real or potential.
> *Context:* the physical, psychological, or sociocultural conditions or circumstances under which communication takes place—the milieu.
> *Goal:* the purpose to be achieved by the message, the anticipated results, the accomplishment, or the outcome of communication.

This technically accurate information alone doesn't seem to help students see how we communicate, however. Presenting students with the above outline wouldn't, by itself, help them write better letters or reports. The problem with most current textbooks is that they merely present communication theory in lots of technical detail, without indicating how the theory can be practically applied.

Gretchen N. Vik, "Bridging the Communication Gap," *ABCA Journal,* Vol. 39, No. 1 (March 1976), pp. 21-24. Reprinted by permission of the American Business Communication Association.

Most business and technical writing students are inherently practical and pragmatic people—if you can *show* them how the theory can be applied to improve their writing, they'll pay attention. If you leave it at the level of theory, they'll ask how much will be on the test and their eyes will tend to glaze over. Fortunately, there are a number of good exercises applying semantic principles to the real world.

A simpler way of presenting communication theory than that described earlier is to say that communication requires a sender, a message, and a receiver. The sender determines the message (including purpose and method of presentation) and takes into account the probable effect of the message on the receiver. This much could be understood by any student, and the pages too often devoted to nuances of theory could be put to better use in applying this brief statement of principles to actual letters and reports.

The two main areas in which the communication gap can be bridged with some ease are: consideration of the audience and presentation of semantic principles. Most books at least touch on the former area in their discussions of the you-attitude and of the psychological principles behind our reactions to refusals. Semantic principles are usually discussed separately from business writing theory, as in Menning and Wilkinson's *Communicating Through Letters and Reports,* where they appear in a concise, readable appendix. Both of these areas could be covered with more emphasis on application, so that the theory of communication would seem more relevant to the subject matter.

CONSIDERATION OF THE AUDIENCE

While the most obvious breakdown in the communication process involves the reader's not getting the meaning the writer intended (often a problem of semantics), some things can be done to make the reader more apt to receive a message properly. As Menning and Wilkinson point out, using good diction, defining technical terms, and using commonly accepted methods of punctuation and formation of clauses are some basic steps to be taken in getting your message across. Paying attention to functional style and being sure to describe the situation clearly and specifically will also reduce message interference.

Jolliffe describes a similar system when he cautions us to write as if a listener might need to ask questions (an advantage of speech over writing, of course)

(1) What do you mean? (do your words mean the same thing for me they do for you?

(2) How do you know? (show me some examples and evidence, qualify your inferences)

(3) What do you want me to do? (I'll have to assess your motives first, but let me know. What's in it for me?)

Jolliffe says that writing ought to be like a clear window—neither ornate and distracting nor cheap and interfering, but inconspicuous, offering a clear view of the subject matter.

Students can best learn to consider their audience if an instructor always makes the reader an assigned part of the letter or report case and stresses you-attitude in both content and approach. Students seem to accept this aspect of the communication process easily.

PRESENTATION OF SEMANTIC PRINCIPLES

Semantic principles aren't so well-received. This area of the communication process needs to be approached with lots of practical applications in hand.

Context

The first aspect of communication that might be discussed is context. Since communication has different physical, psychological, and verbal contexts for both sender and receiver, these areas are sources of communication breakdown.

Not much can be done about the physical context—people's eyesight and hearing problems. Office space or traffic noise, for example, are simply part of the given situation.

Psychological context can be affected to a certain extent by timing letters to arrive on certain better days of the week and by paying attention to you-attitude and the psychology of refusals.

Verbal context, of course, is the real matter of semantics, which might be called the study of the different verbal contexts each person has. This aspect of communication theory definitely has some valuable lessons for the writer of business letters and reports.

If we could operate within the terms of the receiver's personal world, as Jolliffe suggests, communication would be simpler. Since we usually can't do this, as in many business situations where the receiver is known sketchily if at all, the general principles of semantics can help.

Words as Symbols

A most basic principle, discussed in every treatment of semantics I've read, is that words have no meaning and convey no meaning in themselves, that they are merely symbols for commonly accepted concepts. Learning this basic idea would help most students look more closely at what they write. Words are more apt to have personal connotations than common denotations.

One useful exercise to show students the differences in their mental maps of words is to ask them to write five to ten specific features of a certain term as they imagine it. (Suggested terms are *lawyer, college boy, American Indian, President*———.) Obviously class discussion will reveal many differences in the ways different people view the same term.

The common semantic metaphor of the map is also useful here. Jolliffe puts it this way:"Language is to reality as a map is to territory." General words cover large areas and leave out the details; more specific words "cover more differences but less territory." Obviously a successful writer must concern himself with his reader's map as well as his own.

Levels of Abstraction

A second concept of semantics that ought to be discussed in the context of letter and report writing is that of low-and high-level abstractions. High-level abstractions are the hair-trigger words like "communism," "crook," and "homosexual" that have such strong emotional meaning for people that they are best avoided.

Low-level abstractions cause more trouble in actual letter writing practice since they are the words, usually nouns, which name things in groups by ignoring small difference. As Menning and Wilkinson point out, using the most specific word which applied to a concept, such as *typewriter* instead of *business machine,* or even *Smith-Corona* than *typewriter,* helps circumvent the problem of low-level abstractions which separate information and to integrate it with practical problems in writing, as happens in the Potter, Hatch, and Lee texts quoted.

The study of semantics has a place in the business communication course because it produces more careful writers. Wolf ask: "What is accomplished through man's control of communication media unless he learns to understand himself and his uses of symbols which free that self from the prison of its skin?"

An even more pragmatic view is that of Janis, who sees semantics adding an important dimension to the old business writing course: "One of the values of semantics is that it takes the emphasis in language study away from correctness and places it on meaning, where it belongs."

If business communication texts can integrate theory and application when discussing the communication process, students will have an opportunity to become better communicators.

NOTES AND REFERENCES

1. Doris W. Barr, *Effective English for the Career Student,* Belmont, CA: Wadsworth Publishing Company, Inc., 1971. A report writing text which adds information about writing style and approaches—very basic, but realistic as an approach to communication theory in the classroom.
2. Jessamon Dawe and William J. Lord, *Functional Business Communication,* 2nd ed., Englewood Cliffs, NJ: Prentice-Hall, Inc., 1974. A significant amount of space devoted to communication theory.
3. Richard A. Hatch, "On Communication in Business," Western Michigan University: Department of Business Education and Administrative Services, 1974. A short communication text dealing realistically with theory.
4. J. Harold Janis, "Written Communication in an Upgraded Curriculum," *The Journal of Business Communication,* 3, October 1965, 1-11.
5. Harold R. Jolliffe, "Semantics and Its Implications for Teachers of Business Communication," *The Journal of Business Communication,* 1, March 1964, 1-19.
6. Irving J. Lee, *Language Habits in Human Affairs,* New York: Harper and Row, 1941. Still one of the most complete introductory semantics books written—very readable because of all the illustrations.
7. Raymond V. Lesikar, *Report Writing for Business,* 4th ed., Homewood, IL: Richard D. Irwin, Inc., 1973. Chapter 9, "Writing to Communicate: General Characteristics," is helpful on both readability and communication theory.
8. J. H. Menning and C. W. Wilkinson, *Communicating Through Letters and Reports,* 5th ed., Homewood, IL: Richard D. Irwin, Inc., 1972. Interweaves theory and practical application. Has a good appendix on semantics.
9. Robert R. Potter, *Making Sense,* New York: Globe Book Company, 1974. A very good practical semantics text with helpful exercises to reinforce the principles involved.
10. Morris P. Wolf, "Semantics and Redheaded Stepchildren," *The ABWA Bulletin,* 29, April, 1965, 11-19. Emphasizes that our job is the teaching of business communicators not just business communication. He feels that semantics is a necessary part of any course that teaches the communication process.

NONVERBAL MESSAGES

3

After reading the next four selections you will undoubtedly agree that nonverbal communication is one of the most interesting and fascinating areas of study in the field of human communication. Knapp offers an excellent overview of the area in the first selection. In the second selection, Julius Fast relates nonverbal communication to the topic of courtship and romance. This selection is from Fast's book entitled *Body Language* which is a term often used synonomously for the term nonverbal communication.

The third selection by Wahlers and Barker offers an empirical test of the intuitive notion that braless women attract a lot of attention! In the fourth selection, cardiologists Friedman and Rosenman describe the differing nonverbal behaviors of those who are more likely to end up as heart attack victims. This article shows the more serious applications of studying nonverbal messages.

Mark L. Knapp

NONVERBAL COMMUNICATION: BASIC PERSPECTIVES

Those of us who keep our eyes open can read volumes
into what we see going on around us.

—E. Hall

     Herr von Osten purchased a horse in Berlin, Germany in 1900. When von Osten began training his horse, Hans, to count by tapping his front hoof, he had no idea that Hans was soon to become one of the most celebrated horses in history. Hans was a rapid learner and soon progressed from counting to addition, multiplication, division, subtraction, and eventually the solution of problems involving factors and fractions. As if this were not enough, von Osten exhibited Hans to public audiences where he counted the number in the audience or simply the number of people wearing eye glasses. Still responding only with taps, Hans could tell time, use a calendar, display an ability to recall musical pitch, and perform numerous other seemingly fantastic feats. After von Osten taught Hans an alphabet which could be coded into hoofbeats, the horse could answer virtually any question—oral or written. It seemed that Hans, a common horse, had complete comprehension of the German language, the ability to produce the equivalent of words and numerals, and an intelligence beyond that of many human beings.

     Even without the promotion of Madison Avenue, the word spread quickly and soon Hans was known throughout the world. He was soon dubbed "Clever Hans." Because of the obviously profound implications for several scientific fields and because some skeptics thought there was a "gimmick" involved, an investigating committee was established to decide, once and for all, whether there was any deceit involved in Hans' performances. Professors of psychology, physiology, the director of the Berlin Zoological Garden, a director of a circus, veterinarians, and cavalry officers were appointed to this commission of horse experts. An experiment with Hans from which von Osten was absent demonstrated no change in the apparent intelligence of Hans. This was sufficient proof for the commission to announce there was no trickery involved.

     The appointment of a second commission was the beginning of the end for Clever Hans. Von Osten was asked to whisper a number into the horse's left ear while another experimenter whispered a number into the horse's right ear. Hans was told to add the two numbers—an answer none of the onlookers, von Osten, or the experimenter knew. Hans failed. And with further tests he continued to fail. The experimenter, Pfungst, discovered on further experimentation that Hans could only answer a question if someone in his visual field knew the answer.[1] When Hans was given the question, the onlookers assumed an expectant posture and increased their body tension. When Hans reached the correct number of taps, the onlookers would relax and make a slight movement of the head—which was Hans' cue to stop tapping.

The story of Clever Hans is frequently used in discussions concerning the capacity of an animal to learn verbal language. It also seems well suited to an introduction to the field of nonverbal communication. Hans' cleverness was not in his ability to verbalize or understand verbal commands, but in his ability to respond to almost imperceptible and unconscious movements on the part of those surrounding him. It is not unlike that perceptiveness or sensitivity to nonverbal cues exhibited by a Clever Carl, Charles, Frank, or Harold when picking up a girl, closing a business deal, giving an intelligent and industrious image to a professor, knowing when to leave a party, and in a multitude of other common situations. This book is written for the purpose of expanding the reader's conscious awareness of the numerous nonverbal stimuli confronting him in his everyday dialogue with his fellow man. Each chapter will summarize behavioral science research on a specific area of nonverbal communication. First, however, it is necessary to develop a few basic perspectives—a common frame of reference—a lens through which we can view the remaining chapters.

PERSPECTIVES ON DEFINING NONVERBAL COMMUNICATION

Conceptually, the term *nonverbal is* subject to a variety of interpretations—just like the term *communication*. The basic issue seems to be whether the events traditionally studied under the heading *nonverbal* are literally *non* verbal. Ray Birdwhistell, a pioneer in nonverbal research, is reported to have said that studying *nonverbal* communication is like studying *noncardiac* physiology. His point is well taken. It is not easy to dissect human interaction and make one diagnosis which concerns only verbal behavior and another which concerns only nonverbal behavior. The verbal dimension is so intimately woven and so subtly represented in so much of what we have previously labeled *non*verbal that the term does not always adequately describe the behavior under study. Some of the most noteworthy scholars associated with nonverbal study refuse to segregate words from gestures and, hence, work under the broader terms *communication* or *face to face interaction*.

The theoretical position taken by Dance concerning the whole process of communication goes even further in order to call to our attention that perhaps not everything labeled nonverbal is literally nonverbal. Dance might even argue that there is no such thing as uniquely human communication that is nonverbal. He takes the position that all symbols are verbal and that human communication is defined as the eliciting of a response through verbal symbols. He does not deny the fact that we may engage in nonverbal behaviors, but the instant these behaviors are interpreted by another in terms of words, they become verbal phenomena. In the process of making a useful distinction be-

---

[1]O. Pfungst, *Clever Hans, The Horse of Mr. Von Osten* (New York: Holt, Rinehart and Winston, 1911).

tween the terms *vocal* and *verbal,* Dance's point of view concerning nonverbal communication is clarified.

> The confusion of *verbal* and *vocal* in reference to communication exists in a great deal of our literature and dialogue. A verbal symbol can be either vocal or nonvocal. A vocal sound need not always be symbolic. A scream, for instance, may be vocal and nonverbal on the reflex discharge level. On the other hand, a scream, when interpreted by a passerby in terms of circumstances, may be vocal and also may have meaning for the passerby beyond the meaning to the screamer. Thus, the passerby's meaning, being the result of his past actual or vicarious experience, is interpreted by him in terms of words and becomes both vocal and verbal. A traffic signal derives its meaning from the observer's past experiences in learning law and order through words. The traffic signal, then, is nonvocal and verbal. The essential attribute of *verbal* is not the existence of sound in acoustic space, but the representation of abstractions of many specific instances by one sign that then becomes a sign of signs or a symbol.[2]

While many researchers recognize this theoretical and conceptual problem with the term *nonverbal,* their research proceeds. Most of this research is based on the premise that if words are not spoken or written, they become nonverbal in nature. Also included in the term *nonverbal* under this definition are all those nuances which surround words—e.g., tone of voice or type of print. This is frequently called paralanguage. In their early classic, *Nonverbal Communication: Notes on the Visual Perception of Human Relations*, Ruesch and Kees took essentially this point of view. But, in addition, the authors outlined what they considered to be the primary elements in the study of nonverbal communication. This classification system has been highly influential in providing a basis for most of the work done in this field to date.

> In broad terms, nonverbal forms of codification fall into three distinct categories:
> 1. *Sign Language* includes all those forms of codification in which words, numbers, and punctuation signs have been supplanted by gestures; these vary from the "monosyllabic" gesture of the hitchhiker to such complete systems as the language of the deaf.
> 2. *Action Language* embraces all movements that are not used exclusively as signals. Such acts as walking and drinking, for example, have a dual function: on one hand they serve personal needs, and on the other they constitute statements to those who may perceive them.
> 3. *Object Language* comprises all intentional and nonintentional display of material things, such as implements, machines, art objects, architectural structures, and—last but not least—the human body and whatever clothes or covers it. The embodiment of letters as they occur in books and on signs has a material substance, and this aspect of words also has to be considered as object language.[3]

---

[2]F. E. X. Dance, "Toward a Theory of Human Communication," in *Human Communication Theory,* ed. F. E. X. Dance (New York: Holt, Rinehart and Winston, 1967): 290.
[3]J. Ruesch and W. Kees, *Nonverbal Communication: Notes on the Visual Perception of Human Relations* (Berkeley and Los Angeles: University of California Press, 1956): 189.

Another way of defining a field of study is to examine the work that has been done to see if any common directions have been followed. As previously mentioned, one common trend is the assumption that nonverbal communication encompasses those events in which words are not spoken or written. Other recurring trends are exemplified by the following classification system which represents a definition of the field of nonverbal human communication as evidenced in the writing and research available.

Nonverbal Dimensions of Human Communication

I. Body Motion or Kinesic Behavior Body motion, or kinesic behavior, typically includes gestures, movements of the body, limbs, hands, head, feet and legs, facial expressions (smiles), eye behavior (blinking, direction and length of gaze, and pupil dilation) and posture. The furrow of the brow, the slump of a shoulder and the tilt of a head—all are within the purview of kinesics. Obviously, there are different types of nonverbal behavior just as there are different types of verbal behavior. Some nonverbal cues are very specific, some more general; some intended to communicate, some expressive only; some provide information about emotions, others carry information about personality traits or attitudes. In an effort to sort through the relatively unknown world of nonverbal behavior, Ekman and Friesen[4] developed a system for classifying nonverbal behavioral acts. These categories include:

A. *Emblems.* These are nonverbal acts which have a direct verbal translation or dictionary definition—usually consisting of a word or two or a phrase. There is high agreement among members of a culture or subculture on the verbal definition. The gestures used to represent "A-OK" or "Peace" are examples of emblems for a large part of our culture. Toffler notes in his bestseller, *Future Shock,* that some emblems which were perceived as semi-obscene are now becoming more respectable with changing sexual values. He uses the example of the upraised finger—designating "up yours." Emblems are frequently used when verbal channels are blocked (or fail) and are usually used to communicate. The sign language of the deaf, nonverbal gestures used by television production personnel, signals used by two underwater swimmers, or motions made by two people who are too far apart to make audible signals practical—all these are emblems. Our own awareness of emblem usage is about the same as our awareness of word choice.

B. *Illustrators.* These are nonverbal acts which are directly tied to, or accompany, speech—serving to illustrate what is being said verbally. These may be movements which accent or emphasize a word or phrase; movements which sketch a path of thought; movements pointing to present objects; movements depicting a spatial relationship; or movements which depict a bodily action. Illustrators seem to be within our awareness, but not as explicitly as emblems. They are used intentionally to help communicate, but not as deliberately as emblems. They are probably learned by watching others.

C. *Affect Displays.* These are simply facial configurations which display affective states. They can repeat, augment, contradict, or be unrelated to, verbal affective statements. Once the display has occurred, there is usually a

---

[4]P. Ekman and W. V. Friesen, "The Repertoire of Nonverbal Behavior: Categories, Origins, Usage, and Coding," *Semiotica 1* (1969): 49-98.

high degree of awareness, but it can occur without any awareness. Often, affect displays are not intended to communicate, but they can be intentional.

D. *Regulators*. These are nonverbal acts which maintain and regulate the back and forth nature of speaking and listening between two or more interactants. They tell the speaker to continue, repeat, elaborate, hurry up, become more interesting, give the other a chance to talk, etc. They consist mainly of head nods and eye movements, and there seem to be class and cultural differences in usage—improper usage connoting rudeness. These acts are not tied to specific spoken behavior. They seem to be on the periphery of our awareness and are generally difficult to inhibit. They are like overlearned habits and are almost involuntary, but we are very much aware of these signals sent by others. Probably the most familiar regulator is the head nod—the equivalent of the verbal mm-hmm.

E. *Adaptors*. These nonverbal behaviors are perhaps the most difficult to define and involve the most speculation. They are labeled adaptors because they are thought to develop in childhood as adaptive efforts to satisfy needs, perform actions, manage emotions, develop social contacts, or perform a host of other functions. They are not really coded; they are fragments of actual aggressive, sexual or intimate behavior and often reveal personal orientations or characteristics covered by verbal messages. Leg movements can often be adaptors, showing residues of kicking aggression, sexual invitation, or flight. Many of the restless movements of the hands and feet which have typically been considered indicators of anxiety may be residues of adaptors necessary for flight from the interaction. Adaptors are possibly triggered by verbal behavior in a given situation which is associated with conditions occurring when the adaptive habit was first learned. We are typically unaware of adaptors.

II. Physical Characteristics Whereas the previous section was concerned with movement and motion, this category covers things which remain relatively unchanged during the period of interaction. They are influential nonverbal cues which are not movement-bound. Included are such things as: physique or body shape, general attractiveness, body or breath odors, height, weight, hair, and skin color or tone.

III. Touching Behavior For some, kinesic study includes touch behavior; for others, however, actual physical contact constitutes a separate class of events. Some researchers are concerned with touching behavior as an important factor in the child's early development; some are concerned with adult touching behavior. Subcategories may include: stroking, hitting, greetings and farewells, holding, guiding another's movements, and other, more specific instances.

IV. Paralanguage Simply put, paralanguage deals with how something is said and not what is said. It deals with the range of nonverbal vocal cues surrounding common speech behavior. Trager felt paralanguage had the following components:[5]

A. *Voice Qualities*. This includes such things as pitch range, pitch control, rhythm control, tempo, articulation control, resonance, glottis control, and vocal lip control.

---

[5] G.L. Trager, "Paralanguage: A First Approximation," *Studies in Linguistics* 13 (1958): 1-12.

B. *Vocalizations.*

1) *Vocal characterizers.* This includes such things as laughing, crying, sighing, yawning, belching, swallowing, heavily marked inhaling or exhaling, coughing, clearing of the throat, hiccupping, moaning, groaning, yelling, whispering, sneezing, snoring, stretching, etc.

2) *Vocal qualifiers.* This includes intensity (overloud to oversoft), pitch height (overhigh to overlow), and extent (extreme drawl to extreme clipping).

3) *Vocal segregates.* These are such things as "uh-huh," "um," "uh," "ah," and variants thereof.

Related work on such topics as silent pauses (beyond junctures), intruding sounds, speech errors, and latency would probably be included in this category.

V. Proxemics Proxemics is generally considered to be the study of man's use and perception of his social and personal space. Under this heading, we find a body of work called small group ecology which concerns itself with how people use and respond to spatial relationships in formal and informal group settings. Such studies deal with seating arrangements, and spatial arrangements as related to leadership, communication flow, and the task at hand. The influence of architectural features on residential living units and even on communities is also of concern to those who study man's proxemic behavior. On an even broader level, some attention has been given to spatial relationships in crowds and densely populated situations. Man's personal space orientation is sometimes studied in the context of conversational distance—and how it varies according to sex, status, roles, cultural orientation, etc. The term "territoriality" is also frequently used in the study of proxemics to denote the human tendency to stake out personal territory—or untouchable space—much as wild animals and birds do.

VI. Artifacts Artifacts include the manipulation of objects in contact with the interacting persons which may act as nonverbal stimuli. These artifacts include: perfume, clothes, lipstick, eyeglasses, wigs and other hairpieces, false eyelashes, eyeliners, and the whole repertoire of falsies and "beauty" aids.

VII. Environmental Factors Up to this point we have been concerned with the appearance and behavior of the persons involved in communicating. This category concerns those elements which impinge on the human relationship, but which are not directly a part of it. Environmental factors include the furniture, architectural style, interior decorating, lighting conditions, smells, colors, temperature, additional noises or music, etc., within which the interaction occurs. Variations in arrangements, materials, shapes, or surfaces of objects in the interacting environment can be extremely influential on the outcome of an interpersonal relationship. This category also includes what might be called traces of action. For instance, as you observe cigarette butts, orange peels, and waste paper left by the person you will soon interact with, you are forming an impression which will eventually influence your meeting.

PERSPECTIVES ON NONVERBAL COMMUNICATION IN THE TOTAL COMMUNICATION PROCESS

We are constantly being warned against presenting material out of context. Although this was written as a supplement to a treatment of verbal behavior, the fact is that it deals almost exclusively with nonverbal communication. There is a danger that the reader may forget that nonverbal communication cannot be studied in isolation from the total communication process. Verbal and nonverbal communication should be treated as a total and inseparable unit. Birdwhistell makes this point when he says:

> My own research has led me to the point that I am no longer willing to call either linguistic or kinesic systems *communication* systems. All of the emerging data seem to me to support the contention that linguistics and kinesics are *infra*-communicational systems. Only in their interrelationship with each other and with comparable systems from other sensory modalities is the emergent communication system achieved.[6]

Argyle flatly states, "Some of the most important findings in the field of social interaction are about the ways that verbal interaction needs the support of nonverbal communications."[7] What are some of the ways in which verbal and nonverbal systems interrelate? How do nonverbal behaviors support verbal behaviors?[8]

Repeating. Nonverbal communication can simply repeat what was said verbally. For instance, if you told a person he had to go north to find a newspaper stand and then pointed in the proper direction, this would be considered repetition.

Contradicting. Nonverbal behavior can contradict verbal behavior. A classic example is the parent who yells to his child in an angry voice, "Of course I love you!" Or the person who is about to make a public speech whose hands and knees tremble, beads of perspiration form around his brow and he not so confidently states, "I'm not nervous." It has been said that when we receive contradictory messages on the verbal and nonverbal level, we are more likely to trust and believe in the nonverbal message.[9] It is assumed that nonverbal signals are more spontaneous, harder to fake, and less apt to be manipulated. It is probably more accurate to say, however, that some nonverbal behaviors are more spontaneous and harder to fake than others—and that some people are more proficient than others at nonverbal deception.[10] With two contradictory cues—both of which are nonverbal—again we predictably place our reliance on the cues we consider harder to fake. Interestingly, young children seem to give less credence to certain nonverbal cues than do adults when confronted with conflicting verbal and nonverbal messages.[11] Conflicting messages in

---

[6]R.L. Birdwhistell, "Some Body Motion Elements Accompanying Spoken American English," in *Communication: Concepts and Perspectives,* ed. L. Thayer (Washington, D.C.: Spartan Books, 1967), 71.

[7]M. Argyle, *Social Interaction* (New York: Atherton Press, 1969), 70-71.

[8]Cf. P. Ekman, "Communication through Nonverbal Behavior: A Source of Information about an Interpersonal Relationship," in *Affect, Cognition and Personality,* ed. S. S. Tomkins and C. E. Izard (New York: Springer, 1965).

[9]Some evidence to support this notion is found in: E. Tabor, "Decoding of Consistent and Inconsistent Attitudes in Communication," (Ph.D. diss., Illinois Institute of Technology, 1970).

[10]See above for a discussion of our level of awareness of various nonverbal behaviors.

[11]D. E. Bugental, J. W. Kaswan, L. R. Love and M. N. Fox, "Child Versus Adult Perception of Evaluative Messages in Verbal, Vocal, and Visual Channels," *Developmental Psychology* 2 (1970): 367-75.

which the speaker smiled while making a critical statement were interpreted more negatively by children than adults. This was particularly true when the speaker was a woman. Shapiro's work casts a further shadow on the "reliance on nonverbal cues in contradictory situations" theory.[12] Shapiro found student judges to be extremely consistent in their reliance on either linguistic or facial cues when asked to select the affect being communicated from a list of incongruent faces and written messages. This suggests that through experience, some people rely more heavily on the verbal message while others rely on the nonverbal. Although one source of our preferences for verbal or nonverbal cues may be learned experiences, others believe there may also be an even more basic genesis—such as right-left brain dominance.

Substituting. Nonverbal behavior can substitute for verbal messages. When the dejected and downtrodden executive (or janitor) walks into his house after work, his facial expression substitutes for the statement, "I've had a rotten day." With a little practice, wives soon learn to identify a wide range of these substitute nonverbal displays—all the way from "It's been a fantastic, great day!" to "Oh, God, am I miserable!" She does not need to ask for verbal confirmation of her perception. Sometimes, when substitute nonverbal behavior fails, the communicator resorts back to the verbal level. Consider the girl who wants her date to stop "making out" with her. She may stiffen, stare straight ahead, act unresponsive and cool. If the suitor still comes on heavy, she is apt to say something like, "Look Larry, please don't ruin a nice friendship . . . etc."

Complementing. Nonverbal behavior can modify, or elaborate on, verbal messages. A student may reflect an attitude of embarrassment when talking to his professor about his poor performance in class assignments. Further, nonverbal behavior may reflect changes in the relationship between the student and the professor. When a student's slow, quiet verbalizations and relaxed posture change—when posture stiffens and the emotional level of the verbalized statements increases—this may signal changes in the overall relationship between the interactants. Complementary functions of nonverbal communication serve to signal one's attitudes and intentions toward another person.

Accenting. Nonverbal behavior may accent parts of the verbal message much as underlining written words, or *italicizing* them, serves to emphasize them. Movements of the head and hands are frequently used to accent the verbal message. When a father scolds his son about staying out too late at night, he may accent a particular phrase with a firm grip on the son's shoulder and an accompanying frown on his face. In some instances, one set of nonverbal cues can accent other nonverbal cues. Ekman, for instance, found that emotions are primarily exhibited by facial expressions, but that the body carries the most accurate indicators regarding the *level* of arousal.[13]

Relating and Regulating. Nonverbal communication is also used to regulate the communicative flow between the interactants. Some have labeled

---

[12]J. G. Shapiro, "Responsivity to Facial and Linguistic Cues," *Journal of Communication* 18 (1968): 11-17.
[13]P. Ekman, "Body Position, Facial Expression and Verbal Behavior During Interviews," *Journal of Abnormal and Social Psychology* 68 (1964): 295-301. Also: P. Ekman and W. V. Friesen, "Head and Body Cues in the Judgement of Emotion: A Reformulation," *Perceptual and Motor Skills* 24 (1967): 711-24.

this a relational function. A head nod, eye movement, or shift in position—any one of these, or combination of them, may signal the other person to continue to speak or to stop speaking because you want to say something. Speakers generally rely on this feedback to determine how their utterances are being received—or whether the other person is even paying attention.

The future of research in human communication will also require an analysis of verbal and nonverbal behavior as an inseparable unit. Some efforts in this direction have already been made. Harrison[14] and Buehler and Richmond[15] have outlined basic frameworks for the analysis of verbal and nonverbal behavior in two-person settings. Reece and Whitman,[16] among others, are trying to isolate the verbal and nonverbal components which convey interpersonal "warmth." Exline[17] is trying to relate eye behavior to various kinds of verbal material. Agulera[18] found touch gestures by nurses changed the nature of their verbal interaction with patients. Goldman-Eisler[19] is studying the predictability of verbal content following pauses of various types and lengths.

Birdwhistell feels that the whole system of body motion is comparable to spoken language. He reports the existence of kinemes and various types of kinemorphs which combine to form higher level syntactic structures. These kinesic units are comparable to the phoneme, morpheme, and other syntactic units used to analyze spoken language. He even goes so far as to state that a well-trained "linguistic-kinesiologist" should be able to tell what movements a man is making simply by listening to his voice. In like manner, he claims to be able to tell what language the late New York Mayor. Fiorello LaGuardia, was speaking simply by watching his gestures. LaGuardia spoke Italian, Yiddish, and English.

PERSPECTIVES ON THE PREVALENCE AND IMPORTANCE OF NONVERBAL COMMUNICATION

The importance of nonverbal communication would be undeniable if sheer quantity were the only measure. Birdwhistell, generally agreed to be a noted authority on nonverbal behavior, makes some rather astounding estimates of the amount of nonverbal communication taking place. He estimates that the average person actually speaks words for a total of only 10 to 11 minutes daily—the standard spoken sentence taking only about 2.5 seconds.

[14] R. Harrison, "Verbal-Nonverbal Interaction Analysis: The Substructure of an Interview" (Paper presented to the Association for Education in Journalism, Berkeley, Calif., August 1969).

[15] R. E. Buehler and J. F. Richmond, "Interpersonal Communication Behavior Analysis: A Research Method," *Journal of Communication* 13 (1963): 146-55.

[16] M. Reece and R. Whitman, "Expressive Movements, Warmth, and Verbal Reinforcement," *Journal of Abnormal and Social Psychology* 64 (1962): 234-36.

[17] R. V. Exline, *et al.*, "Visual Interaction in Relation to Machiavellianism and an Unethical Act," *American Psychologist* 16 (1961): 396. *Also see* R. V. Exline, D. Gray and D. Schuette, "Visual Behavior in a Dyad as Affected by Interview Content and Sex of Respondent," *Journal of Personality and Social Psychology* 1 (1965): 201-9.

[18] D. C. Agulera, "Relationship Between Physical Contact and Verbal Interaction Between Nurses and Patients," *Journal of Psychiatric Nursing and Mental Health Services* 5 (1967): 5-21.

[19] F. Goldman-Eisler, *Psycholinguistics: Experiments in Spontaneous Speech* (New York: Academic Press, 1968).

He goes on to say that in a normal two-person conversation, the verbal components carry less than 35% of the social meaning of the situation; more than 65% is carried on the nonverbal band.

Another way of looking at the quantity of nonverbal messages is to note the various systems man uses to communicate. Hall outlines ten separate kinds of human activity which he calls "primary message systems."[20] He suggests that only one involves language. Ruesch and Kees discuss at least seven different systems—personal appearance and dress, gestures or deliberate movements, random action, traces of action, vocal sounds, spoken words, and written words. Only two of the seven involve words.[21]

It is not my purpose here to argue the importance of the various human message systems, but to put the nonverbal world in perspective. It is safe to say that the study of human communication has for too long ignored a significant part of the process.

Further testimony to the prevalence and importance of nonverbal communication is available if we scrutinize specific facets of our society: the use of nonverbal cues in psychiatry, teaching the deaf, doctor-nurse communication during operations, disturbed nonverbal communication, audience-speaker nonverbal communication, advertising, music, our use of time, art, pictures, dance, nonverbal aspects of written and printed language, nonverbal cues in deceptive communications, communicating across cultures, communicating across ethnic groups within a culture, drum and whistle languages—the list is interminable.[22] This same idea can be illustrated by briefly noting the role of nonverbal communication in four areas: televised politics, classroom behavior, behavioral research, and courtship behavior.

Televised Politics. The tired, overweight, physically unappealing political boss is slowly being replaced by the young, good looking, vigorous candidate who can capture the public's vote with an assist from his nonverbal attraction. We currently watch between 30 and 40 hours of television each week. Television has certainly helped to structure some of our nonverbal perceptions, and more and more political candidates recognize the tremendous influence these perceptions may have on the eventual election outcome. Perhaps the most frightening and vivid example of the role of nonverbal communication in televised politics is found in McGinniss' book, *The Selling of the President 1968:*

> Television seems particularly useful to the politician who can be charming but lacks ideas . . . On television it matters less that he does not have ideas. His personality is what the viewers want to share. He need be neither statesman nor crusader; he must only show up on time. Success and failure are easily measured: how often is he invited back? Often enough and he reaches his goal—to advance from "politician" to "celebrity," a status jump bestowed by grateful viewers who feel that finally they have been given basis for making a choice.
>
> The TV candidate, then, is measured not against his predecessors —not against a standard of performance established by two centuries

---

[20] E. T. Hall, *The Silent Language* (Garden City, N.Y.: Doubleday, 1959).

[21] Ruesch and Kees, *Nonverbal Communication.*

[22] T. Stern, "Drum and Whistle Languages: An Analysis of Speech Surrogates," *American Anthropologist* 59 (1957): 487-506.

of democracy—but against Mike Douglas. How well does he handle himself? Does he mumble, does he twitch, does he make me laugh? Do I feel warm inside?

It does not surprise us, then, to note John Lindsay, as Mayor of New York City, making frequent visits to Johnny Carson's show; or to see Robert Finch, presidential advisor, appearing on an antidrug episode of "The Name of the Game"; or to find the Vice President of the United States, Spiro T. Agnew, introducing the 1970 fall season of "The Red Skelton Show." Fortunately, the media experts do not yet control all the variables as the fall, 1970, elections indicated. The batting average for the top public relations and media experts, both Democratic and Republican, was only about .500.

Classroom Behavior. The classroom is a veritable goldmine of nonverbal behavior which has been relatively untapped by scientific probes. Acceptance and understanding of ideas and feelings on the part of both teacher and student, encouraging and criticizing, silence, questioning, etc.—all involve nonverbal elements. Consider the following instances as representative of the variety of classroom nonverbal cues:

(1) the frantic hand waver who is sure he has the correct answer
(2) the student who is sure he does not know the answer and tries to avoid any eye contact with the teacher
(3) the effects of student dress and hair length on teacher-student interaction
(4) facial expressions—threatening gestures, and tone of voice are frequently used for discipline in elementary schools
(5) the teacher who requests student questioning and criticism, but whose nonverbal actions make it clear he will not be receptive
(6) absence from class communicates
(7) a teacher's trust of his students is sometimes indicated by his arrangement of seating and his monitoring behavior during examinations
(8) the variety of techniques used by students to make sleeping appear to be studying or listening
(9) the professor who announces he has plenty of time for student conferences, but whose fidgeting and glancing at his watch suggest otherwise
(10) teachers who try to assess visual feedback to determine student comprehension[23]
(11) even classroom design (wall colors, space between seats, windows) has an influence on student participation in the classroom.

The subtle nonverbal influences in the classroom can sometimes have dramatic results as Rosenthal and Jacobson found out.[24] Briefly, here is what happened: Rosenthal and Jacobson gave I.Q. tests to elementary school pupils prior to their entering for the fall term. *Randomly* (not according to scores) some students were labeled as high scorers on an "intellectual blooming test"

---

[23] At least one study suggests even experienced teachers are not very successful at this. Cf. J. Jecker, N. Maccoby, M. Breitrose, and E. Rose, "Teacher Accuracy in Assessing Cognitive Visual Feedback from Students," *Journal of Applied Psychology* 48 (1964): 393-97.
[24] R. Rosenthal and L. Jacobson, *Pygmalion in the Classroom* (New York: Holt, Rinehart and Winston, 1968)

which indicated they would show unusual intellectual development in the following year. Teachers were given this information. These students showed a sharp rise on I.Q. tests given at the end of the year. The experimenters attribute this to teacher expectations and to the way these "special" students were treated.

> To summarize our speculations, we may say that by what she said, by how and when she said it, by her facial expressions, postures, and perhaps by her touch, the teacher may have communicated to the children of the experimental group that she expected improved intellectual performance. Such communications together with possible changes in teaching techniques may have helped the child learn by changing his self concept, his expectations of his own behavior, and his motivation, as well as his cognitive style and skills.[25]

Behavioral Research. Closely related to Rosenthal's work on nonverbal classroom behavior is his expose of how nonverbal cues in behavioral science experiments often influence the experimental results. This concept is sometimes called "experimenter bias."

Rosenthal once asked, "Covert communications occur routinely in all other dyadic interactions; why then, should they not occur in the dyad composed of the experimenter and his subject?"[26] With this as a guiding premise, he has thoroughly explored the nonverbal dimensions of what happens when experimenter and subject get together.[27] A few findings from his work will illustrate:

(1) Considerable evidence is available to show that male and female experimenters sometimes obtain significantly different data from subjects. It has been noted that male experimenters behave in an "interested" manner toward female subjects—spending more time in preparation behavior, leaning much closer. Female subjects are more protectively treated during investigations involving tension and stress. Female subjects gain more attention and consideration than males.

(2) In some instances, black experimenters have been able to obtain different responses on questionnaires and GSR equipment than white experimenters.

(3) Changes in the appearance of an interviewer, designed to make her more or less "Jewish," changed the responses to a public survey containing anti-Semitic items.

(4) High status experimenters sometimes obtain different responses than low status ones.

---

[25] *Ibid.*, p. 180. Another experiment was designed in which different experimenters were told that their rats (though from the same population) were either "Maze-Bright" or "Maze-Dull" in relation to their ability to learn a maze. Those experimenters expecting better performance of the rats obtained it. Cf. R. Rosenthal and K. Fode, "Psychology of the Scientist: V. Three Experiments in Experimenter Bias," *Psychological Reports* 12 (1963): 491-511.

[26] R. Rosenthal, "Covert Communication in the Psychological Experiment," *Psychological Bulletin* 67 (1967): 357.

[27] R. Rosenthal, *Experimenter Effects in Behavioral Research* (New York: Appleton-Century-Crofts, 1966).

(5) The experimenter's need for approval, dominance, authoritarianism, warmth or coldness; prior contact with the subjects; and amount of research experience will frequently influence the dyadic relationship and hence, the results of the experiment.

(6) Sometimes the subjects will act as a source of behaviors later manifested by the experimenter. Take, for instance, the particularly obnoxious subject who affects an experimenter's entire day of testing—making him hostile and moody.

Courtship Behavior. One of many contemporary comments on nonverbal courtship behavior is found in the following excerpts from the Beatles' song, "Something" (Copyright © 1969 Harrisongs Ltd. Written by George Harrison. Used by permission. All rights reserved. International copyright secured.):

> Something in the way she moves
> Attracts me like no other lover
> Something in the way she woos me . . .
>
> Somewhere in her smile she knows
> That I don't need no other lover
> Something in her style that shows me . . .
>
> You're asking me will my love grow . . .
>
> You stick around, now
> It may show . . .

As the song suggests, we know there is "something" which is highly influential in our nonverbal courtship behavior. Like other areas of nonverbal study, however, we are still at a very early stage in quantifying these patterns of behavior. On a purely intuitive level, we know that there are some men and some women who can exude such messages as "I'm available," "I'm knowledgeable," or "I want you" without saying a word. For the male, it may be such things as his clothes, sideburns, length of hair, an arrogant grace, a thrust of his hips, touch gestures, extra long eye contact, carefully looking at the woman's figure, open gestures and movements to offset closed ones exhibited by the woman, gaining close proximity, a subtleness which will allow both parties to deny that either had committed themselves to a courtship ritual, making the woman feel secure, wanted, "like a woman," or showing excitement and desire in fleeting facial expressions. For the woman, it may be such things as sitting with her legs symbolically open, crossing her legs to expose a thigh, engaging in flirtatious glances, stroking her thighs, protruding breasts, using appealing perfume, showing the "pouting mouth" in her facial expressions, opening her palm to the male, using a tone of voice which has an "invitation behind the words," or any of a multitude of other cues and rituals—some of which vary with status, subculture, region of the country, etc. A study by some students in Milwaukee of a number of "singles' bars" suggested that a cigar was taboo for any male wishing to pick up a female in these places. Other particularly important behaviors for males operating in this context seemed to be looking the female in the eyes often; dressing slightly on the "mod" side, but generally avoiding extremes in dress; and staying with one girl for the entire evening.

Another group of Milwaukee undergraduate students focused on nonverbal courtship behavior of homosexuals and found many similarities to heterosexual courtship rituals. Homosexuals were found to lavishly decorate their living quarters to impress their partners, use clothing for attraction and identification, and use eye behavior to communicate intentions. Scheflen has outlined four categories of heterosexual nonverbal courtship behavior—courtship readiness, preening behavior, positional cues, and actions of appeal or invitation.[28] The Milwaukee students found these to be useful categories in analyzing homosexual nonverbal courtship behavior too. Contrary to the popular stereotype, most homosexuals do not have effeminate and lisping characteristics. This raises the interesting question of what cues are used for identification purposes between two homosexuals. Certainly the environmental context may be very influential (gay bars), but other cues are also used. For instance, slang terms, brief bodily contact (leg to leg), and other body movements such as certain lilts of the head or hands have been reported. In public places, however, the most common and effective signals are extended eye glances. Uninterested males will most likely avoid these long, lingering glances while those who maintain such eye contact suggest they are open for further interaction.

Nielsen, citing Birdwhistell, has described the "courtship dance" of the American adolescent.[29] He claims to have identified 24 steps between the "initial contact between the young male and female and the coitional act." He explains that these steps have an order to them. By this he means that when a boy begins holding a girl's hand, he must wait until she presses his hand (signaling a go-ahead) before he can take the next step of allowing his fingers to intertwine with hers. Girls and boys are labeled "fast" or "slow" according to whether they follow the order of the steps. If a step is skipped or reversed in the order, the person who does so is labeled "fast." If a person ignores the signal to move on to the next step, or takes actions to prevent the next step, he or she is considered "slow." This ordering would suggest that only after the initial kiss may the male attempt to approach the female's breast. She will probably block his approach with her upper arm against her side since protocol forbids approaching the breast from the front. The male really does not expect to reach the breast until after a considerable amount of additional kissing.

Up to this point, we have concentrated on the nonverbal courtship behavior of unmarried men and women. Certainly there are additional volumes to be written on marital nonverbal courtship behavior patterns. The whole repertoire of messages for inviting or avoiding sexual intercourse is largely nonverbal. Some observers, for instance, have noted that "staying up to watch the late show" is a common method of saying "not tonight."

PERSPECTIVES ON THE ORIGINS AND UNIVERSALITY OF NONVERBAL BEHAVIOR

The ontogenetic development of human speech is a well-known process; the development and origin of nonverbal behaviors is much less clear. We do know that during the first two years of a child's life, he exhibits an extensive repertoire of nonverbal signals to communicate with those around him. We also know he is learning to interpret various nonverbal signals he receives from others.

Ekman and Friesen speculate that there are three sources for our various nonverbal behaviors: (1) inherited neurological programs, (2) experi-

---

[28] A. E. Scheflen, "Quasi-Courtship Behavior in Psychotherapy," *Psychiatry* 28 (1965): 245-57.

[29] G. Nielsen, *Studies in Self-Confrontation* (Copenhagen: Munksgaard; Cleveland: Howard Allen, 1962): 70-71.

ences common to all members of the species—e.g., regardless of culture the hands will be used to place food in the mouth, and (3) experience which varies with culture, class, family, or individual.[30] Generally, nonverbal behaviors are partly instinctive, partly taught, and partly imitative. The origins of the specific nonverbal behaviors mentioned earlier are as follows:

> *Emblems* are learned in conjunction with a specific culture. They are specifically taught as verbal language is taught.
>
> *Illustrators* are socially learned by imitation. They vary with ethnicity, and cultural and class differences will be found in type and frequency.
>
> *Regulators* are learned, but it is not certain when.
>
> *Affect displays* show a relationship between facial musculature, affect and some of the evokers, which is neurologically programmed. Some evokers, blends, display rules, and consequences are socially learned.
>
> *Adaptors* are habits first learned to deal with sensation, excretion, ingestion, grooming and affect; to maintain prototypic interpersonal relationships; or to perform instrumental tasks.

The fact that Ekman and Friesen think some affect displays may not be culture-bound raises a long-standing question in nonverbal communication theory and research.[31] Birdwhistell, who claims his research began with a search for universal gestures, said flatly in a 1970 *New York Times* interview: "There are no universal gestures. As far as we know, there is no single facial expression, stance, or body position which conveys the same meaning in all societies." Davitz, however, presents evidence which indicates at least some expressive facial patterns are not learned—their emergence depending primarily on physical maturation.

> This conclusion is further supported by studies of congenitally blind subjects, whose opportunities for learning facial expression by imitation are obviously limited.[32]

Perhaps the most conclusive evidence supporting the universality of facial expressions is found in the work of Ekman and his colleagues.[33] Photos of faces expressing happiness, fear, surprise, sadness, anger, disgust, and interest were easily identified by observers in at least six different countries—some of which were very isolated and primitive. Ekman reasoned that previous studies which showed persons from different literate cultures associating the same emotion concepts with the same facial behaviors did not prove universality. The exposure of such persons to the mass media might have taught them

---

[30]Ekman and Friesen, "Repertoire of Nonverbal Behavior."

[31]Darwin also argued that some affect states were universal to mankind, cf. C. Darwin, *The Expression of the Emotions in Men and Animals* (New York: Appleton-Century-Crofts 1896).

[32]J. R. Davitz, ed., *The Communication of Emotional Meaning* (New York: McGraw-Hill, 1964): 19-20.

[33]P. Ekman and W. V. Friesen, "Constants Across Cultures in the Face and Emotion," *Journal of Personality and Social Psychology* 17 (1971): 124-29. Also: P. Ekman, "Universals and Cultural Differences in Facial Expressions of Emotion," in *Nebraska Symposium on Motivation*, ed. J. Cole (Lincoln: University of Nebraska Press, 1972).

to recognize unique aspects of faces in other cultures. However, in several studies with preliterate cultures (New Guinea) which did not have widespread contact with mass media, Ekman found results comparable to those found in literate Eastern and Western cultures. In these studies, stories were told to the subjects who were then asked to select one of three facial photos which reflected the emotion of the story. Thus, there does seem to be a universal association between particular facial muscular patterns and discrete emotions. Remember, that this is only a specific element of universality and does not suggest that all aspects of facial affect displays are universal—as Ekman and Friesen testify:

> . . . We believe that, while the facial muscles which move when a particular affect is aroused are the same across cultures, the evoking stimuli, the linked effects, the display rules and the behavioral consequences all can vary enormously from one culture to another.[34]

In fact, Ekman and Friesen have suggested an alternative to the totally inherited theory. They propose that perhaps affective facial displays evolve in the same way for each individual during the course of his development. For instance, the disgust affect display may evolve from each person's movement of the mouth and nose involved in ejecting a bad taste or smell.

SUMMARY

The term *nonverbal* is commonly used to describe all human communication events which transcend spoken or written words, and many of these nonverbal events and behaviors are interpreted through verbal symbols. Therefore they are not truly *non*-verbal. The theoretical writings and research on nonverbal communication can be broken down into the following seven areas:

(1) body motion or kinesics (emblems, illustrators, affect displays, regulators, and adaptors)
(2) physical characteristics
(3) touching behavior
(4) paralanguage (vocal qualities and vocalizations)
(5) proxemics
(6) artifacts
(7) environment.

Nonverbal communication should not be studied as an isolated unit, but as an inseparable part of the total communication process. Nonverbal communication may serve to repeat, contradict, substitute, complement, accent, or regulate verbal communication. Nonverbal communication is important because of the role it plays in the total communication system, the tremendous quantity of informational cues it gives in any particular situation, and because of its use in fundamental areas of our daily life. Nonverbal behavior is partly taught, partly imitative, and partly instinctive. There is a growing body of evidence which suggests a pancultural (or universal) element in emotional facial behavior, but this does not suggest there are not cultural differences in such things as the circumstances which elicit an emotion, the display rules which govern the management of facial behavior in certain settings, and the action consequences of an emotion.

---

[34] Ekman and Friesen, "Repertoire of Nonverbal Behavior," p. 73.

Julius Fast

THE SILENT LANGUAGE OF LOVE

STANCE, GLANCE AND ADVANCE

Mike is a ladies' man, someone who is never at a loss for a girl. Mike can enter a party full of strangers and within ten minutes end up on intimate terms with one of the girls. Within half an hour he has cut her out of the pack and is on his way home with her—to his or her place, depending on which is closer.

How does Mike do it? Other men who have spent half the evening drumming up enough courage to approach a girl, will see Mike come in and take over quickly and effectively. But they don't know why.

Ask the girls and they'll shrug. "I don't know. He just has his antennae out, I guess. I get signals, and I answer them, and the first thing I know. . . ."

Mike is not particularly good looking. He's smart enough, but that's not his attraction. It seems that Mike almost has a sixth sense about him. If there's an available girl Mike will find her, or she will find him.

What does Mike have?

Well, if he hasn't looks or brilliance, he has something far more important for this type of encounter. Mike has an unconscious command of body language and he uses it expertly. When Mike saunters into a room he signals his message automatically. "I'm available, I'm masculine. I'm aggressive and knowledgeable." And then when he zeroes in on his chosen subject, the signals go, "I'm interested in you. You attract me. There's something exciting about you and I want to find out what it is."

Watch Mike in action. Watch him make contact and signal his availability. We all know at least one Mike, and we all envy him his ability. What is the body language he uses?

Well, Mike's appeal, Mike's nonverbal clarity, is compounded of many things. His appearance is part of it. Not the appearance he was born with, that's rather ordinary, but the way Mike has rearranged that appearance to transmit his message. There is, when you look at Mike carefully, a definite sexuality about him.

"Of course," a knowing woman will say, "Mike is a very sexy man." But sexy how? Not in his features.

Pressed further, the woman will explain, "It's something about him, something he has, a sort of aura."

Actually it's nothing of the sort, nothing so vague as an aura. In part it's the way Mike dresses, the type of pants he chooses, his shirts and jackets and ties, the way he combs his hair, the length of his sideburns—these all contribute to the immediate picture, but even more important than this is the way Mike stands and walks.

One woman described it as an "easy grace." A man who knew Mike was not so kind. "He's greasy." What came through as pleasing to the woman was transmitted as disturbing or challenging and therefore distasteful to the man, and he reacted by characterizing the quality contemptuously.

Yet Mike does move with grace, an arrogant sort of grace that could well arouse a man's envy and a woman's excitement. A few actors have that same movement, Paul Newman, Marlon Brando, Rip Torn, and with it they can transmit an obvious sexual message. The message can be broken down into the way they hold themselves, their stance or posture, and the easy confidence of their motion. The man who has that walk needs little else to turn a woman's head.

But Mike has more. He has dozens of little gestures, perhaps unconscious ones, that send out elaborations of his sexual message. When Mike leans up against a mantel in a room to look around at the women, his hips are thrust forward slightly, as if they were cantilevered, and his legs are usually apart. There is something in this stance that spells sex.

Watch Mike when he stands like this. He will lock his thumbs in his belt right above the pockets, and his fingers will point down toward his genitals. You have surely seen the same stance a hundred times in western movies, usually not taken by the hero, but by the sexy bad guy as he lounges against a corral fence, the picture of threatening sexuality, the villain the men hate and the women—well, what they feel is a lot more complex than hate or desire or fear, and yet it's a mixture of all these things. With his blatant body language, his leather chaps, his cantilevered groin and pointing fingers he is sending out a crude, obvious but effective signal. "I am a sexual threat. I am a dangerous man for a woman to be alone with. I am all man and I want you!"

But his body language doesn't stop there. This much serves to signal his intentions, to create an atmosphere, an aura if you will. This fascinates the available women and interests or even irritates the non-available ones.

Mike himself explained how he proceeded after this. "I size up the women, the ones who want it. How? It's easy. By the way they stand or sit. And then I make my choice and I catch her eye. If she's interested she'll respond. If not, I forget her."

"How do you catch her eye?"

"I hold the glance a little longer than I should, since I don't really know her. I won't let her eyes slide away, and I narrow mine—sort of."

But there is even more to Mike's approach than the insistent eye, as I observed one evening at a party. Mike has an uncanny instinct for sizing up a woman's defensive body language and insistently breaking it down. Are her arms clasped defensively? He opens his. Is her posture rigid? He relaxes as they talk. Is her face pinched and drawn? He smiles and loosens his face.

In short, he answers her body signals with opposite and complementary signals of his own, and by doing this intrudes himself into her awareness. He brushes aside her body language pretenses, and because unconsciously she really wants to open herself up, she opens up to Mike.

Mike moves in on a woman. When he has made signal contact, when his body language gets the message of his availability across, his next step is physical invasion, but physical invasion without touch.

He cuts into the woman's territory or body zone. He comes close enough for her to be uneasy, and yet not close enough for her to logically object. Mike doesn't touch his victim needlessly. His closeness, his intrusion into her territory, is enough to change the situation between them.

Then Mike carries his invasion even further by visual intrusion as they talk. What they say really doesn't matter much. Mike's eyes do far more talking than his voice. They linger on the woman's throat, on her breasts, her body. They linger sensuously and with promise. Mike touches his tongue to his lips, narrows his eyes, and invariably the woman becomes uneasy and excited. Remember, she's not just any woman, but that particular susceptible woman who has responded to Mike's opening gambit. She has returned his flattering attentions, and now she is in too deep to protest.

And anyway, what could she protest against? Just what has Mike done? He hasn't touched her. He hasn't made any suggestive remark. He is, by all the standards of society, a perfect gentleman. If his eyes are a bit too hot, a bit too bold, this is still a matter of interpretation. If the girl doesn't like it she has only to be rude and move off.

But why shouldn't the girl like it? Mike is flattering her with his attention. In effect he is saying, "You interest me. I want to know you better, more intimately. You're not like other women. You're the only woman here I care about."

For, in addition to his flattering attention to this woman, Mike never makes the mistake of spreading his interest. He narrows his focus and speaks to only one woman, and he makes the impact of his body language all the stronger for it. Half the time, when Mike leaves with the girl of his choice, she hardly needs any persuasion. By that time a simple, "Let's go!" is enough.

IS SHE AVAILABLE?

How does Mike single out his victim? What body language does an available girl at a party use to say, "I'm available. I'm interested. I can be had"? There must be a definite set of signals because Mike rarely makes a mistake.

A girl in our society has an additional problem in this game of sexual encounters. No matter how available she may be, it's considered pretty square to let anyone know it. This would instantly put her value down and cheapen her. And yet, unconsciously, she must let her intent be known. How does she do it?

A big part of the way she transmits her message is also in stance, posture or movement. An available woman moves in a studied way. A man may label it posing, another woman, affectation, but the movement of her body, hips and shoulders telegraph her availability. She may sit with her legs apart, symbolically open and inviting, or she may affect a gesture in which one hand touches her breast in a near caress. She may stroke her thighs as she talks or walk with a languorous roll to her hips. Some of her movements are studied and conscious, some completely unconscious.

A few generations ago female availability was broadly burlesqued by Mae West's "come up and see me sometime" routine. A later generation turned to the baby-face and hushed and breathless voice quality of a Marilyn Monroe —a tarnished innocence. Today, in a more cynical age, it is again blatant sexuality. Someone like Raquel Welch spells out the message. But these are the obvious, motion picture messages. On a subtler, living room level, the level on which Mike operates, the message is more discreet, often so discreet that the man who is ignorant of body language misses it completely. Even the man who knows a little about the subject may be misled. For example, the woman who crosses her arms across her chest may be transmitting the classic signal, "I am closed to any advance. I will not listen to you, or hear you."

This is a common interpretation of closed arms, and it is one with which most psychologists are familiar. As an example of this, there was a recent story in the papers about Dr. Spock addressing a class at the Police Academy. The audience of police were extremely hostile to the good doctor, in spite of the fact that he was responsible for the way most of them and their children had been brought up. They demonstrated their hostility verbally in their discussion, but also much more obviously in body language. In the news photo, every policeman sat with his arms crossed tightly over his chest, his face hard and closed.

Very clearly they were saying, "I am sitting here with a closed mind. No matter what you say I'm unwilling to listen. We just can't meet." This is the classical interpretation of crossed arms.

But there is another equally valid interpretation. Crossed arms may say, "I am frustrated. I am not getting what I need. I am closed in, locked in. Let me out. I can be approached and am readily available."

While the man who knows only a little about body language may misinterpret this gesture, the man well educated in body language will get the correct message from the accompanying signals the girl sends out. Is her face pinched and tight with frustration? Is she sitting stiffly instead of in a relaxed position? Does she avert her eye when you try to catch it?

All the body signals must be added up to a correct total if a man is to use body language effectively.

The aggressively available woman acts in a predictable fashion too. She has a number of effective tricks of body language to telegraph her availability. As Mike does, she uses territorial intrusion to make her point. She will sit uncomfortably close to the man she is after, taking advantage of the uneasiness such closeness arouses. As the man shifts and fidgets, unaware of why he is disturbed, she will move in with other signals, using his uneasiness as a means of throwing him off balance.

While a man on the make cannot touch the woman if he is to play the game fairly, it is perfectly permissible for a woman on the make, at this stage of the game, to touch the man. This touch can exaggerate the uneasiness of the man into whose territory she has cut.

A touch on the arm can be a disarming blow. "Do you have a match?" Steadying the hand that holds it to her cigarette can allow a moment of flesh-to-flesh contact that may be effectively troubling.

The contact of a woman's thigh, or her hand carelessly brushed against a man's thigh can be devastating if it is applied at just the right moment.

The aggressive approach by a woman can utilize not only body language—the adjustment of a skirt as she sits close, the uncrossing of her legs, the thrusting forward of her breasts, a pouting mouth—it can also utilize smell. The right perfume in the right amount, to give an elusive but exciting scent, is an important part of the aggressive approach.

IS THE FACE WORTH SAVING?

But sight, touch and smell are still less than the complete arsenal of the woman on the warpath. Sound is a very definite part of the approach. It is not always what she says, but the tone of her voice, the invitation behind the words, the pitch and the intimate, caressing quality of the sound.

The French actresses understand this well, but French is a language that lends itself to sexuality, no matter what is being said. One of the most amusing off-Broadway revue sketches I have ever seen consisted of an actor and actress doing a "scene" from a French movie. Each recited a list of vegetables in French, but the tone of voice, cadence and vocal innuendo dripped sexuality.

This, as we described earlier in the book, is the use of one communication band to carry two messages. In the area of love and sex it is a very common use. For the aggressively available woman it can serve to throw a man off guard. This is a trick used by both men and woman in the aggressive sexual pursuit. If you throw your quarry off balance, make him or her uneasy, moving in for the kill becomes relatively easy.

The trick of using the voice to carry one innocuous spoken message and another more meaningful, and much stronger, unspoken message is particularly effective because the quarry, male or female, cannot protest by the rules of the game. The aggressor, if protest is made, can always draw back and say, with some truth, "But what did I do? What did I say?"

There is a face-saving device in this, for no matter how hot the pursuit of love or sex, it cannot be done with the risk of losing face. For many people, particularly if they are insecure, losing face is a devastating and humiliating occurence. The sexual aggressor, if he or she is truly successful at the trade, is concerned with face-saving in his victim only as a means of manipulating his quarry. To be sexually aggressive, a man or woman must have enough self-assurance, enough security, to function without the need of face-saving devices.

On the opposite side of the coin, the sexually insecure person, the quarry in the inevitable hunt, desperately needs to avoid humiliation, to save face. This puts her at a tremendous disadvantage in the game. The aggressor can manipulate the quarry, holding loss of face as a threat.

When, for example, the aggressor moves in on the quarry's territory and, using a sexually seductive voice, speaks in obvious banalities, what is the quarry to do? Move back and risk the raised eyebrow. "What did you think I wanted?"

To assume that the aggressor is after *her* sexually is to import more worth to *herself* than *she* truly believes *she* has. To be let down after this would be too humiliating to bear. Suppose *she* were truly misinterpreting *his* motives? So, in most cases, the aggressor gets away with *his* ploy.

The same type of interaction is used by the deviate sexual aggressor outside of a social situation. The male subway-sexual deviate who attempts to fondle or touch a female rider in a crowd depends on her fright and insecurity to keep her quiet. The same dynamics are in action, and the fear of losing face may prevent her from protesting. She endures the minor annoyance of a groping pervert or an exposing pervert in order not to attract attention to herself.

This is so much an expected reaction that many sexual perverts who achieve satisfaction from exposing themselves count on the embarrassment and shame of their victims. Should the victim react by laughing or by any show of amusement, or even by aggressively approaching him, it would be a devastating experience for the deviate.

PICKUPS, AC AND DC

On the theme of deviates, among both male homosexuals and lesbians there are definite body language signals that can establish intimate communication. Homosexuals "cruising" on a street can identify a sympathetic soul without exchanging a word.

"Making contact is relatively simple," a young homosexual recently explained in a survey. "The first thing to do is to identify your man, and it's hard to tell you how it's done, because there are so many little signals. Some of it is the way he walks, though many of us walk like perfectly normal men. Mostly, I guess, it's the eye contact. You look and you know. He holds your eye just a little too long, and then his eye may travel down your body. The quick glance to the crotch and away is a sure giveaway."

Discussing his own signals, he explains, "I walk past and then look back. If there's any interest he'll look back too. Then I slow down, stop to look at a store window. Then we'll drift back towards each other . . . and contact!"

The signals are rigid and formalized, and sometimes they are unspoken but on the verbal band, though not related to the words. Dr. Goffman tells of a homosexual who stopped into a "gay" bar for a drink but had no interest in picking anyone up. He took out a cigarette, but found he had no matches. He suddenly realized that to ask anyone at the bar for a match was the understood signal, "I am interested. Are you?"

In the end he bought a pack of matches from the bartender.

The homosexual's signals for initiating contact are not far divorced from the normal man's signals for picking up a girl. A long time ago, when I was a soldier on leave in Boston, a soldier friend cajoled me into coming out with him to "pick up some dames."

I had had no experience at this, but I had to play the "bigshot" since I couldn't admit my ignorance. I went along and watched my friend carefully. Within half an hour he had "picked up" five girls and selected two for us. His technique was built on body language.

Walking along the street, or more properly, sauntering along, he would catch a prospect's eye, hold it a bit longer than was necessary and lift one eyebrow. If the girl faltered in her stride, stopped to look at her compact, to fix her stockings or window-shop down the street, it was one of a number of return signals that meant, "I am aware of you and possibly interested. Let's pursue this further."

My friend would then break stride, turn and follow behind the girl for a block. The following without making contact was a necessary part of the ritual and allowed him to begin vocal contact, to comment to me, a third party, on her dress, her walk, her looks—all in semi-humorous terms, a face-saving device to avoid offense.

At first she would pretend his advances were unwelcome. If this stage lasted too long it would be mutually agreed that his advances really were unwelcome. If, however, she giggled or answered him, or commented on him to her girl friend, if she had one, then it indicated a growing interest.

Eventually the pickup ended with my friend side-by-side with the girl, talking her into an apparently reluctant familiarity. I have seen the very same technique used today among teen-agers and it is one in which every step is rigidly outlined and the game must be played out from start to finish. At any point negotiations can be easily broken off by either partner without loss of face to the other. This is a stringent requirement of a successful and smooth pickup.

There is something ritualistically similar to this in the opening ceremony of certain encounters among animal species. Watch two pigeons in the park as the male circles, pouts and goes through a formal pickup while the female pretends indifference. A very definite body language is in use and in the same way humans approach each other in courtship with definite body language.

Dr. Gerhard Nielsen of the Psychological Laboratory at the University of Copenhagen describes in his book, *Studies in Self-Confrontation,* the extremely important use of body language in what he calls the "courtship dance" of the American adolescent.

Breaking the procedure of courtship down to a cold, clinical level, Dr. Nielsen found twenty-four steps between the "initial contact between the young male and female and the coitional act." These steps by the man, he decided, and the counter steps taken by the girl had a "coercive order." He explains this by saying that when a boy takes the step of holding a girl's hand, he must wait until she presses his hand, signaling a go-ahead, before he can take the next step of allowing his fingers to intertwine with hers.

Step must follow step until he can casually put his arm around her shoulder. He may move his hand down her back then and approach her breast from the side. She, in turn, can block this approach with her upper arm against her side.

After the initial kiss, and only then, he may try to move toward her breast again, but he does not really expect to reach it until a good deal of kissing has taken place. Protocol forbids him to approach the breast from the front, even ás it forbids the first kiss before the initial hand-holding.

Dr. Neilsen suggests that the boy or girl is labeled "fast" or "slow" in terms of the order of each step, not the time taken for each step. "Skipping steps or reversing their order is fast," in the same way that ignoring the signal to move on to the next step, or not permitting the next step, is slow.

CHOOSE YOUR POSTURE

Dr. Albert E. Scheflen, professor of psychiatry at the Albert Einstein College of Medicine in New York City, has studied and charted patterns of courtship and what he calls "quasi-courtship" in human beings. This quasi-courtship is the use of courting or flirting or sex to achieve non-sexual goals.

All human behavior is patterned and systematic, according to Dr. Scheflen, and it is also made up of regular, small segments arranged into larger units. This is equally true for sexual behavior, and in a study of the elements that make up our sexual relations to each other, Dr. Scheflen found that in business meetings, at parties, in school and in many other gatherings, people used these sexual elements, even though they had no sexual goal in mind.

He came to the conclusion that either Americans behave sexually when they get together on a non-sexual basis, or else—and more likely—the sexual behavior has certain qualifying body language signals when it is not used with the ultimate goal of sexual intercourse.

Just what are these sexual patterns of behavior? Well, according to Dr. Scheflen's investigations, when a man and a woman prepare for a sexual encounter, although they are unaware of what they are doing, they go through a number of body changes that bring them into a state of readiness.

The muscles of their bodies become slightly tensed and "ready for action." Body sagging disappears, and they stand up straighter, more erect and alert. There is less "jowling" in their faces and "bagging" around their eyes. Their posture becomes more youthful, and their stomachs are pulled in, their leg muscles tightened. Even their eyes seem brighter while their skins may blush or grow pale. There may even be changes in their body odors, harking back to a more primitive time when smell was a tremendously important sense in sexual encounters.

As these changes take place, the man or woman may begin to use certain gestures which Dr. Scheflen calls "preening behavior." A woman will stroke her hair or check her makeup, rearrange her clothes or push her hair away from her face, while a man may comb his hair, button his coat, readjust his clothes, pull up his socks, arrange his tie or straighten the crease in his trousers.

These are all body language signals that say, "I am interested. I like you. Notice me. I am an attractive man—an attractive woman . . . "

The second step in these sexual encounters consists of positioning. Watch a man and a woman at a party, a couple who are getting to know one another and feel a mounting sexual interest in each other. How do they sit? They will arrange their bodies and heads to face one another. They will lean toward each other and try to block off any third person. They may do this by using their arms to close a circle, or by crossing their feet toward each other to block out anyone else.

Sometimes, if such a couple are sharing a sofa and a third person is on a facing chair, they will be torn between two compulsions. One is the desire to close in their own spaces, to include only themselves, and the other is the social responsibility of having to include the third person. They may solve their dilemma by having the best of both worlds. They may cross their legs to signal to each other that they are a closed circle. The one on the right will cross his right leg over his left. The one on the left will cross her left leg over her right. In effect this closes the two of them off from the third—from the waist down. However, social responsibility to the third person may make them arrange the top parts of their bodies directly facing him, thus opening themselves to him.

When one woman at a gathering wants to get a man into an intimate situation where the two of them can form a closed unit, she acts as the sexually aggressive woman does, but to a lesser degree. She utilizes body language that includes flirting glances, holding his eyes, putting her head to one side, rolling her hips, crossing her legs to reveal part of her thigh, putting a hand on her hip or exposing her wrist or palm. All of these are accepted signals that get a message across without words. "Come and sit near me. I find you attractive. I would like to know you better."

Now let us take a situation without sexual overtones. In a conference room at a big industrial firm, a male and a female executive discuss production costs with other officials. They may go through what appear to be these same sexual encounter signals. They are using body language that in other circumstances would invite sexual advances, and yet quite obviously these two have their minds entirely on the business matter in hand. Are they masking their true feelings and do they really have a sexual desire for each other? Or are we misinterpreting their body language?

In a college seminar it appears, to an uninitiated eye, that one of the girl students is using body language to send signals to the professor, signals that invite a sexual encounter. He in turn reacts as if he were agreeable. Are they in fact flirting, or are these really non-sexual signals? Or is there something wrong with our interpretation of body language?

A group psychotherapy seminar has a group therapist who uses body language to make "advances" to one of the women. Is he stepping out of line and violating his code of ethics? Or is this part of his therapy? Or again, are the signals confused?

After careful study of these and similar situations, Dr. Scheflen found that often sexual signals were sent out when the people involved had no intention of getting into any sexual encounter. However, he found that the body language signals sent out when a sexual encounter was expected as the end result of a meeting were not quite the same as those sent out for non-sexual endings. There were subtle differences that announced, "I am interested in you and I want to do business with you, but this is not a sexual matter."

SEMI-SEXUAL ENCOUNTERS

How do we make it clear to each other that the encounter is to be non-sexual? We do it by sending another sign along with the signal, a bit of body language over and above the obvious body language, another case of two signals on one communications band.

One method for letting a partner know that the sexual signals are not to be taken seriously is to refer, in some way, to the fact that this is a business meeting, or a classroom, or a psychotherapy group. It could be something as simple as a gesture or a movement of the eyes or head toward someone in authority, or toward the other members of the gathering.

Another trick to separate sex from business is to make the sexual body language signal incomplete, to omit an important part of it. Two people sitting close together at a business meeting may adopt a sexual relationship by facing each other, but may turn part of their bodies away, or put their arms out to include others in their private circle. They may break partner contact with their eyes, or raise their voices to include everyone else in the room.

In each case a vital element must be missing from the sexual encounter. The missing element may be eye linkage, a low and private voice, arms arranged to include only the partner or any of a number of other intimacies.

Another way of putting the situation on a non-sexual level is to use disclaimers, to refer in talk to a wife, a boyfriend, a fiancée. This brings the situation into proper focus and tells the partner, "We are friends, not lovers."

This goes back to Dr. Scheflen's belief that behavior occurs in specified units that make up whole patterns. If some of the units are omitted, the finished pattern is different. In this case it is changed from sexual to non-sexual, but still with a strong man-woman interaction. A certain business routine takes place, but it is spiced by a strong flavor of half-teasing sexuality. The participants, without any expectation of sexual gratification, are still exploiting the fact that there is a sexual difference between them. The businessman uses sexual body language signals to get a certain relationship across. The intellectual uses it as a teaching aid, and the therapist uses it to help a psychological situation, but they are all aware that they are simply manipulating their genders, not aiming at sexual gratification.

There is, however, no guarantee that in any of these situations sexuality will not develop. There have been enough teachers responding sexually to pupils, businessmen to businesswomen and therapists to patients to give all of these encounters a certain piquancy and even promise.

These semi-sexual encounters occur so frequently that they are an innate part of our culture. Not only do they take place out of the home, but they also occur between parents and children, hosts and guests, even between two women or two men. The one thing that must always be made clear in this sexual-non-sexual relationship is that it is not for real. From the beginning the qualifications or disclaimers must be in effect. There should, if it is done properly, be no possibility of one partner suddenly waking up to say, "But I thought you meant . . .''; and of the other having to protest, "Oh no, it wasn't that way at all.''

Dr. Scheflen notes that there are some psychotherapists who use this flirtation behavior very consciously to involve their patients. A disinterested female patient may be made to talk openly by a sexual approach on the part of her therapist, sexual of course in terms of body language. He may arrange his tie, his sock or his hair in a preening manner to transmit sexual interest, but he must, of course, make his true non-sexual position known.

Dr. Scheflen describes a situation of a family visiting a therapist, a mother, daughter, grandmother and father. Whenever the therapist would talk to the daughter or grandmother, the mother, who sat between them, would begin to transmit sexual signals in body language. This would serve to draw the therapist's attention back to her, a sort of flirting procedure that is very common among women when they are not the center of attention. She would pout, cross her legs and extend them, place her hand on her hips and lean her body forward.

When the therapist unconsciously responded to her "advances" by arranging his tie or hair or leaning forward, both the girl and the grandmother on either side of the mother would cross their legs, placing the crossed leg in front of the mother from either side and, in effect, "boxing her in." She, in turn, would stop her sexual signals and lean back.

Perhaps the most interesting thing about this entire charade was that the "boxing in" by daughter and grandmother was always done at a signal from the father. The signal—waving his crossed foot up and down! And all of this was done by therapist, women and father without any of them being aware of their own signaling.

From a careful study of sexual-non-sexual behavior, Scheflen concludes that it usually occurs between two people when one becomes preoccupied or turns away from the other for some reason. In a large group, a family, a business gathering or a classroom, it also happens when one member is ignored or excluded by the others. The excluded member may "preen" in a sexual way to get back into the group. When one member of a group withdraws it may also be used by the rest of the group to call him back.

The important part in all of this is to know the signals, to know the limiting or qualifying signals that separate real sexual advances from non-sexual. The two, Scheflen believes, are easily confused. Indeed there are people who regularly confuse both the sending and receiving of these sexual signals and their qualifiers. There are people who, for psychological reasons, cannot follow through a sexual encounter, but still act in a sexually seductive manner, particularly when they should not.

These people not only provoke sexual advances, but see such advances in others when no such advances are intended. This is the typical "tease" all of us know or the girl who is sure everyone has designs on her.

On the other hand, Scheflen lists those people who are not aware of the qualifying signals telling them that the advance is not really sexual. These people freeze up in ordinary non-sexual situations and withdraw.

How the body language for these situations is learned and how we know the correct interpretations, the correct disclaimers and qualifiers to make sexual advances non-sexual, how we learn all of this is hard to explain. Some is taught and some is absorbed from the culture. When, for one reason or another, an individual has been divorced from his society and hasn't been taught the proper interpretations of these signals, he may face a good deal of trouble. For him body language may be unknown on a conscious level and unused on an unconscious level.

Kathy J. Wahlers and Larry L. Barker

BRALESSNESS AND NONVERBAL COMMUNICATION

Social changes usually are accompanied by controversy. The current braless trend is no exception. Much of the braless fashion controversy centers on the sexual aspects of dress, particularly the way the female bosom is (or is not) emphasized. Without concern for the fashion world, the Women's Liberation Movement has adopted bralessness as a symbol for social equality. By giving up their bras these women symbolize that they want liberation from the male stereotype of the feminine role.[1]

An incidental effect of bralessness, whether inspired by fashion, comfort or Women's Liberation is the decision by observers of "whether to look or not to look." This decision affects eye contact in interpersonal settings and has a potential effect on numerous additional nonverbal interpersonal communication variables. Another incidental effect of bralessness is the tendency on the part of some observers to apply preconceived stereotypes to braless girls. Thus, the impact of bralessness on nonverbal interpersonal communication appears to be a socially relevant and contemporary area of communication research.

REVIEW OF LITERATURE

Experimental studies have revealed the extent to which nonverbal communication complements or contradicts verbal communication.[2] The study of human bodily movement, kinesics, indicates that both the appearance and the body action of the source communicate messages to receivers.[3]

Studies of impression formation suggest that in a few seconds the receiver gains sufficient information from a visual inspection of facial expression, gestures, physique, and style of dress to form a clear image of the source and to guide his own responses to him. Although the perception of another person usually changes as new information is gathered about him, one's first impression of a person may color all subsequent information.[4]

Kathy J. Wahlers and Larry L. Barker, "Bralessness and Nonverbal Communication," *Central States Speech Journal*, Vol. 24, No. 3 (Fall 1973) pp. 222-226. Reprinted by permission.
[1]Denton F. Morrison and Carlin Paige Holden, "Why Women Are Burning Their Bras," *Sexual Behavior*, II (November 2, 1972), 24.
[2]See e.g., Paul Ekman, "Communication Through Nonverbal Behavior: A Source of Information About an Interpersonal Relationship," in S. S. Tompkins and C. E. Izard, eds. *Affect, Cognition, and Personality* (New York: Springer, 1965), pp. 390-442. Ray L. Birdwhistell, "Some Relations Between American Kinesics and Spoken American English," in A. G. Smith, ed. *Communication and Culture* (New York: Holt, Rinchart and Winston, 1966), pp. 182-189.
[3]See e.g., Ekman. Ray L. Birdwhistell, "Communication as a Multi-Channel System" in D. L. Sills, ed. *International Encyclopedia of the Social Sciences* (New York: Crowell-Collier and Macmillan, in press).
[4]A. Paul Hare, *Handbook of Small Group Research* (New York: Free Press, 1962).

The majority of the studies reported in the literature which deal with style of dress have been concerned with the functional use and purchase of clothing rather than the social aspects of clothing.[5] The experimental studies that have investigated clothing and sociological variables have related style of dress to status, occupation, conformity and motivation, and personal traits.[6] Even small details of grooming such as the wearing of lipstick or glasses have been found to affect personal impressions.[7] In addition differences between males and females in impression formation based on dress were found in a study by Hamid.[8] Whether warranted or not, impression formation based on style of dress seems to affect interpersonal perceptions.

It would appear that bralessness could potentially affect perceptions of others (particularly with respect to communication behaviors). Therefore, the central objective of this study was to assess effects of bralessness on nonverbal communication behaviors in message senders and receivers.[9]

1. Do message senders and receivers perceive differences in nonverbal communication behaviors when communicating with a braless girl?
2. If the nonverbal communication behaviors are perceived to differ when a girl is braless, how are they different?
3. When communicating with a braless girl, are nonverbal communication behaviors of males perceived to be different from females?[10]
4. Are the nonverbal communication behaviors of braless girls perceived to be different when they are communicating with others?
5. If the nonverbal communication behaviors of girls are perceived to be different when they are braless, how are they different?

---

[5] See e.g., K. Dunlap, "The Development and Function of Clothing," *Journal of General Psychology*, I (1928), 64-78. J. C. Flügell, *Psychology of Clothes* (London: Hogarth Press, 1930); and S. Evelyn Evans, "Motivations Underlying Clothing Selection and Wearing," *Journal of Home Economics*, LVI (1964), 739-743.

[6] See e.g., T. F. Hoult, "Experimental Measurement of Clothing as a Factor in Some Social Ratings of Selected American Men," *American Sociological Review*, XIX (1954), 324-328. M. Lefkowitz, R. R. Blake and J. S. Mouton, "Statue Factors in Pedestrian Violation of Traffic Signals," *Journal of Abnormal and Social Psychology*, LI (1955), 707-708; M. L. Rosencranz, "Clothing Symbolism," *Journal of Home Economics*, LIV (1962), 18-22, R. Sybers and M. E. Roach, "Clothing and Human Behavior" *Journal of Home Economics*, LIV (1962), 184-187; L. R. Aiken, Jr., "The Relationships of Dress to Selected Measures of Personality in Undergraduate Women," *Journal of Social Psychology*, LIX (1963), 119-128; H. I. Douty, "The Influence of Clothing on Perceptions of Persons" *Journal of Home Economics*, LV (1963), 197-202.

[7] W. McKeachie, "Lipstick as a Determinant of First Impressions of Personality: An Experiment for the General Psychology Course," *Journal of Social Psychology*, XXXVI (1952), 241-244, and G. Thornton, "The Effect of Wearing Glasses Upon Judgments of Personality Traits of Persons Seen Briefly," *Journal of Applied Psychology*, XXVIII (1944), 203-207.

[8] P. Hamid, "Style of Dress as a Perceptual Cue in Impression Formation," *Perceptual and Motor Skills*, XXVI (1968), 904-906.

[9] It should be obvious that nonverbal communication encompasses many variables which could potentially relate to such an investigation. For example, body (e.g., breast) size, shape and type, posture and facial expressions may affect perceptions of a braless girl and should be examined in further research.

[10] Results of the pilot study indicated differences according to sex and year in school.

METHOD

Subjects

Subjects for this study were selected from students attending the Florida State University. Two different groups of subjects were employed in this investigation:

1. Braless girls (n = 42). Forty-two interviewees were selected from the population of braless girls walking across the Florida State University campus.
2. Questionnaire respondents (n = 329). A stratified sample was employed in selecting the questionnaire respondents. Each of four interviewers was asked to administer the questionnaire to approximately equal numbers of males and females in each of the five university levels (freshman through graduate). When the quota for one level was reached, the interviewers stopped administering the questionnaire to respondents in that category.

Administration of Interview Schedule and Questionnaire

Two sets of interviews were conducted for this study. The two sets of interviews were designed to determine perceived changes in nonverbal communication behaviors as a function of bralessness. Pilot tests (n = 100) of the interview schedule and questionnaire resulted in several suggestions for changes in the wording of questions and for structuring item alternatives.[11]

Two female interviewers employed a structured interview schedule in the first set of interviews with braless girls (N = 42). Each interviewer explained that she was assisting with a research project in the Department of Communication concerning the braless trend and asked if the potential interviewee would answer a few questions. Following an affirmative reply, the interviewer asked if the potential interviewee ever went braless in public (to validate the assumption that the interviewee was braless at the time). Following an affirmative response (there were no negative replies), the interviewer proceeded with the interview.

Two female interviewers (wearing bras)[12] and two male interviewers employed a structured questionnaire in the second set of interviews with the questionnaire respondents (n = 329). Each interviewer interviewed an approximately equal number of male and female respondents in each of the five university levels (freshman through graduate) to control for possible bias due to sex of the interviewer. Each interviewer explained that he was assisting with a research project in the Department of Communication concerning the braless trend and asked if the potential respondent would answer a few questions. Following an affirmative reply, the interviewer proceeded with the interview.

A series of training sessions was conducted for all interviewers. The behavior of the interviewer, methods for gaining respondent participation and

---

[11]Carole Chamberlain, Preliminary Study of the Braless Trend, The Florida State University, Department of Communication, Tallahassee, 1970.

[12]It is possible that responses obtained by the interviewers wearing bras would have been different if they had been braless.

valid responses were discussed.[13] The interviewers also practiced interviewing techniques prior to conducting the interviews.

Analysis of Data

To analyze the perceived effects of bralessness on nonverbal communication behavior, the results of the two sets of interviews were coded and classified. Percentages based on the total number of usable responses were derived for each item alternative. Because all of the braless interviewees responded to each item, the percentages computed were based on the total number of interviews (n = 42). Not all of the questionnaire respondents in the *general* population responded to all items and the base number for those percentages varied from item to item.

RESULTS

Interviews with Braless Girls

Seventeen per cent of the braless interviewees perceived embarrassment in the people with whom they communicate. Embarrassment while communicating when they initially began to go braless was perceived by 64 per cent of the interviewees. However, only five per cent of the interviewees indicated that they were embarrassed at the time of the interview. Tension in others while communicating was perceived by 26 per cent of the interviewees. A change in eye contact in interpersonal settings (e.g., on a one-to-one or small group basis) was perceived both in males (52 per cent of the braless interviewees reported observing changes in the eye contact of males) and in females (35 per cent of the braless interviewees reported observing changes in the eye contact of females). The braless interviewees also reported observing changes in the eye contact of males (52 per cent of the interviewees reported changes) and females (26 per cent of the interviewees reported changes) in impersonal (e.g., large groups or passing on the street) settings.

The following perceived changes in the eye contact of *males* in interpersonal settings were reported by 52 per cent of the interviewees: longer eye contact (18 per cent of the braless interviewees) eyes frequently dropping to the breast area (56 per cent), eyes avoiding the breast area (5 per cent), and eyes looking in other directions (18 per cent). These changes in the eye contact of males in interpersonal settings were perceived as nervousness or tension by 27 per cent of the braless interviewees and 36 per cent indicated that the changes made them feel uncomfortable.

A perceived change in the eye contact of *females* in interpersonal settings was reported by 35 per cent of the braless interviewees. The following specific changes were reported: shorter eye contact (13 per cent), longer eye contact (13 per cent), eyes frequently dropping to the breast area (20 per cent), and eyes avoiding the breast area (27 per cent). Changes in the eye contact of females in interpersonal settings were perceived as nervousness or tension by 33 per cent of the braless interviewees and 7 per cent indicated that the changes made them feel uncomfortable.

---

[13]S. A. Richardson, B. S. Dohrenwend and D. Klein, *Interviewing: Its Forms and Functions* (New York: Basic Books, 1965), pp. 108-137, 198-206, 218-291.

Longer eye contact of *males* in impersonal settings was perceived by 46 per cent of the braless interviewees who noted changes and 55 per cent reported observing eyes frequently dropping to the breast area. These changes in the eye contact of males in impersonal settings were perceived as nervousness or tension by 14 per cent of the braless interviewees and 32 per cent indicated that the changes made them feel uncomfortable.

Shorter eye contact of *females* in impersonal settings was reported by 9 per cent of the interviewees who noted changes. Longer eye contact was perceived by 55 per cent and 27 per cent reported observing eyes frequently dropping to the breast area. These changes in the eye contact of females in impersonal settings were perceived as nervousness or tension by 46 per cent of the braless interviewees and 99 per cent indicated that the changes made them feel uncomfortable.

Interviews with Questionnaire Respondents

Follow-up interviews with questionnaire respondents verified, generally, the information previously reported and indicates a high percentage of nervous gestures by male respondents and a moderate level of tension in the respondents themselves.

The results of the study, though not conclusive, provide the following responses to the research questions posed earlier in the section.

(1) Message senders and receivers tend to perceive differences in nonverbal communication behaviors when communicating with braless girls.
(2) Message senders and receivers tend to perceive differences in the following: eye contact (in interpersonal and impersonal communication settings), nervous gestures or movements, stuttering or pauses and movements indicating tension, embarrassment and self-consciousness.
(3) The nonverbal communication behaviors of males tend to differ from females. There appear to be differences in eye contact (males tend to look more at the breast area than females) and gestures or movements which indicate nervousness or tension (males appear to experience these to a greater extent).
(4) Braless girls and the people with whom they communicate tend to perceive differences in the nonverbal communication behaviors of braless girls.
(5) Braless girls tend to feel embarrassed when they initially go braless. Braless girls may exhibit nervous gestures and movements, little eye contact, and self-consciousness.

DISCUSSION

The finding that eye contact tended to be affected by bralessness was expected. Societal norms have tended to make the breast a "privileged" area of the female body which, in turn, has made it more attractive to males. Females try to avoid being caught looking at or paying an undue amount of attention to the breasts of other females. The fact that both males and females reacted to bralessness in a predictable manner, i.e., males tend to look more at the breast area than at the eyes when a girl is braless (often without making a conscious effort to do so), and girls attempt to avoid looking at the breast area, also indicate that the responses to the questions asked possess a substantial degree of face validity.

The reports of nervous tension in males created by communicating with a braless girl indicate that, although a male's natural tendency might be to want to interact more frequently with a braless girl, the fear that an abnormal interest in the breast area would be detected creates tension. The tension is expressed through such means as nervous gestures, vocalized pauses, and/or stuttering. Social desirability would have tended to make the responses to questions related to nervousness more conservative.

Girls who decide to go braless must be aware that it may affect the eye contact and comfort of males with whom they want to communicate. They also must be prepared to note changes in the nonverbal behavior of some of their female acquaintances. Since the braless trend is now a part of our culture, its potential effects on communication should be noted both by girls who elect to go braless and by those with whom they communicate.

Meyer Friedman and Ray Rosenman

HOW TO TELL A TYPE A FROM A TYPE B

From the very time we began to think that a particular behavior complex bore responsibility for an increased risk of coronary artery and heart disease, we have been developing and refining methods of identifying individuals characterized by such patterns. Clearly the best method, and the one we use most to this day, is an interview conducted by trained personnel. At the moment, we have several interviewers especially skilled at spotting Type A behavior using a standardized questionnaire. The questions themselves, of course, are far less important than the *manner* of response to them. We find it necessary to emphasize this point repeatedly to those asking to have our list of twenty or so questions in order to run their own tests. Type A and Type B persons may give identical answers, but the *way* they give them is sufficient for our interviewers to differentiate the types almost all of the time.

In an attempt to make the classification process still less "subjective," we have tried using a voice analysis technique. Its basis is a two-paragraph diatribe, presumably the words used by a military commander exhorting his troops before a battle. This is the text:

> This is the way that you and me, every God damned one of us are going to lick the hell out of whoever stands in our way. And I don't give a damn whether you like what I'm telling you or not. This is the way I say it's got to be done. First, we're going to smack them hard with mortar fire, understand? I want you to pour it on them! Let the bastards feel it get hot, really hot around them. Singe the hell out of them! Scorch the bastards, fry them, burn their guts out. Make ashes out of them.
>
> After the mortars, I'll tell you when to advance. And when I give the signal, don't crawl, you run forward! Remember, it's your skin or theirs! All right, enough talk, now let's get the lead out of our pants and get going. Hey! One more thing, good luck!

A subject is invited to first read the monologue over to himself silently, until he is sure he can read it aloud without stumbling. Then he is asked to read it aloud, pretending that he is in his own home, alone. After this is done, and recorded, he is asked to imagine that he is the officer on the battlefield and to read it again.

A variety of tests are used to analyze the results. The most vivid by far are the electronically recorded voice-prints, which display in visual form the oscillations of each subject's voice during the readings. The Type B subject shows very little expression while reading to himself, and even during the more rapid hortatory reading inflects key words only moderately. The Type A subject, on the other hand, throws himself into the project with a certain violence. Even the trial reading displays wide oscillations caused by his typically harsh, explosive speech rhythms. His hortatory reading sends the needle flipping wildly.

This sharply aggressive manner of speech is one of the most common telltale signs of a Type A individual. Other signs are rather more subtle—for example, in many people a slight darkening of pigmentation around the eyes is a sign of certain pituitary secretions, an indication in turn of reaction to stress. But ordinarily the pattern is obvious without recourse to such points. Indeed, identification is easy when a person with a *fully developed* complex presents himself.

Yet even then, if the procedure is wrong, the investigator can be tricked. Several years ago we thought we had devised a clever objective test for screening Type A's. Subjects were asked to listen to a girl incoherently and maddeningly relating a story with no point whatsoever. As they listened, their breathing and body movements (such as wriggling or fist clenching) were carefully monitored by a polygraph machine. It seemed obvious that a Type A would show his impatience readily. But to our surprise a large-scale test failed. What we had forgotten was the Type A man's ability to simply quit listening if he was bored, and how easy it is for him to pretend to be listening when he is actually thinking about something else.

The following section is intended to help you determine for yourself whether you are a Type A or Type B personality. If you are honest in your self appraisal—and if you are actually aware of your own traits and habits—we believe that you will not have too much trouble accomplishing this. The details of the behavior pattern vary, of course, according to many factors—education, age, social position. But most of you will be able to spot yourselves. Incidentally, we have found that Type A persons are by and large more common, and that if you are not quite sure about yourself, chances are that you, too, are Type A —not fully developed, perhaps, but bad enough to think about changing. And after you have assessed yourself, ask a friend or your spouse whether your self-assessment was accurate. If you disagree, *they* are probably right.

YOU POSSESS TYPE A BEHAVIOR PATTERN:

1. If you have (a) a habit of explosively accentuating various key words in your ordinary speech even when there is no real need for such accentuation, and (b) a tendency to utter the last few words of your sentences far more rapidly than the opening words. The vocal explosiveness betrays the excess aggression or hostility you may be harboring. The hurrying of the ends of sentences mirrors your underlying impatience with spending even the time required for your own speech.
2. If you *always* move, walk, and eat rapidly.
3. If you feel (particularly if you openly exhibit to others) an impatience with the rate at which most events take place. You are suffering from this sort of impatience if you find it difficult to restrain yourself from hurrying the speech of others and resort to the device of saying very quickly over and over again, "Uh huh, uh huh," or, "Yes yes, yes yes," to someone who is talking, unconsciously urging him to "get on with" or hasten his rate of speaking. You are also suffering from impatience if you attempt to finish the sentences of persons speaking to you before they can.

Others signs of this sort of impatience: if you become *unduly* irritated
or even enraged when a car ahead of you in your lane runs at a pace
you consider too slow; if you find it languishing to wait in a line or to
wait your turn to be seated at a restaurant; if you find it intolerable
to watch others perform tasks you know you can do faster; if you
become impatient with yourself as you are obliged to perform repetitious duties (making out bank deposit slips, writing checks, washing
and cleaning dishes, and so on), which are necessary but take you
away from doing things you really have an interest in doing; if you find
yourself hurrying your own reading or always attempting to obtain
condensations or summaries of truly interesting and worthwhile literature.

4. If you indulge in *polyphasic* thought or performance, frequently striving to think of or do two or more things simultaneously. For example,
   if while trying to listen to another person's speech you persist in
   continuing to think about an irrelevant subject, you are indulging in
   polyphasic thought. Similarly, if while golfing or fishing you continue
   to ponder your business or professional problems, or if while using an
   electric razor you attempt also to eat your breakfast or drive your car,
   or if while driving your car you attempt to dictate letters for your
   secretary, you are indulging in polyphasic performance. This is one of
   the commonest traits in the Type A man. Nor is he always satisfied
   with doing just two things at one time. We have known subjects who
   not only shaved and ate simultaneously, but also managed to read a
   business or professional journal at the same time.

5. If you find it *always* difficult to refrain from talking about or bringing
   the theme of any conversation around to those subjects which especially interest and intrigue you, and when unable to accomplish this
   maneuver, you pretend to listen but really remain preoccupied with
   your own thoughts.

6. If you almost always feel vaguely guilty when you relax and do absolutely nothing for several hours to several days.

7. If you no longer observe the more important or interesting or lovely
   objects that you encounter in your milieu. For example, if you enter
   a strange office, store, or home, and after leaving any of these places
   you cannot recall what was in them, you no longer are observing well
   —or for that matter enjoying life very much.

8. If you do not have any time to spare to become the things worth *being*
   because you are so preoccupied with getting the things worth *having.*

9. If you attempt to schedule more and more in less and less time, and
   in doing so make fewer and fewer allowances for unforeseen contingencies. A concomitant of this is a *chronic sense of time urgency,* one
   of the core components of Type A Behavior Pattern.

10. If, on meeting another severely afflicted Type A person, instead of
    feeling compassion for his affliction you find yourself compelled to
    "challenge" him. This is a telltale trait because no one arouses the
    aggressive and/or hostile feelings of one Type A subject more quickly
    than another Type A subject.

11. If you resort to certain characteristic gestures or nervous tics. For
    example, if in conversation you frequently clench your fist, or bang

your hand upon a table or pound one fist into the palm of your other hand in order to emphasize a conversational point, you are exhibiting Type A gestures. Similarly, if the corners of your mouth spasmodically, in tic-like fashion, jerk backward slightly exposing your teeth, or if you habitually clench your jaw, or even grind your teeth, you are subject to muscular phenomena suggesting the presence of a continuous *struggle*, which is, of course, the kernel of the Type A Behavior Pattern.

12. If you believe that whatever success you have enjoyed has been due in good part to your ability to get things done faster than your fellow men and if you are afraid to stop doing everything faster and faster.

13. If you find yourself increasingly and ineluctably committed to translating and evaluating not only your own but also the activities of others in terms of "numbers."

The characteristics above mark the fully developed, hardcore Type A. Many people properly classified as Type A exhibit these characteristics in a lesser degree, however. If you are a moderately afflicted Type A subject, for example, you rarely feel or display much hostility. Your aggressiveness, although in excess, has still not evolved into free-floating rancor. You do not bristle with the barely governable rage that seethes so often just below the surface of the personality of the full Type A person.

Similarly, your impatience is not of towering proportions. You may attempt to squeeze more and more events into smaller and smaller pieces of time at work but often you can avoid this practice in off hours. You do not feel that you have to propel your "bicycle" faster and faster to keep your balance once your business or professional day has ended. At such times, like fire wagon horses unharnessed after returning from a fire, you may become almost torpid. But again like fire horses, who used to neigh and stomp their hooves just as soon as they heard the first peal of the fire alarm bell, so you, on hearing the alarm clock in the morning, shed your indolence and begin to hustle, bustle, and resume your strife with time.

Nor as a moderate Type A are you *obsessively* involved in the acquisition of sheer numbers. You are still aware of the many nonnumerate, charming aspects of full-bodied, full-souled living, even if you cannot completely enjoy and lose yourself in them.

YOU POSSESS TYPE B BEHAVIOR PATTERN:

1. If you are completely free of *all* the habits and exhibit none of the traits we have listed that harass the severely afflicted Type A person.

2. If you never suffer from a sense of time urgency with its accompanying impatience.

3. If you harbor no free-floating hostility, and you feel no need to display or discuss either your achievements or accomplishments unless such exposure is demanded by the situation.

4. If, when you play, you do so to find fun and relaxation, not to exhibit your superiority at any cost.

5. If you can relax without guilt, just as you can work without agitation.

The Type B person is far more aware of his capabilities than concerned about what peers and superiors may think of his actions. Unlike the Type A person, who really is never quite certain of his virtues and cannot ever quite face up to his deficiencies, you as a Type B know fairly well the value of your virtues and have resigned yourself to the restrictions that your deficiencies set upon you. You seek and succeed in finding your self-confidence by a process of candid self-appraisal. The Type A man seeks but never quite succeeds in finding self-confidence because he looks for it in the acquisition of an ever-increasing set of "numbers."

You, too, may strive for the things worth having. Indeed, as the "tortoise" (which the Type A "rabbit" more or less always believes you are) you may, in the final stretch, obtain a greater share of the things worth having than your Type A counterpart. But usually (if you have not been too critically wounded by the ethos of our times) you also attempt to become at least some of the things worth being. In any event, you do not build your life's ladder with rungs composed solely of numbers.

You may not be a completely developed Type B, but if you are relatively free of all the habits enslaving the Type A subject, and if you exhibit relatively rarely any of his traits, then you may still be classed as a Type B. You may occasionally feel a sense of time urgency, but if you do, it will be associated exclusively with your vocational and never with your avocational activities. Also, even at work, you will not feel this stress except during those limited periods when the demands of your position make it logical to feel that time is short. For example, if you are an accountant, you may well feel a sense of time urgency during the first two weeks of April.

But precisely like a fully developed Type B person, you, too, never suffer from the presence of free-floating hostility nor do you habitually attempt to speed things up like a Type A. You, too, strive to acquire the things worth having, but again, you will not do so at the expense of totally disregarding the pursuit of the things worth being.

We have presumed to slice the spectrum of personality types rather sharply, and possibly, rather arbitrarily. Even in our increasingly standardized society, human beings possess personalities that cannot be nearly so precisely categorized as has been done here. Behavior types tend to run together to some extent. Then, too, there are some people (but no more than about 10 percent of an urban population) who possess some habits and exhibit some traits that are Type A and some that are Type B. Ordinarily, though, it is not difficult to recognize and differentiate persons with Type A Behavior Pattern from persons with Type B.

Theologians and psychologists may object vigorously to the implication obviously inherent in this section that large numbers of human beings are "typable." They would insist (though the Harvard psychologist B. F. Skinner might not) that man has available to him, and frequently acts upon, myriads of different responses to identical challenges. This is so in respect to many Type B subjects. But it certainly is not true of a man whose personality has eroded to the point where his choice of responses is actually limited. Type A persons, having suffered such erosion, rarely vary in their responses to specific challenges of their milieu. Their original endowment of free choice has been supplanted by a sad enslavement and absorption in the acquisition of "numbers."

In attempting to assess yourself, we should again like to suggest that before you make your final decision whether you are a Type A or B person, you request the advice and opinion of your spouse, or a relative or friend who knows you well. We have observed that many Type A persons are totally unaware of either the presence or effects of their behavior pattern. They do not notice their restlessness, their tense facial muscles, their tics, or their strident-staccato manner of speaking. Nor are they always aware of their free-floating hostility —when it is present—if only because they can rationalize it so beautifully. Some Type A persons are not even aware of their sense of time urgency; it has been present so long that it seems a part of their personality. For that matter, they may be understandably reluctant to recognize, as enslaving and spiritu-ally devastating, habits and traits that only yesterday were held in high esteem by all—including Horatio Alger and his prosperous friends.

TWO-PERSON COMMUNICATION____ 4

People most often take part in two-person or dyadic communication unless, of course, they are isolated. The first selection, Marie Shear's artistic description of a female's brief encounter with a male in "Free Meat Talks Back," may amuse you on the surface and make you pause to think later. And you may enjoy Potter's "Natural One-Downness of Patient" (second), an explanation of how medical doctors maintain a superior air in dealings with individual patients.

A few years ago, Joseph (Jo) Luft and Harry (Hari) Ingram created a model of interpersonal awareness "The Johari Window" which has received great notice. You can read Luft's own explanation of this model in the third segment, "Brief Summary of the Johari Awareness Model."

Maybe you restrict your association of the term "interview" to formal situations such as hiring or firing. Not so, say Goyer, Redding and Rickey in the fourth selection, "An Introduction to Interviewing." Many two-person encounters amount to an interview.

Marie Shear

FREE MEAT TALKS BACK

. . . Hello-babied by strangers, ogled on the street,
[women are] objects of ridicule and contempt; even [our]
most neutral transaction is usually accompanied by
abuse.

Naomi Weisstein

"Why We Aren't Laughing . . . Any More"
Ms. Magazine

The day after I read Weisstein's first-rate essay, I went to my usual candy store to buy a couple of magazines. As I mused over an article on the failings of the President, my reverie was broken by a middle-aged man whose neat jacket, shirt, and tie stood out among the shapeless clothes commonly seen at Nostrand and Church Avenues in Flatbush.

"Hiya, sweetheart," he says. (He can't mean me. I'm a dog. Remember last year, when I wore my new halter dress to work for the first time and the frankfurter-seller on Desbrosses Street crowded me, looked directly at my breasts, and murmured, "Pathetic." Double-take, He *does* mean me.) He is not the roguish stranger with whom one gladly exchanges sixty seconds of mutually heartening persiflage. The man is a sallow grub with a tin gizzard behind his presentable front. He isn't flirting; he doesn't like women well enough for that. He's collecting tribute.

An involuntary smile does not smear itself across my puss. Congratulating myself, I stare at the collector, then return to my magazine. Methodically, he greets every other woman in the store. One of them responds with an obedient pleasantry, and he rewards her by letting her be.

His rounds completed, the collector focuses on me again. He begins sympathetically. Obviously, he says, something's bothering you or you'd be smiling at me. I say nothing. Then a new tack: "You must be Jewish." (Huh?) "I like Jews." The grub elaborates upon this nonsequitur for a while. I say nothing and go to the counter to ask where *Rolling Stone* is kept. By now, my unresponsiveness has nettled him slightly; other women are handy, but he was fastened on the holdout. He keeps talking at me until he has tired of sympathy and Semitism. As I wait to pay the counter-man for the magazines I've picked, the collector leans to his left so that his body presses against my right side in the awkward space among the stacks of Sunday newspapers, and he tries a third theme—the Freud Was Right number: "You must have a problem," he says.

Instead of backing away, I literally stand my ground (*mirabile dictu*) My ribs are trembling, and something behind my sternum is cold from fright, but a strong voice comes out of my mouth (*mazl tov*): "My only problem is that you won't mind your own business." In print, after the fact, the words are banal, but they are a fine defiance on the spot. He is silent for a fraction of a second. Drawn up to an authoritative 5'1 ½ " and still trembling, I go on: " . . . and stop leaning on me! What do you think I am—*free meat?!*" (O, admirable roar. The trembling has stopped.)

Success. He is not pressing against my body now. And he is angry. Angry at me in particular. Not impersonally cloying. Bullyingly angry at me. Really concentrating. "Go to hell!" he blasts into my face.

So far, the counter-man has confined himself to a ruefully amused glance at me; I tell him loud and clear that I have had enough; he tells the grub to "take a walk" and gets a bellicose reply.

I have paid for the magazines and am ready to go, but I'm not leaving first. I'm still too frightened to see or hear how the other customers are reacting, but I am not leaving first. The grub slams his paper cup of soda down onto the counter and unleashes the ultimate compliment: "BITCH!" Then he leaves. First.

This time.

Stephen Potter

NATURAL ONE-DOWNNESS OF PATIENT

What chance, it may well be asked, has even the lay Lifeman against the Doctor? The Doctor holds all the cards, and can choose his own way of playing them. Right at the start, when answering Patient's original phone call, for instance, he can, and generally does, say, "Dr. Meadows speaking," in a frightfully hollow and echoing voice, as if he was expecting a summons to sign a death certificate. Alternatively, a paralysingly brisk voice can be used suggesting that Doctor is busier than Patient in normal life, and in a more important way.

Doctor: Hallo, yes. Finchingfield here . . . Well, it will have to be rather late this morning. I'll see what I can do.

In the bedroom, the Irish type of M.D.man is tidier, better, or at any rate more crisply dressed than the Patient, and is able to suggest by his manner not only that Patient's room is surprisingly disordered, but that he, the Doctor, goes in for a more up-to-date type of pajamas than the ones he observes Patient to be wearing.

The Patient starts perkily enough:

Layman: Thank you, doctor. I was coming home rather late last night from the House of Commons . . .

M.D.man: Thank you . . . now if you'll just let me put these . . . hair brushes and things off the bed for you . . . that's right . . .

Layman: I was coming home rather late. Army Act, really—

M.D.man: Now just undo the top button of your shirt or whatever it is you're wearing . . .

Layman: I say I was coming . . .

M.D.man: Now if you've got some hot water—really hot—and a clean towel.

Layman: Yes, just outside. The Postmaster General . . .

M.D.man: Open your mouth please.

To increase the one-downness, bring in the washing-the-hands gambit immediately after touching hands with Patient. Unpleasant infectant possibilities can be suggested.

The old, now discarded, bedside mannership is still used when Doctor wishes to subdue the sensitive patient suffering from an eclipsing headache. Doctor used to begin a constant fire of hollowly exploding clubroom stories, so involved in their climax that only the keenest attention revealed the point of expected laughter. We now teach that the M.D.man should show an *inaccurate familiarity with the patient's own tastes or profession.* He can suggest, for instance, that some prized first edition "might be worth something some day," or, if his patient is a horseman, tell him that the first syllable in "Pytchley" is long. For actor-patients, Doctor can tell the story of how as a young student he dressed up as Principal Boy in the Middlesex Hospital Pantomime when a member of the Middlesex Mauve Merriments.

After this opening treatment, Doctor may, *under certain circumstances,* ask Patient his symptoms. But he will let it be seen that he is not listening to what Patient is saying, and may place his hand on Patient's wrist, or, better, stomach, as if to suggest that he as Doctor can tell more through the sensitive tip of one finger than from listening to the layman's self-deceiving, ill-observed, and hysterically redundant *impressions* of what is wrong with him.

Many good M.D.men make a point of shepherding their patients into the consulting room where, by his way of averting his head as Patient is undressing, Doctor can suggest criticism of his choice of underclothes, socks, &c. The doctor is well. You are longing for a cigarette. And you are ill. And in more ways than in mere physical health.

Nevertheless the following Friendly Consulting Room Approach[1] is basically better. Suppose your patient comes in with, say, a chronic outbreak of warts on the back of the neck. He will be disposed to make light of this. *Allow him to, but frighten him at the same time,* by little asides to invisible nurses. Thus:

M.D.man: Well, you are a pretty sight. Now, just lower your shirt.
Layman: (enjoying himself): Not very pretty for sunbathing at Annecy next
    summer. I thought . . .
M.D.man: Better take it right off. Ah, you lucky man. You know the lake, do
    you? *(Lowering voice)*Nurse, get me a Watson-Dunn, will you?
Layman: Yes, I love it, we go every year . . .
M.D.man (pressing buzzer): The food of course is marvellous. *(Speaking calmly
    into some machine)* Oh Barker, get me the light syringe from the
    steriliser—yes, the dual. Yes, we must get you right for that.
Layman: But it's not anything . . .
M.D.man: Nothing serious, I'm sure. Now bend down. Yes, Annecy—and you
    know Talloires? . . . Now nurse, if you'll just stand by while we have
    a look. Quadriceps please . . . and—oh, thank you, Barker. Better get
    the hydrogeniser going *(compressed air sound can be imitated by some
    assistant in the background going "zzzz" through his teeth).* Yes,
    there's a little restaurant—right down please—the Georges Bise
    . . . Now.

At the end, with a charming "au revoir," M.D.man, instead of telling him what is wrong, can stare, last thing, at frightened Patient's left eye through a specially contrived speculum which startles Patient with a view of Doctor's own eye, enlarged, inverted, and bloodshot.

---

[1]This gambit was invented by a well-known actor, with medical tastes. Shunning publicity, he yet allows me to say that it was evolved in Rome during the filming of *Quo Vadis.* He was in charge of the St. John's Ambulance Tent, block L, during the scenes when the lions were eating the Christians—largely faked. He himself was playing the part of the Emperor Ustinian.

Joseph Luft

BRIEF SUMMARY OF THE JOHARI AWARENESS MODEL

The four quadrants represent the total person in relation to other persons. The basis for division into quadrants is awareness of behavior, feelings, and motivation. Sometimes awareness is shared, sometimes not. An act, a feeling, or a motive is assigned to a particular quadrant based on who knows about it. As awareness changes, the quadrant to which the psychological state is assigned changes. The following definitions and principles are substantially the same as those in *Group Processes* (Luft, 1963, pp. 10-11). Each quadrant is defined:

1. Quadrant 1, the open quadrant, refers to behavior, feelings, and motivation known to self and to others.
2. Quadrant 2, the blind quadrant, refers to behavior, feelings, and motivation known to others but not to self.
3. Quadrant 3, the hidden quadrant, refers to behavior, feelings, and motivation known to self but not to others.
4. Quadrant 4, the unknown quadrant, refers to behavior, feelings, and motivation known neither to self nor to others.

There are eleven principles of change:

1. A change in any one quadrant will affect all other quadrants.
2. It takes energy to hide, deny, or be blind to behavior which is involved in interaction.

3. Threat tends to decrease awareness; mutual trust tends to increase awareness.

4. Forced awareness (exposure) is undesirable and usually ineffective.

5. Interpersonal learning means a change has taken place so that quadrant 1 is larger, and one or more of the other quadrants has grown smaller.

6. Working with others is facilitated by a large enough area of free activity. It means more of the resources and skills of the persons involved can be applied to the task at hand.

7. The smaller the first quadrant, the poorer the communication.

8. There is universal curiosity about the unknown area, but this is held in check by custom, social training, and diverse fears.

9. Sensitivity means appreciating the covert aspects of behavior, in quadrants 2, 3, and 4, and respecting the desire of others to keep them so.

10. Learning about group processes, as they are being experienced, helps to increase awareness (enlarging quadrant 1) for the group as a whole as well as for individual members.

11. The value system of a group and its membership may be noted in the way *unknowns* in life of the group are confronted.

Robert Goyer, Charles Redding, and John Rickey

AN INTRODUCTION TO INTERVIEWING

What is an interview? What unique features set it apart from public speaking? from social conversation? from group discussion?

It is obvious that interviewing, like public speaking and conversation and discussion, is a form of *oral communication.* The first question to be answered, then, is: What do we mean by "communication"? Perhaps the simplest way of defining communication is to say that it is *the process of sending and receiving messages.* But further questions now arise. What are messages? Modern communication theory offers a number of highly technical and sophisticated answers to this crucial question. For present purposes, however, it will be useful to say that a message is *any* stimulus which is interpreted in a meaningful way by the person receiving it.

Such a position carries with it a number of provocative implications. For example, messages can obviously consist of many things besides words: facial expressions, tone of voice, gestures, manner of walking or sitting down, and inanimate objects (such as office furnishings, uniforms, and landscaping). Furthermore, inaction and silence—when some action or some utterance is expected—can obviously be messages. Thus, A may *interpret* B's raising of an eyebrow as "B is silently laughing at me"; or C may *interpret* D's hasty grabbing of a pencil and making notes as "D is pouncing on some error I've just made"; or E may interpret F's silence as "F disapproves of me." All these interpretations, in the mind of the receiver, are *messages.*

A few moments of thought will quickly demonstrate that messages can be classified not only as verbal and nonverbal, but as intentional and unintentional (so far as the sender is concerned). For instance, the person whose knees shake and whose hand trembles is conveying messages he no doubt would rather not convey: that he is unsure of himself, or that he is perhaps dishonest. A company may proclaim an "open door" policy; but employees may easily get the unintentional message that the door is really closed if elaborate arrangements are necessary in order to make an appointment, or if there are several secretaries and receptionists to cope with, or if the office furnishings are ostentatiously "plushy." In the "close-up" situation of the typical interview, the possibilities of sending unintentional messages (arising from such factors as movements of facial muscles, posture, clothing, and vocal quality) are almost infinite.

It also becomes apparent that the only message upon which the receiver can form a judgment to take an action is the message *he receives;* and the message he receives in many cases can be quite different from the message the sender intended to send. The receiver can interpret messages only in terms of his own experiences, his own learnings, his own point of view, his own vocabulary, and his own motives. No two people can be exactly alike in these respects; hence, no two people can interpret any stimulus in exactly the same manner. The skilled interviewer is particularly aware of these facts, and realizes that it is fruitless to complain about the other person's "stupidity" or "bull-headedness" when he has been "misunderstood." He realizes that, in order to be understood, it is necessary to talk—as much as humanly possible —in the other person's language; that is, to adapt his messages to the *receiver's* way of looking at the world.

An interview, then, is an event in which messages are constantly being sent and received; these messages may be nonverbal as well as verbal; they may be unintentional as well as intentional; and, most crucial of all, the messages as understood by the receiver can never be exactly identical to the messages as intended by the sender.

But, of course, these basic considerations of communication theory apply to public speaking and discussion and conversation as well as to the interview. In what respects does the interview differ from these other forms of oral communication?

Perhaps this question is best answered if we examine a proposed definition of the interview:

> *The interview is a form of oral communication involving two parties, at least one of whom has a preconceived and serious purpose, and both of whom speak and listen from time to time.*

Let us dissect this definition and focus attention upon several crucial terms.

1. *Two parties.* This term implies, obviously, that the interview is a *bi-polar* situation—there are no "third" or "fourth" parties to act as arbiters or to form majority combinations. Each "party" is typically a single person; however, it is possible to regard "group interviews" and "board interviews" as essentially bi-polar, even though one of the parties in each of these cases is made up of two or more persons.
2. *At least one of whom has a preconceived and serious purpose.* This term indicates that an event cannot be regarded as an interview if *neither* party comes to it without some advance thought and without some purpose (even though vaguely conceived) he wishes to accomplish. Further, the word "serious" is used here to suggest that the purpose goes beyond the enjoyment of each other's company, or beyond trivial and transitory interests.
3. *Both of whom speak and listen from time to time.* This term probably implies the most basic differentiating feature of the interview, for it is really a non-technical way of describing the constant two-way *interaction* that must take place between the two parties. The literature or the subject repeatedly emphasizes interaction as the *sine qua non* of interviewing. If one person does all—or almost all—of the talking, and the other person does all—or almost all—of the listening, what is probably taking place is not an interview at all, but a public speech to an audience of one. The "high-pressure" salesman who rattles off a memorized "pitch" to the captive housewife at the door is not really

engaging in an interview, but in a public speech. Public speaking, it can be said with little exaggeration, is primarily a *one*-way form of communication: one person, the speaker, initiates virtually all the messages; the audience occupies its time primarily in receiving his messages. For this reason, a highly successful platform speaker may easily be a total failure as an interviewer; he is not psychologically attuned to a situation in which he must be as alert and as constant a message-receiver as he is a message-sender.

Furthermore, not only is the interviewer a listener as well as a speaker, he is also compelled to make *moment-to-moment adaptations* to the verbal and nonverbal messages constantly being sent to him by the other person. He cannot, therefore, depend upon a "cut-and-dried" advance outline. Nor can he depend merely upon words; he must be sensitive to a multitude of nonverbal cues. As Roethlisberger and Dickson[1] pointed out many years ago, he must be aware of "latent" meanings as well as "manifest" meanings; that is, he must be able to "read between the lines," and to go behind the other person's mere words to his real *meanings*.

All this is involved in the innocent-looking word "listening." The interviewer listens not only to the obvious ("manifest") meanings of words; he observes all the available nonverbal stimuli and constantly attempts to understand what the other person is "really" trying to say (or to conceal); and on the basis of this never-ending listening and observing, he makes *instantaneous decisions*—decisions which, in turn, determine what he is to say next and what he is to do next in order to make the best possible adaptation to the other party. The interviewer cannot arbitrarily stop the communication process and take a recess while he ponders how to interpret the other person and what to say. (It is true, of course, that the interviewer can make better decisions and better adaptations if he has had an opportunity, *in advance of the interview*, to study the other person, to analyze the subject-matter, and to consider a wide variety of possible decisions.)

The "ideal" interviewer, then, is a person who is adept at translating his own thoughts and purposes into appropriate verbal and nonverbal symbols; who is highly sensitive to the verbal and nonverbal messages being sent by the other party; and who is able to make constant adaptations to the behavior of the other party. He is both message-sender and message-receiver; he is both talker and listener; he is both active and passive; and above all he is highly flexible.

"ANATOMY" OF THE INTERVIEW

In order to analyze and discuss any phenomenon, it is usually essential to break the phenomenon up into parts and to attach labels to the parts. The interview is an uncommonly fluid event which resists efforts to "pin it down" or to chop it up into neatly wrapped packages. Very seldom can real-life interviews be subdivided into stable units; furthermore, interviews take place in so many different contexts and with so many different purposes that it is

---

[1] Roethlisberger, F.J., and Dickson, W.J., *Management and the Worker*. (Cambridge: Harvard University Press, 1939), pp. 270-279.

practically impossible to suggest a single structural scheme appropriate for all types of interviews.

However, there are a few aspects of interviewing which can readily be identified, which are reasonably universal in their application, and which are relevant to the practical study of the subject. These will be discussed below, under the three headings: Purposes, Participants, and Parts.

Interview Purposes

There are, of course, two parties in every interview; therefore, there are usually two sets of specific purposes. Furthermore, the purposes of one party or the other will frequently shift during the course of a single interview. Nevertheless, it is possible to suggest a rough classification of interviews in terms of the *dominant* purpose governing the behavior of *that person in the interview who has the chief responsibility for achieving a "successful" outcome.* Such a classification follows:

1. *Information-getting.* The interviewer is primarily concerned with obtaining information (typically beliefs, attitudes, feelings, etc.) from the interviewee. Common examples are public-opinion polls and research surveys.
2. *Information-giving.* The interviewer is concerned here with instructing or explaining. This type of interview occurs, for example, when a person engages in on-the-job "coaching," or gives work instructions, or inducts an employee into a new job.
3. *Advocacy.* One person—the persuader—attempts here to modify the beliefs, attitudes, or actions of a second person—the persuadee—on a subject involving a difference of opinion (or at least of feeling) between the two parties. The persuader, in other words, is attempting to get the persuadee to adopt his point of view, or his feeling, about something. Perhaps the most obvious everyday example of persuasive interviewing is the encounter between a salesman and a prospective customer. A persuasive interview is also taking place when a subordinate attempts to induce his "boss" to accept a proposal, or when a client attempts to secure a loan from a banker. Other examples will spring to mind, since our lives are full of instances in which one person is trying to get a second person to agree with him, or to take a specified action. In many persuasive interviews, it should be noted, there may be a common *ultimate* purpose shared by both parties: the satisfaction of a "need" that is felt by both.
4. *Problem-solving.* This interview typically involves both information and persuasion. It is characterized by the fact that neither party ordinarily enters it with a preconceived solution to the problem; each person is attempting to *find* a solution, and is willing to get all the assistance he can from the person in doing this. Actually, this interview is a two-person discussion or conference, where the basic purposes of both parties should be the same.
5. *Counseling.* This interview situation also resembles the persuasive in some ways. In fact, it could be regarded as a very special type of persuasion in that one person (the counselor) is attempting to effect

some kind of modification of behavior on the part of the other (the counselee, or client). However, in the most typical counseling situations—as distinguished from the simple persuasion and problem-solving types described above—the counselor does *not* attempt to convince the counselee to accept his own conclusions or interpretations; rather, at least in the more frequent (usually *non*directive) counseling interviews, he permits the counselee to take most of the initiative in deciding what to talk about and how to talk about it. Thus, the counselor strives to create a situation in which the counselee *gains insight* into his own problems, and (hopefully) solves his own problems. It should be understood that counseling interviews deal with the *personal* problems of the counselee, whereas other kinds of problems (involving far less "ego-involvement") are dealt with in the persuasive or problem-solving interviews previously described. Hence, counseling requires an unusual degree of psychological sophistication and maturity on the part of the counselor.

6. *Employment (or job-application)*. This is a specialized interview, involving elements of information and persuasion. It is characterized particularly by the fact that each party must secure crucial information from the other, and that either or both parties may attempt to persuade the other (the applicant, that he is the best candidate for the job; the employer, that this is the best job the applicant could take). It requires skillful use of questioning and the ability to make shrewd evaluations of personality and character from interview responses.

7. *Receiving complaints*. This again is a specialized interview, combining features of persuasion, information-getting, information-giving, problem-solving, and counseling. The purpose of the complaint-receiver is to provide as much satisfaction of the grievance as the circumstances will permit, while at the same time maintaining optimum "human relations."

8. *Correcting or reprimanding*. This is another specialized interview, requiring unusual proficiency on the part of the interviewer (typically a superior dealing with a subordinate). The purpose is to induce a change in the behavior of the interviewee—preferably on his own initiative and based on his own insight—while at the same time preserving his "ego" and retaining his loyalty to the organization.

9. *Appraisal (or performance review)*. As another specialized interview, this one most closely resembles counseling. The literature on the subject of appraisal is a large one, and it reflects a wide diversity of opinions on how the interview should be conducted. The purpose is to inform the subordinate how well he is meeting the criteria of his job assignment, and to counsel him on his future performance.

10. *Stress interviews, including cross-examinations*. There are a number of situations—including police interrogation, courtroom examinations, and selection of personnel in certain kinds of military assignments—in which the purpose is to observe how the interviewee will respond under varying kinds of psychological "pressure," or to extract responses from a reluctant witness. Obviously, this course will not concern itself with such interviews; but the student should recognize their existence.

Participants in the Interview

There exists no universally recognized terminology for designating the two parties in an interview, applicable to all the various interviewing situations and purposes. The most common terms, of course, are *interviewer* and *interviewee*. However, these are not readily transferable to such situations as advocacy or problem-solving. Some authors have used the terms *conferrer* and *conferee;* but these appear to be most meaningful in the persuasive or problem-solving contexts; they are not necessarily satisfactory when used to describe the two parties in informational, counseling, complaint, employment, or reprimand interviews. In interviews featuring persuasion, the most appropriate terms are probably *persuader* and *persuadee*. And in counseling situations, the terms *counselor* and *counselee* are most frequently encountered.

The only solution to this problem of mixed terminology seems to be the use of different sets of terms for different kinds of interviews. Regardless of the particular terms used, however, it is *generally* (not always) true that *one* party carries the *chief* responsibility for achieving a "successful" outcome of the interview. What is "successful," naturally, will vary with the type of interview. In some situations—especially those emphasizing information or persuasion—this party bearing most of the responsibility may be said to have a "psychological burden of proof." Furthermore, in most interviews, one of the two parties is likely to have the chief *power of decision* (although, again, this function is sometimes equally shared between the two, as in the employment interview). The question may be asked, who has the chief responsibility for achieving a successful outcome in the counseling interview? The answer seems clearly to be: it is the counselor who is primarily responsible for attempting to conduct the interview in such a way that the counselee achieves optimum insight into his problems. Similarly, for example, the information-gatherer in the typical polling situation, bears the burden of having to plan his questions and conduct himself in such a manner that the most complete and appropriate answers are elicited from the respondent.

As a matter of mere convenience, the capital letter R will be used in this article to designate one of the parties in any kind of interview; the letter E, to designate the other. These letters will be understood to refer to the terms listed below, ending respectively in "r" or "e."

TABLE 1

Type of Interview	*"R"*	*"E"*
Information-getting	Interviewer	Interviewee
Advocacy	Persuader	Persuadee
Problem-solving	Conferrer	Conferee
Counseling	Counselor	Client
Employment (job application)	Employer	Applicant
Reprimand	Interviewer (giving reprimand)	Interviewee (receiving reprimand)

By now, it should be apparent to the thoughtful reader that burden of proof, or responsibility for the success of the interview, or power of decision-making may shift in special cases from one party to the other, or in some instances may be equally shared by both parties. The employment interview is particularly a case in point. Here, as is well known, the employer may frequently be attempting to "sell" his company to the job applicant—especially in a "tight" labor market. Also, however, the job applicant—especially when there is competition from other applicants for the same position—must "sell" his qualifications or services to the employer. Likewise, in the complaint situation, the complainant is literally a persuader; he wishes to persuade the other person that he has a grievance which requires correction; as a persuader, then, he may carry a "burden of proof." But the interviewer who hears the complaint also has an obligation—a psychological burden of proof—to give the complainant as much satisfaction as the facts of the case warrant; he also must do much persuasion.

In *most* of the "E" roles mentioned, the party so named has the power of decision—in the information-getting (poll) interview, for example, the respondent, and only the respondent, can decide whether to answer the questions or not; in the reprimand or appraisal interviews, the interviewee can decide whether he will "accept" the reprimand or the evaluation; and in the counseling interview, the counselee is, in the final analysis, the only one who can decide whether he will entertain certain interpretations of his own conduct. Certainly, in all persuasive types of interviews, the persuadee is the one who has the power of deciding whether to be persuaded. However, in the employment interview, *both* parties have the power of decision: the employer, whether to hire the applicant; the interviewee, whether to take the job. The student, therefore, is warned that he must carefully analyze the functions of each participant in every kind of interview; it is unsafe to assume any standardized or universal functions for either "R" or "E," applicable to all kinds of interview situations.

One thing needs to be said, however: in *every* interview, there are *role-relationships* between the two parties that exist from the very start. Sometimes the roles may change as the interview develops. But if either party is uncertain what role either he himself, or the other person, is to play, communication is seriously affected. For example, in a polling situation, it is essential that the interviewer make clear to the respondent exactly what is going on; that he explain the purpose of the questions, the uses to which the answers are to be put, and the general way in which both parties are to conduct themselves. Similarly, if roles are not clarified, job applicants or counselees or persons being reprimanded (etc.) may misunderstand what is expected of them, with grave consequences for the communication that may take place between the two parties. Generally speaking the "*R*" party is the one who should take the initiative, *early* in the interview, to clarify the roles of both persons.

Parts of the Interview

It is not practical to partition the average interview into several clearly delineated parts, as is usually the case with a platform speech. It must be remembered that the interview, much more than the public speech, is a constantly changing affair, the product of moment-by-moment interaction between two parties.

However, in most cases, at least three identifiable parts of the interview may be discerned: the opening moments, the main "body," and the closing moments. Obviously, there can be no hard-and-fast time limits for any of these three parts. What is involved here is a *psychological,* not a time or mechanical, differentiation. In other words, it is suggested that there are *unique* psychological problems (attention-getting, rapport-building, orienting, conciliating, etc.) facing the two parties in the opening portion of the interview; similarly, there are unique tasks which must be accomplished in the body, and in the closing portion. To facilitate discussion of these matters, this course will therefore utilize the terms: *opening, body,* and *close.*[2] For each type of interview studied, appropriate ways of handling each of these three parts (by each of the two parties) will be examined.

SOME COMMON TECHNIQUES FOR THE OPENING

Note to the student: The following list is merely for convenient reference, and to save time during class. Obviously, it is suggestive rather than prescriptive; no such list can be complete.

1. Brief statement or rapid summary of a problem (need) facing E and/or R. (Appropriate with E who is *vaguely* aware of problem, but not too well informed on details.)
2. Brief explanation of how you (R) happened to learn that a problem exists—coupled with suggestion that E will want to discuss it. (Avoids appearance of lecturing or talking down to E; encourages spirit of cooperative, objective discussion of a *mutual* problem.)
3. Statement of an incentive (goal or outcome) desired by E, that may reasonably be expected *if* your proposal is accepted. (Potentially the most powerful opening of all; *but* easily abused—frequently "corny," too obvious, or exaggerated. Avoid sounding like a high-pressure "sales pitch." Emphasize honesty and sincerity!)
4. Request for advice or assistance on a problem—from E. (Good when it is *sincere! Don't* use it as a slick gimmick!)
5. Statement of a striking, dramatic fact. (Again, potentially very powerful. But can be "corny"! Must be sincere, logically justified, and related to motivations of E; can easily be tied in with Number 3—incentives. Particularly appropriate when real emergency exists and when E is apathetic, must be aroused.)
6. Reference to the known position of E on a given problem situation. (This is the common-ground approach. Excellent to use when E has taken a public position, or has already asked R to bring in proposals, etc.)
7. Reference to the *background* (causes, origin, etc.) *leading up to a* problem (but not stating problem itself), when E is fairly familiar with this background. (Another application of common ground. May be useful when E is expected to react in a hostile manner as soon as he discovers what your proposal really is.)
8. Statement of person who sent you to see E. (Appropriate when E is a stranger, and an "entree" is necessary; can be used, of course, only when *true*—and when third party is respected by E.)

---

[2] In the literature on interviewing, the student may encounter such terms as "approach," "reception," "discussion," and "dismissal." These finer distinctions will not be observed in this selection because of their limited applications to specific types of interviews.

9. Statement of company, organization, or group you represent. (Appropriate when added prestige is needed, or when necessary to explain why there.)
10. Request for a specified, *brief* period of time (e.g., "ten minutes of your time"). (Caution! Can be too apologetic! To be used only when necessary, dealing with impatient, irritable, or very busy E.)
11. Question (various types: direct interrogation; leading, yes-response, etc.). (Advantage: compels E to respond in some manner. But many pitfalls. Can easily be tactless, abrupt, or too obvious. Should be related to E's motives, mood, background, etc. A "question-opening" can easily become a *non-directive* one.)

NOTE: Although these opening techniques may be adapted to a wide variety of interviews, it should be observed that they are especially appropriate for the persuader (R) when initiating a *persuasive* interview.

BIBLIOGRAPHY

1. Bingham, W., Moore, B., and Gustad, J., *How To Interview* (New York: Harper & Brothers, 1959), (4th rev. ed.). pp. 3-16 in Chapter 1, pp. 37-51 in Chapter 2, pp. 62-69 in Chapter 3.
2. Fenlason, A., Ferguson, G., & Abrahamson, A., *Essentials in Interviewing* (New York: Harper and Row, 1962). Chapters 1-5.
3. Kahn, R.L., and Cannell, C.F., *The Dynamics of Interviewing* (New York: John Wiley & Sons, Inc., 1957). Chapters 1 and 2.
4. Richardson, S., Dohrenwend, B., & Klein, D., *Interviewing: Its Forms and Functions* (New York: Basic Books, Inc., 1965). Chapters 2 and 3.

SMALL GROUP COMMUNICATION _____ 5

The following selections give you varied glimpses of what happens in small group interactions. First, Gouran demonstrates four different ways to study the complex activity of group leadership.

Second in "Functional Roles of Group Members," Benne and Sheats highlight the importance of the many roles necessary to the functioning of groups; they maintain that some small-group scholars concentrate on leadership by one person and overlook the leadership potential of other group members.

Have you ever heard about Parkinson's Law concerning the amounts of time groups devote to projects? Now you can read about it as explained by the law giver himself in Parkinson's "High Finance or the Point of Vanishing Interest" from *Parkinson's Law*.

Fourth, still another concept—that of changing habits through group interaction—comes from the pen of one of the pioneers in group dynamics, Lewin, a German psychologist who moved to the USA. This selection, "Group Decision," demonstrates empirically the value of group discussion as a persuasive technique compared to the public speaking method.

Finally, a *Psychology Today* article by Janis, "Groupthink," indicates that group processes have their negative aspects as well as their positive. He discusses such national disasters as Vietnam and Pearl Harbor. He also suggests that the decision-making processes in Washington need re-examination.

Dennis S. Gouran

CONCEPTUAL AND METHODOLOGICAL APPROACHES TO THE STUDY OF LEADERSHIP

Despite the voluminous amount of research on leadership, empirical findings to date have not contained as much of interest for communication specialists as some would like. The purpose of this article is to discuss conceptual and methodological perspectives for leadership research that hopefully will yield more of the kind of information that is relevant to the interests of our discipline than much of the existing research has.

Examining the scholarly literature on leadership, one rather quickly discovers four discernible approaches to study of the phenomenon, including what have been described as the trait, stylistic, situational, and functional approaches. Since many of the studies emanating from these research approaches have been summarized by Bormann,[1] Cartwright and Zander,[2] and Hollander,[3] the following discussion of previous contributions will be comparatively brief. The emphasis rather will be on the relative strengths and weaknesses of each approach as exemplified by particular studies.

Research based on the trait approach has frequently grown out of the long held assumption that leaders are born, not made. Apparently accepting the validity of this assumption, some early social psychologists attempted to study leadership by simply identifying the personality variables which theoretically would distinguish leaders from nonleaders. What for centuries had been a commonly held assumption, however, began to be rejected as research findings accumulated. Bird, for example, found in his survey of research designed to identify the unique traits of leaders that only five per cent of those discovered were common to four or more investigations.[4]

Borgatta, Couch, and Bales conducted a study,[5] which is frequently cited in support of the trait approach. These investigators found that individu-

Dennis S. Gouran, "Conceptual and Methodological Approaches to the Study of Leadership," *Central States Speech Journal,* Vol. 21, No. 4 (Winter 1970), pp. 217-223. Reprinted by permission of the Central States Speech Association.

[1] Ernest G. Bormann, *Discussion and Group Methods: Theory and Practice* (New York: Harper and Row, 1969), pp. 244-248.

[2] Dorwin Cartwright and Alvin Zander, eds., *Group Dynamics: Research and Theory,* 3rd ed. (New York: Harper & Row, 1968), pp. 301-315.

[3] Edwin P. Hollander, *Leaders, Groups, and Influence* (New York: Oxford University Press, 1964), pp. 3-15.

[4] Cartwright and Zander, p. 303.

[5] Edgar Borgatta *et al.,* "Some Findings Relevant to the Great Man Theory of Leadership," *American Sociological Review,* XIX (1954), 755-759.

als rated high by other group members on task ability, individual assertiveness, and social acceptability after participation in a problem-solving discussion continued to emerge and be recognized as leaders in subsequent sessions. After one carefully examines the study, however, these results seem to be less impressive. Close scrutiny reveals that of the original 126 subjects, only eleven met the investigators' criterion of leadership, and only seven of these remained leaders throughout as many as three group sessions. More importantly, the tasks in every work session in which the leaders participated were highly similar. This similarity in task from one trial to another, of course, did not allow for a very rigorous test of the generalizability of leadership from situation to situation.

Perhaps the most encouraging support for the trait approach is the conclusion reached by Stogdill. His review of leadership research indicated that leaders generally excel non-leaders in intelligence, scholarship, dependability and responsibility, activity and social participation, and socio-economic status.[6] In spite of the findings reported by Stogdill, Hollander,[7] Cartwright and Zander,[8] and Gouldner[9] suggest that the approach has fallen into disfavor and in recent years has been largely abandoned.

Among all of the studies of leadership traits, the one having possibly the greatest interest for communication scholars is Geier's.[10] In an investigation of leadership emergence, he identified five negative traits associated with failure to achieve the position of leader in small group discussions. These traits included being uninformed, non-participation, extreme rigidity, authoritarian behavior, and offensive verbalization. With more concentration on communication traits and less on personality variables, the genre of trait research could once again become fashionable.

A second approach to the study of leadership was given impetus by the now classic investigations of White and Lippitt.[11] Focusing on what leaders do rather than on their personalities, White and Lippitt studied leadership in three different social climates. The styles of leadership behavior examined included what the investigators labelled authoritarian, democratic, and *laissez-faire*. The democratic style proved to be superior to the others in a number of respects, including the level of group cohesiveness developed, the amount of independent behavior exhibited by the subjects, and the degree of satisfaction with group activities.

Other investigators, while often using terminology different from White and Lippitt's, have studied leadership styles and have generally found the democratic style to be superior in terms of its relative effects on certain dependent variables of interest. Berkowitz, for example, discovered that groups having more permissive leaders developed higher levels of cohesiveness than groups with less permissive leadership.[12] In a similar study, Hare reported

---

[6]Ralph Stodgill, "Personal Factors Associated with Leadership: A Survey of the Literature," *Journal of Psychology,* XXV (1948), 1-14.
[7]Hollander, p. 4.
[8]Cartwright and Zander, pp. 302-304.
[9]A. W. Gouldner, ed., *Studies in Leadership* (New York: Harper, 1950), pp. 23-45.
[10]John G. Geier, "A Trait Approach to the Study of Leadership in Small Groups," *Journal of Communication,* XVII (1967), 316-323.
[11]Ralph White and Ronald Lippitt, *Autocracy and Democracy* (New York: Harper, 1960).
[12]Leonard Berkowitz, "Sharing Leadership in Small Decision-Making Groups," *Journal of Abnormal and Social Psychology,* XLVIII (1953), 231-238.

finding participatory leadership superior to supervisory leadership in producing opinion change.[13] Finally, in a non-laboratory setting, Coch and French discovered that employee participation in some decision-making activities in the Harwood Manufacturing Corporation had a significant effect in reducing resistance to change in working conditions.[14]

Careful scrutiny of research growing out of the stylistic approach reveals two fairly common tendencies. First, the democratic and participatory styles at their best are frequently studied in relation to more autocratic styles at their worst. This tendency is particularly evident in the White and Lippitt study. The title of the book in which they report their research is *Democracy and Autocracy,* yet what they actually studied was democratic behavior verses authoritarian behavior.[15] While authoritarianism may be a characteristic of many autocrats, it is far from being a necessary characteristic. For example, one can retain complete responsibility for making a decision that will be binding on the members of the group, but the exercise of such control would not necessitate prohibiting expressions of others' opinions.

A second tendency evident in this body of research involves the investigators' confusion over what is meant by participation and democratic behavior. In some studies, it includes a role for non-leaders in decision-making activities. In others, it involves no opportunity to exert influence, but only token participation. The confusion is perhaps best exemplified in the Coch and French study.[16] What they called "total participation" amounted to the Harwood employees approving or disapproving a plan which the management had proposed. No formal decision, however, was reached by the group, nor were any of the employees permitted to participate in the development of the plan.

Perhaps some of the questionable aspects of stylistic research on leadership could be overcome by more careful manipulations of the various styles investigated. A recent study by Sargent and Miller[17] may have significant implications in this respect. Comparing leaders who preferred the autocratic style with others who preferred the democratic, they found the two types differed along a number of communication dimensions. Autocratic leaders' statements were more task-oriented, more concerned with achievement of their own preferred outcomes, and less favorably disposed to other member participation than democratic leaders'. These findings could be the basis for development of a set of criteria for manipulating leadership styles, thereby allowing for more rigorous tests of the effects of different styles on group outcomes.

Despite improvements in the quality of stylistic research which a study like Sargent and Miller's may permit, it is unlikely that we will ever discover one style of leadership to be consistently more effective than others. Korten has argued that the style which is most appropriate for the achieve-

---

[13] A. Paul Hare, "Small Group Discussions with Participatory and Supervisory Leadership," *Journal of Abnormal and Social Psychology,* XLVIII (1953), 273-275.

[14] Lester Coch and John R. French, Jr., "Overcoming Resistance to Change," *Human Relations,* XI (1948), 512-532.

[15] White and Lippitt.

[16] Coch and French.

[17] James F. Sargent and Gerald R. Miller, "Some Differences in the Communication Behaviors of Autocratic and Democratic Group Leaders." (Paper presented at the Speech Association of America Convention, December 28, 1969, New York.)

ment of a specific set of objectives will depend on a number of situational variables.[18] For example, when group goals are more important than individual goals and when ambiguities obscure the paths to achieving such goals, authoritarian leadership will be sought. When ambiguities are not stress-inducing, however, and the attainment of group goals is perceived as unnecessary for the attainment of individual goals, more democratic forms of leadership will be sought.

While the stylistic approach to leadership has indeed been more fruitful than the trait approach, the position developed by Korten reflects what seems to be the major inadequacy in the study of leadership styles. As a result, leadership research has increasingly become a product of the situational approach. In a sense, this approach combines the best features of both of the previous ones. According to Bormann, its underlying assumption is that leadership is "a function of the traits (personality variables) of the members, the purpose of the group, the internal and external pressures on the group, and the *inter-actions of the members.*"[19]

Perhaps the most well known exponent of the situational school is Fiedler.[20] His years of research with groups performing diverse tasks in a variety of social settings revealed that the successful exercise of leadership is not uniformly related to a particular style or personality type. On the contrary, Fiedler reports having found successful leadership to be the result of individuals in key positions employing a style demanded by the situation and the degree of psychological distance between them and other group members. Other studies by Burke,[21] Mulder and Stemerding,[22] and Shaw and Blum[23] have produced similar findings.

As Haiman notes, one can easily form the impression from research based on the situational approach that leadership effectiveness depends so heavily on specific situational factors that no general principles can be discovered.[24] More important, however, is the general failure of investigators to specify the critical behavior factors in the exercise of influence as they vary from situation to situation. For example, Fiedler found that psychologically close leaders experience greater success in extremely favorable and unfavorable situations while psychologically distant leaders enjoy greater success in only moderately favorable situations.[25] His explanation for this difference is that psychologically distant leaders, being more task-oriented, can function

---

[18] David C. Korten, "Situational Determinants of Leadership Structure," *Journal of Conflict Resolution,* VI (1962), 222-235.

[19] Bormann, p. 246.

[20] Fred E. Fiedler, "Personality and Situational Determinants of Leadership Effectiveness," in Cartwright and Zander, pp. 362-380.

[21] W. Warner Burke, "Leadership Behavior as a Function of the Leader, the Follower, and the Situation," *Journal of Personality,* XXXIII (1965), 60-81.

[22] Mauk Mulder and Ad Stemerding, "Threat, Attraction to Group, and Need for Strong Leadership," *Human Relations,* XVI (1963), 317-334.

[23] Marvin E. Shaw and Michael J. Blum, "Effects of Leadership Style upon Group Performance as a Function of Task Structure," *Journal of Personality and Social Psychology,* III (1966), 238-242.

[24] Franklyn Haiman, *Group Leadership and Democratic Action* (Boston: Houghton Mifflin, 1951), pp. 10-11.

[25] Fiedler, p. 375.

better under circumstances which do not create a need for dealing with inter-personal problems. Conversely, psychologically close leaders can function bet-ter in those situations which demand attention to interpersonal problems. This explanation, however, does not help one to identify what specific differences in the behavior of close and distant leaders exist and, more important, which behaviors contribute most to these respective types of leaders' success.

A final approach to leadership research involves the identification of group functions which promote the achievement of specific objectives. Cattell was one of the earliest theorists to espouse the functional position. He argues that any group member exerts leadership if the properties (syntality) of the group are modified by his presence.[26] More recently, Bavelas, in defense of the functional approach, has asserted that we need to define the leadership func-tions that must be performed in various situations and "regard as leadership those acts which perform them."[27]

The major problem with the functional approach so far has been that it has not yielded a set of functions that are uniquely related to leadership, nor has it identified those behaviors which most consistently contribute to the achievement of group goals. As Cartwright and Zander point out, the trend in this body of research has been simply "to identify the various group functions, without deciding finally whether or not to label each specifically as a function of leadership."[28] This tendency is particularly evident in the pioneering re-search efforts reported by Krech and Crutchfield[29] and Shartle.[30] Within the last few years, however, a new trend has begun to emerge with scholars at-tempting to discover what determines the development of group functions, their allocation, and the consequences resulting from their execution.[31]

Of the four approaches to leadership research just reviewed, the func-tional approach appears to have the greatest promise for significant develop-ments in future research. Despite the differences among the trait, stylistic, and situational approaches, they seem to have two things in common which, in this writer's judgment, render them relatively less useful than the functional ap-proach. First, they focus on individuals as leaders as they affect group behavior rather than on leadership as a total process of achieving goals. Second, because of the centrality of particular individuals in these approaches, the research which has grown out of them provides at best only limited information about the ways in which group goals are achieved; that is, we learn about the behav-ior and contributions of only one or two group members, but not much about other contributions which may be at least as important as those made by the so-called leaders.

Most of the research growing out of the functional approach has been more concerned with the distribution and execution of many different kinds of

---

[26] Raymond Cattell, "New Concepts for Measuring Leadership in Terms of Group Syntal-ity," *Human Relations,* IV (1951), 378-383.

[27] Alex Bavelas, "Leadership: Man and Function," *Administrative Science Quarterly,* IV (1960), p. 494.

[28] Cartwright and Zander.

[29] David Krech and Richard S. Crutchfield, *Theories and Problems of Social Psychology* (New York: McGraw-Hill, 1948), cited in Cartwright and Zander, p. 305.

[30] C. L. Shartle, *Executive Performance and Leadership* (Englewood Cliffs, N.J.: Prentice-Hall, 1956), cited in Cartwright and Zander, p. 305.

[31] Cartwright and Zander, p. 305.

activities in groups and organizations than with communication acts exclusively. In addition, many of the functions studied have been defined in terms of variables that are too global to be of much interest in communication research. Two of the functions sometimes studied, for example, are planning and maintenance. More emphasis should be placed on the statements which group members make and, more particularly, on the measurable properties of those kinds of statements which seem to be in evidence whenever a group achieves one of its goals and absent when it does not.

The notion of studying statements in leadership research is, of course, by no means a new one, nor is the functional approach the only one of the four reviewed which is amenable to such a methodological strategy. The earlier mentioned studies by Geier[32] and by Sargent and Miller[33] rather clearly focused on the kinds of statements made by leaders. The emphasis in these studies, however, was not on the characteristics of statements related to the achievement of group goals.

To focus on the statement as the unit of interest in leadership research will necessitate developing a meaningful set of descriptive characteristics with which to make evaluations. One system which already exists is Bales' Interaction Process Analysis.[34] Because of its availability and because of the considerable amount of research that has employed it, IPA would obviously be useful in the type of research being proposed. There are some problems associated with Bales' system of analysis, however, which have led some people to believe that new methodological approaches and strategies need to be developed in order to move our research substantially forward. The author has argued elsewhere that IPA suffers in at least two important respects.[35] First, the categories are mutually exclusive, which precludes looking at the same statement from more than one perspective. Many statements made in a discussion, however, serve several functions and could be classified in more than one way. Second, the system does not lend itself to precise statistical analysis. One is limited to comparing the relative proportions of certain kinds of statements emanating from different groups.

Unfortunately, it is not possible at present to offer as well a defined system of analysis with which to replace Bales' as might be desirable. However, some promising methodological research has been completed recently which might eventually lead to the development of a more useful analytical system than Interaction Process Analysis. In separate studies, Taylor,[36] Russell,[37] and Gouran[38] have had judges rate discussion statements on a substantial

---

[32] Geier.

[33] Sargent and Miller.

[34] For the most recent version of Interaction Process Analysis Techniques, see Robert F. Bales, *Personality and Interpersonal Behavior* (New York: Holt, Rinehart and Winston, 1970).

[35] Dennis S. Gouran, *An Investigation to Identify the Critical Variables Related to Consensus in Group Discussions of Questions of Policy* (Washington, D.C.: Educational Research Information Center, 1969), p. 6.

[36] K. Phillip Taylor, "An Investigation of Majority Verbal Behavior Toward Opinions of Deviant Members in Group Discussions of Policy (Ph.D. dissertation, Indiana University, 1969), pp. 37-62.

[37] Hugh C. Russell, "An Investigation of Leadership Maintenance Behavior" (Ph.D. dissertation, Indiana University, 1970), pp. 30-61.

[38] Gouran, pp. 9-14.

number of variables. In each case the task of the judges was to determine the extent to which the statements exhibited each of several different properties, such as opinionatedness, clarity, provocativeness, and informativeness. These data were then factor analyzed, and subsequent examination of the results in the separate studies has revealed the emergence of three rather stable factors which could be called goal facilitation, social-emotional behavior, and communication skills. Each of these factors was common to at least two of the studies. The first dimension was characterized by such variables as orientation, cooperativeness, and objectivity; the second by emotionality, defensiveness, and argumentativeness; and the third by clarity, informativeness, and clarification.

The three factors and related variables just described could form the basis of a new analytical system for use in future leadership research. Over time, such a system would undoubtedly undergo considerable revision and refinement as investigators continue to tap more of the dimensions of group processes, better define the variables which represent them, and improve the methods of detecting their presence in discussion statements. Until a more refined system does evolve, however, considerable headway in leadership research can still be made. The remainder of this discussion will explain and exemplify the form which this research might take.

For the immediate future, perhaps more of our leadership research should be investigatory than experimental. At present, we do not have sound bases for making the kinds of predictive statements demanded in experimental research. Well designed and carefully executed investigations could provide the kind of information with which it would be possible to generate research hypotheses which subsequently could be experimentally tested.

The question which naturally arises is, "What type of investigatory research should be done?" Perhaps initially, the most fruitful strategy is to compare groups which have achieved their goals with those which have failed to achieve them in terms of the kinds of communication variables previously mentioned. For example, if problem-solving were a goal of interest, one might try to discover if groups which are successful in this activity make statements which are consistently clearer, more objective, and more informative than groups which are unsuccessful. Discovering differences, of course, could be coincidental, but one would at least have some basis for making an intelligent prediction about the effects of certain kinds of communication behavior on the achievement of a group goal.

An actual example of the success of this proposed strategy might help to make it more acceptable. In an investigation of variables related to consensus, the author discovered that the statements of consensus groups manifested generally higher levels of orientation than those of non-consensus groups.[39] As a result, in a subsequent experiment, Knutson had a basis for predicting that groups having high orientation statements deliberately injected into their discussions would come closer to consensus on a question of policy than groups without such statements.[40]

---

[39] *Ibid.*, pp. 63-64.

[40] Thomas J. Knutson, "An Experimental Study of the Effects of Statements Giving Orientation on the Probability of Reaching Consensus on Group Discussions of Questions of Policy" (Ph.D. dissertation, Indiana University 1970).

The characteristics of the communication behaviors associated with the achievement of consensus on questions of policy, of course, are not the only ones of interest. Those related to the achievement of other kinds of goals, such as the development of cohesiveness, conciliation, increased sensitivity, accuracy of communication, and information gain, would also be worthy of study. The purpose of this article, however, has not been to indicate specific studies which need to be undertaken. Rather, it has been to encourage a particular way of looking at leadership and to develop a general methodological strategy for research. The precise features of leadership that should be examined, of course, will depend on the judgment of individual researchers and the uses to which they wish to put the knowledge they might uncover.

While much remains to be learned about the phenomenon of leadership, hopefully the focus which has been suggested and the strategy which has been outlined will help achieve this end. The knowledge that might be obtained from this kind of approach would be valuable in the development of a fruitful theory of group communication and would have significant practical implications as well.

Kenneth D. Benne and Paul Sheats

FUNCTIONAL ROLES OF GROUP MEMBERS

THE RELATIVE NEGLECT OF MEMBER ROLES IN GROUP TRAINING

Efforts to improve group functioning through training have traditionally emphasized the training of group leadership. And frequently this training has been directed toward the improvement of the skills of the leader in transmitting information and in manipulating groups. Little direct attention seems to have been given to the training of group members in the membership roles required for effective group growth and production. The present discussion is based on the conviction that both effective group training and adequate research into the effectiveness of group training methods must give attention to the identification, analysis, and practice of leader *and* member roles, seen as co-relative aspects of over-all group growth and production.

Certain assumptions have undergirded the tendency to isolate the leadership role from membership roles and to neglect the latter in processes of group training. 1) "Leadership" has been identified with traits and qualities inherent within the "leader" personality. Such traits and qualities can be developed, it is assumed, in isolation from the functioning of members in a group setting. The present treatment sees the leadership role in terms of functions to be performed within a group in helping that group to grow and to work productively. No sharp distinction can be made between leadership and membership functions, between leader and member roles. Groups may operate with various degrees of diffusion of "leadership" functions among group members or of concentration of such functions in one member or a few members. Ideally, of course, the concept of leadership emphasized here is that of a multilaterally shared responsibility. In any event, effectiveness in the leader role is a matter of leader-member relationship. And one side of a relationship cannot be effectively trained in isolation from the retraining of the other side of that relationship. 2) It has been assumed that the "leader" is uniquely responsible for the quality and amount of production by the group. The "leader" must see to it that the "right" group goals are set, that the group jobs get done, that members are "motivated" to participate. On this view, membership roles are of secondary importance. "Membership" is tacitly identified with "followership." The present discussion assumes that the quality and amount of group production is the "responsibility" of the group. The setting of goals and the marshalling of resources to move toward these goals is a group responsibility in which all members of a mature group come variously to share. The functions to be performed both in building and maintaining group-centered activity and in effective production by the group are primarily member roles.

Kenneth D. Benne and Paul Sheats, "Functional Roles of Group Members," *Journal of Social Issues*, Vol. 4, No. 2 (Spring 1948), pp. 41-49. Reprinted by permission of the Society for the Psychological Study of Social Issues.

Leadership functions can be defined in terms of facilitating identification, acceptance, development and allocation of these group-required roles by the group. 3) There has frequently been a confusion between the roles which members enact within a group and the individual personalities of the group members. That there are relationships between the personality structures and needs of group members and the range and quality of group membership roles which members can learn to perform is not denied. On the contrary, the importance of studies designed to describe and explain and to increase our control of these relationships is affirmed. But, at the level of group functioning, member roles, relevant to group growth and accomplishment, must be clearly distinguished from the use of the group environment by individuals to satisfy individual and group-irrelevant needs, if clear diagnosis of member-roles required by the group and adequate training of members to perform group-required roles are to be advanced. Neglect of this distinction has been associated traditionally with the neglect of the analysis of member roles in group growth and production.

A CLASSIFICATION OF MEMBER ROLES

The following analysis of functional member roles was developed in connection with the First National Training Laboratory in Group Development, 1947. It follows closely the analysis of participation functions used in coding the content of group records for research purposes. A similar analysis operated in faculty efforts to train group members in their functional roles during the course of the laboratory.[1]

The member-roles identified in this analysis are classified into three broad groupings.

(1) *Group task roles.* Participant roles here are related to the task which the group is deciding to undertake or has undertaken. Their purpose is to facilitate and coordinate group effort in the selection and definition of a common problem and in the solution of that problem.

(2) *Group building and maintenance roles.* The roles in this category are oriented toward the functioning of the group as a group. They are designed to alter or maintain the group way of working, to strengthen, regulate and perpetuate the group as a group.

(3) *Individual roles.* This category does not classify member-roles as such, since the "participations" denoted here are directed toward the satisfaction of the "participant's" individual needs. Their purpose is some individual goal which is not relevant either to the group task or to the functioning of the group as a group. Such participations are, of course, highly relevant to the problem of group training, insofar as such training is directed toward improving group maturity or group task efficiency.

---

[1] A somewhat different analysis of member-participations, in terms of categories used by interaction-observers in observation of group processes in the First National Training Laboratory, is described in the *Preliminary Report* of the laboratory, pages 122-132. The number of categories used by interaction observers was "directed primarily by limitations of observer load."

GROUP TASK ROLES

The following analysis assumes that the task of the discussion group is to select, define and solve common problems. The roles are identified in relation to functions of facilitation and coordination of group problem-solving activities. Each member may of course enact more than one role in any given unit of participation and a wide range of roles in successive participations. Any or all of these roles may be played at times by the group "leader" as well as by various members.

a. The *initiator-contributor* suggests or proposes to the group new ideas or a changed way of regarding the group problem or goal. The novelty proposed may take the form of suggestions of a new group goal or a new definition of the problem. It may take the form of a suggested solution or some way of handling a difficulty that the group has encountered. Or it may take the form of a proposed new procedure for the group, a new way of organizing the group for the task ahead.

b. The *information seeker* asks for clarification of suggestions made in terms of their factual adequacy, for authoritative information and facts pertinent to the problem being discussed.

c. The *opinion seeker* asks not primarily for the facts of the case but for a clarification of the values pertinent to what the group is undertaking or of values involved in a suggestion made or in alternative suggestions.

d. The *information giver* offers facts or generalizations which are "authoritative" or relates his own experience pertinently to the group problem.

e. The *opinion giver* states his belief or opinion pertinently to a suggestion made or to alternative suggestions. The emphasis is on his proposal of what should become the group's view of pertinent values, not primarily upon relevant facts or information.

f. The *elaborator* spells out suggestions in terms of examples or developed meanings, offers a rationale for suggestions previously made and tries to deduce how an idea or suggestion would work out if adopted by the group.

g. The *coordinator* shows or clarifies the relationships among various ideas and suggestions, tries to pull ideas and suggestions together or tries to coordinate the activities of various members or sub-groups.

h. The *orienter* defines the position of the group with respect to its goals by summarizing what has occurred, points to departures from agreed upon directions or goals, or raises questions about the direction which the group discussion is taking.

i. The *evaluator-critic* subjects the accomplishment of the group to some standard or set of standards of group-functioning in the context of the group task. Thus, he may evaluate or question the "practicality," the "logic," the "facts" or the "procedure" of a suggestion or of some unit of group discussion.

j. The *energizer* prods the group to action or decision, attempts to stimulate or arouse the group to "greater" or "higher quality" activity.

    k. The *procedural technician* expedites group movement by doing things for the group—performing routine tasks, e.g., distributing materials, or manipulating objects for the group, e.g., rearranging the seating or running the recording machine, etc.

    l. The *recorder* writes down suggestions, makes a record of group decisions, or writes down the product of discussion. The recorder role is the "group memory."

GROUP BUILDING AND MAINTENANCE ROLES

Here the analysis of member-functions is oriented to those participations which have for their purpose the building of group-centered attitudes and orientation among the members of a group or the maintenance and perpetuation of such group-centered behavior. A given contribution may involve several roles and a member or the "leader" may perform various roles in successive contributions.

    a. The *encourager* praises, agrees with and accepts the contribution of others. He indicates warmth and solidarity in his attitude toward other group members, offers commendation and praise and in various ways indicates understanding and acceptance of other points of view, ideas and suggestions.

    b. The *harmonizer* mediates the differences between other members, attempts to reconcile disagreements, relieves tension in conflict situations through jesting or pouring oil on the troubled waters, etc.

    c. The *compromiser* operates from within a conflict in which his idea or position is involved. He may offer compromise by yielding status, admitting his error, by disciplining himself to maintain group harmony, or by "coming half-way" in moving along with the group.

    d. The *gate-keeper and expediter* attempts to keep communcation channels open by encouraging or facilitating the participation of others ("we haven't got the ideas of Mr. X yet," etc.) or by proposing regulation of the flow of communication ("why don't we limit the length of our contributions so that everyone will have a chance to contribute?" etc.)

    e. The *standard setter* or *ego ideal* expresses standards for the group to attempt to achieve in its functioning or applies standards in evaluating the quality of group processes.

    f. The *group-observer* and *commentator* keeps records of various aspects of group process and feeds such data with proposed interpretations into the group's evaluation of its own procedures.

    g. The *follower* goes along with the movement of the group, more or less passively accepting the ideas of others, serving as an audience in group discussion and decision.

"INDIVIDUAL" ROLES

Attempts by "members" of a group to satisfy individual needs which are irrelevant to the group task and which are non-oriented or negatively oriented to group building and maintenance set problems of group and member training. A high incidence of "individual-centered" as opposed to "group-centered" participation in a group always calls for self-diagnosis of the group. The diagnosis may reveal one or several of a number of conditions—low level of skill-training among members, including the group leader; the prevalence of "authoritarian" and "laissez faire" points of view toward group functioning in the group; a low level of group maturity, discipline and morale; an inappropriately chosen and inadequately defined group task, etc. Whatever the diagnosis, it is in this setting that the training needs of the group are to be discovered and group training efforts to meet these needs are to be defined. The outright "suppression" of "individual roles" will deprive the group of data needed for really adequate self-diagnosis and therapy.

a. The *aggressor* may work in many ways—deflating the status of others, expressing disapproval of the values, acts or feelings of others, attacking the group or the problem it is working on, joking aggressively, showing envy toward another's contribution by trying to take credit for it, etc.

b. The *blocker* tends to be negativistic and stubbornly resistant, disagreeing and opposing without or beyond "reason" and attempting to maintain or bring back an issue after the group has rejected or by-passed it.

c. The *recognition-seeker* works in various ways to call attention to himself, whether through boasting, reporting on personal achievements, acting in unusual ways, struggling to prevent his being placed in an "inferior" position, etc.

d. The *self-confessor* uses the audience opportunity which the group setting provides to express personal, non-group oriented, "feeling," "insight," "ideology," etc.

e. The *playboy* makes a display of his lack of involvement in the group's processes. This may take the form of cynicism, nonchalance, horseplay and other more or less studied forms of "out of field" behavior.

f. The *dominator* tries to assert authority or superiority in manipulating the group or certain members of the group. This domination may take the form of flattery, of asserting a superior status or right to attention, giving directions authoritatively, interrupting the contributions of others, etc.

g. The *help-seeker* attempts to call forth "sympathy" response from other group members or from the whole group, whether through expressions of insecurity, personal confusion or depreciation of himself beyond "reason."

h. The *special interest pleader* speaks for the "small business man," the "grass roots" community, the "housewife," "labor," etc., usually cloaking his own prejudices or biases in the stereotype which best fits his individual need.

THE PROBLEM OF MEMBER ROLE REQUIREDNESS

Identification of group task roles and of group building and maintenance roles which do actually function in processes of group discussion raises but does not answer the further question of what roles are required for "optimum" group growth and productivity. Certainly the discovery and validation of answers to this question have a high priority in any advancing science of group training and development. No attempt will be made here to review the bearing of the analyzed data from the First National Training Laboratory in Group Development on this point.

It may be useful in this discussion, however, to comment on two conditions which effective work on the problem of role requiredness must meet. First, an answer to the problem of optimum task role requirements must be projected against a scheme of the process of group production. Groups in different stages of an act of problem selection and solution will have different role requirements. For example, a group early in the stages of problem selection which is attempting to lay out a range of possible problems to be worked on, will probably have relatively less need for the roles of "evaluator-critic," "energizer" and "coordinator" than a group which has selected and discussed its problem and is shaping its decision. The combination and balance of task role requirements is a function of the group's stage of progress with respect to its task. Second, the group building role requirements of a group are a function of its stage of development—its level of group maturity. For example, a "young" group will probably require less of the role of the "standard setter" than a more mature group. Too high a level of aspiration may frustrate a "young" group where a more mature group will be able to take the same level of aspiration in its stride. Again the role of "group observer and commentator" must be carefully adapted to the level of maturity of the group. Probably the distinction between "group" and "individual" roles can be drawn much more sharply in a relatively mature than in a "young" group.

Meanwhile, group trainers cannot wait for a fully developed science of group training before they undertake to diagnose the role requirements of the groups with which they work and help these groups to share in such diagnosis. Each group which is attempting to improve the quality of its functioning as a group must be helped to diagnose its role requirements and must attempt to train members to fill the required roles effectively. This describes one of the principal objectives of training of group members.

THE PROBLEM OF ROLE FLEXIBILITY

The previous group experience of members, where this experience has included little conscious attention to the variety of roles involved in effective group production and development, has frequently stereotyped the member into a limited range of roles. These he plays in all group discussions whether or not the group situation requires them. Some members see themselves primarily as "evaluator-critics" and play this role in and out of season. Others may play the roles of "encourager" or of "energizer" or of "information giver" with only small sensitivity to the role requirements of a given group situation. The development of skill and insight in diagnosing role requirements has already been mentioned as an objective of group member training. An equally · important objective is the development of role flexibility, of skill and security in a wide range of member roles, on the part of all group members.

A science of group training, as it develops, must be concerned with the relationships between the personality structures of group members and the character and range of member roles which various personality structures support and permit. A science of group training must seek to discover and accept the limitations which group training per se encounters in altering personality structures in the service of greater role flexibility on the part of all members of a group. Even though we recognize the importance of this caution, the objective of developing role flexibility remains an important objective of group member training.

METHODS OF GROUP MEMBER TRAINING

The objectives in training group members have been identified. Some of the kinds of resistances encountered in training group members to diagnose the role requirements of a group situation and to acquire skill in a variety of member roles have been suggested. Before analyzing briefly the methods used for group member training in the First National Training Laboratory, a few additional comments on resistances to member training may be useful. The problem of group training is actually a problem of retraining. Members of a training group have had other group experiences. They bring to the training experience attitudes toward group work, more or less conscious skills for dealing with leaders and other members, and a more or less highly developed rationale of group processes. These may or may not support processes of democratic operation in the training group. Where they do not, they function as resistances to retraining. Again, trainees are inclined to make little or no distinction between the roles they perform in a group and their personalities. Criticism of the role a group member plays is perceived as criticism of "himself." Methods must be found to reduce ego-defensiveness toward criticism of member roles. Finally, training groups must be helped to make a distinction between group feeling and group productivity. Groups which attain a state of good group feeling often perceive attempts to diagnose and criticize their level of productivity as threats to this feeling of group warmth and solidarity.

(1) Each Basic Skill Training group in the Laboratory used self-observation and diagnosis of its own growth and development as a primary means of member training.

    (a) Sensitization to the variety of roles involved in and required by group functioning began during the introduction of members to the group. In one BST group, this early sensitization to member role variety and role requiredness began with the "leader's" summarizing, as part of his introduction of himself to the group, certain of the member roles in which he was usually cast by groups and other roles which he found it difficult to play, even when needed by the group. He asked the group's help in criticizing and improving his skill in those roles where he felt weakest. Other members followed suit. Various members showed widely different degrees of sensitivity to the operation of member roles in groups and to the degree of their own proficiency in different roles. This introduction procedure gave the group a partial listing of member roles for later use and supplementation, initial self-assessments of member strengths and weaknesses and diagnostic material concerning the degree of group self-sophistication among the members. The training job had come to be seen by most members as a retraining job.

    (b) A description of the use of training observers in group self-evaluation sessions is given in the next paper in this issue. At this point, only the central importance which self-evaluation sessions played in member training needs to be stressed. Research observers fed observational data concerning group functioning into periodic discussions by the group of its strengths and weaknesses as a group. Much of these data concerned role requirements for the job the group had been attempting, which roles had been present, which roles had probably been needed. "Individual" roles were identified and interpreted in an objective and non-blaming manner. Out of these discussions, group members came to identify various kinds of member roles, to relate role requiredness to stages in group production and in group growth and to assess the range of roles each was able to play well when required. Out of these discussions came group decisions concerning the supplying of needed roles in the next session. Member commitments concerning behavior in future sessions also came out of these evaluations. These took the form both of silent commitments and of public commitments in which the help of the group was requested.

(c) Recordings of segments of the group's discussion were used by most Basic Skill Training groups. Groups listened to themselves, diagnosed the member and leader functions involved and assessed the adequacy of these.

(2) Role-played sessions in each group, although they were pointed content-wise to the skills of the change-agent, offered important material for the diagnosis of member roles and of role requiredness. These sessions offered an important supplement to group self-diagnosis and evaluation. It is easier for members to get perspective on their participation in a role-played episode of group process than it is on their own participation in a "real" group. The former is not perceived as "real." The role is more easily disengaged for purposes of analysis and evaluation from the person playing the role. Ego-defensiveness toward the role as enacted is reduced. Role-playing sessions also provided practice opportunity to members in a variety of roles.

(3) Practice by group members of the role of *observer-commentator* is especially valuable in developing skill in diagnosing member roles and in assessing the role requirements of a group situation. In several groups, each member in turn served as observer, supplementing the work of the research observers in evaluation sessions. Such members worked more or less closely with the anecdotal observer for the group on skill-problems encountered. Practice opportunity in the *observer-commentator* role was also provided in clinic group meetings in the afternoon.

SUMMARY

Training in group membership roles requires the identification and analysis of various member roles actually enacted in group processes. It involves further the analysis of group situations in terms of roles required in relation both to a schema of group production and to a conception of group growth and development. A group's self-observation and self-evaluation of its own processes provides useful content and practice opportunity in member training. Practice in enacting a wider range of required roles and in role flexibility can come out of member commitment to such practice with help from the group in evaluating and improving the required skills. Member training is typically retraining and resistances to retraining can be reduced by creating a non-blaming and objective atmosphere in group self-evaluation and by using role-playing of group processes for diagnosis and practice. The training objectives of developing skill in the diagnosis of group role requirements and developing role flexibility among members also indicate important research areas for a science of group training.

Cyril N. Parkinson

HIGH FINANCE OR THE POINT OF VANISHING INTEREST

People who understand high finance are of two kinds: those who have vast fortunes of their own and those who have nothing at all. To the actual millionaire a million dollars is something real and comprehensible. To the applied mathematician and the lecturer in economics (assuming both to be practically starving) a million dollars is at least as real as a thousand, they having never possessed either sum. But the world is full of people who fall between these two categories, knowing nothing of millions but well accustomed to think in thousands, and it is of these that finance committees are mostly comprised. The result is a phenomenon that has often been observed but never yet investigated. It might be termed the Law of Triviality. Briefly stated, it means that the time spent on any item of the agenda will be in inverse proportion to the sum involved.

On second thoughts, the statement that this law has never been investigated is not entirely accurate. Some work has actually been done in this field, but the investigators pursued a line of inquiry that led them nowhere. They assumed that the greatest significance should attach to the order in which items of the agenda are taken. They assumed, further, that most of the available time will be spent on items one to seven and that the later items will be allowed automatically to pass. The result is well known. The derision with which Dr. Guggenheim's lecture was received at the Muttworth Conference may have been thought excessive at the time, but all further discussions on this topic have tended to show that his critics were right. Years had been wasted in a research of which the basic assumptions were wrong. We realize now that position on the agenda is a minor consideration, so far, at least, as this problem is concerned. We consider also that Dr. Guggenheim was lucky to escape, as he did, in his underwear. Had he dared to put his lame conclusions before the later conference in September, he would have faced something more than derision. The view would have been taken that he was deliberately wasting time.

If we are to make further progress in this investigation we must ignore all that has so far been done. We must start at the beginning and understand fully the way in which a finance committee actually works. For the sake of the general reader this can be put in dramatic form thus:

Chairman—We come now to Item Nine. Our Treasurer, Mr. McPhail, will
report.

Mr. McPhail—The estimate for the Atomic Reactor is before you, sir, set forth
in Appendix H of the subcommittee's report. You will see that the

general design and layout has been approved by Professor McFission.
The total cost will amount to $10,000,000. The contractors, Messrs.
McNab and McHash, consider that the work should be complete by
April, 1959. Mr. McFee, the consulting engineer, warns us that we
should not count on completion before October, at the earliest. In this
view he is supported by Dr. McHeap, the well-known geophysicist, who
refers to the probable need for piling at the lower end of the site. The
plan of the main building is before you—see Appendix IX—and the
blueprint is laid on the table. I shall be glad to give any further
information that members of this committee may require.

Chairman—Thank you, Mr. McPhail, for your very lucid explanation of the
plan as proposed. I will now invite the members present to give us
their views.

It is necessary to pause at this point and consider what views the
members are likely to have. Let us suppose that they number eleven, including
the Chairman but excluding the Secretary. Of these eleven members, four—
including the chairman—do not know what a reactor is. Of the remainder,
three do not know what it is for. Of those who know its purpose, only two have
the least idea of what it should cost. One of these is Mr. Isaacson, the other is
Mr. Brickworth. Either is in a position to say something. We may suppose that
Mr. Isaacson is the first to speak.

Mr. Isaacson—Well, Mr. Chairman. I could wish that I felt more confidence in
our contractors and consultant. Had we gone to Professor Levi in the
first instance, and had the contract been given to Messrs. David and
Goliath, I should have been happier about the whole scheme. Mr.
Lyon-Daniels would not have wasted our time with wild guesses about
the possible delay in completion, and Dr. Moses Bullrush would have
told us definitely whether piling would be wanted or not.

Chairman—I am sure we all appreciate Mr. Isaacson's anxiety to complete this
work in the best possible way. I feel, however, that it is rather late in
the day to call in new technical advisers. I admit that the main contract has still to be signed, but we have already spent very large sums.
If we reject the advice for which we have paid, we shall have to pay
as much again.

(Other members murmur agreement.)

Mr. Isaacson—I should like my observation to be minuted.

Chairman—Certainly. Perhaps Mr. Brickworth also has something to say on
this matter?

Now Mr. Brickworth is almost the only man there who knows what
he is talking about. There is a great deal he could say. He distrusts that round
figure of $10,000,000. Why should it come out to exactly that? Why need they
demolish the old building to make room for the new approach? Why is so large
a sum set aside for "contingencies"? And who is McHeap, anyway? Is he the
man who was sued last year by the Trickle and Driedup Oil Corporation? But
Brickworth does not know where to begin. The other members could not read
the blueprint if he referred to it. He would have to begin by explaining what
a reactor is and no one there would admit that he did not already know. Better
to say nothing.

Mr. Brickworth—I have no comment to make.

Chairman—Does any other member wish to speak? Very well. I may take it then that the plans and estimates are approved? Thank you. May I now sign the main contract on your behalf? (*Murmur of agreement*) Thank you. We can now move on to Item Ten.

Allowing a few seconds for rustling papers and unrolling diagrams, the time spent on Item Nine will have been just two minutes and a half. The meeting is going well. But some members feel uneasy about Item Nine. They wonder inwardly whether they have really been pulling their weight. It is too late to query that reactor scheme, but they would like to demonstrate, before the meeting ends, that they are alive to all that is going on.

Chairman—Item Ten. Bicycle shed for the use of the clerical staff. An estimate has been received from Messrs. Bodger and Woodworm, who undertake to complete the work for the sum of $2350. Plans and specification are before you, gentlemen.

Mr. Softleigh—Surely, Mr. Chairman, this sum is excessive. I note that the roof is to be of aluminum. Would not asbestos be cheaper?

Mr. Holdfast—I agree with Mr. Softleigh about the cost, but the roof should, in my opinion, be of galvanized iron. I incline to think that the shed could be built for $2000, or even less.

Mr. Daring—I would go further, Mr. Chairman. I question whether this shed is really necessary. We do too much for our staff as it is. They are never satisfied, that is the trouble. They will be wanting garages next.

Mr. Holdfast—No, I can't support Mr. Daring on this occasion. I think that the shed is needed. It is a question of material and cost . . .

The debate is fairly launched. A sum of $2350 is well within everybody's comprehension. Everyone can visualize a bicycle shed. Discussion goes on, therefore, for forty-five minutes, with the possible result of saving some $300. Members at length sit back with a feeling of achievement.

Chairman—Item Eleven. Refreshments supplied at meetings of the Joint Welfare Committee. Monthly, $4.75.

Mr. Softleigh—What type of refreshment is supplied on these occasions?

Chairman—Coffee, I understand.

Mr. Holdfast—And this means an annual charge of—let me see—$57?

Chairman—That is so.

Mr. Daring—Well, really, Mr. Chairman. I question whether this is justified. How long do these meetings last?

Now begins an even more acrimonious debate. There may be members of the committee who might fail to distinguish between asbestos and galvanized iron, but every man there knows about coffee—what it is, how it should be made, where it should be bought—and whether indeed it should be bought at all. This item on the agenda will occupy the members for an hour and a quarter, and they will end by asking the Secretary to procure further information, leaving the matter to be decided at the next meeting.

It would be natural to ask at this point whether a still smaller sum —$20, perhaps, or $10—would occupy the Finance Committee for a proportionately longer time. On this point, it must be admitted, we are still ignorant. Our tentative conclusion must be that there is a point at which the whole tendency is reversed, the committee members concluding that the sum is beneath their notice. Research has still to establish the point at which this reversal occurs. The transition from the $50 debate (an hour and a quarter) to the $20 debate (two and a half minutes) is indeed an abrupt one. It would be the more interesting to establish the exact point at which it occurs. More than that, it would be of practical value. Supposing, for example, that the point of vanishing interest is represented by the sum of $35, the Treasurer with an item of $62.80 on the agenda might well decide to present it as two items, one of $30.00 and the other of $32.80, with an evident saving in time and effort.

Conclusions at this juncture can be merely tentative, but there is some reason to suppose that the point of vanishing interest represents the sum the individual committee member is willing to lose on a bet or subscribe to a charity. An inquiry on these lines conducted on racecourses and in Methodist chapels, might go far toward solving the problem. Far greater difficulty may be encountered in attempting to discover the exact point at which the sum involved becomes too large to discuss at all. One thing apparent, however, is that the time spent on $10,000,000 and on $10 may well prove to be the same. The present estimated time of two and a half minutes is by no means exact, but there is clearly a space of time—something between two and four and a half minutes—which suffices equally for the largest and the smallest sums.

Much further investigation remains to be done, but the final results, when published, cannot fail to be of absorbing interest and of immediate value to mankind.

Kurt Lewin

GROUP DECISION

LECTURE COMPARED WITH GROUP DECISION (RED CROSS GROUPS)

A preliminary experiment in changing food habits[1] was conducted with six Red Cross groups of volunteers organized for home nursing. Groups ranged in size from 13 to 17 members. The objective was to increase the use of beef hearts, sweetbreads, and kidneys.* If one considers the psychological forces which kept housewives from using these intestinals, one is tempted to think of rather deep-seated aversions requiring something like psychoanalytical treatment. Doubtless a change in this respect is a much more difficult task than, for instance, the introduction of a new vegetable such as escarole. There were, however, only 45 minutes available.

In three of the groups attractive lectures were given which linked the problem of nutrition with the war effort, emphasized the vitamin and mineral value of the three meats, giving detailed explanations with the aid of charts. Both the health and economic aspects were stressed. The preparation of these meats was discussed in detail as well as techniques for avoiding those characteristics to which aversions were oriented (odor, texture, appearance, etc.). Mimeographed recipes were distributed. The lecturer was able to arouse the interest of the groups by giving hints of her own methods for preparing these "delicious dishes," and her success with her own family.

For the other three groups Mr. Alex Bavelas developed the following procedure of group decision. Again the problem of nutrition was linked with that of the war effort and general health. After a few minutes, a discussion was started to see whether housewives could be induced to participate in a program of change without attempting any high-pressure salesmanship. The group discussion about "housewives like themselves" led to an elaboration of the obstacles which a change in general and particularly change toward sweetbreads, beef hearts, and kidneys would encounter, such as the dislike of the husband, the smell during cooking, etc. The nutrition expert offered the same remedies and recipes for preparation which were presented in the lectures to the other groups. But in these groups preparation techniques were offered after the groups had become sufficiently involved to be interested in knowing whether certain obstacles could be removed.

From *Readings in Social Psychology* by Eleanor E. Maccoby, Theodore M. Newcomb and Eugene Hartley. Copyright 1947, 1972, © 1958 by Holt, Rinehart and Winston, Inc. Reprinted by permission of Holt, Rinehart and Winston.
[1]The studies on nutrition discussed in this article were conducted at the Child Welfare Research Station of the State University of Iowa for the Food Habits Committee of the National Research Council (Executive Secretary, Margaret Mead).
*Editors' Note: This study was conducted during World War II when meat was being sent to troops overseas and civilians were having to ration food and supplies to support the war effort.

In the earlier part of the meeting a census was taken on how many women had served any of these foods in the past. At the end of the meeting, the women were asked by a showing of hands who was willing to try one of these meats within the next week.

A follow-up showed that only 3 percent of the women who heard the lectures served one of the meats never served before, whereas after group decision 32 percent served one of them (Fig. 5-1).

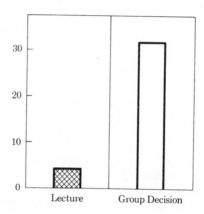

FIG. 5-1. *Percentage of individuals serving type of food never served before, after lecture and after group decision.*

If one is to understand the basis of this striking difference, several factors may have to be considered.

Degree of Involvement

Lecturing is a procedure in which the audience is chiefly passive. The discussion, if conducted correctly, is likely to lead to a much higher degree of involvement. The procedure of group decision in this experiment follows a step-by-step method designed *(a)* to secure high involvement and *(b)* not to impede freedom of decision. The problem of food changes was discussed in regard to "housewives like yourselves" rather than in regard to themselves. This minimized resistance to considering the problems and possibilities in an objective, unprejudiced manner, in much the same way as such resistance has been minimized in interviews which use projective techniques, or in a socio-drama which uses an assumed situation of role playing rather than a real situation.

Motivation and Decision

The prevalent theory in psychology assumes action to be the direct result of motivation. I am inclined to think that we will have to modify this theory. We will have to study the particular conditions under which a motivating constellation leads or does not lead to a decision or to an equivalent process through which a state of "considerations" (indecisiveness) is changed into a state where the individual has "made up his mind" and is ready for action, although he may not act at that moment.

The act of decision is one of those transitions. A change from a situation of undecided conflict to decision does not mean merely that the forces toward one alternative become stronger than those toward the other alternative. If this were the case, the resultant force should frequently be extremely small. A decision rather means that the potency of one alternative has become zero or is so decidedly diminished that the other alternative and the corresponding forces dominate the situation. This alternative itself might be a compromise. After the decision people may feel sorry and change their decision. We cannot speak of a real decision, however, before one alternative has become dominant so far as action is concerned. If the opposing forces in a conflict merely change so that the forces in one direction become slightly greater than in the other direction, a state of blockage or extremely inhibited action results rather than that clear one-sided action which follows a real decision.

Lecturing may lead to a high degree of interest. It may affect the motivation of the listener. But it seldom brings about a definite decision on the part of the listener to take a certain action at a specific time. A lecture is not often conducive to decision.

Evidence from everyday experience and from some preliminary experiments by Bavelas in a factory indicate that even group discussions, although usually leading to a higher degree of involvement, as a rule do not lead to a decision. It is very important to emphasize this point. Although group discussion is in many respects different from lectures, it shows no fundamental difference on this point.

Of course, there is a great difference in asking for a decision after a lecture or after a discussion. Since discussion involves active participation of the audience and a chance to express motivations corresponding to different alternatives, the audience might be more ready "to make up its mind," that is, to make a decision after a group discussion than after a lecture. A group discussion gives the leader a better indication of where the audience stands and what particular obstacles have to be overcome.

In the experiment on hand, we are dealing with a group decision after discussion. The decision, itself, takes but a minute or two. (It was done through raising of hands as an answer to the question: Who would like to serve kidney, sweetbreads, beef hearts next week?) The act of decision, however, should be viewed as a very important process of giving dominance to one of the alternatives, serving or not serving. It has an effect of freezing this motivational constellation for action. We will return to this point later.

Individual versus Group

The experiment does not try to bring about a change of food habits by an approach to the individual, as such. Nor does it use the "mass approach" characteristic of radio and newspaper propaganda. Closer scrutiny shows that both the mass approach and the individual approach place the individual in a quasi-private, psychologically isolated situation with himself and his own ideas. Although he may, physically, be part of a group listening to a lecture, for example, he finds himself, psychologically speaking, in an "individual situation."

The present experiment approaches the individual as a member of a face-to-face group. We know, for instance, from experiments in level of aspiration[2] that goal setting is strongly dependent on group standards. Experience in leadership training and in many areas of re-education, such as re-education regarding alcoholism or delinquency[3] indicates that it is easier to change the ideology and social practice of a small group handled together than of single individuals. One of the reasons why "group carried changes" are more readily brought about seems to be the unwillingness of the individual to depart too far from group standards; he is likely to change only if the group changes. We will return to this problem.

One may try to link the greater effectiveness of group decision procedures to the fact that the lecture reaches the individual in a more individualistic fashion than group discussion. If a change of sentiment of the group becomes apparent during the discussion, the individual will be more ready to come along.

It should be stressed that in our case the decision which follows the group discussion does not have the character of a decision in regard to a group goal; it is rather a decision about individual goals in a group setting.

Expectation

The difference between the results of the lectures and the group decision may be due to the fact that only after group decision did the discussion leader mention that an inquiry would be made later as to whether a new food was introduced into the family diet.

Leader Personality

The difference in effectiveness may be due to differences in leader personality. The nutritionist and the housewife who did the lecturing were persons of recognized ability, experience, and success. Still, Mr. Bavelas, who led the discussion and subsequent decision, is an experienced group worker and doubtless of unusual ability in this field.

To determine which of these or other factors are important, a number of systematic variations have to be carried out. To determine, for instance, the role of the decision as such, one can compare the effect of group discussion with and without decision. To study the role of group involvement and the possibility of sensing the changing group sentiment, one could introduce decisions after both, lecture and discussion, and compare their effects.

The following experiments represent partly analytical variations, partly repetitions with somewhat different material.

LECTURE VERSUS GROUP DECISION (NEIGHBORHOOD GROUPS)

Dana Klisurich, under the direction of Marian Radke, conducted experiments with 6 groups of housewives composed of 6-9 members per group. She compared the effect of a lecture with that of group decision. The topic for

---

[2] K. Lewin, "Behavior and Development as a Function of the Total Situation" in L. Carmichael (ed.), *Manual of Child Psychology* (New York: John Wiley, 1946), pp. 791-844.
[3] K. Lewin and P. Grabbe (eds.), "Problems of Re-education," *J. Soc. Issues,* (August) 1945, I, No. 3.

these groups was increasing home consumption of milk, in the form of fresh or evaporated milk or both.[4]

The procedure followed closely that described above. Again there was no attempt at high-pressure salesmanship. The group discussion proceeded in a step-by-step way, starting again with "what housewives in general might do" and only then leading to the individuals present. The lecture was kept as interesting as possible. The knowledge transmitted was the same for lecture and group decision.

A check-up was made after two weeks and after four weeks. As in the previous experiments, group decision showed considerably greater effectiveness, both after two weeks and after four weeks and for both fresh and evaporated milk (Figs. 5-2 and 5-3). This experiment permits the following conclusions:

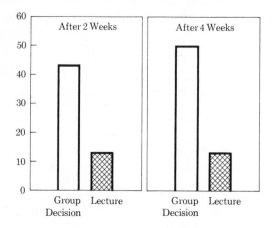

FIG. 5-2. *Percentage of mothers reporting an increase in the consumption of fresh milk.*

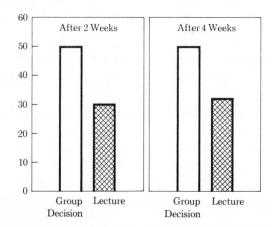

FIG. 5-3. *Percentage of mothers reporting an increase in the consumption of evaporated milk.*

[4]M. Radke and D. Klisurich, Experiments in Changing Food Habits. Unpublished manuscript.

1. It shows that the greater effectiveness of the group decision in the first experiment is not merely the result of the personality or training of the leader. The leader was a lively person, interested in people, but she did not have particular training in group work. She had been carefully advised and had had a try-out in the group decision procedure. As mentioned above, the leader in lecture and group decision was the same person.

2. The experiment shows that the different effectiveness of the two procedures is not limited to the foods considered in the first experiment.

3. It is interesting that the greater effectiveness of group decision was observable not only after one week but after two and four weeks. Consumption after group decision kept constant during that period. After the lecture it showed an insignificant increase from the second to the fourth week. The degree of permanency is obviously a very important aspect of any changes in group life. We will come back to this point.

4. As in the first experiment, the subjects were informed about a future check-up after group decision but not after the lecture. After the second week, however, both groups knew that a check-up had been made and neither of them was informed that a second check-up would follow.

5. It is important to know whether group decision is effective only with tightly knit groups. It should be noticed that in the second experiment the groups were composed of housewives who either lived in the same neighborhood or visited the nutrition information service of the community center. They were not members of a club meeting regularly as were the Red Cross groups in the first experiment. On the other hand, a good proportion of these housewives knew each other. This indicates that decision in a group setting seems to be effective even if the group is not a permanent organization.

INDIVIDUAL INSTRUCTION VERSUS GROUP DECISION

For a number of years, the state hospital in Iowa City has given advice to mothers on feeding of their babies. Under this program, farm mothers who have their first child at the hospital meet with a nutritionist for from 20-25 minutes before discharge from the hospital to discuss feeding. The mother receives printed advice on the composition of the formula and is instructed in the importance of orange juice and cod liver oil.

There had been indication that the effect of this nutrition program was not very satisfactory. An experiment was carried out by Dana Klisurich under the direction of Marian Radke to compare the effectiveness of this procedure with that of group decision.[5]

With some mothers individual instruction was used as before. Others were divided into groups of six for instruction on and discussion of baby feeding. The manner of reaching a decision at the end of this group meeting was similar to that used in the previous experiments. The time for the six mothers together was the same as for one individual, about 25 minutes.

---

[5] M. Radke and D. Klisurich, Experiments in Changing Food Habits. Unpublished manuscript.

After two weeks and after four weeks, a check was made on the degree to which each mother followed the advice on cod liver oil and orange juice. Figs. 5-4 and 5-5 show the percentage of individuals who completely followed the advice. The group decision method proved far superior to the individual instruction. After four weeks every mother who participated in group decision followed exactly the prescribed diet in regard to orange juice.

The following specific results might be mentioned:

1. The greater effect of group decision in this experiment is particularly interesting. Individual instruction is a setting in which the individual gets more attention from the instructor. Therefore, one might expect the individual to become more deeply involved and the instruction to be fitted more adequately to the need and sentiment of each individual. After all, the instructor devotes the same amount of time to one individual as he does to six in group decision. The result can be interpreted to mean either that the amount of individual involvement is greater in group decision or that the decision in the group setting is itself the decisive factor.

2. Most of the mothers were not acquainted with each other. They returned to farms which were widely separated. Most of them had no contact with each other during the following four weeks. The previous experiment had already indicated that the effectiveness of group decision did not seem to be limited to well-established groups. In this experiment the absence of social relations among the mothers before and after the group meeting is even more clear cut.

3. The data thus far do not permit reliable quantitative, over-all comparisons. However, they point to certain interesting problems and possibilities. In comparing the various experiments concerning the data two weeks after group decision, one finds that the percentage of housewives who served kidneys, beef hearts or sweetbreads is relatively similar to the percentage of housewives who increased the consumption of fresh milk or evaporated milk or of mothers who followed completely the diet of cod liver oil with their babies. The percentages lie between 32 and 50. The percentage in regard to orange juice for the baby is clearly higher, namely, 85 percent. These results are surprising in several respects. Mothers are usually eager to do all they can for their babies. This may explain why a group decision in regard to orange juice had such a strong effect. Why, however, was this effect not equally strong on cod liver oil? Perhaps, giving the baby cod liver oil is hampered by the mothers' own dislike of this food. Kidneys, beef hearts, and sweetbreads are foods for which the dislike seems to be particularly deep-seated. If the amount of dislike is the main resistance to change, one would expect probably a greater difference between these foods and, for instance, a change in regard to fresh milk. Of course, these meats are particularly cheap and the group decision leader was particularly qualified.

4. The change after lectures is in all cases smaller than after group decision. However, the rank order of the percentage of change after lectures follows the rank order after group decision, namely (from low to high), glandular meat, fresh milk, cod liver oil for the baby, evapo-

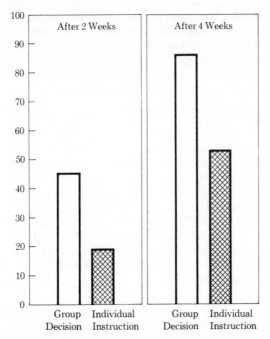

FIG. 5-4. *Percentage of mothers following completely group decision or individual instruction in giving cod liver oil.*

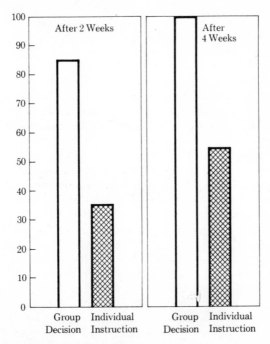

FIG. 5-5. *Percentage of mothers following completely group decision or individual instruction in giving orange juice.*

rated milk for the family, orange juice for the baby.

The constancy of this rank order may be interpreted to mean that one can ascribe to each of these foods—under the given circumstances and for these particular populations—a specific degree of "resistance to change." The "force toward change" resulting from group decision is greater than the force resulting from lecture. This leads to a difference in the amount (or frequency) of change for the same food without changing the rank order of the various foods. The rank order is determined by the relative strength of their resistance to change.

5. Comparing the second and the fourth week, we notice that the level of consumption remains the same or increases insignificantly after group decision and lecture regarding evaporated or fresh milk. A pronounced increase occurs after group decision and after individual instruction on cod liver oil and orange juice, that is, in all cases regarding infant feeding. This seems to be a perplexing phenomenon if one considers that no additional instruction or group decision was introduced. On the whole, one may be inclined to expect weakening effect of group decision with time and therefore a decrease rather than an increase of the curve.

Irving L. Janis
GROUPTHINK

"How could we have been so stupid?" President John F. Kennedy asked after he and a close group of advisers had blundered into the Bay of Pigs invasion. For the last two years I have been studying that question, as it applies not only to the Bay of Pigs decision-makers but also to those who led the United States into such other major fiascos as the failure to be prepared for the attack on Pearl Harbor, the Korean War stalemate and the escalation of the Vietnam War.

Stupidity certainly is not the explanation. The men who participated in making the Bay of Pigs decision, for instance, comprised one of the greatest arrays of intellectual talent in the history of American Government—Dean Rusk, Robert McNamara, Douglas Dillon, Robert Kennedy, McGeorge Bundy, Arthur Schlesinger Jr., Allen Dulles and others.

It also seemed to me that explanations were incomplete if they concentrated only on disturbances in the behavior of each individual within a decision-making body: temporary emotional states of elation, fear, or anger that reduce a man's mental efficiency, for example, or chronic blind spots arising from a man's social prejudices or idiosyncratic biases.

I preferred to broaden the picture by looking at the fiascos from the standpoint of group dynamics as it has been explored over the past three decades, first by the great social psychologist Kurt Lewin and later in many experimental situations by myself and other behavioral scientists. My conclusion after poring over hundreds of relevant documents—historical reports about formal group meetings and informal conversations among the members—is that the groups that committed the fiascos were victims of what I call "groupthink."

"Groupy"

In each case study, I was surprised to discover the extent to which each group displayed the typical phenomena of social conformity that are regularly encountered in studies of group dynamics among ordinary citizens. For example, some of the phenomena appear to be completely in line with findings from social-psychological experiments showing that powerful social pressures are brought to bear by the members of a cohesive group whenever a dissident begins to voice his objections to a group consensus. Other phenomena are reminiscent of the shared illusions observed in encounter groups and friendship cliques when the members simultaneously reach a peak of "groupy" feelings.

Above all, there are numerous indications pointing to the development of group norms that bolster morale at the expense of critical thinking. One of the most common norms appears to be that of remaining loyal to the group by sticking with the policies to which the group has already committed itself, even when those policies are obviously working out badly and have unintended consequences that disturb the conscience of each member. This is one of the key characteristics of groupthink.

1984

I use the term groupthink as a quick and easy way to refer to the mode of thinking that persons engage in when *concurrence-seeking* becomes so dominant in a cohesive ingroup that it tends to override realistic appraisal of alternative courses of action. Groupthink is a term of the same order as the words in the newspeak vocabulary George Orwell used in his dismaying world of *1984*. In that context, groupthink takes on an invidious connotation. Exactly such a connotation is intended, since the term refers to a deterioration in mental efficiency, reality testing and moral judgments as a result of group pressures.

The symptoms of groupthink arise when the members of decision-making groups become motivated to avoid being too harsh in their judgments of their leaders' or their colleagues' ideas. They adopt a soft line of criticism, even in their own thinking. At their meetings, all the members are amiable and seek complete concurrence on every important issue, with no bickering or conflict to spoil the cozy, "we-feeling" atmosphere.

Kill

Paradoxically, soft-headed groups are often hard-hearted when it comes to dealing with outgroups or enemies. They find it relatively easy to resort to dehumanizing solutions—they will readily authorize bombing attacks that kill large numbers of civilians in the name of the noble cause of persuading an unfriendly government to negotiate at the peace table. They are unlikely to pursue the more difficult and controversial issues that arise when alternatives to a harsh military solution come up for discussion. Nor are they inclined to raise ethical issues that carry the implication that *this fine group of ours, with its humanitarianism and its high-minded principles, might be capable of adopting a course of action that is inhumane and immoral.*

Norms

There is evidence from a number of social-psychological studies that as the members of a group feel more accepted by the others, which is a central feature of increased group cohesiveness, they display less overt conformity to group norms. Thus we would expect that the more cohesive a group becomes, the less the members will feel constrained to censor what they say out of fear of being socially punished for antagonizing the leader or any of their fellow members.

In contrast, the groupthink type of conformity tends to increase as group cohesiveness increases. Groupthink involves nondeliberate suppression of critical thoughts as a result of internalization of the group's norms, which is quite different from deliberate suppression on the basis of external threats of social punishment. The more cohesive the group, the greater the inner compulsion on the part of each member to avoid creating disunity, which inclines him to believe in the soundness of whatever proposals are promoted by the leader or by a majority of the group's members.

In a cohesive group, the danger is not so much that each individual will fail to reveal his objections to what the others propose but that he will think the proposal is a good one, without attempting to carry out a careful, critical scrutiny of the pros and cons of the alternatives. When groupthink becomes dominant, there also is considerable suppression of deviant thoughts, but it takes the form of each person's deciding that his misgivings are not relevant and should be set aside, that the benefit of the doubt regarding any lingering uncertainties should be given to the group consensus.

Stress

I do not mean to imply that all cohesive groups necessarily suffer from groupthink. All ingroups may have a mild tendency toward groupthink, displaying one or another of the symptoms from time to time, but it need not be so dominant as to influence the quality of the group's final decision. Neither do I mean to imply that there is anything necessarily inefficient or harmful about group decisions in general. On the contrary, a group whose members have properly defined roles, with traditions concerning the procedures to follow in pursuing a critical inquiry, probably is capable of making better decisions than any individual group member working alone.

The problem is that the advantages of having decisions made by groups are often lost because of powerful psychological pressures that arise when the members work closely together, share the same set of values and, above all, face a crisis situation that puts everyone under intense stress.

The main principle of groupthink, which I offer in the spirit of Parkinson's Law, is this: *The more amiability and esprit de corps there is among the members of a policy-making ingroup, the greater the danger that independent critical thinking will be replaced by groupthink, which is likely to result in irrational and dehumanizing actions directed against outgroups.*

Symptoms

In my studies of high-level governmental decision-makers, both civilian and military, I have found eight main symptoms of groupthink.
Invulnerability. Most or all of the members of the ingroup share an *illusion* of invulnerability that provides for them some degree of reassurance about obvious dangers and leads them to become overoptimistic and willing to take extraordinary risks. It also causes them to fail to respond to clear warnings of danger.

The Kennedy ingroup, which uncritically accepted the Central Intelligence Agency's disastrous Bay of Pigs plan, operated on the false assumption that they could keep secret the fact that the United States was responsible for the invasion of Cuba. Even after news of the plan began to leak out, their belief remained unshaken. They failed even to consider the danger that awaited them: a worldwide revulsion against the U.S.

A similar attitude appeared among the members of President Lyndon B. Johnson's ingroup, the "Tuesday Cabinet," which kept escalating the Vietnam War despite repeated setbacks and failures. "There was a belief," Bill Moyers commented after he resigned, "that if we indicated a willingness to use our power, they [the North Vietnamese] would get the message and back away from an all-out confrontation. . . . There was a confidence—it was never bragged about, it was just there—that when the chips were really down, the other people would fold."

A most poignant example of an illusion of invulnerability involves the ingroup around Admiral H. E. Kimmel, which failed to prepare for the possibility of a Japanese attack on Pearl Harbor despite repeated warnings. Informed by his intelligence chief that radio contact with Japanese aircraft carriers had been lost, Kimmel joked about it: "What, you don't know where the carriers are? Do you mean to say that they could be rounding Diamond Head (at Honolulu) and you wouldn't know it?" The carriers were in fact moving full-steam toward Kimmel's command post at the time. Laughing together about a danger signal, which labels it as a purely laughing matter, is a characteristic manifestation of groupthink.

Rationale. As we see, victims of groupthink ignore warnings; they also collectively construct rationalizations in order to discount warnings and other forms of negative feedback that, taken seriously, might lead the group members to reconsider their assumptions each time they recommit themselves to past decisions. Why did the Johnson ingroup avoid reconsidering its escalation policy when time and again the expectations on which they based their decisions turned out to be wrong? James C. Thompson Jr., a Harvard historian who spent five years as an observing participant in both the State Department and the White House, tells us that the policymakers avoided critical discussion of their prior decisions and continually invented new rationalizations so that they could sincerely recommit themselves to defeating the North Vietnamese.

In the fall of 1964, before the bombing of North Vietnam began, some of the policymakers predicted that six weeks of air strikes would induce the North Vietnamese to seek peace talks. When someone asked, "What if they don't?" the answer was that another four weeks certainly would do the trick.

Later, after each setback, the ingroup agreed that by investing just a bit more effort (by stepping up the bomb tonnage a bit, for instance), their course of action would prove to be right. *The Pentagon Papers* bear out these observations.

In *The Limits of Intervention,* Townsend Hoopes, who was acting Secretary of the Air Force under Johnson, says that Walt W. Rostow in particular showed a remarkable capacity for what has been called "instant rationalization." According to Hoopes, Rostow buttressed the group's optimism about being on the road to victory by culling selected scraps of evidence from news reports or, if necessary, by inventing "plausible" forecasts that had no basis in evidence at all.

Admiral Kimmel's group rationalized away their warnings, too. Right up to December 7, 1941, they convinced themselves that the Japanese would never dare attempt a full-scale surprise assault against Hawaii because Japan's leaders would realize that it would precipitate an all-out war which the United States would surely win. They made no attempt to look at the situation through the eyes of the Japanese leaders—another manifestation of groupthink.

Morality. Victims of groupthink believe unquestioningly in the inherent morality of their ingroup; this belief inclines the members to ignore the ethical or moral consequences of their decisions.

Evidence that this symptom is at work usually is of a negative kind —the things that are left unsaid in group meetings. At least two influential persons had doubts about the morality of the Bay of Pigs adventure. One of them, Arthur Schlesinger Jr., presented his strong objections in a memorandum to President Kennedy and Secretary of State Rusk but suppressed them when he attended meetings of the Kennedy team. The other, Senator J. William Fulbright, was not a member of the group, but the President invited him to express his misgivings in a speech to the policymakers. However, when Fulbright finished speaking the President moved on to other agenda items.

David Kraslow and Stuart H. Loory, in *The Secret Search for Peace in Vietnam,* report that during 1966 President Johnson's ingroup was concerned primarily with selecting bomb targets in North Vietnam. They based their selections on four factors—the military advantage, the risk to American aircraft and pilots, the danger of forcing other countries into the fighting, and the danger of heavy civilian casualties. At their regular Tuesday luncheons, they weighed these factors the way school teachers grade examination papers, averaging them out. Though evidence on this point is scant, I suspect that the group's ritualistic adherence to a standardized procedure induced the members to feel morally justified in their destructive way of dealing with the Vietnamese people—after all, the danger of heavy civilian casualties from U.S. air strikes was taken into account on their checklists.

Stereotypes. Victims of groupthink hold stereotyped views of the leaders of enemy groups: they are so evil that genuine attempts at negotiating differences with them are unwarranted, or they are too weak or too stupid to deal effectively with whatever attempts the ingroup makes to defeat their purposes, no matter how risky the attempts are.

Kennedy's groupthinkers believed that Premier Fidel Castro's air force was so ineffectual that obsolete B-26s could knock it out completely in a surprise attack before the invasion began. They also believed that Castro's army was so weak that a small Cuban-exile brigade could establish a well-protected beachhead at the Bay of Pigs. In addition, they believed that Castro was not smart enough to put down any possible internal uprisings in support of the exiles. They were wrong on all three assumptions. Though much of the blame was attributable to faulty intelligence, the point is that none of Kennedy's advisers even questioned the CIA planners about these assumptions.

The Johnson advisers' sloganistic thinking about "the Communist apparatus" that was "working all around the world" (as Dean Rusk put it) led them to overlook the powerful nationalistic strivings of the North Vietnamese government and its efforts to ward off Chinese domination. The crudest of all stereotypes used by Johnson's inner circle to justify their policies was the domino theory ("If we don't stop the Reds in South Vietnam, tomorrow they will be in Hawaii and next week they will be in San Francisco," Johnson once said). The group so firmly accepted this stereotype that it became almost impossible for any adviser to introduce a more sophisticated viewpoint.

In the documents on Pearl Harbor, it is clear to see that the Navy commanders stationed in Hawaii had a naive image of Japan as a midget that would not dare to strike a blow against a powerful giant.

Pressure. Victims of groupthink apply direct pressure to any individual who momentarily expresses doubts about any of the group's shared illusions or who questions the validity of the arguments supporting a policy alternative favored by the majority. This gambit reinforces the concurrence-seeking norm that loyal members are expected to maintain.

President Kennedy probably was more active than anyone else in raising skeptical questions during the Bay of Pigs meetings, and yet he seems to have encouraged the group's docile, uncritical acceptance of defective arguments in favor of the CIA's plan. At every meeting, he allowed the CIA representatives to dominate the discussion. He permitted them to give their immediate refutations in response to each tentative doubt that one of the others expressed, instead of asking whether anyone shared the doubt or wanted to pursue the implications of the new worrisome issue that had just been raised. And at the most crucial meeting, when he was calling on each member to give his vote for or against the plan, he did not call on Arthur Schlesinger, the one man there who was known by the President to have serious misgivings.

Historian Thomson informs us that whenever a member of Johnson's ingroup began to express doubts, the group used subtle social pressures to "domesticate" him. To start with, the dissenter was made to feel at home, provided that he lived up to two restrictions: 1) that he did not voice his doubts to outsiders, which would play into the hands of the opposition; and 2) that he kept his criticisms within the bounds of acceptable deviation, which meant not challenging any of the fundamental assumptions that went into the group's prior commitments. One such "domesticated dissenter" was Bill Moyers. When Moyers arrived at a meeting, Thomson tells us, the President greeted him with, "Well, here comes Mr. Stop-the-Bombing."

Self-censorship. Victims of groupthink avoid deviating from what appears to be group consensus; they keep silent about their misgivings and even minimize to themselves the importance of their doubts.

As we have seen, Schlesinger was not at all hesitant about presenting his strong objections to the Bay of Pigs plan in a memorandum to the President and the Secretary of State. But he became keenly aware of his tendency to suppress objections at the White House meetings. "In the months after the Bay of Pigs I bitterly reproached myself for having kept so silent during those crucial discussions in the cabinet room," Schlesinger writes in *A Thousand Days*. "I can only explain my failure to do more than raise a few timid questions by reporting that one's impulse to blow the whistle on this nonsense was simply undone by the circumstances of the discussion."

Unanimity. Victims of groupthink share an *illusion* of unanimity within the group concerning almost all judgments expressed by members who speak in favor of the majority view. This symptom results partly from the preceding one, whose effects are augmented by the false assumption that any individual who remains silent during any part of the discussion is in full accord with what the others are saying.

When a group of persons who respect each other's opinions arrives at a unanimous view, each member is likely to feel that the belief must be true. This reliance on consensual validation within the group tends to replace individual critical thinking and reality testing, unless there are clear-cut disagreements among the members. In contemplating a course of action such as the invasion of Cuba, it is painful for the members to confront disagreements within their group, particularly if it becomes apparent that there are widely divergent views about whether the preferred course of action is too risky to undertake at all. Such disagreements are likely to arouse anxieties about making a serious error. Once the sense of unanimity is shattered, the members no longer can feel complacently confident about the decision they are inclined to make. Each man must then face the annoying realization that there are troublesome uncertainties and he must diligently seek out the best information he can get in order to decide for himself exactly how serious the risks might be. This is one of the unpleasant consequences of being in a group of hard-headed, critical thinkers.

To avoid such an unpleasant state, the members often become inclined, without quite realizing it, to prevent latent disagreements from surfacing when they are about to initiate a risky course of action. The group leader and the members support each other in playing up the areas of convergence in their thinking, at the expense of fully exploring divergencies that might reveal unsettled issues.

"Our meetings took place in a curious atmosphere of assumed consensus," Schlesinger writes. His additional comments clearly show that, curiously, the consensus was an illusion—an illusion that could be maintained only because the major participants did not reveal their own reasoning or discuss their idiosyncratic assumptions and vague reservations. Evidence from several sources makes it clear that even the three principals—President Kennedy, Rusk and McNamara—had widely differing assumptions about the invasion plan.

Mindguards. Victims of groupthink sometimes appoint themselves as mindguards to protect the leader and fellow members from adverse information that might break the complacency they shared about the effectiveness and morality of past decisions. At a large birthday party for his wife, Attorney General Robert F. Kennedy, who had been constantly informed about the Cuban invasion plan, took Schlesinger aside and asked him why he was opposed. Kennedy listened coldly and said, "You may be right or you may be wrong, but the President has made his mind up. Don't push it any further. Now is the time for everyone to help him all they can."

Rusk also functioned as a highly effective mindguard by failing to transmit to the group the strong objections of three "outsiders" who had learned of the invasion plan—Undersecretary of State Chester Bowles, USIA Director Edward R. Murrow, and Rusk's intelligence chief, Roger Hilsman. Had Rusk done so, their warnings might have reinforced Schlesinger's memorandum and jolted some of Kennedy's ingroup, if not the President himself, into reconsidering the decision.

Products

When a group of executives frequently displays most or all of these interrelated symptoms, a detailed study of their deliberations is likely to reveal a number of immediate consequences. These consequences are, in effect, products of poor decision-making practices because they lead to inadequate solutions to the problems under discussion.

1. The group limits its discussions to a few alternative courses of action (often only two) without an initial survey of all the alternatives that might be worthy of consideration.
2. The group fails to reexamine the course of action initially preferred by the majority after they learn of risks and drawbacks they had not considered originally.
3. The members spend little or no time discussing whether there are nonobvious gains they may have overlooked or ways of reducing the

   seemingly prohibitive costs that made rejected alternatives appear undesirable to them.

4. Members make little or no attempt to obtain information from experts within their own organizations who might be able to supply more precise estimates of potential losses and gains.

5. Members show positive interest in facts and opinions that support their preferred policy; they tend to ignore facts and opinions that do not.

6. Members spend little time deliberating about how the chosen policy might be hindered by bureaucratic inertia, sabotaged by political opponents, or temporarily derailed by common accidents. Consequently, they fail to work out contingency plans to cope with foreseeable setbacks that could endanger the overall success of their chosen course.

Support

The search for an explanation of why groupthink occurs has led me through a quagmire of complicated theoretical issues in the murky area of human motivation. My belief, based on recent social psychological research, is that we can best understand the various symptoms of groupthink as a mutual effort among the group members to maintain self-esteem and emotional equanimity by providing social support to each other, especially at times when they share responsibility for making vital decisions.

Even when no important decision is pending, the typical administrator will begin to doubt the wisdom and morality of his past decisions each time he receives information about setbacks, particularly if the information is accompanied by negative feedback from prominent men who originally had been his supporters. It should not be surprising, therefore, to find that individual members strive to develop unanimity and esprit de corps that will help bolster each other's morale, to create an optimistic outlook about the success of pending decisions, and to reaffirm the positive value of past policies to which all of them are committed.

Pride

Shared illusions of invulnerability, for example, can reduce anxiety about taking risks. Rationalizations help members believe that the risks are really not so bad after all. The assumption of inherent morality helps the members to avoid feelings of shame or guilt. Negative stereotypes function as stress-reducing devices to enhance a sense of moral righteousness as well as pride in a lofty mission.

The mutual enhancement of self-esteem and morale may have functional value in enabling the members to maintain their capacity to take action, but it has maladaptive consequences insofar as concurrence-seeking tendencies interfere with critical, rational capacities and lead to serious errors of judgment.

While I have limited my study to decision-making bodies in Government, groupthink symptoms appear in business, industry and any other field where small, cohesive groups make the decisions. It is vital, then, for all sorts of people—and especially group leaders—to know what steps they can take to prevent groupthink.

Remedies

To counterpoint my case studies of the major fiascos, I have also investigated two highly successful group enterprises, the formulation of the Marshall Plan in the Truman Administration and the handling of the Cuban missile crisis by President Kennedy and his advisers. I have found it instructive to examine the steps Kennedy took to change his group's decision-making processes. These changes ensured that the mistakes made by his Bay of Pigs ingroup were not repeated by the missile-crisis ingroup, even though the membership of both groups was essentially the same.

The following recommendations for preventing groupthink incorporate many of the good practices I discovered to be characteristic of the Marshall Plan and missile-crisis groups:

1. The leader of a policy-forming group should assign the role of critical evaluator to each member, encouraging the group to give high priority to open airing of objections and doubts. This practice needs to be reinforced by the leader's acceptance of criticism of his own judgments in order to discourage members from soft-pedaling their disagreements and from allowing their striving for concurrence to inhibit critical thinking.

2. When the key members of a hierarchy assign a policy-planning mission to any group within their organization, they should adopt an impartial stance instead of stating preferences and expectations at the beginning. This will encourage open inquiry and impartial probing of a wide range of policy alternatives.

3. The organization routinely should set up several outside policy-planning and evaluation groups to work on the same policy question, each deliberating under a different leader. This can prevent the insulation of an ingroup.

4. At intervals before the group reaches a final consensus, the leader should require each member to discuss the group's deliberations with associates in his own unit of the organization—assuming that those associates can be trusted to adhere to the same security regulations that govern the policymakers—and then to report back their reactions to the group.

5. The group should invite one or more outside experts to each meeting on a staggered basis and encourage the experts to challenge the views of the core members.

6. At every general meeting of the group, whenever the agenda calls for an evaluation of policy alternatives, at least one member should play devil's advocate, functioning as a good lawyer in challenging the testimony of those who advocate the majority position.

7. Whenever the policy issue involves relations with a rival nation or organization, the group should devote a sizable block of time, perhaps an entire session, to a survey of all warning signals from the rivals and should write alternative scenarios on the rivals' intentions.

8. When the group is surveying policy alternatives for feasibility and effectiveness, it should from time to time divide into two or more subgroups to meet separately, under different chairmen, and then come back together to hammer out differences.

9. After reaching a preliminary consensus about what seems to be the best policy, the group should hold a "second-chance" meeting at which every member expresses as vividly as he can all his residual doubts, and rethinks the entire issue before making a definitive choice.

HOW

These recommendations have their disadvantages. To encourage the open airing of objections, for instance, might lead to prolonged and costly debates when a rapidly growing crisis requires immediate solution. It also could cause rejection, depression and anger. A leader's failure to set a norm might create cleavage between leader and members that could develop into a disruptive power struggle if the leader looks on the emerging consensus as anathema. Setting up outside evaluation groups might increase the risk of security leakage. Still, inventive executives who know their way around the organizational maze probably can figure out how to apply one or another of the prescriptions successfully, without harmful side effects.

They also could benefit from the advice of outside experts in the administrative and behavioral sciences. Though these experts have much to offer, they have had few chances to work on policy-making machinery within large organizations. As matters now stand, executives innovate only when they need new procedures to avoid repeating serious errors that have deflated their self-images.

In this era of atomic warheads, urban disorganization and ecocatastrophes, it seems to me that policymakers should collaborate with behavioral scientists and give top priority to preventing groupthink and its attendant fiascos.

PUBLIC
COMMUNICATION_____6

In the first selection, Mills and Bauer offer a practical and helpful set of guidelines to follow in planning a speech. The outline form at the end of their selection is especially helpful for organizing your material. In the second selection, we offer some description of the types of supporting materials which can be used to develop the ideas a speaker would like to convey.

In the third selection, Applbaum and Anatol review some of the research findings relevant to the message aspects of public communication. In the fourth selection, Barker offers some specific suggestions for developing our skills as receivers. We think listening is an often neglected facet of public communication.

Glen E. Mills and Otto F. Bauer

PUTTING A SPEECH TOGETHER

Speechmaking is a total, unified process involving many components of attitude, knowledge, and skill. Its complexity is such that the total process cannot be learned at once. It must for pedagogical reasons be divided into manageable units such as we find in this and other textbooks.

DETERMINE THE GENERAL PURPOSE

Sometimes the general or primary purpose is a speaker's first concern, while at other times it is considered after the general subject is selected. In case either a subject or a purpose is assigned, there is no question about priority; the speaker begins with what he has been given.

Speeches that amount to anything are made for purposes, goals, or ends that represent the kinds of responses sought by speakers from their listeners. These purposes may be either rhetorical or non-rhetorical. However compelling a non-rhetorical purpose (such as impressing a boss or getting a grade) may be, it lies outside our purview here. We are concerned with speeches to inform, to entertain, and to persuade.

These purposes are often mixed and sometimes subdivided. For instance, a primarily persuasive speech is likely to have an informative secondary purpose. Also, a persuasive speech may reinforce an existing belief, change a belief, or move to action. However, in the interest of clarity we shall discuss the three general purposes as if they were unmixed.

A speech to inform is intended to clarify concepts or processes, to enlighten the understanding, to add knowledge, or to stimulate thought. It often appears as a report, and it is supposed to give correct, unbiased information. An explanation of a state primary election would be a case in point.

A speech to entertain is intended to create a diversion or to provide enjoyment, but not necessarily through the use of stories and humor. An account of an interesting true adventure could be made entertaining. The techniques can be more important than the subject in determining whether the speech will entertain.

A speech to persuade may only stimulate, reinforce or excite existing attitudes, or impress a believing audience. It may go further and convince listeners to modify attitudes, accept a new idea, or endorse a solution. Some say a speech may also be designed to confuse. Finally, a persuasive speech may actuate, which means to move persons beyond the endorsement of an idea to the taking of some action on its behalf. Some of the books handle these subdivisions separately.

SELECT THE GENERAL SUBJECT

. . . here we are concerned with the analysis of audience, occasion, and speaker as determinants of general subjects. This is done with the understanding that these kinds of analysis are also related to the other steps in putting a speech together: choosing specific subjects, formulating specific purposes, stating central ideas, and so forth.

Analyze the Audience

It is no accident that most speech reference textbooks offer advice on audience analysis. No doubt most inexperienced persons would think it a matter of common sense to ask who is going to hear them speak. But just how much and what sorts of analysis are feasible to perform are more complex problems. The important thing is to be audience-centered at this stage, whether the audience is your speech class or not. It pays to find common bonds for use in adaptation. What interests these listeners? What concerns them? What do they know about certain matters? What do they think is worthwhile? What are they "touchy" about?

When some of these variables seem important, and when it is feasible to estimate them, try to learn what you can about your listeners in terms of:

(1) knowledge
(2) beliefs and attitudes (neutral, friendly, indifferent, opposed, and mixed)
(3) expectations for this event
(4) cultural, social, educational, and linguistic status
(5) occupations and other affiliations,
(6) avocations and hobbies
(7) size of audience,
(8) age and sex distribution

How can this be done? Most often a speaker observes in advance or asks others who seem to know the people. But when one has a captive audience, as in a school, a camp, or a prison, he can do a more sophisticated analysis. Likert-type attitude scales and objective information tests have been used occasionally. When much class time is available for this activity, a three-step procedure can be used:

(1) A speaker gives a short oral report on his intended proposition, main points, etc., or he merely mentions the controversy and its background
(2) In a brief forum period he estimates the interest, knowledge, and attitudes of the class
(3) He then continues his preparation, making adaptations alone or in consultation with the teacher.[1]

Analyze the Occasion

If you have freedom to choose your subject, the nature of the meeting and your purpose in being there may determine or at least suggest a subject. When the meeting is occasioned by a Red Cross drive, a town's centennial, or

---

[1]Kully, R., and Brockriede, W. "An Exercise in Audience Analysis," *Central States Speech Journal*, XIV (1963), 292-4.

a speech contest on patriotism, certain general subjects are implied. Even if the nature of the occasion fails to provide a subject, it can at least suggest guidelines as to what would be appropriate or timely. Several questions come to mind: What is the occasion about? Why me? How large an event is it to be? Will attendance be voluntary? What will be the conditions in terms of time limit, program content, place, acoustics, and the like?

Analyze Yourself

On what are you qualified, or on what can you soon become qualified, to speak? Can you bring some originality to it? Does the subject seem worthwhile to you? Are you enthusiastic about it? Answers to these questions can be approached through a kind of self-survey. Explore your interests in terms of hobbies, courses, current affairs, and sensitivity to your environment. Check out your background in home life, schooling, reading, and experiences on jobs or in travel. Finally, what of your ability to handle the subjects that occur to you?

NARROW THE SUBJECT AND THE PURPOSE

Choose a Specific Subject

Usually this means limiting or narrowing the selected general subject, but whether it does or not, we must realize that the analysis of a subject begins here. Some limitation is frequently necessary because the general subject is too broad for the speaker, the time limit, or other factors. Modern art, automation, and Africa are instances of this. The African subject could be reduced to the Congo and still further to the prospects for political stability in the Congo.

Time limitations and the nature of the speaking occasion must be taken into account. If the Congolese problem proves to be too much for four minutes, if that is the limit, narrow it further or give a series of two or more talks on it. There are occasions which call for broad subjects, as in inspirational addresses, and there are some which demand narrow ones, as in persuasive speeches for specific actions.

Limitations may also be imposed by your audience. The usefulness of some topics within your general subject can be seriously affected by such variables as education, intelligence, experience, occupation, attention span, and the curve of forgetting. These hints echo the earlier advice on audience analysis.

Your own knowledge and purpose as a speaker obviously impose limitations upon your choice of a specific subject. If the purpose is impressiveness, controversial topics should be used sparingly. If it is entertainment, sad topics are inappropriate. Use whatever is within your competence and will contribute to the realization of your purpose.

Sometimes this advice will require you to broaden rather than narrow your subject. Suppose a friend tells you he has been "cut off" by his family because he defied a parental ultimatum and majored in dramatics instead of engineering. At first you are moved to inveigh against this parental pigheadedness, but on second thought you decide to broaden your subject and talk on the wisdom of "leaving the door ajar" in a controversy: "Never Say 'Never' in Negotiations."

Formulate a Specific Purpose

This is your declaration, mainly for your own guidance, of what you want to do with the audience. It will be treated in relation to the narrowing of subjects and purposes. First, a specific purpose should be expressed in an infinitive phrase: "To instruct my classmates in Speech 100 so that they will be able to apply artificial respiration." This is like writing a note to yourself but not necessarily stating it to the audience in so many words. Secondly, it is not the central idea, as you will see in the next paragraph. Thirdly, it limits the scope of the speech by stating the speaker's intention or the precise response sought. Thus the phrasing is audience-centered. Finally, the specific purpose serves as a guide to preparation, particularly analysis and investigation. As Seneca observed centuries ago, "When a man does not know to what port he is steering, no wind is favorable to him."

State the Central Idea

We first stress the difference between central idea and specific purpose. A central idea is expressed in terms of speech content, while a specific purpose states the desired audience response. Some writers call the central idea a theme, core, thesis, or proposition, depending upon the kind of speech they are dealing with. In any case it is a unifying thought which, when it is written in an outline, is placed somewhere ahead of the body or discussion section. This subject sentence should be simple, concise, complete, and declarative. In other words, it conveys a single idea positively.

Note this progression which illustrates the foregoing steps in this chapter:

> General Purpose—To persuade
> General Subject—Voting
> Specific Subject—Importance of voting
> Specific Purpose—To move my classmates in Speech 100 to vote in next week's campus election.
> Central Idea—Get out and vote in the campus election next Friday.

ARRANGE THE MATERIALS

Set Out the Main Points

These topics, which were derived by analyzing the subject, serve to develop the central idea. Questions concerning what these points are and how many there should be have been answered. Now we shall add that these main points, which bear Roman numerals in outlines, are major divisions which directly support the central idea by proving, explaining, or illustrating it. These topics are to be related to each other without overlapping or duplication; they are presumably coordinate, meaning similar in rank and importance. Finally, when composing these main points, make them terse, vivid, and appealing to audience interests.

State the Subpoints

Being of the second order of magnitude, so to speak, these items serve to prove, explain, or illustrate the main points. These lesser points must be

Speech Outline

NAME _____ SECTION _____ DATE _____

(12th Step)   TITLE of Speech _____

SUBJECT

(2nd Step)   State your general subject:

(3rd Step)   State your specific subject:

PURPOSE

(1st Step)   State your general purpose:

(4th Step)   State your specific purpose:

CENTRAL IDEA

(5th Step)   State the central idea and partition it into its MAIN POINTS.

I.

II.

III.

INTRODUCTION

(10th Step)   Write the introduction as you plan to give it.

This introduction will:

_____ Arouse attention. _____ Gain good will. _____ Lead into the subject.

NAME _____ SECTION _____ DATE _____

BODY

(6th Step)   State the first main point.

I.

(7th Step)   Choose subpoints which develop the first
             main point.

A.

(8th Step)   Give statistics, illustrations, testimony, etc.,
             which support the subpoints

1.

2.

B.

1.

2.

(11th Step) Write a transition between the first and
             second main points.

NOTICE: Repeat steps 6, 7, and 8 for additional main
        points.

II.

A.

1.

2.

B.

1.

2.

Describe your *tactics* of
persuasion for a(n)

a. Believing audience.
b. Neutral audience.
c. Opposing audience.
d. Apathetic audience.

NAME _____ SECTION _____ DATE _____

(11th Step) Write a transition between the second and third main points.

Describe your *tactics* of persuasion for a(n)

III.

A.

  1.

  2.

B.

  1.

  2.

a. Believing audience.
b. Neutral audience.
c. Opposing audience.
d. Apathetic audience.

CONCLUSION

(9th Step) Write the conclusion as you plan to give it.

This conclusion will:

___ Summarize. ___ Restate central idea. ___ Make final appeal. ___ Indicate desired action.

Bibliography: State sources; use correct bibliographical form.

  1.

  2.

  3.

  4.

Instructor's Critique

NAME _____ SECTION _____ DATE _____

SUBJECT _____ ASSIGNMENT _____ TIME _____

                                                    GRADE _____

Basic Principles	Comments
MASTER THE CONTENT	
Subject	
Analysis	
Information	
Inferences	
ORGANIZE MATERIALS CAREFULLY	
Specific Purpose	
Central Idea	
Introduction	
Main Points	
Conclusion	
MAKE YOUR LANGUAGE COUNT	
Clarity	
Eloquence	
DEVELOP EFFECTIVE DELIVERY	
Body	
Voice	
OTHER COMMENTS:	

coordinate among themselves, but any of them can be subdivided in turn. Any supporting materials which are listed in the next major section of this chapter appear in these subpoints or in their subdivisions. Customarily there are two or more subpoints per point, but on rare occasions one will suffice. Capital letters usually identify the first rank of subpoints in outlines.

Select a Pattern of Arrangement

Before you select any pattern, think of it as a means and not an end. It is just another device to help you to get your central idea across. Even so, it helps you to outline better, and it makes for a consistent viewpoint in the speech. Many textbooks explain these patterns: time order, space order, partition of a theme, increasing-difficulty orders, topical-classification order, issues and values (for persuasion), extended-analogy order, and repetition of a pattern.

Follow the Principles of Outlining

These principles apply to all outlining, but there may be less confusion as you consult two or more books if you keep in mind three ways of classifying one outline: (1) topical or logical, (2) words, phrases, or sentences, and (3) preparation or presentation. In a topical outline, the subtopics explain or illustrate their immediately superior points, while in a logical outline each subpoint is connected to its superior point by "because" for the purpose of designating a probative relationship. In order for this connective to make sense, complete sentences must be used. Topical outlines often have words and phrases as points. A classification based solely upon words, phrases, or sentences requires no further exposition. The main difference between a preparation outline and a presentation outline is the length, detail, and completeness of the former.

At least six principles apply to all classes of outlines. The first is simpleness, or one idea per point:

I. Married women should not be hired because
   A. Their jobs are needed by others.

Second is coordination, which means the points have a generic relationship as in A-B-C below:

I. Protestant churches in Podunk
   A. Presbyterian
   B. Methodist
   C. Baptist

The third is subordination, which may be seen in the relationship of A, B, and C to I above. Fourth is discreteness or the distinctness of each point. There is no merging or overlapping:

I. How to seed a lawn
   A. Rake the ground
   B. Sow seed
   C. Fertilize
   D. Roll the surface
   E. Water regularly

The fifth principle is sequence, which calls for a significant order of progression as in any of the patterns of arrangement above. Symbolization to identify the rank of each point in terms of coordination and subordination is the sixth principle of all outlining. It is demonstrated above.

SUPPORT THE TOPICS

Support or development is taken to include all materials and methods a speaker uses to make each topic (point) specific, concrete, vivid, credible, moving, clear, amusing, or whatever else is intended.

How does one know which materials he needs and where they belong in his speech? The preceding steps in putting a speech together have cumulatively guided the speaker to the time when he must add supporting substance to the framework. Through analysis he has determined which points he will use and must develop, and through investigation he presumably has found the materials of development.

In the non-inferential category, which includes all but the kinds of reasoning, there are description, explanation, instances and illustrations, factual statements, comparison and contrast, authoritative testimony, quotations and proverbs, stories, and audio-visual aids. The inferential supports, as treated in this book, are analogy, causal relation, sign, and generalization. However, as we remarked earlier, both the non-inferential and the inferential supports are variously named and grouped in the ten reference works.

SUPPLY THE FINISHING TOUCHES

Compose the Conclusion

The functions of the final lines of a speech are such that the conclusion is often composed before the introduction. In various ways the closing remarks focus upon the central idea: by pointing up the main topics, by clarifying through application or illustration, by facilitating action, by summarizing, or by leaving a positive impression of the speaker. These are frequently overlapping or even mixed in actual practice, as the names of the types of conclusions will suggest. Several writers distinguish among the types they call summary (repetition or restatement), epitome, inspirational, hortatory, application, challenge, and quotation conclusions.

Some hints on content and style will be summarized here. Among the typical contents of conclusions are quotations, forecasts, striking remarks, questions, review or restatement, and direct ethical appeal. The general rule is that a conclusion does not take a new step in the development of the central idea. Nor should it be abrupt, anticlimactic, complex, or apologetic. Instead, it should be shorter than the introduction, smooth in style, consistent with the body in tone, and *sound* like a conclusion. For these reasons it is a good idea to write the conclusion of an extemporaneous speech.

Compose the Introduction

Opening remarks serve to introduce the speaker and his message to the audience. If there is an introducer, there is less of this for the main speaker to do. In any case there is something to be done to achieve attention and rapport, although the problem of contact varies enormously among audiences and speakers. If the audience needs some background to understand the subject, the introduction should provide it. Then, of course, the subject is set out, unless an indirect order is being used for effect. Finally, the introduction leads into the body or discussion.

It typically does so by announcing the subject outright, explaining the context, or motivating attention. Among the specific devices that are available are challenging questions, startling statement, personal reference, apt quotation or anecdote, narrated event, reference to timeliness of subject, expression of appreciation, pleasantry or humor, reference to present setting, and adaptation to preceding remarks.

In using any of these, beware of the temptation to be trite, pompous, misleading, or apologetic. Strive to be interesting, and work for a confident but modest tone. Because it is so important as well as so difficult to get started right, try writing some of your introductions.

Work on Transitions

Have you heard a jerky speech recently? Or given one? If so, you can attribute some of the fault to the neglect of transitions. These are words, phrases, and sentences that serve as bridges between the introduction and the body, between points in the body, and between the body and the conclusion. They will be dull, trite, or mechanical if you don't give them some thought. "My second point is," "and another thing," and "and then" sound familiar, don't they?

It is well to think of transitions as signposts which point forward to the first topic but both ways between topics one and two. While pointing they indicate coordination or subordination. For coordination we use *furthermore, moreover, however, and yet, also,* and *finally.* For subordination we use *because, since, for, therefore, for example, let me explain,* and the like.

Title the Speech

When a speech is to be publicized, or when an introducer is going to present the speaker, a title is worth thinking about. It takes imagination or cleverness to invent attractive titles, but perhaps a few hints will help. We are told that a title should be short (seven or fewer words), pertinent to the subject, appropriate to the context, "catchy" but not "cute," and suggestive.

QUESTIONS

(For oral or written reports). Prepare a descriptive, critical, content analysis of one of the specimen speeches in this book or elsewhere. Identify and evaluate as many of the following items as the teacher specifies. Sometimes these items of critical apparatus are divided among several individuals or committees:

(a) general purpose, (b) general subject (in relation to the three-fold analysis), (c) specific subject, (d) specific purpose, (e) central idea, (f) outline of main points and principal subpoints, (g) pattern of arrangement, (h) forms of support used, (i) conclusion, (j) introduction, (k) transitions, (l) the title.

Robert M. Carter and Stewart L. Tubbs

SUPPORTING MATERIALS FOR PUBLIC COMMUNICATION

Once a speaker has selected a topic and determined a central idea for a speech, the question becomes "How do I develop or expand on the central idea?" As we saw in the selection by Mills and Bauer, the speaker must then determine the main points and subpoints he or she wants to use to elaborate on the central idea. Once these points have been determined, the next step is to choose the appropriate supporting materials which will help make the points more memorable.

There are basically four methods of support which a speaker might want to use. These include (1) examples, (2) statistics, (3) quotations, and (4) analogies. Before we take a closer look at each of these, keep in mind that all four types of supporting materials can be made even more vivid by the use of audio-visual aids. Examples or statistics can be made more dramatic through the use of such nonverbal means as photographs, drawings, charts or graphs. Examples and quotations can be made more vivid through the use of audio tape recorders which allow the listener to hear the original source. At least one research study (Nelson and VanderMeer, 1953) has shown that the use of visual aids in informative speeches significantly increases audience retention of the speaker's points. To repeat, each of the four methods of support may be further strengthened by using an audio-visual aid in combination with the method of support.

EXAMPLES

Imagine that as you sit listening to a boring lecture, you begin to escape into sleep. Just at that moment you hear the speaker say, "Here's an example." You rouse yourself to listen to a bit more. You vaguely recall that the lecture deals with "Off-beat People". You hear, "A noted homosexual woman of the nineteenth century, Rosa Bonheur, gained more fame than any other painter for her representations of animals." Now you have one eye open. And when the speaker goes on to how "Examples of homoerotic males include the Greek general who conquered the known world, Alexander the Great, and the leading Artist of the Italian Renaissance, Michaelangelo," you find yourself attentive.

Often, examples bring the obscure into the understandable area of your consciousness. A lecture on the development of the integrated circuit (IC) leaves you cold until the speaker holds up a pocket calculator explaining that only with the IC can such a miniaturization happen. He then provides the example of outer space vehicles where the same condition pertains.

Consider the impact on young ears of Aesop's fables. A fable amounts to a story example with animals representing people. Perhaps without the story examples, we would never have heard of Aesop's teachings.

And what of the parable example? In the New Testament, Jesus illustrated his teachings about morality in the form of parables.

Someone may tell you that a two-line poem can sometimes make a point, but if he or she presents one as an example, you may remember it longer:

Executive with starched white collar,
What dreams have died to bring in dollar?

STATISTICS

Many ideas can be explained in a quantitative fashion. If we state that the divorce rate is increasing in America that is one thing. However, if we state that the divorce rate has doubled in the last ten years we are using a statistic to quantify the first statement. In one persuasive speech about hotdogs, a speaker stated that about 40 percent of the content of a hotdog is water. He went on to examine all of the other ingredients in hotdogs and the percentage of the total which they represented. He used a real hotdog to show the total and sliced off different sized segments to show the approximate percentages of protein, filler, water, etc.

In a speech on job satisfaction, the speaker used statistics combined with a visual aid to persuasively argue that most people are satisfied with their jobs and that the level of job satisfaction has not changed significantly over the past two decades.

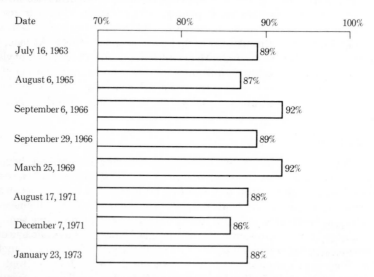

FIG.6-1. *Percentage of "Satisfied" Workers, 1963-1973, based on eight Gallup Polls (men only, ages 21 through 65)*

QUOTATIONS

Now suppose you are preparing a speech, and you want to make a point about how word symbols can mean different things in varying contexts. It may help if you simply quote a dictionary (Merriam-Webster's New Collegiate, 1951 edition). The words you have in mind are conversation and criminal.

"CONVERSATION: . . . social interchange . . . "
"CRIMINAL: . . . a felon . . . "

Still quoting, you turn to:

> "CRIMINAL CONVERSATION: . . . unlawful intercourse with a married woman; adultery . . . "

You have made your point with the authority of a leading dictionary with the simple use of quotation.

We have all read that Nineteenth Century speeches possessed a flowery oratorical style, but we may really believe it if a speaker quotes some passages from speeches delivered then. Consider these excerpts from T. B. Reed's *Modern Eloquence,* Philadelphia: John D. Morris, 1900—

> William M. Evarts (1881) "It is with great pride, as well as with great pleasure, that I respond to the call [to speak] in behalf of the merchants of the United States, through this ancient guild of the Chamber of Commerce, in paying their tribute of honor and applause to the French nation, that was present as a nation in the contest of our Revolution, and is present here [New York City] as a nation by its representatives today; and to the great Frenchmen that were present with their personal heroism in the struggles of the Revolution, and are present here in their personal descendants, to see the fruits of that Revolution, and to receive our respectful greeting; and to the Germans who were present, where they could not have been spared in the great trials of our feeble nation in its struggle against the greatest power in the world, and who are here, by the descendants of those heroic Germans, to join in this feast of freedom and of glory."

> Thomas H. Huxley (1883) " . . . I have noticed of late years a great and growing tendency among those who were once jestingly said to have been born in a pre-scientific age to look upon science as an invading and aggressive force, which if it had its own way would oust from the universe all other pursuits."

Contrast these with today's speeches, and you see our point.

ANALOGIES

An analogy is a comparison between two similar phenomena. Analogies may be either literal or figurative. A literal analogy makes a comparison between two things that are quite similar, while a figurative analogy compares things that are more different than alike.

One speaker employed a literal analogy by arguing that the leader of a work group was like the captain of a football team. He or she had to command the respect of the followers in order to have sufficient leadership influence. Literal analogies are often more valid but less colorful than figurative analogies.

A figurative analogy was used by one speaker who was trying to convince his audience to improve the nutritional aspects of their diet. He argued that just as a car needs gasoline with the proper octane rating for its engine, so too does the human body need the appropriate nutritional ingredients for its systems to run effectively. Another figurative analogy is the idea that "you shouldn't change horses in midstream." This saying applies to political elections in that to continue with the incumbent is better than changing to a lesser known candidate.

Analogies often provide a very interesting and influential type of supporting material; however, sooner or later most analogies do break down due to the differences between things being compared.

In summary, supporting materials include four types: (1) examples, (2) statistics, (3) quotations, and (4) analogies. Keep in mind that these may be used in combination, you need not limit yourself to only one in any given speech.

REFERENCES

H. E. Nelson and A. W. VanderMeer, "Varied Sound Tracks on Animated Film," *Speech Monographs*, XX (1953), 261-267.

Ronald L. Applbaum and Karl W. E. Anatol

THE EFFECTS OF THE MESSAGE ON PERSUASIVE COMMUNICATION

In the preceding chapter, we found that a great percentage of our daily activity is spent communicating—reading, writing, speaking, and listening. A source transmits by speaking or writing his persuasive ideas to a receiver. In turn, the receiver listens to or reads these persuasive appeals. The source's ideas are communicated to the receiver through a *message*. A persuasive message may be transmitted in many forms: a speech, conversation, telephone call, textbook, letter, photograph, billboard, and so on.

Messages are composed of symbols, verbal and nonverbal, which can elicit particular meanings and responses from receivers. In persuasion, the source develops a message with a specific response in mind. For successful persuasion, the meaning given the symbols composing the message must be similar for source and receiver; persuasive communication is dependent upon the use of symbolic messages having shared meaning for sources and receivers. Imagine a persuasive situation in which a husband is talking to his wife at home. He slouches into a chair, hands trembling, voice quivering, and shouts the following: "Sue, I'm worried. The Governor has said we'll get a raise, but you know how two-faced he can be. Inflation is so bad we may be forced to cut down on our activities. Will you help me write a letter to our state senator urging him to support our proposed raise?"

A number of messages may have been communicated by the husband to his wife in this persuasive situation. The quivering voice, trembling hands, and slouching into the chair acting as nonverbal symbols may have indicated to the wife that her husband was tense, nervous, and disturbed. The oral-verbal message may have provided additional information indicating his specific distress and the behavioral response he desired. For his persuasive appeal to be successful, it must be assumed that the wife correctly interpreted the nonverbal symbols and, thereby, established the correct context for the subsequent verbal communication. Second, it must be assumed that she understood the oral message. For example, the husband states that inflation may "cut down on our activities" or "you know how two-faced he can be." The wife must share the meanings of these two ideas for the message to make sense and provide justification for the intended response. Unless the meanings of the messages are shared by source and receiver, attempts at persuasion are fruitless.

Let's imagine, once more, sitting around a dinner table with friends talking about a politician we've just heard on television. The politician's speech is his persuasive message. In attempting to explain our reaction to the speech we might suggest, "he shouldn't have put his best arguments last," or "he sounded disorganized." These evaluative judgments reflect a concern over the form or organization of the message. Messages do not exist as single words, but are created from the placement or ordering of groups of words (paragraphs, chapters, arguments, summaries, and so on) to provide the specific meaning of the persuasive communication for the receiver. We might also suggest, "his message attempted to frighten us," or "he only stated his side." These reactions reflect a recognition of the importance of the contents of the message in a persuasive communication. The source must decide what materials will appeal to the receiver and, thus, encourage the receiver to accept the source's position. At other times our reactions to the politician's speech may run from, "I don't like the way he sounds" to, "he's rather pompous, don't you think?" These reactions reflect a concern for the manner in which the message is presented to the receiver. The source decides how best to present his organized content to the receiver. The presentation of a message is sometimes called *delivery*. However, in today's society, the term delivery has a more restricted meaning —the presentation of a formal speech or lecture.

This essay is divided into three sections: (1) form of the message; (2) content of the message; and (3) presentation of the message. We will consider only message variables relating to persuasion. Although we will examine each message variable in isolation, it must be emphasized that message variables do not exist in isolation; they are only one part of the total message. In turn, the message, while discussed separately from source, channel, receiver, and situation, never occurs without the presence and effect of these other persuasive elements. It is beyond the scope of this text to investigate all message variables and their interrelationships within the persuasive situation. We will examine only those message variables that have been extensively researched and appear to affect attitude or behavior change.

FORM OF THE MESSAGE

Why organize a message? Why not just give an individual the right information? He'll change the way he feels, believes, or behaves. The assumption that providing information without consideration of its form will change attitudes is widely held but not always correct. Despite all the money and time spent by advertisers devising persuasive appeals based on this assumption, most of their work is wasted. Adding new information without consideration of its form is an effective agent of change in very specialized situations, that is, when information refers to some person, object, or thing for which we have no existing attitudes. This is indeed a rare situation. New information that contradicts an existing attitude is usually distorted to fit our existing cognitive structures. Jack Haskins (1966) in a review of advertising and psychological literature found "no relationship between what a person learned, knew, or recalled on one hand, and what he did or how he felt on the other . . . Telling him *(the receiver)* the facts" does not necessarily influence his attitudes or behavior.

One variable that does affect the persuasive appeal of information (new or old) is the message's organization. Since communication is a process, and each communication effort is a unique attempt at expressing a message, the organization of a message is a situational phenomenon. A speaker organizes his message according to the situation. In our examination of message organization, we limit discussion to the form of a message as it applies to introductions, conclusions, ordered versus disordered messages, and the question of primacy-recency.

Introductions—Conclusions

It is difficult to conclude whether an introduction is needed or what type of introduction is preferred in a persuasive situation. It would be foolish to assume that introductions are of no value when so many speakers use them and so many teachers of speech communication recommend their use. However, reaching any conclusions about the effectiveness of introductions is difficult. Since what comes before something else in a message has an effect on what follows and since the introduction of speakers has an effect on the audience's attitude toward the speaker and his subject matter, it is obvious that introductory material in a message will have an effect on the other parts of the message, the perception of the source and message by the receiver, the retention of the message by the receiver, and the persuasive impact of the message on the receiver.

Introductions appear to have a persuasive effect upon the receiver. Allyn and Festinger (1961) found that when receivers holding a position strongly were told in advance about the content of a communication arguing against their position, they had less change in attitude than when they were not told about the communication content. The introduction also interacts with the source to affect the receiver's attitudes. Receivers change less when a disliked source in his introduction announces his persuasive intention than when he does not *mention* his intent (Mills and Aronson 1965). In the same regard, receivers change more when a well-liked source admits his persuasive intent. Despite these findings, we still do not have conclusive evidence of either the effect or need for introductions. The inclusion of an introduction is a situational phenomenon that seems related to the issue, the source credibility, and receiver involvement in the topic.

The use of conclusions in messages is no less a situational phenomenon than introductions. It has been suggested that the effectiveness of conclusions is influenced by the kind of communication, audience, issue, and degree of explicitness with which the conclusions are drawn (Hovland, Janis, and Kelley 1953; Cohen 1964; Karlin and Abelson 1970).

We might ask, is it better for the source to state his conclusions explicitly or let the receiver draw his own conclusions? Hovland and Mandel (1952) presented receivers with two messages that were exactly the same except that one drew the conclusions at the end (explicit) and the other did not (implicit). They found that more receivers changed their opinions in the direction advocated by the source when the conclusions were explicitly stated. Cooper and Dinerman (1951), working with a film presentation, discovered that implicit messages influenced the more intelligent members of the audience but not the less intelligent. It has also been found that stating conclusions in a message is more effective in changing the opinions of the less intelligent (Thistlethwaite, deHaan, and Kamenetsky 1955). The more intelligent may resent having conclusions drawn for them, particularly when they are obvious conclusions. However, where an issue is highly complex, stating the conclusion explicitly may be more effective (Krech, Crutchfield and Ballachey 1962). What if the receivers do not favor the source's position? In this situation, Weiss and Steenbock (1965) found that a persuasive message presenting conclusions is more effective in changing attitudes.

The findings would seem to indicate that when using highly complex messages, addressing less intelligent receivers, or when receivers are initially unfavorable, it may be wise to state the conclusions explicitly. When dealing with an intelligent audience, particularly with simple problems, it would be best to have implicit conclusions. In some situations, the audience may view a statement of conclusions as "propaganda" and become more hostile or suspicious, thus resisting any persuasive attempts.

We have all been confronted with the communicator who asks us directly to take some form of action or adopt a certain belief. We might ask, Where should a direct appeal be placed in persuasive messages? Appeals for receiver change appear more effective if they are placed in the conclusion rather than anywhere else in the message (Leventhal and Singer 1966). While conclusions that ask for a large amount of change produce more change than conclusions asking for less change, the change attained is less than the speaker asks for (Hovland and Pritzker 1957).

Ordered versus Disordered Messages

Should a speech be presented in some orderly manner or not? Smith (1951) found that minor disorganization has no significant effect on attitude change, but major reorganization (rearranging major units of the speech such as the introduction, transitions, and conclusions) leads to significantly less attitude change than when the material is presented in correct order. Thompson (1960) and Darnell (1963), on the other hand, found differences in retention due to rearrangement (rearranging sentences within various parts of a speech), but no differences in attitude change.

Baker (1965) manipulated "disorganization cues," having the speaker apologize in the speech for his lack of organization, and found no significant differences in attitude change between groups hearing the organized or disorganized messages. However, most research indicates that the presence of disorganization brings about a reduction in attitude change (McCrosky and Mehrley 1969; Jones and Serlousky 1971).

The disorganization of a speech appears to affect attitude change, an audience's retention of a message, and the source's evaluation, but it is not clear if disorganization affects the listener's understanding of the message. Beighley (1952), who randomly rearranged paragraphs in the presentation of two speeches, found no significant differences in comprehension due to the rearrangements. In contrast, Johnson (1970) found that the disorganized speech led to significantly less comprehension than did the organized version.

It should be obvious that not all the answers regarding the effect of order in a message have been found. The conflicting results may be due to factors not yet thoroughly investigated. For the present, it seems that logical order in a speech as perceived by the receiver is more persuasive and may lead to better comprehension, while helping the source appear more credible.

Order of Arguments

Let's imagine we have a persuasive message to which we want a group of receivers to respond. In this message are a number of very important arguments we want the audience to remember. Hopefully, these arguments will provide the impetus for the desired change. Where do we place the arguments? Tannenbaum (1954) exposed groups of receivers to a tape-recorded news program containing twelve news items. He rotated the news items so that each group heard a different order of items. Receivers were then tested to see how many news items they could recall. Recall was better for items at the beginning and end of the newscast, but not items in the middle. In addition, Shaw (1961) found that what is said first or last (versus in between) can influence actual behavior even if some of the communication is forgotten. We might ask ourselves, Which position is more effective in enhancing the impact of vital information? Unfortunately, research results are conflicting and no final conclusion can be made regarding whether the opening or closing parts of a communication should include the more important material (Cromwell 1950; Sponberg 1946). It has been suggested that when an audience is not interested in the communication, the major arguments should be placed first. Where interest is high, it seems advisable to place the arguments last. The placement of important information first for a relatively disinterested audience may arouse or maintain interest. If the important arguments are placed last, the audience may lose all motivation and not pay attention to the persuasive appeal (Karlins and Abelson 1970).

Let's imagine that we intend to deliver a persuasive appeal utilizing both sides of the issue. We might ask, Where do I present the side I favor—first or last? This question has received a great deal of attention in persuasion research and is called the *primacy-recency* problem. The specific question investigated asks, Will the message presented first (primacy) or last (recency) have the greatest effect on attitude and behavior change?

Early research by Lund (1925) indicated that arguments presented first were significantly more effective in producing attitude change than arguments presented second. In 1952, Hovland and Mandel replicated the Lund study. However, their results were entirely opposite. Recency, not primacy, seemed to be more effective in the persuasive process. Hovland, Janis and Kelley (1953) concluded that it was unlikely that either presenting strong arguments first followed by weaker arguments or putting weaker arguments first and important arguments last would invariably turn out to be superior. They felt that other factors might well produce varying outcomes and suggested that some of the important factors were receiver attention, learning, and acceptance of the arguments. Putting major arguments first would be more effective when the receiver is not too interested in the persuasive appeal, but when attention and desire to learn are present, then ending with the strongest arguments would be more effective. Cohen (1964) added that "the advantages of one order over the other depend on the particular conditions under which the communication is presented, including the predispositions of the audience and the type of material being presented."

Let's examine several generalizations drawn from a review of primacy-recency literature (Cohen 1964). When two sides of an issue are to be presented by different communicators, being the first speaker may not be advantageous. The message's effect may be tempered by various conditions (time, place, audience, and so on). However, when one speaker presents two sides of an issue in one presentation, we are usually more influenced by the side he presents first.

The receiver will play an important role in determining the proper placement of arguments. When we make a public response about our position after hearing one side of an argument, the second side we hear is less effective in changing our attitudes. This may be based on our need for social acceptance. Once we publicly take a position it may be difficult for us to change for fear we will be viewed as inconsistent and/or dishonest. If our needs are aroused before a communication and the communication satisfies these needs, the communication is more readily acceptable than if we perceive the need after the communication. If some specific need is aroused within us we are eager to listen and apply any information presented that will satisfy that need. If, on the other hand, the need arousal follows the information, it may be difficult for us to reconstruct the information in our minds and then apply it to the need. If, early in a speech, a communicator presents ideas with which we can readily agree, we may find ourselves accepting those ideas and becoming more responsive to him as a communicator. This responsiveness may make us less critical of later ideas and views with which we cannot readily agree. Whereas, if ideas with which we disagree are presented first, we may become more critical of the communicator, hence becoming even more critical of acceptable ideas presented later in the speech. If we are listening to a communicator whom we respect, we are influenced more when he presents the arguments for his position first, followed by the arguments against his position. We are less likely to be influenced if he presents the arguments against his position first and follows with arguments for his position.

Our ability to handle and retain information plays a role in determining the effectiveness of argument placement. When we receive a series of communications about a variety of subjects the primacy factor seems to operate at first but diminishes as the series of communications progresses. There seems to be a limitation as to how much information our minds are capable of handling at any given time. When we are receiving a great deal of unrelated information at once, we have a tendency to remember what we hear first, but as the mass of information continues to build up, subsequent information tends to inhibit the effectiveness of material received earlier. When one side of an issue is presented and there is a time lag before the other side is presented, there is a maximum forgetting of the first side and minimum forgetting for the second, so that the last side presented has an advantage. When two sides are presented at the same time, both sides have equal forgetting potential. Under this condition, the first issue presented has an advantage.

In summary, Cohen states that "taken as a whole, the findings regarding primacy and recency seem to rule out any universal principle of primacy in persuasion." Rosnow and Robinson (1967) make the following statement regarding the possibility of either a law of primacy or recency—

> Instead of a general "law" of primacy or recency, we have today an assortment of miscellaneous variables, some which tend to produce primacy ("primacy-bound variables"), others of which, to produce recency ("recency-bound variables"). Still others produce either order effect, depending on their utilization or temporal placement in a two-sided communication ("free variables"). Non-salient, controversial topics, interesting subject matter, and highly familiar issues tend toward primacy. Salient topics, uninteresting subject matter, and mod-

erately unfamiliar issues tend to yield recency. If arguments for one side are perceived more strongly than arguments for the other, then the side with the stronger arguments has the advantage—"strength" being the free variable. Another free variable is "reinforcement." When incidents that are perceived as rewarding or satisfying are initiated close in time to a persuasive communication, opinions tend to change in the direction of the arguments closer to the rewarding incident. When an incident is dissatisfying, or punishing, opinions tend to change in the direction of the arguments farther in time from it.

In this section, we discussed the organization of a message including information on introductions, conclusions, ordered versus disordered messages, placement order of arguments, and primacy-recency. In the next section, we will examine the content of the communication, the specific information that the source transmits to the receiver. We will attempt to discover what types of information or persuasive appeals have the greatest influence upon attitude and behavior change.

CONTENT OF THE MESSAGE

When we attempt to persuade another person or group, we are not only concerned with *how* we order the available information, but also *what* information we select or disregard as we formulate our persuasive message. In this section, we will be concerned with the content or substance of the messages, we will examine the use of evidence, one-sided versus two-sided messages, fear appeals, emotional versus factual appeals, and humor.

Evidence

Many textbooks currently available on persuasion and persuasive speaking recommend that a speaker utilize documented supporting materials in order to produce attitude or behavior change. However, research in this area has produced conflicting results regarding the value of including evidence in a persuasive message (McCroskey 1969; Gilkinson, Paulson, and Sikkink 1954; Anderson 1958; Dresser 1962, 1963).

While there is much research that still needs to be done in regard to the effect of evidence in a persuasive message, a few generalizations can be drawn. The effect of evidence in a message seems closely related to the perceived credibility of the source. A less credible source seems to gain credibility by the inclusion of evidence, while a more credible source does not seem to profit much from it. If, however, a highly credible source is speaking after a message that included evidence has already been given on his subject, then he loses credibility if he does not include evidence in the message. The effects of the inclusion of evidence seem related to the topic, with some topics being enhanced by the inclusion of evidence and others not. If we are listening to a speaker who is trying to convince us that we should brush our teeth, the topic may need little or no evidence for support. If the speaker is trying to convince us that integration will lead to the removal of racial prejudice, evidence to support this topic seems essential. The effect of the inclusion of evidence seems to be influenced by the delivery of the source, with poor delivery lowering the impact of the inclusion of the evidence. The effect of the evidence seems to be influenced by the intelligence of the audience members, with the more intelligent receivers being influenced more by the evidence. An audience's familiarity with the evidence presented seems to have an impact on the effect that the evidence has. For example, if we had just completed reading articles supporting the contention that integration reduces racial prejudice, we would be more receptive to a speaker citing such evidence than if we had not been exposed to this material before. Finally, the effect of evidence will be influenced by whether the receivers perceive the evidence as "good" evidence or not. For example, if we are listening to a speaker quoting evidence on a specific topic, that evidence should seem to us to be relevant to the topic and from an acceptable source, such as the AMA on a medical issue. If we do not perceive the evidence to be relevant and acceptable we would be inclined to discount the speaker's message (see McCroskey 1969).

We might ask two additional questions: (1) Does the intelligence of the audience relate to the effect of evidence in a message? and (2) Does evidence play a role in counter-persuasion? Kline (1969) found that the effect of evidence varied with the receiver's intelligence. That is to say, the inclusion of factual evidence and the specificity of that evidence will make more difference for receivers of high intelligence than for those of low intelligence. In regard to counter-persuasion, McCroskey (1970) found that evidence does appear to serve as an inhibitor to future counter-persuasion.

It seems obvious that the research on the effect of evidence in a message underscores the interaction occurring in the persuasive process. We have seen that evidence interrelates with the source, the receiver, the perceptual processes of both, the presentation of the message, and the other elements of the persuasive process.

One-Sided versus Two-Sided Messages

In an earlier section of this selection the effects of placing strongest arguments at the beginning of a message (primacy) or at the end of a message (recency) were examined. We will now question whether one side of an issue or two sides of an issue should be included in the message. We realize that most issues have at least two sides. Therefore, we must make a decision whether to discuss both sides.

Hovland, Lumsdaine and Sheffield (1949) investigated whether it is more effective to present evidence supporting the main goal of the persuasive appeal or to include opposing arguments too. Their results indicated that, for receivers initially opposed to the position presented by the message, giving both sides of the issue was more effective. For receivers initially favoring the stand taken by the message, the one-sided presentation was more effective. A further study by Lumsdaine and Janis (1953) exposed subjects to counter-arguments after having them initially exposed to one-sided and two-sided messages. Their results indicated that those who had been exposed to the two-sided presentation were more resistant to counter-propaganda than those exposed to the one-sided communication. In a more recent study, McGinnes (1966) provides cross-cultural support for the earlier Hovland, Lumsdaine and Sheffield study. Using Japanese university students, he found that two-sided communication was superior to one-sided appeals when individuals were initially opposed to the position advocated. For those students who initially agreed with the speaker's position, the one-sided communication tended to be more effective.

The educational level of the receiver appears to play a role in whether a speaker should use a one-sided or two-sided message. The two-sided presentation is more effective for better educated men, while the one-sided presentation is more effective with less educated. When the amount of education and initial position are examined together, the one-sided communication is more effective with the less educated subjects who initially favored the position advocated in the message, while the two-sided communication was more effective with the better educated subjects regardless of their initial position (Hovland, Lumsdaine and Sheffield 1949). However, an investigation by Bettinghaus and Basehart (1969) found no support for the generalization that two-sided messages are more effective than one-sided messages for changing attitudes of more highly educated individuals.

Thistlethwaite and Kamenetsky (1955) found that using two-sided messages leads to less change in attitudes when receivers are not previously aware of the opposing arguments, but failure to include both sides will weaken the effect if receivers are previously aware of the opposing arguments.

From research done on inoculation effects and on the issue of one-sided versus two-sided messages, the following generalizations seem appropriate (Karlin and Abelson 1970). One-sided messages seem to be more effective when the audience is aware of the source's persuasive attempts, when the audience is generally friendly to the source, when one position is all that will be presented, when the audience is not aware of counter-arguments, and is not expected to hear counter-arguments, or when only immediate, temporary opinion change is desired. Two-sided messages seem to be more effective when the audience initially disagrees with the communicator, when the audience is aware of counter-arguments before the presentation or will be exposed to them, when the audience members are more intelligent, and where the communicator wants to be fair and objective in his message.

Fear Appeals

In a Los Angeles mayoral race several years ago, one of the candidates, the incumbent, attempted to scare voters into voting against his opponent. He charged that his opponent was a political radical and that his election would ruin the city. In this particular election, the incumbent's use of fear appeals was not successful and he was soundly defeated at the polls. The use of fear appeals in speaking situations is not a new phenomenon. Aristotle, the father of rhetorical theory, discusses the use in Greek persuasive speaking in his classic work, *The Rhetoric.* It would appear that the use of fear appeals can be both successful and unsuccessful in the persuasive situation. Therefore, to fully understand the value and use of persuasive appeals to fear, there are several questions we must answer: Are appeals to fear generally successful in the persuasive situation? Are there different types of fear appeals? When are fear appeals successful or unsuccessful? Within the last three decades a great deal of research has been centered around answering these questions.

Janis and Feshbach (1953) examined three types of fear appeals and their effect in producing change among groups of high school students regarding dental hygiene. Group one received a strongly threatening lecture which included the possibility of cancer among the many consequences of poor oral hygiene. The second group received a mildly threatening lecture that condemned people who neglected their mouths to nothing worse than a few cavities. The third group received a lecture with an intermediate degree of fear. They found that the more threatening the lecture, the more worry students expressed immediately after the lecture. After a period of one week, however, they found that the group subjected to the least amount of fear was found to have conformed most to the message. They concluded that under conditions where people will be exposed to competing communications dealing with the same issue, the use of a strong threat appeal will tend to be less effective than a minimal threat appeal in producing attitude change. We might suggest that high fear appeals produce more threat and receivers are more likely to employ defense mechanisms. Thus, they become more resistant to high fear appeals in a message.

However, mild fear appeals are not always the superior form of fear appeal in producing attitude or behavior change. Leventhal and Niles (1964), for instance, found that a low fear appeal message was more effective than moderate or high fear appeals in enforcing an individual's intentions to stop smoking. Leventhal and Watts (1966) exposed audiences at a state fair to high, medium, and low fear appeals on the topic of antismoking. In their persuasive message, they recommended that the audience stop smoking and take an X-ray at a nearby mobile unit to detect the presence of cancer. They found that audiences exposed to the high fear appeals stopped smoking more significantly than those exposed to the other fear appeal conditions. However, the audiences exposed to the low fear appeals were more likely to have the chest X-ray. They suggested that extreme fear produced an avoidance reaction within the audience members that forced them to avoid the possibility of further fear coming from X-ray. Thus, the high fear appeal group selected an alternate method for reducing the threat—they stopped smoking.

Dabbs and Leventhal (1966) examined the effect of high and low fear communication upon the attitudes and behavior of college students exposed to written materials. The researchers recommended in the messages that the students should receive a tetanus inoculation. Students exposed to high fear appeals were more likely to want and obtain shots than individuals who received the low fear appeal messages. "The manipulation of fear . . . . influenced both intentions to take shots and actual shot-taking behavior . . . A positive relationship between fear arousal and persuasion was observed." Kraus, El-Assal and De Fleur (1966) also found that high fear appeals were very successful in modifying behavior using the mass media as the agent for transmitting the message.

It would appear that the personality of the receiver interacts with the level of fear in the message. Some individuals may not be able to avoid high fear appeals because they are unable to develop adequate defense mechanisms. Niles (1964) found that students who rated themselves "highly vulnerable" to a communication on antismoking showed more attitude change toward stopping smoking when exposed to moderate fear appeals than to high or low fear appeals. On the other hand, "low vulnerable" subjects showed more attitude change when exposed to an increase in fear arousing appeals in the message. Dabbs and Leventhal (1966), in the study reported earlier, found that individuals of "high self-esteem" complied with the recommendations of the researchers. Individuals who were classified as "low self-esteem" complied equally well to both high and low fear appeals.

The effectiveness of fear appeals appears to be related to a number of other factors as well. Berkowitz and Cottingham (1960) found a strong fear appeal more effective than a weak appeal when the communication was of low interest value or low relevance to the audience. The dramatic nature of the high fear appeal may make the message more interesting. Insko, Arkoff, and Insko (1965), examining the effects of fear appeal on attitudes toward smoking, concluded that audiences exposed to high fear appeals were quicker to make inferences from the message that diseases caused by smoking could and would affect them and, therefore, the high fear appeal was more effective in producing immediate attitude change. Miller and Hewgill (1964) found that a high credibility source using a high fear message was more effective than when he used a low fear message. His credibility may make the appeal more believable or lend more credence to the information provided, thus making it more difficult for the receiver to discredit the influence attempt. Powell (1965) discovered that a strong fear appeal posing a threat to the receiver's family produced a greater change in attitude than a mild appeal. Our defense mechanisms may not be able to cope as easily with a threat to a loved one as a threat to ourselves. Simonson and Lundy (1966) found that irrelevant fear facilitated the acceptance of a persuasive message. They suggested that this might have occurred because irrelevant fear served as a distractor.

Many factors influence the effectiveness of fear appeals in the persuasive situation. Some studies indicate that mild appeals are more effective, while other studies indicate the reverse. Fear appeals seem to be effective in changing behavior when: (1) immediate action can be taken on recommendations included in the appeal and (2) specific instructions are provided for carrying out the message's recommendations (Leventhal, Jones and Trembly 1966; Leventhal, Singer and Jones 1965). Cronkhite (1969) recommends that the communicator present a specific plan of action and demonstrate that it is effective and feasible whenever a strong fear is used. The source may use the strong fear appeal followed by a specific plan of action with confidence when his receivers have a history of being able to cope with their problems and when the suggested action is aggressive in nature, does not create a further threat, and does not appear too difficult. The fear appeal should be realistic enough that the receiver cannot easily say it does not concern him and should not present an excess of fear that might appear ridiculous rather than frightening.

Emotional versus Factual Appeals

We often hear individuals say that it is better to appeal to the heart than the head. Many people feel that a speaker is more successful in producing attitude change if he appeals to the emotions of his audience. Whether emotional or factual appeals are more successful in producing attitude and behavior change is difficult to answer. Hartman (1936) examined the effectiveness of appeals in soliciting votes for Socialist candidates in the 1936 elections. He found that written pamphlets using emotional appeals were more successful than factual appeals in getting individuals to vote for the Socialist candidates. The Opinion Research Corporation (1952) prepared booklets attempting to marshal opinion against excess profits taxes. The booklet with emotional arguments was more successful than the booklet using factual arguments.

Weiss (1960) found the opposite effect. He prepared three written messages with the same conclusion—criminals should be severely punished for their crimes—and three different forms of supporting evidence: one message utilized emotional appeals, a second message used factual appeals, and the third message combined emotional and factual arguments. He found that factual arguments were more effective than emotional arguments in changing opinions. In addition, no differences of opinion existed between students reading factual or emotional-factual messages. However, the persuasive advantage of factual arguments was only temporary. Two weeks after the initial testing, students expressed similar opinions about the treatment of criminals—regardless of the appeal read. Several other studies have also found partial support for the superiority of factual appeals (Bowers 1963; Carmichael and Cronkhite 1965; Weiss and Lieberman 1959). Carmichael and Cronkhite (1965) suggest that the effectiveness of the appeal is sometimes dependent on the mood of the audience. It would appear that no type of appeal is always superior. Much depends on the issue to be discussed and the composition of the audience.

Humor

Many politicians and advertisers use humor to persuade their audience. The humor used by Truman and the Kennedy brothers has been suggested as a factor contributing to their political success. Approximately forty-two percent of television commercials use some humor (Markiewicz 1972). Cannan (1914) stated: "No tyrant, no tyrannous idea ever came crashing to earth but it was first wounded with shafts of satire: no free man, no free idea ever rose to the heights but it endured them." However, Feinberg (1967) states: "The notion that satire has played an important part in reforming society is probably a delusion satirists themselves know better." We might ask ourselves, Does a humorous persuasive message increase the amount of persuasion?

Gruner (1965, 1966) found that humor (at least satire) was not a potent persuasive device in messages. However, the initial opinion of receivers might determine when a humorous message is more persuasive. It is suggested that humor functions as a distractor; receivers initially opposed to a message position would be more persuaded by a humorous rather than a serious message. Those initially neutral or in favor of the position would be equally persuaded by either a humorous or serious message (Haaland and Verbeatesan 1968; Osterhouse and Brock 1970; Zimbardo, et al. 1970). However, it is possible that receivers generally laugh more at those whom they do not sympathize or identify with. When the humor in a message supports the message position, those who are initially opposed to the position might not be amused, and might react against the persuasive attempt. Those initially opposed to a position should be less persuaded by a humorous than a serious message. Satire may operate as a reinforcer of attitudes. "When people already hold opinions which satire expresses, these opinions are reinforced." However, "The satirist who expresses unpopular views has no social effect, no matter how entertaining he may be" (Feinberg 1967). People enjoy humor directed against "enemy" reference groups and least enjoy humor ridiculing their own reference groups (Priest and Abraham 1970). Gruner (1972) found support for the contention that satire can and does operate as a reinforcer of previous attitudes in oral communication situations.

Markiewicz (1972) found that a humorous source was rated more trustworthy than a serious one. If humor enhances the image of a source, the effect of humor would more likely be evident with low credibility or disliked sources. A low credibility source might utilize humor to raise his image before his audience and, therefore, improve his chances of persuading the audience to his particular position.

We have centered our discussion of message content on the use of evidence, one-sided versus two-sided messages, fear appeals, factual versus emotional appeals, and humor. This in no way exhausts the list of message content variables that can and do operate in the persuasive situation. However, these other variables—for example, the use of metaphor—have not been researched thoroughly enough as yet to draw meaningful generalizations to the persuasive situation. We will now proceed from dealing with *what* is said in a message to *how* something is said in a persuasive message. We will examine how the presentation of a message affects the persuasive situation.

PRESENTATION OF A MESSAGE

In this section of the essay we will examine how the manner in which a message is presented to an audience or group of individuals will influence the persuasive process. We will examine how active versus passive listener participation, audience distractors, and general delivery affect attitude and behavior change.

Active versus Passive Participation

Let's imagine a situation in which you desire to persuade an audience that air pollution can be controlled by the development of rapid transit systems. You have a choice—you can talk to the audience about your position or you can ask your listeners to write an essay on the subject. Would you be more successful in giving the talk or allowing the audience to participate actively in the persuasive process? Watts (1967) examined this problem. It was found that, initially, both active and passive participation can lead to opinion change. However, over time, the active participants showed greater persistence of the initially produced opinion change. Furthermore, active participation leads to greater involvement and superior recall of the topic and side supported.

Karlin and Abelson (1970) present a sample of diverse research situations in which active participation is superior to passive participation in producing attitude and behavior change—

(2) Active participation, in the form of group discussion, is often more effective than passive participation (hearing lectures or reading appeals) in changing attitudes (Hereford, 1963; Lewin, 1953). . . . (4) Active participation in T-groups or sensitivity training leads to marked behavior modification (Rubin, 1967). (5) A person who actively (rather than passively) learns about a situation often changes his attitudes about that situation. Thus, visitors who took guided tours through a state school for mental defectives changed their opinions about the patients and the institution (Kimbrell & Luckey, 1964); and children who studied Spanish had more positive attitudes toward Spanish-speaking peoples than children lacking such education (Riestra & Johnson, 1964).

We might conclude from these findings that the effect of a persuasive appeal is enhanced by requiring active, rather than passive, participation by the receiver.

Distractors

Let's imagine ourselves at a school cafeteria. A friend invites us to have dinner with him and during the meal asks us to support a petition he is circulating around campus. Our friend has used a method of distraction (eating our dinner) in order to enhance his persuasive attempt.

Leon Festinger and Nathan Maccoby (1964) had two groups of fraternity men listen to an antifraternity message while watching a movie. One group viewed the film of a speaker giving the antifraternity lecture; the second group watched an irrelevant silent comedy while listening to the sound track of the first film. They found that the distracted group (those watching the comedy film) were more persuaded by the message—expressing more antifraternity attitudes. Haaland and Verbeatesan (1968), however, found less attitude change when receivers were subjected to visual and behavioral distraction while listening to a persuasive communication. The type of distraction experienced by the receiver may be an important factor in the persuasive process. "Generally, persuasive appeals become more powerful when presented in conjunction with moderately distracting stimuli which positively reinforce the individual" (Karlin and Abelson 1970). Food and sex appear to operate as positive reinforcements for receivers. Using these stimuli as detractors may enhance the effectiveness of persuasive appeals (Janis, Kaye and Kirschner 1965; Zimbardo, Ebbesen and Fraser 1968). Negative reinforcements (foul odors) are generally ineffective in enhancing the persuasive process.

General Delivery

The manner in which a speaker delivers his message to an audience has a tremendous influence over the effectiveness of that persuasive effort. Heinberg (1963) found delivery to be almost twice as important as content in determining general effectiveness of introductions and also three times as influential as content in determining effectiveness in attempts to have an idea accepted. Delivery includes the way a message is spoken and presented to an audience. It also includes the nonverbal aspects such as the way the source looks when he presents a message, facial expressions, gestures, and the like.

It appears that delivery can influence the degree of attitude change that takes place in the listener. Heyworth (1942) found that fluency and effectiveness were highly correlated. Bettinghaus (1961) found that effective delivery contributed to persuasiveness in the presentation of a message. While McCroskey and Arnold (1969) did not find an effect on immediate attitude change attributable to delivery quality for live, video-taped, or audio-taped speakers, they did find a delivery effect on delayed attitude change. In addition they found that when good delivery was coupled with good message quality, it produced immediate positive attitude change; but when good delivery was coupled with poor message quality, it did not. While it has been found that nonfluency has no effect on immediate attitude change, McCroskey and Mehrley (1969) found that "extensive nonfluencies seriously restrict the amount of attitude change any source can produce."

Effective delivery also appears to enhance a speaker's credibility (Bettinghaus 1961). McCroskey and Arnold (1969) found that the quality of delivery had a significant effect on perceived source credibility. Assuming that source credibility plays an important role in producing the impetus for attitude change, it would behoove the source to evaluate the effectiveness of his delivery style.

PROPOSITIONS

1. Information by itself does not always produce persuasive change.
2. New information may be an agent of change when the receiver has no existing attitudes concerning the attitude object.
3. Message organization will influence attitude change.
4. The organization of a message is a situational phenomenon.
5. Introductions have a persuasive effect on receivers.
    a. Introductions alerting receivers that the message will argue against their position produce less attitude change.
    b. Receivers change less when a disliked source announces his persuasive intent.
    c. Receivers change more when a well-liked source admits his persuasive intent.
6. The conclusion of a message will have a persuasive effect on receivers.
    a. Conclusions should be stated explicitly when using complex messages, addressing less intelligent receivers, and when receivers are initially favorable toward the message position.
    b. Conclusions should be stated implicitly when the problem is simple and the receivers are intelligent.
    c. If the receivers view the conclusions as propaganda, they may resist persuasive appeals.
    d. Direct appeals for change should be placed in the conclusion of a message.
    e. Conclusions asking for a great amount of change produce more change than conclusions asking for less change.
7. Message disorganization reduces the amount of attitude change, audience's retention of a message, and the source's evaluation.
8. Receiver recall is better for materials placed at the beginning and end of the message.
9. No universal rule of primacy or recency exists in persuasive situations.
    a. There is no advantage in being the first communicator when two sides of an issue are presented by two different speakers.
    b. When a receiver makes a public response about his position after hearing one side of an argument, the second side is less effective in changing attitudes.
    c. When one speaker presents two sides of an issue in one presentation, we are usually more influenced by the side presented first.
    d. When a receiver's needs are aroused before a communication satisfies these needs, the communication is more readily acceptable than if the need arousal follows the communication.
    e. Attitudes change more when desirable ideas precede undesirable ideas.

    f.   The pro-con order is more effective than the con-pro order when an authoritative communicator presents both sides.

    g.   If a time lag exists between the presentation of two sides of an issue, the side presented last has an advantage.

    h.   When no time lag exists between presentation of two sides of an issue, the first side has an advantage.

    i.   When a receiver hears a series of communications about a variety of subjects, primacy operates at first but diminishes as the series of communications progresses.

    j.   Salient topics, uninteresting subjects, and moderately unfamiliar issues tend to yield recency effects.

    k.   Nonsalient, controversial topics, interesting subject matter, and highly familiar issues tend toward primacy effects.

    l.   The placement of reward or punishment in a message will affect primacy-recency effects.

10. The content of a message will affect attitude and behavior change.

11. Evidence may play a role in producing a persuasive change.

    a.   A less credible source gains credibility with inclusion of evidence.

    b.   A highly credible source can lose credibility if he does not include evidence.

    c.   The effect of evidence will be influenced by the message topic.

    d.   The inclusion of evidence is influenced by the delivery of the source.

    e.   Intelligent receivers are influenced more by evidence.

    f.   Receivers are influenced by evidence with which they are familiar.

    g.   The evidence must be perceived to be relevant and acceptable or the receiver may discount the message.

    h.   The medium of transmission used to convey the evidence does not affect the potential influence of that evidence.

12. The presentation of one or more sides of an issue may affect the persuasive process.

    a.   Two-sided messages are more effective when receivers initially oppose the message position.

    b.   One-sided messages are more effective when receivers initially favor the position taken by the message.

    c.   Receivers exposed to two-sided presentations are more resistant to counter-propaganda.

    d.   Two-sided presentations are more effective with better educated men, while one-sided presentations are more effective with less educated men.

    e.   Failure to include both sides of an issue may weaken the persuasive attempt, if receivers are aware of the opposing arguments.

13. Fear appeals may affect the persuasive process.

    a.   The level of fear producing change is influenced by the personality of the receiver and the message topic.

    b.   Fear appeals are effective in changing behavior when immediate action can be taken on appeal recommendations and specific instructions are provided for carrying out the recommendations.

14. Neither emotional nor factual appeals are universally effective in persuasive situations.
15. Humor may affect the persuasive process.
    a. Humor as a distractor may produce greater attitude change.
    b. Satire may operate as a reinforcer of attitudes.
16. The presentation of a message affects the persuasive process.
17. Active participation is more effective than passive participation in producing attitude and behavior change.
18. Presentation distractors may enhance the effectiveness of persuasion.
19. The manner of delivery used by a speaker may influence his persuasive attempt.
    a. Extensive nonfluencies may restrict the amount of attitude change any source can produce.
    b. The quality of delivery may affect source credibility.

BIBLIOGRAPHY

Bettinghaus, E. P. *Persuasive Communication.* 2d ed. New York: Holt, Rinehart and Winston, 1973. Chapter 5 provides a very basic explanation of the code system used in persuasive messages.

Karlin, M. and H. I. Abelson. *Persuasion: How Opinions and Attitudes Are Changed.* New York: Springer Pub. Co., Inc., 1970, pp. 5-40. An examination of major issues and studies of persuasive messages.

Miller, G. R. and M. Burgoon. *New Techniques of Persuasion.* New York: Harper & Row, 1973. An examination of recent theory and research not usually found in basic persuasion texts. Topics of particular interest are: (1) uses and limitations of counterattitudinal advocacy and (2) inducing resistance to persuasion.

Larry L. Barker

IMPROVING YOUR LISTENING BEHAVIOR

SOME SPECIFIC SUGGESTIONS FOR LISTENING IMPROVEMENT

Be Mentally and Physically Prepared to Listen

This suggestion may be obvious, but active listening involves being physically and mentally "in shapes." We take for granted that athletes involved in active competition must prepare their minds and bodies for the sport in which they are engaged. However, few people view listening as an activity which demands being in condition. Your attention span is directly related to your physical and mental condition at a given moment. If you are tired, your capacity to listen actively and effectively is reduced.

Think about the Topic in Advance When Possible

In the case of classroom lectures it is often possible to read ahead about the lecture topic and devote some conscious thought to the issues in advance. The same holds true, to a lesser extent, when you plan to attend a public speech or public discussion. You should try to provide an opportunity to review in your mind considerations regarding the topic about which you will be listening. This suggestion is based on learning research, which supports the contention that, if you are somewhat familiar with a topic before you attempt to learn more about it, your learning takes place more efficiently and is generally longer lasting.

Behave as You Think a Good Listener Should Behave

A partial summary of desirable listening behaviors might include:

1. Concentrating all of your physical and mental energy on listening
2. Avoiding interrupting the speaker when possible
3. Demonstrating interest and alertness
4. Seeking areas of agreement with the speaker when possible
5. Searching for meanings and avoiding arguing about words
6. Demonstrating patience because you understand that you can listen faster than the speaker can speak
7. Providing clear and unambiguous feedback to the speaker
8. Repressing the tendency to respond emotionally to what is said
9. Asking questions when you do not understand something
10. Withholding evaluation of the message until the speaker is finished— and you are sure you understand the message

---

Larry L. Barker, *Listening Behavior,* © 1971, pp. 73-84. Reprinted by permission of Prentice-Hall, Inc., Englewood Cliffs, New Jersey.

Try to imitate those behaviors which lead to effective listening. In addition, observe other people who are good listeners and model your own behavior in listening settings after them. In this particular instance, imitation not only may be a sincere form of flattery, it also may help you become a better listener.

Determine the Personal Value of the Topic for You

This suggestion is designed to make you a "selfish listener." It is based upon the assumption that initial motivation to listen may not be sufficient without some added active effort on your part to perceive what may be gained by listening to the message. Search for ways in which you can use the information. Look for potential economic benefits, personal satisfaction, or new interests and insights. In other words, strive to make listening to the topic appear vital or rewarding for you.

Listen for Main Points

The key word in this suggestion is "main." Look for those points which, in your estimation, represent the primary theme of the message, that is, the central idea the speaker is trying to impart. It is impossible to remember everything a speaker says. Therefore, try to isolate major points and do not attempt to memorize all of the sub-points. This suggestion, if followed, should help you begin to quickly identify important elements in the speaker's message while screening out less important points.

Practice Listening to Difficult Expository Material

This is, perhaps, more of an exercise than a suggestion; but it has been found that by applying good listening habits to difficult listening, listening under normal circumstances can be improved. This same principle applies to other areas of mental and physical improvement. For example, if you practice shooting a basketball into a hoop smaller than regulation size, theoretically it should be easier to make baskets in a hoop of normal size. If you find you are an effective listener in extremely difficult listening settings, it is very probable you will be even more effective when listening under normal conditions.

Concentrate—Do Not Let Your Thoughts Wander

Listening is an activity which is usually performed at relatively high speeds. Speaking can be performed at a variety of speeds, most of them considerably lower than normal listening speeds.

The listener should be aware of the difference between the rate of speech and the rate of thinking and should use the time lag effectively rather than letting it destroy the listening process. Some specific suggestions can help the listener use this time lag constructively to enhance the listening process.

1. *Identify the developmental techniques used by the speaker.* This means, look at examples used, order of arrangement, and the mechanics of the message itself in an attempt to determine how the message is constructed and how it combines a set of ideas into a coherent unit (or if it does not combine ideas into a coherent unit).
2. *Review previous points.* Use the time lag to review in your mind the points the speaker has made already. This may help you learn the

material more completely and reinforce ideas the speaker has made
so you can relate them to other parts of his message.

3. *Search for deeper meanings than you received upon hearing the message for the first time.* Some words may have secondary or connotative meanings which you did not identify at first. Search the message for words which may have hidden meanings and apply these new meanings to the rest of the speaker's message.

4. *Anticipate what the speaker will say next.* This sort of second guessing could be a bad listening habit if the listener does not compare what the speaker actually says with what he anticipated was going to be said. However, this suggestion can be useful if you try to evaluate what has been said, predict what will be said, and compare the actual message transmitted with that which you predicted. This active mental activity also can help reinforce the speaker's ideas in your mind and keep your attention focused on the message.

Obviously, you cannot engage in all four of these mental activities simultaneously. If you were to try, you probably would completely lose track of the speaker's message. You need to decide initially which of the activities should prove most beneficial in a given listening setting. This decision should be based, in part, on your specific purpose for listening.

Build Your Vocabulary as Much as Possible

This suggestion has been stressed by educators for several years. Comprehension is directly related to a listener's having meaningful associations for the word symbols. In other words, listeners must have a sufficiently developed vocabulary to understand most of what the speaker is saying. In some instances it may even be necessary to learn a "new" vocabulary before attempting to listen. In the classroom you may need to review a new set of definitions or terms, or learn some key words which will be used throughout the course, in order to understand what the teacher is saying. A foreign language course provides a good example of the need to have a sufficient vocabulary in order to understand what is happening in class. This is why most language courses begin by having students memorize certain words; new words are then gradually added as they are used in the daily lesson.

Be Flexible in Your Views

Do not be close-minded. Examine your own views. Make sure the views you hold that are inflexible are held for a very good reason; and try to keep in mind that there may be other, contradictory views which may have some merit even if you cannot give them total acceptance. If you approach all listening situations with an open mind, you can only profit.

Compensate for Emotion-Rousing Words

Some words evoke "signal reactions" (i.e., reactions which are a function of habit or conditioning) as opposed to cognitive deliberation. We must be aware of those particular words which affect us emotionally—for example, "sex," "nigger," "teacher," and most "four-letter" words—and attempt to compensate at the cognitive level for them. Following are some specific suggestions to help compensate for emotion-rousing words.

(a) *Identify, prior to listening, those words that affect you emotionally.* This step simply involves making yourself aware of specific words which you know stimulate signal reactions.

(b) *Attempt to analyze why the words affect you the way they do.* What past experiences or encounters have created for you unique meanings for certain words?

(c) *Try to reduce their impact upon you by using a "defense" mechanism.* One which is popularly suggested to help avoid emotional reactions to certain words is called "rationalization." Rationalization involves attempting to convince yourself that the word really is not such a bad word or it does not have any real referent. Another technique is to repress certain meanings of emotionally laden words and substitute new meanings. No matter what defense mechanisms you use, try to eliminate, insofar as possible, a conditioned or signal reaction to a word. Try to determine objectively what meaning the word holds for the speaker. (*See also* Mabry's "A Multivariate Investigation of Profane Language.")

Compensate for Main Ideas to Which You React Emotionally

This is similar to the point above in that there also are certain trains of thought, main points, or ideas to which we may react emotionally. For example, a listener may react very emotionally when the topic of compulsory arbitration in unions is discussed, because he is a long-standing union member. Students may react emotionally when the topic of grades is discussed, and so forth.

When you hear an issue being discussed to which you have an apparent emotional reaction, there are several suggestions which may help you compensate for your initial bias.

1. *Defer judgment.* This is a principle suggested by Osborn (1962) in his text *Applied Imagination.* He suggests that in order to be a creative thinker, problem solver, or listener you must learn to withhold evaluation of ideas until you have listened to everything the speaker has to say. This suggestion often is difficult to employ because of prior experiences, positive or negative, that you may have had with certain ideas. However, if you can successfully employ the principle of deferred judgment you will become a more effective and appreciated listener.

2. *Empathize.* This involves taking the speaker's point of view while you listen, and trying to discover why he says what he says. In essence, identify with the speaker, search for his reasons, views, and arguments which differ from your own but which, from his point of view, may nevertheless hold some validity.

3. *Place your own personal feelings in perspective.* Try to realize that your past experiences, including your cultural and educational background, have molded you into a unique human being. As a result, you hold certain views which may be different from the views that others hold. Nevertheless, you must evaluate your own perceptions and feelings in light of those the speaker is trying to communicate. If you can critically evaluate your own views and feelings, you may be able to discover how they relate to or differ from those of the speaker.

KEEP THESE POINTS IN MIND WHEN YOU LISTEN

The previous suggestions relate to specific aspects of listening improvement. Following are some questions you should constantly keep in mind in all listening settings. If you can answer all of them at the end of each listening experience, the probability is high that you have listened successfully.

What Does the Speaker Really Mean?

This question was implied earlier, but is important to ask at all listening levels. Since you hold different meanings for words than the speaker as a result of differing past experiences, you must search actively to discover what message the speaker really is trying to communicate through his word symbols.

Have Some Elements of the Message Been Left Out?

People often speak without paying careful attention to the way they use certain words. Similarly, they often take for granted that the listener will fill in missing information in the message. The omission of information may be intentional or it may be subconscious on the part of the speaker. Therefore, you, the listener, have to take the active role in finding out what elements the speaker may have left out, which might help clarify and add meaning to his message.

What Are the Bases for the Speaker's Evidence?

This question implies that you must evaluate critically the reasons why a speaker advocates certain points. Is his evidence based on firsthand observation (perhaps this class of data may be called "facts") or is it based primarily on personal opinion? If on opinion, is the speaker an expert (thought to have a valued opinion on the subject) or are his opinions based on inferences or secondhand observations? Is the speaker's evidence consistent with what you may know? Is it based on careful study or cursory observation? All of these considerations contribute to the validity of the speaker's arguments. As you begin to search and evaluate the speaker's evidence, you become more critically aware of the quality and importance of his ideas.

SOME HINTS FOR NOTE TAKING[1]

Closely related to the listening process is the process of taking notes. Note taking is employed frequently in classroom settings, but also may be exercised in other public speaking or semiformal listening situations. Below are several suggestions designed to improve your note taking ability.

Determine Whether or Not to Take Notes

Notes may be useful in some settings, but unnecessary, and even distracting, in others. Your purpose for listening should determine whether or not you need to take notes. If you feel you may need to refer to the information at a future time, the notes probably are necessary. However, if the information is for immediate use (e.g., announcements about the day's schedule at a sum-

---

[1] Some of the suggestions in this section are derived, with some adaptation, from Lewis and Nichols (1965).

mer workshop), it may be more effective simply to listen carefully without taking notes. Your own ability to comprehend and retain information is a variable which also must be taken into account. If you have high concentration and retention abilities, you probably will need to take relatively few notes. However, if you have difficulty remembering information the day after it is presented, you probably should get out the notepad.

Decide What Type of Notes Are Necessary

There are at least three different types of notes which people may elect to take. They differ in purpose and specificity. These three common types are key words, partial outline, and complete outline.

1. *Key words.* When you primarily want to remember some specific points in the message, key word notes are probably the most efficient. For example, if you wanted to remember an entertaining story about a member of Students for a Demorcratic Society who attended a meeting of the John Birch Society by mistake, so you could retell it later, you might elect to write the key words, "SDS at Birch meeting," on your notepad. Key words are used to help provide cues for ideas which were presented during the listening setting. However, unless you can positively associate the meaning with the key words, they are not of value.
2. *Partial Outline.* If you decide that there are several important elements you should remember in a message, it probably is desirable to take notes in partial outline form. The points in the message which seem important to you are noted rather completely and other points which you do not deem important are not recorded. For example, if you are auditing a class on statistics and your professor illustrates how to compute a mean, median, and mode, you may decide that you want to remember only how to compute the mode. Consequently, you record in your notes only that portion of the lecture that relates to your specific interest. The notes you take are complete, but they do not represent all of the message that was presented.
3. *Complete Outline.* In many lecture classes it is important to record most of what is presented in class. This is because you often will be expected to remember specific information later on tests. In such classes, and in other settings where you may need to have a complete record of what was said, a complete set of notes in outline form is necessary.

The key is to determine in advance what form of notes you will need to take in a given listening setting, and then adapt your note taking accordingly. If you modify your note taking according to the demands of the situation, you will make most efficient and effective use of your energy.

Keep Notes Clear

This involves not only using brief sentences and statements of ideas which are understandable after you have written them, but involves such technical details as not cluttering the page, not scribbling, and not writing side comments. Use the paper efficiently; do not crowd words together.

Keep Notes Brief

This suggestion speaks for itself. The briefer your notes, the less time you will be spending writing. This means you also will be less likely to miss what the speaker says.

Note as Quickly as Possible the Organizational Pattern (or Lack of Pattern) of the Speaker

First, be aware of the fact that many speakers have no discernible organizational pattern. There is a tendency for some note takers to try to organize notes on the basis of their own organizational patterns rather than the speaker's. For example, you may prefer outlining with Roman numeral I, followed by A and B, 1 and 2, a and b, and so forth. However, if the speaker is simply talking in random fashion without much formal organization, artificially imposing an organizational pattern on his message may distort this message. Therefore, it is important to note quickly if the speaker is employing a formal organizational pattern and adapt your own note taking to his pattern.

Review Your Notes Later

This suggestion is extremely important in a learning theory framework because by reviewing information frequently it is possible to retain information more permanently. Ideas that we hear once tend to be forgotten within 24 hours. Without some review they may be lost to us forever. Another reason for reviewing your notes soon after taking them is that you may remember some subtleties at that point which you might not remember when reading your notes at some future time.

APPRECIATIVE LISTENING SUGGESTIONS

The previous suggestions refer primarily to critical and discriminative listening settings. The suggestions below are designed to improve appreciative listening behavior in social or informal settings.

1. *Determine what you enjoy listening to most.* This suggestion requires a self-analysis to discover those listening situations in which you find yourself most frequently involved by choice.
2. *Analyze why you enjoy these listening settings.* Determining the reasons why you enjoy particular situations may help you more fully understand your listening preferences.
3. *Compare your own likes in listening with those of others.* By comparing your own likes with those of others you can derive some social reinforcement for the types of listening you enjoy.
4. *Be curious.* Have an inquisitive mind about everything you hear. Try to be constantly creative and noncritical in the way you approach listening settings.
5. *Read and consult to learn more about those areas in which you enjoy listening.* Find out as much as you can about the subject (or music) to which you like to listen. Get more out of listening by being mentally prepared regarding the subject prior to engaging in listening.

AN IDEAL ENVIRONMENT FOR LISTENING

In some situations you may have control over the listening environment. The following suggestions may be helpful in structuring the environment for effective listening. Teachers generally have control over classroom listening environments; consequently, several of the specific suggestions that follow are derived from classroom listening.

Establish a Comfortable, Quiet, Relaxed Atmosphere in the Room

Listening is usually more successful when there are few physical distractions. It is possible to create an atmosphere that is so comfortable that the listener may become sleepy or drowsy. However, it is more probable that noise and other elements in the environment will distract the listener. These elements should be controlled.

Make Sure the Audience Senses a Clear Purpose for Listening

This may involve a brief explanation or preview on your part of what is ideally supposed to take place in the listening setting. The reason for this suggestion is obvious. When motivation is present (that is, perception of personal purpose), listening effectiveness is increased.

Prepare the Listeners for What They Are About to Hear

This involves more than just providing them with a purpose for listening. It involves giving them some background in the content area of the message—e.g., define critical terms or provide a conceptual framework for the message.

Break Up Long Periods of Listening with Other Activities

How long a person can listen depends on many factors, such as his immediate physical condition, the air temperature, humidity, time of day, and so forth. For adult listeners a maximum time period for concentrated listening probably should be one hour, or less, if possible. If you are in control of a situation in which listening is to take place, you should intersperse other activities, hopefully involving physical action, so that the listeners can seek a diversion, become relaxed, and become mentally and physically prepared for the next listening session.

Many bad listening habits often are practiced simultaneously. Similarly, many of the suggestions in this chapter for improving your listening effectiveness interrelate. For example, when you concentrate hard on what the speaker is saying you also are likely to be searching for main points, and behaving like a good listener should behave. Similarly, if you are truly flexible in your views you are likely to try not to let yourself become overstimulated by emotional words or ideas.

In conclusion, these suggestions are intended primarily to provide a basis for listening improvement. They are by no means exhaustive, and all of them may not apply in every listening situation. The objectives will have been realized if you have carefully examined each suggestion, applied it to your own personality and listening behavior, and assessed its usefulness. Remember, understanding concepts about listening without trying to improve your own listening behavior is of little value.

SUMMARY

Sensitivity to listening problems is probably the most effective means of improving listening behavior. However, several "common sense" suggestions also can help interested listeners become more effective in a variety of listening settings. Among the suggestions to help improve listening are the following:

(1) be physically and mentally prepared to listen
(2) think about the topic in advance when possible
(3) behave as good listeners should behave
(4) determine the personal value of the topic for you
(5) listen for main points
(6) practice listening to difficult expository material
(7) concentrate—do not let your thoughts wander
(8) build your vocabulary as much as possible
(9) be flexible in your views
(10) compensate for emotion-rousing words
(11) compensate for main ideas to which you react emotionally.

Some general questions to keep in mind while listening are:

(1) What does the speaker really mean?
(2) Have some elements of the message been left out?
(3) What are the bases for the speaker's evidence?

Some hints for note taking include:

(1) determine whether or not to take notes
(2) decide what type of notes are necessary
(3) keep notes clear
(4) keep notes brief
(5) note as quickly as possible the organizational pattern (or lack of pattern) of the speaker
(6) review your notes later.

The previous suggestions relate primarily to critical and discriminative listening settings. The following suggestions relate to appreciative listening:

(1) determine what you enjoy listening to most
(2) analyze why you enjoy these listening settings
(3) compare your own likes in listening with those of others
(4) be curious
(5) read and consult to learn more about those areas in which you enjoy listening.

When listeners have an opportunity to modify the listening environment to enhance the probability of effective listening they should

(1) establish a comfortable and quiet, relaxed atmosphere in the room (but not too comfortable)
(2) make sure the audience senses a clear purpose for listening
(3) prepare listeners for what they are about to hear
(4) break up long periods of listening with other activities.

COMMUNICATION IN ORGANIZATIONS

7

People's contentment with jobs in organizations depends largely on the amount and quality of communication. This also determines how they feel toward each other about cooperating on tasks. Messages need to flow freely upward, downward and laterally (horizontally) between and among individuals and departments. Goldhaber amplifies on these complexities in "Organizational Communication, —State of the Art 1975" in which he suggests a possible means of improvement.

In "Organization Communications," Blagdon and Spataro classify the many barriers to effective organizational communication. In addition, they summarize the lines and channels of communication flow including communication networks.

A supportive climate for open communication in organizations allows employees to make their needs and wants known without fear of recrimination from "above." Tubbs takes up this topic focusing on the crucial importance of the supportive climate in "Leadership Issues in Organizational Communication."

If a top manager desires information from the "bottom" of the hierarchy, he or she may receive spurious or phony data. Betsy and Gabriel Gelb spell out this problem and make suggestions for improvement in "Strategies to Overcome Phony Feedback."

One company experimented by removing the time clock and punch cards as well as the blue-collar, white collar barrier and set up a new employee self-rating system in an effort to improve employee attitudes as well as productivity. Sullivan reports what happened in "Tearing Down the Barriers."

Gerald M. Goldhaber

ORGANIZATIONAL COMMUNICATION

The age of "future shock" is upon us. We are all subjected to instant travel, instant change and instant communication. Today we can send a man to the moon in less time than it takes for a parcel post package to travel from Boston to San Francisco. Within five minutes we can talk on the telephone to almost any part of the world. Satellite networks enable us to be eyewitness observers at the funeral of a world leader, the landing of a spaceship on the moon, or even a full-scale war—without ever leaving our living rooms.

Despite many space-age communication victories, however, we still witness the moral decay of our government and political institutions, the disintegration of our families, and the bankruptcy of our businesses. It appears that advances in technological communications are not positively related to successful interpersonal communication. In fact, the relationship between the two may be inverse.

In 1956 William Whyte labeled most of us "organization men" because of the large amount of time we spend within organizations. In 1973, Harry Levinson claimed that this is still true, that "90 percent of those who work do so in organizations." When we add the time we spend in civic and social clubs, religious and educational institutions, hospitals, banks, etc., it is relatively simple to conclude that all of us today are organization men and women.

Since we spend most of our waking time in organizations, it is obvious that the problems of our cities, universities, and businesses are problems of organizations. One might hypothesize that given the technology to conquer outer space, we should be able to master the daily "people problems" we face in our complex organizations. One might hypothesize that given our current social psychological and clinical-medical models of handling people, we would be able to minimize intra- and intergroup conflict and the morale and motivation problems associated with managing complex organizations.

Yet despite the research reported by our nation's leading organizational experts advocating new approaches to structuring organizations and managing people, most organizations today rigidly adhere to the military model with control directed from the top of the hierarchy. Despite the findings of our behavioral scientists, most organizations maintain detailed job descriptions and specific goal-oriented objectives with an absolute minimum of flexibility. To compound the problem, many managers, fresh from a "sensitivity training session" or a "group dynamics workshop" or an "organization development seminar," claim to be "new people with a changed outlook on life and their job." It only takes a few weeks (or days) for them to return to their old

Gerald M. Goldhaber, Vice President of the International Communication Association. Speech delivered at the International Symposium in Communication, Monterrey, Mexico, October 29, 1975. From *Vital Speeches of the Day*, Vol. 42, No. 9 (February 15, 1976), pp. 268-273. Permission granted for reprinting by *Vital Speeches of the Day*.

ways of management based upon "carrot and stick" philosophies of dealing with people. Levinson calls this the "jackass fallacy" and predicts that organizational crises will continue as long as managers, superiors, and leaders maintain this basic attitudinal structure of "The powerful treating the powerless as objects as they maintain anachronistic organizational structures that destroy the individual's sense of worth and accomplishment." The evidence ("increased inefficiency, lowered productivity, heightened absenteeism, theft, and sometimes outright sabotage") would seem to support Levinson's conclusion that our organizations are still in a state of crisis which will ultimately result in both their destruction and the alienation of our youth.

Since 1938, when Chester Barnard defined the main task of an executive as that of communication, it has been demonstrated continuously that organization man (and woman) is a communicating person. To illustrate this, I'd like to quote from a recent Newsday story:

Edward Carlson, chairman and chief executive officer of United Airlines, travels an estimated 200,000 miles a year, using much of that time to communicate with approximately 50,000 employees. Carlson, who stops frequently to hold formal meetings, informal chats or just shake hands, has called the program "visible management." He has encouraged company managers to also make themselves as "visible" as possible, and the company feels that the program has helped considerably in United's major financial turnaround of recent years.

Various national surveys have shown that United's "visible management" policy is a rarity in business. Communications within private companies generally are poor and neglected and sometimes a severe problem, despite the fact that managers spend an estimated 75 percent of their time in some form of communication.

Before Carlson took charge people were poorly informed; they didn't understand why certain policies were necessary. A poorly informed workforce is not a very productive one. United lost $41 million in 1970 and Carlson joined the company that December. After edging back slowly at first, United, *in the height of the energy crisis,* had a record $86.3 million in profits.

"We work pretty hard at communications—all of us," Carlson said recently. "In my visits I constantly encourage employees to raise problems and suggestions. In turn, we are careful to respond to their ideas, because we really do care about what our employees are thinking."

Many organizations, however, frequently are not even conscious of communications problems. During the last fifteen years many speech and speech communication departments have begun offering courses to study this phenomenon of people communicating in organizations. In 1970 Wright and Sherman conducted a survey of speech communication graduate programs offering courses in organizational communication. Among the conclusions of the survey were the following:

1. 54 percent of the sample indicated that they either offer or planned soon to offer at least one course in organizational communication.
2. Classes in organizational communication typically enroll fulltime students in speech communication, as well as students from a variety of departments and colleges (usually business).
3. The areas of emphasis for organizational communication courses were relatively equally dispersed among theory, research, and application.

4. The most frequently studied organization setting was business and industrial organizations.
5. A majority of the completed questionnaires indicated that more courses should be offered in the area of organizational communication.

Downs and Larimer conducted a similar survey and reported —

1. 61 percent of their sample offer courses in organizational communication (mostly 1 or 2 courses/department).
2. 40 percent of their sample offer a major or a minor concentration in this area.
3. 60 percent of the course offerings have been originated in the last five years.
4. 35 percent of their sample report mostly non-speech majors as enrollees in the organizational communication courses.

It is apparent from the results of these surveys, that the field of organizational communication has shown remarkable growth in just a few years. All indications are that this growth will continue in the coming decade. Students who enter the field of communication are demanding an education which will lead directly to a future occupation or profession (other than more education). Organizational communication as a field would appear to answer these student demands. But what is organizational communication? What does it include and exclude?

I recently surveyed the literature and found over 50 "organizational communication" experts, each with their own definition of the field. This conceptual disparity is further illustrated by Downs and Larimer's finding that the following 21 areas of subject matter are currently being taught in organizational communication courses: Downward Communication, Upward Communication, Organization Theory, Horizontal Communication, Decision Making, Small Group Communication, Leadership, Research Techniques, Motivation, Interviewing, Change and Innovation, Conflict Management, Organizational Development, Conference Techniques, Management Theory, Consultation Training, Listening, Job Satisfaction, Public Speaking, Writing, Sensitivity Training.

What does all this mean? It is apparent that definitions, approaches to and perceptions of organizational communication are legion. It is apparent that organizational communication can mean and refer to whatever the author wants. Despite this wide variety of viewpoints, a few common strands can be detected in many of the fifty perceptions:

1. Organizational communication occurs within a complex open system which is influenced by and influences its environment.
2. Organizational communication involves messages, their flow, purpose, direction and media.
3. Organizational communication involves people, their attitudes, feelings, relationships and skills.

These propositions lead to my definition of organizational communication: *Organizational communication is the flow of messages within a network of interdependent relationships.* This perception of the field of organizational communication includes four key concepts, each of which I will now define and illustrate briefly: *messages, networks, interdependent,* and *relationship.*

Messages

The following messages were taken from letters of wives, husbands, mothers and fathers, on file at the San Antonio Veterans Administration:

"Both sides of my parents are poor and I can't expect nothing from them, as my mother has been in bed for one year with the same doctor, and won't change."

"Please send me a letter and tell me if my husband has made application for a wife and baby."

"I can't get any pay. I has 6 children, can you tell me why this is?"

"I am forwarding you my marriage certificate and my 2 children, one is a mistake as you can plainly see."

"I am annoyed to find out that you branded my child as illiterate, it is a dirty lie as I married his father a week before he was born."

"You changed my little boy to a girl, does this make a difference?"

"In accordance with your instructions, I have given birth to twins in the enclosed envelope."

"My husband had his project cut off 2 weeks ago and I haven't had any relief since."

Undoubtedly, the senders of the above letters may not have had the same meanings in their minds as may be interpreted by some readers. In fact, many of the senders probably would deny any other possible interpretation of their messages *except* the one they intended. How often do we assign a meaning to a message and assume that because we know what it means, so shouldn't everyone else? In a popularly used teaching film on communication, a manager is upset with his employee for not following his *explicit* instructions for completing a "model job." When the worker joyfully displayed his electrical-mechanical simulation "model," his boss angrily shouted, "I didn't ask you for this!" The employee, now frightened by his employer's loud, shrill voice and fast moving gestures, proclaimed, "But boss, you asked me to produce a model job, and that's what I did!" The now almost violent boss screamed, "But I didn't mean that you should build a model. I meant that you should do a model job, a good job, an excellent job!" The employee interrupted, "But boss, that's not what you said!" In a final shout of despair, the boss yelled, *"Don't listen to what I say, listen to what I mean!"*

In organizational communication we study the flow of messages throughout organizations. Organizational message behavior can be examined according to several taxonomies: language modality; intended receivers; method of diffusion; purpose of flow. *Language modality* differentiates *verbal* from *nonverbal* messages. Examples of verbal messages in organizations are: letters, speeches, conversations. With verbal messages we are most interested in studying the exact word choice used in the speech, letter, or conversation. Nonverbal messages are primarily unspoken or unwritten. Examples of nonverbal messages are: body language (eye movement, gesturing, etc.); physical characteristics (height, weight, hair length); touching behavior (hand-shaking, stroking, hitting); vocal cues (tone, pitch, rhythm); personal space (spatial arrangements, territoriality); objects (glasses, wigs, clothing); environment (room size, furniture, music).

Intended receivers include those people either within or outside the organization. The former examines messages intended for internal use, the latter for external. Examples of internal message systems include memos, bulletins, meetings. External message behavior is illustrated by advertising campaigns, public relations efforts, sales efforts, civic duties, etc. Internal messages are intended for consumption by the employees of the organization.

Method of diffusion identifies the particular communication activity employed during the sending of the messages to other people. Diffusion implies that messages are spread throughout the organization (either widely or narrowly). Here we are interested in how messages are spread. Most organizational communication diffusion methods can be divided into two general categories: those using "software" and those using "hardware" for dissemination. The latter depend upon electrical or mechanical *power* to make them function; the former depend upon our individual abilities and skills (particularly thinking, writing, speaking, and listening). Software methods are such oral (face-to-face) communication activities as conversations, meetings, interviews, discussions, and such written activities as memos, letters, bulletins, reports, proposals, etc. Examples of hardware are such *technological* activities as telephone, teletype, microfilm, radio, walkie-talkie, videotape, computer.

Purpose of flow refers to *why* messages are sent and received in organizations and *what* specific function they serve. Redding (1967) suggested three general reasons for message flow within an organization: task, maintenance, and human. Task messages relate to those products, services, or activities of specific concern to the organization—for example, messages about improving sales, markets, quality of service, quality of products, etc. Maintenance messages, such as policy or regulation messages, help the organization to remain alive and perpetuate itself. Human messages are directed at people within the organization, their attitudes, morale, satisfaction, and fulfillment.

Thus, in any organization, we recognize the different modalities, audiences, diffusion methods and purposes of messages. Since we are primarily concerned with *speech communication* phenomena within organizations, our discussion of message behavior includes: *verbal/nonverbal messages orally diffused to internal audiences for task, maintenance, and human purposes.*

Networks

The following message was communicated from a Colonel to a Major: "At nine o'clock tomorrow there will be an eclipse of the sun, something which does not occur every day. Get the men to fall out in the company street in their fatigues so that they will see this rare phenomenon, and I will then explain it to them. Now, in case of rain, we will not be able to see anything, of course, so then take the men to the gym."

The Major passed on the message to the Captain: "By order of the Colonel tomorrow at nine o'clock there will be an eclipse of the sun. If it rains, you will not be able to see it from the company street, so, then, in fatigues, the eclipse of the sun will take place in the gym, something which does not occur every day."

The Captain then said to the Lieutenant: "By order of the Colonel in fatigues tomorrow, at nine o'clock in the morning the inauguration of the eclipse of the sun will take place in the gym. The Colonel will give the order if it should rain, something which does occur every day."

The Lieutenant then told the Sergeant: "Tomorrow at nine, the Colonel in fatigues will eclipse the sun in the gym, as it occurs every day if it's a nice day. If it rains, then this occurs in the company street."

The Sergeant then assured the Corporal: "Tomorrow at nine, the eclipse of the colonel in fatigues will take place because of the sun. If it rains in the gym, something which does not take place every day, you will fall out in the company street."

Finally, one Private said to another Private: "Tomorrow, if it rains, it looks as if the sun will eclipse the Colonel in the gym. It's a shame that this does not occur every day."

This example illustrates the most commonly written about pattern of communication within an organization—that which exists downward from superior to subordinate and so on until the message is diffused throughout the organization. By no means, however, is this pattern the only one used in most organizations. Organizations are composed of a series of people who occupy certain positions or roles. The flow of messages between and among these people exists over pathways called communication networks. It is entirely possible for a communication network to exist which includes only two people, a few people, or the entire organization, Many factors influence the nature and scope of the network:

> *role relationship*—is the employee communicating according to a formally prescribed role or via an informal one?
> *direction of the message flow*—is the message flowing up, down, across, or diagonally throughout the organization?
> *serial nature of message flow*—are details of the message being omitted, added, highlighted or modified?
> *content of the message*—is the message verbal or nonverbal, task, maintenance or human in purpose, hard or soft in diffusion method?

Interdependence

Earlier I defined an organization as an open system whose parts all related to its whole and its environment. I say that the nature of this relationship is interdependent or interlocking because all parts within the system affect and are affected by each other. This means that a change in any one part of the system will affect all other parts of the system. This means also that, in a sense, communication networks within an organization can be seen as *overlapping* one another.

Implications for the concept of interdependence center on the relationships between the people who occupy the various organizational roles. For example, when a manager makes a decision, he would be wise to account for the implications of his decision on the entire organization. Of course, one way to account for the interdependent relationships affected by and affecting a decision is to communicate all possible messages to all possible people within the organization. Naturally, this would cause the organization to collapse from information overload. On the other hand, too little information communicated may affect other variables such as morale, attitude, production, and turnover. Somewhere there exists an appropriate amount of messages which proves effective at maintaining the organization's existence without succumbing to overload in the system. To further illustrate the concept of interdependence I will describe an incident which occurred at the University of New Mexico.

A graduate teaching assistant once read a poem containing profane language to his English class. Word of this act reached one member of the New Mexico Legislature who loudly denounced the instructor, his deeds, and the entire university for apparently condoning this act. The legislator ultimately introduced a resolution into the legislature calling for a reduction of the university's budget to *one dollar.* Although the motion failed, public attitudes toward the university were negatively affected for several years. Even today seven years after the incident, some members of the public reported in an attitude survey that they still "hold it against the university for allowing swearing in class."

Relationships

The last of the four key concepts inherent in my definition of organizational communication is *"relationship."* Exactly what relationships are important for study in an organization? Since an organization is an open, living social system, its connecting parts function at the hands of people. In other words, the networks through which messages travel in organizations are connected by people. Thus, we are interested, by studying roles, positions and nets, in studying the relationships among people. Human relationships within the organization are studied by focusing on the communication behavior of the people involved in the relationship. We study the effects of these behaviors upon specific relationships within the organization's subparts as they interact with each other. We study employee attitudes, skills, and overall morale as they affect and are affected by their organizational relationships.

When we focus on the the major ways people relate to one another in an organization, we usually identify three: the dyad (two people interacting); the small group (3 to approximately 12 people interacting); and public relationships (interaction with large groups).

If we agree that organizational communication is the flow of messages within a network of interdependent relationships, what is the current state of our knowledge about organizational communication? After three decades of research, what have we learned about the way people send and receive messages in complex organizations? One scholar, attempting to answer that question, (Redding, 1972) has concluded that the "road to a valid and a practical understanding of human communication behavior in living organizations . . . is barely more than a tow-path for most of its length, full of holes and interrupted by numerous unfinished sections as well as many washed-out bridges!" Redding went on to add, *"The total output of reasonably scientific, empirically-data-based-research efforts is very small indeed!"* If Redding is correct, and I suspect he is, then we haven't learned very much in thirty years!

Possible reasons for this lack of generalizable conclusions related to organizational communication theory building may be found in the methodologies employed by the researchers themselves. Careful reviews of the organizational communication literature reveal that most studies have used survey or interview techniques, have been done in organizations with relatively small (but available) samples, have ignored the multivariate approach crucial to the complete understanding of an organization and its multiplicity of interdependent variables, have not carefully adhered to basic psychometric methods when using or designing measuring instruments, and have not replicated their procedures in a variety of different organizations.

Recognizing this lack of generalizability of conclusions about organizational communication, a group of researchers within the International Communication Association began, in 1972, the Communication Audit Project. For the past four years and led by myself, Gary Richetto of the Williams Companies of Tulsa, Oklahoma, and Harry Dennis of the Executive Committee of Milwaukee, Wisconsin, over 100 researchers from six countries have contributed to this project whose goals are to:

1. Establish a normed data bank to enable comparisons to be made between organizations on their communication systems;
2. Establish, through these comparative studies, a general external validation of many organizational communication theories and propositions;
3. Provide research outlets for faculty and professionals and graduate students;
4. Establish the Intl. Communication Association as a visible center for organizational communication measurement.

The "communication audit" methodology of the ICA has several advantages not found in most research reported in the literature:

1. It uses a variety of measurement techniques (5) to converge upon a core of communication behavior;
2. It relies upon cooperation from several large organizations providing a large sample for the data base;
3. It allows several multivariate comparisons among key organizational variables, especially by interfacing the findings of the five measurement techniques;
4. It has been carefully and rigorously developed after four years of library research and five pilot-tests in a wide variety of organizations;
5. Its standardized measurement procedures allow for research replication and generalizability of findings.

During the past year, the "communication audit" has been successfully pilot-tested in five organizations (a utility company, a hospital, a manufacturing company, a school system, and a U.S. Senator's office) with total samples exceeding 2,000 employees. As a result of our pilot-tests, we have now been able to improve the validity and reliability of our instruments as well as maximize the efficiency of our entire audit procedure. We are currently making plans to do additional audits in the United States, Finland, England, Canada, and Mexico.

Although we have been involved in pilot-tests of our audit procedure, we have begun to notice some commonalities among our conclusions about organizational communication in our clients' organizations. Although some caution should be used in citing these findings, they do represent conclusions drawn from five different organizations, the data of which were all collected using standardized procedures and common instruments. I would like to conclude by mentioning some of our more commonly reported and repeated findings:

1. Most employees seem to like their immediate work environment and the people with whom they work closest—their work groups and immediate supervisors, but aren't that satisfied with their organization at large, its reward system, and their contributions to the organization as a whole.
2. Most employees are receiving the information they *need* to do their

daily jobs, but are not receiving all the information they *want,* particularly related to organization-wide concerns, problems, goals, decisions and mistakes; the exception is the manufacturing company where downward communication was very effective on almost all subjects.

3. Opportunities exist for employees to voice their opinions upward, particularly about work activity and staff progress, but the existence of adequate and appropriate *follow-up* is definitely lacking at the top of most organizations; especially missing is the opportunity for adequate upward flow related to evaluating supervisors' performance.

4. Horizontal communication, particularly information sharing between work groups, is weak or nonexistent, creating some problems of mistrust and unnecessary conflict and/or competition.

5. Face-to-face and written channels of communication appear to operate more effectively than such hardware as bulletin boards, videotape presentations, telephones, computer printouts.

6. Employees are least satisfied with information sources most removed from their immediate work environment (top management, their boss' superiors) and most satisfied with sources closest to their daily work performance (their boss, co-workers).

7. Of the four traits related to the quality of information (clarity, appropriateness, timeliness, believability), only timeliness—getting messages on time—appears to be a problem, particularly related to messages originating from top management.

8. The overall communication climate was more negative than positive for most of the organizations.

9. The most important communication problems experienced by employees related to the inadequacy or absence of information needed and/or wanted to do a good job, the misuse of authority or incorrectly following procedures to do a job, and ineffective interpersonal relationships due to personality clashes or poor cooperation.

10. In the larger organizations (over 500 employees) many employees are relatively isolated from both the necessary and incidental information flow.

We realize that these findings are only the beginning. Our ultimate goal is to build a data bank large enough to allow most organizations to compare themselves on key communication behaviors. We live in an age of organizations. We are all affected by organizations every day. Organizations as communication systems are in a state of crisis mainly due to archaic structures and faulty communication. If we are to move beyond the "tow-path" of our current research status, if we are to improve the daily flow of information in organizations, if we are to build our data bank of valid and reliable findings, then we must embark upon an international cooperative research endeavor, heretofore unseen among communication professionals. Researchers must sacrifice individual designs and personal glories so that a commonly employed methodology, resulting in externally valid findings, will allow our theories of organizational communication to be built upon a foundation of hard data. This, I submit to you, is the state of our art today and our challenge for the coming three decades of tomorrow.

Charles Blagdon and Lucian Spataro

ORGANIZATION COMMUNICATIONS

BARRIERS TO COMMUNICATION

In this report, barriers to communication are classified into two areas: (1) management philosophy and organizational environment, and (2) interpersonal barriers. In the real world, however, these divisions are not realistic, but they serve to simplify the analysis.

I.

Organizational barriers are crucial barriers to any communications network.

A. The nature, dynamics, and functions of the organization itself may be important barriers to the effective or efficient communication of information. This can happen in four ways:

1. The *physical distance* between members of an organization, both in terms of activity locus and organizational structure, presents a very obvious barrier to communication.
2. The *specialization of jobs,* which characterizes the act of organizing, has the effect of complicating and thus perplexing the exchange of information in organizations.
3. *Power and status relationships* may serve to impede the free flow of information in an organization. The superior-subordinate relationship has a direct effect upon communication.
4. *Information "ownership"* is a barrier which must be overcome. As long as a greater value is placed upon achievement by position rather than achievement by cooperation, there will appear to be power accruing to the "owner" of vital information.

II.

Management philosophy and organizational environment set the stage for the dynamic functioning of the communication system.

A. One of the most awesome barriers to organizational communication is the barrier of "unconcern." The business communicator who does not recognize the need to communicate well is doomed to varied kinds of problems in our economic and social order.

1. Managers often fail to transmit needed messages because they assume everyone knows, because they are lazy, because they procrastinate, or

Charles Blagdon and Lucian Spataro, "Organization Communications," *ABCA Journal,* Vol. 36, No. 3 (September 1973) pp. 12-15, 24-27. Reprinted by permission of the American Business Communication Association.

because they have a tendency to hog information. Since one cannot communicate everything, it is necessary to select, and this leaves the door wide open to selecting nothing.

2. Many organizations simply do not expect substantial two-way communication. Some executives' view of two-way communication consists of orders going downward and reports flowing upward.

B. Communications fail when they are intended to mislead. To illustrate this "unsound objective barrier," some companies engage in economic education programs for their employees, but their major purpose is to get the employees to accept doctrines and concepts held by managers rather than to educate the workers.

C. Organizational barriers in general are compounded by the fact that no one is responsible for seeing to it that communication takes place. Willingness to communicate is not enough; someone must be in charge of the function. His job is not to relieve everyone else from communicating but rather to aid them in their communications. Hence, the "functional responsibility" barrier expands the need for communication experts.

D. Executives mistake the form of communication for its substance. They often pay too much attention to media and devices and too little attention to purpose and content, thus, "media barrier."

E. Too great emphasis on the written word can be a barrier. Some administrators seem to make a fundamental mistake in considering the mimeograph or printing press as a substitute for sound face-to-face relationships. There cannot be any real communication in the form of bulletins, magazines, newspapers, booklets, and the like unless there is a relationship characterized by a fair degree of mutual trust and confidence. Such a relationship is based on attitude and behavior rather than words.

III.

Interpersonal barriers arise because of individual differences.

A. People often fail to communicate because they attach different meanings to the same word. This "barrier of semantics" is caused by the fact that meanings occur in the minds of individuals and these meanings are influenced by the totality of an individual's past experiences. No panacea for this semantic illness exists. But if a communicator will stop and question his words in the light of what they may mean to his recipient, a sizeable step toward clear communication can be taken. Such faults as vagueness, poorly chosen words, careless omission, lack of coherence, bad organization of ideas, jargon, and failure to clarify implications plague communication irrespective of how it is delivered.

B. The "tendency to evaluate" barrier occurs when individuals evaluate utterances within their particular frame of reference. Where feelings and emotions are involved, this barrier is likely to be heightened. The gateway to avoiding this barrier is to listen with understanding, i.e., examine the idea and attitude from the other person's point of view. Three major difficulties hinder the willingness to see things from another's point of view.

1. If a person is really willing to enter the private world of another individual and see the way life appears to him, the empathizer runs the risk of being changed himself. The risk of being changed is one of

the most frightening prospects facing many humans today.

2. It is just when emotions are strongest that it is most difficult to achieve the frame of reference of the other person. Rogers has found that this obstacle of heightened emotions can be reduced by employing a neutral third party to clarify the views and attitudes that each party holds.

3. Today's civilization does not yet have enough faith in the social sciences to use their findings.

C. In written communication particularly are found many polysyllabic and awesome words—words which are perfectly good English words, yet words which create an aura of "apartness." Because the communicator may be fearful of using words which might be beneath his economic and social level, he fails to communicate. This barrier is called the "status anxiety" barrier.

D. The barriers of "status relationships" and "distrust" are closely related to the "status anxiety" barrier.

1. Superior-subordinate relationships in a formal structure inhibit free flow of communication. The subordinate tends to tell the superior what the latter is interested in, not to disclose what he does not want to hear, and to cover up problems and mistakes which may reflect on the subordinate. To overcome this barrier, it is necessary to de-emphasize status and create an atmosphere in which all parties will mutually accept criticism, welcome suggestions, and admit problems.

2. Some superiors make a habit of changing or modifying their messages. Repeated experience with this can cause a subordinate to delay action or to act unenthusiastically.

E. Communication which solidifies the *status quo* is more acceptable and therefore more tempting, but it is not always the most valuable type of communication. This *status quo* barrier results in a tendency to carry good news only.

F. The "fear barrier" includes fear of misinterpretation, fear of distortion, fear of exposing a lack of knowledge, and fear of reprisal. However, actual distortion, actual misinterpretation, and actual reprisal, not just the fear of them are even greater barriers to communication. The failure of superiors to keep a subordinate informed may sustain these fears.

IV.

These "barriers" just mentioned are in a sense interpersonal barriers to communication; however, they arise from the nature, dynamics and functions of the organization itself. There are those barriers which arise from interpersonal contacts outside any obvious influence of the organization.

A. The first of these is referred to as *climate* of the interpersonal contact or relationship.

1. The total complex of feelings and sentiments of a relationship may be referred to as its climate.

2. This climate depends mostly upon actions and intentions, not upon words.

B. People take *values and standards* from the group to which they belong or to which they aspire. When the values of the originator and the receiver conflict, exchange of information will be difficult, and occasionally impossible. Misinterpretation and misunderstanding can easily occur.

C. Closely related to values and standards is the barrier presented by the conflicting or antagonistic *attitude* of the persons interacting.

1. A negative attitude toward the communicator or toward the content of the message will likely cause the intended receiver to misunderstand, or perhaps to ignore, the message.
2. There is evidence from research in mental health that one's attitude toward himself has a great deal to do with how accurately he is able to get information from the outside world and how accurately he is able to transmit it.

D. One other interpersonal barrier to which little attention has been given is that of the *effect and influence of mass communication.*

BIBLIOGRAPHY

Bass, B.M., *Organizational Psychology,* Allyn and Bacon, Inc., New York, 1960, pp. 186-201.

Brock, Luther A., "Overcoming Barriers to Communication," *North Texas State University Business Studies,* Spring 1965, pp. 60-62.

Fischer, Frank E., "A New Look at Management Communication," *Personnel,* Vol. 30, No. 6 (May 1955), pp. 487-495.

Goetzinger, Charles and Milton Valentine, "Problems in Executive Interpersonal Communication," *Personnel Administration,* Vol. 27, No. 2 (March-April 1964), pp. 24-29.

Hoslett, Schuyler Dean, "Barriers to Communication," *Personnel,* Vol. 28, No. 2 (September 1951), pp. 108-114.

Koontz, Harold and Cyril O'Donnel, *Principles of Management,* Third Edition, McGraw-Hill Book Co., New York, 1964, 637 pp.

Mason, Edward S. (Ed.), *The Corporation in Modern Society,* Harvard University Press, Cambridge, 1959, pp. 266-271.

Read, William H., "Communication in Organizations: Some Problems and Misconceptions," *Personnel Administration,* Vol. 26, No. 2 (March-April 1963), pp. 4-10.

Rogers, Carl R. and F. J. Roethlisberger, "Barriers and Gateways to Communication," *Harvard Business Review,* Vol. 30, No. 4 (July-August 1952), pp. 46-52.

Schramm, Wilbur (Ed.), *The Process and Effects of Mass Communication,* University of Illinois Press, Urbana, 1954, pp. 185-206.

Stieglitz, Harold, "Barriers to Communication," *Management Record,* Vol. 20 (January 1958), pp. 2-5.

LINES AND CHANNELS OF COMMUNICATION

I.

Communications link the supervising persons with subordinates.

A. They provide for the dissemination of ideas, orders, instructions, etc.

B. They provide for the receipt of ideas, advice, special reports, problems, etc.

II.

There are several "types" of formal communication channels.

A. A *formal channel* is consciously established and is thought of as one which ordinarily "carries" occupational or professional information.

B. An *organizational channel* is one which is established by and in the construction of the organization; therefore, it corresponds to the lines drawn between offices and functions on the organization chart.

C. *Lines of authority* connect the physical organization's hierarchy of command.

D. *Lines of power* are those which arise out of one person's willingness to be guided in his thought or behavior by another person.

E. *Intergroup channels* are established by the respective group leaders to "carry" those messages pertinent to the individual interests of each group, to their relationship and its changes, to the implications of conflict and/or cooperation, etc.

F. *Intragroup channels* are leadership channels within the group which "carry" information pertinent to the group's locomotion, operations, ideologies, norms, values, etc.

III.

Formal channels of communication can be viewed as proceeding in three directions: downward, upward, and laterally.

A. Downward communications are primarily directive.

1. Since the locus of authority in a business is at the top of the structure and is delegated downward through the organization, the burden of communication is directed from the top down.
2. The process of delegation itself is a form of downward communication.
3. Downward communication helps tie the levels of the organization together.
4. It is the instrument by which an executive puts his delegated authority to effective use.
5. It is the role of the supervisor to decide what his subordinates need to know, and to make sure that they get this information regularly in sufficient quantities, and in useful form.
6. The information must be communicated quickly enough for the subordinate to act in response to it.
7. Downward communications initiate actions by subordinates.

B. Upward communication is primarily nondirective.

1. It reports results or gives information, but cannot initiate activity.
2. Upward communication exists primarily to the degree that it is encouraged and permitted by the superior executive.
3. The minimum communication necessary is that which will enable the superior to check his own downward communication.
   a. To know that downward communications are being received and carried out.
   b. To know how to modify or discontinue them.
4. Each supervising executive has a basic responsibility of knowing how to encourage adequate upward communication.
5. Each employee has the responsibility of knowing how, when, and what to communicate in an upward direction.

C. Lateral communication has few implications of authority and status.

1. Landsberger's view is that the function of horizontal relationship is to facilitate the solutions of problems arising from the division of labor.
   a. The nature of horizontal relationships is determined by the individual position-holders' having different organizational subgoals, but interdependent activities that need to be blended.
   b. Conflict and disagreement may be frequent and inevitable, but useful.
   c. Much goes on in the horizontal pattern of communications before the vertical processes are called upon to mediate a conflict or bring about actions and decisions.
   d. The problems of an organization determine to a large extent the frequency and content of horizontal interactions and exert pressure toward solving the problem.
   e. These problems determine the stands taken by the departmental units and the strengths by which they are defended.
2. Dalton has reached some conclusions in some respects opposite to those of Landsberger.
   a. While interdepartmental conflicts may have positive value, it is an unintended or accidental consequence.
   b. He views horizontal relationships and interdepartmental conflicts primarily as results of intense personal rivalries and ambitions.
   c. Cliques form to take sides in the struggle, not determined by departmental lines but by informal factors. Organizational problems are of only secondary importance.
3. Simpson, in an empirical study of superior-subordinate relationships, views horizontal communications as determined primarily by the state of technology, thus de-emphasizing the frequency or content of horizontal interactions.
   a. He believes vertical communication has been over-emphasized.
   b. He has found that communications among foremen were mainly horizontal because of the mechanized nature of the work.

IV.

"Communication nets" is a concept that will be developed further.

A. Bavelas, Leavitt, and others have made studies of patterns other than the pyramid-shaped, hierarchical organization structure.

B. These patterns or nets are illustrated on the next page.[1]

C. It was established that difficulty of organizing is greatest in circle groups, next in all-channel groups, and least in wheel groups.

D. These findings indicate that there is not necessarily a direct connection between complete freedom to communicate and effective functioning. Some communication restrictions may improve effectiveness.

E. Findings also show how communication relates to the evolution of hierarchy and other patterns of organizational structure.

---

[1] Harold Guetzkow and Herbert A. Simon, "The Impact of Certain Communication Nets Upon Organization and Performance in Task-Oriented Groups," *Management Science,* Vol. 1, Nos. 3 and 4 (April-July 1955), page 237.

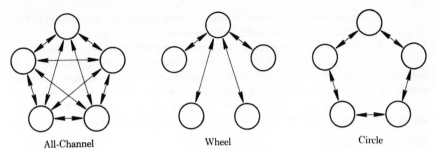

All-Channel   Wheel   Circle

V.

The design of an organizational hierarchy implies the structuring of communication channels.

WHAT IS AHEAD IN INFORMATION TECHNOLOGY?

I.

The impact of information systems throughout the organization is increasing. With technical developments in speed, accuracy, flexibility, and capacity of equipment and processes, the makeup of the corporate information system will be markedly changed.

II.

Several developments will come about.
   A. Future information systems will be more versatile and will more nearly parallel the real flow of information within an organization.
      1. The heart of a typical system will be a communications "center" to direct incoming and outgoing data from a central point or points to the entire organization.
      2. As costs of long-distance data communications are reduced, the variety of services available will be greatly increased.
         a.   Future management information reports will be generated by high speed printers, on screens, and by voice.
         b.   Computers will communicate with each other.

   B. Information systems will tend increasingly to be "real time"; that is, they will reflect important and routine events as they occur.
   C. Storage and retrieval of technical, management, and general data will become increasingly important aspects of information systems.
      1. Indexing and handling of the relationship between the machine system and the data will be the most difficult.
      2. The task is to develop a systems methodology.

III.

Functions involving day-to-day decisions and data analysis exist regardless of variations in management philosophy. It is on these *functions* and *the way they are performed* that information technology will have one of its major impacts, whether the functions are considered those of the top manager or those of his subordinates.

A. Management will have new tools, new problems, new opportunities as a result of future developments in information technology.

B. Increased management skills in human relations will be called for.

C. Increasing importance will be placed on the manager's ability to communicate rapidly and intelligibly, to gain acceptance for change and innovation, and to motivate and lead people in new and varying directions.

D. The manager of the future will need all the computer help he can get in coping with the greatly increased complexity of his communications job.

BIBLIOGRAPHY

Books

Dalton, Melville, *Men Who Manage,* John Wiley and Sons, Inc., New York, 1959, 340 pages.

McFarland, Dalton E., *Management: Principles and Practices,* 2nd ed., The MacMillan Company, New York, 1964, 684 pages.

Thayer, Lee O., *Administrative Communication,* Richard D. Irwin, Inc., Homewood, Illinois, 1961, 252 pages.

Periodicals

Bavelas, A., "Communication Patterns in Task-Oriented Groups," *Journal of Acoustical Society of America,* Vol. 22, No. 3 (1950), pp. 725-730.

Bavelas, A., "A Mathematical Model for Group Structures," *Applied Anthropology,* Vol. 7, No. 3 (Summer 1948), pp. 16-30.

Guetzhow, Harold and Herbert A. Simon, "The Impact of Certain Communication Nets Upon Organization and Performance in Task-Oriented Groups," *Management Science,* Vol. 1, Nos. 3 and 4 (April-July 1955), p. 237.

Landsberger, Henry A., "The Horizontal Dimensions in Bureaucracy," *Administrative Science Quarterly,* Vol. 6, No. 3 (December 1961), pp. 299-332.

Leavitt, H. J., "Some Effects of Certain Communication Patterns on Group Performance," *Journal of Abnormal and Social Psychology,* Vol. 46, No. 1 (1951), pp. 38-50.

Simpson, Richard L., "Vertical and Horizontal Communication in Organizations," *Administrative Science Quarterly,* Vol. 4, No. 3 (December 4, 1959), pp. 188-196.

Stewart L. Tubbs

LEADERSHIP ISSUES IN ORGANIZATIONAL COMMUNICATION

TO: All Personnel

SUBJECT: Early Retirement Program

As a result of automation as well as declining workload, Management must of necessity take steps to reduce our workforce. A reduction in force plan has been developed which appears to be the most equitable under the circumstances. Under the plan, older employees will be placed in early retirement, thus permitting the retention of employees who represent the future of the company. Therefore a program to phase out older personnel by the end of the current fiscal year via early retirement will be placed into effect immediately. The program will be known as RAPE (Retired Aged Personnel Early). Employees who are RAPED will be given the opportunity to seek other jobs within the company, provided that while they are being RAPED they request a review of their employment records before actual retirement takes place. This phase of the operation is called SCREW (Survey of Capabilities of Retired Early Workers).

All employees who have been RAPED and SCREWED may also apply for a final review.

This will be called SHAFT (Study by Higher Authority Following Termination).

Program policy dictates the employees may be RAPED once, SCREWED twice; but may get the SHAFT as many times as the company deems appropriate.

PERSONNEL DEPARTMENT

This fictitious memo is a typical example of the ways subordinates poke fun at their organization, and by doing so better cope with their environment. This is also an example of a way in which the informal organization functions.

A paper presented at the Spring Conference of the Michigan Speech Association, Oakland, April 1976.

A leader representing the formal organization may sometimes find his/her effectiveness undermined by the informal organization. Thus, the quality of interpersonal communication between leader and subordinates becomes very important.

Although the connection between leadership style and employee productivity and satisfaction is not always totally predictable, a growing body of evidence suggests that the leader with a supportive interpersonal style tends to be more effective. Most all of us are familiar with Gibb's (1961) classic article indicating that Supportive climates produce more effective communication than Defensive.

It took me some time before I realized that Gibb's findings [refer to Jack Gibb's "Defensive Communication" in Chapter One] apply not only to the interpersonal and small group contexts, but to the interpersonal and small group communication which occurs in organizations too! I think a lot of us have been brainwashed to think that the task demands of an organization disallow the supportive style. More and more I have been finding that this isn't necessarily so.

Meyer, Kay, and French (1965) found that the supportive supervisor got better results from performance appraisal interviews, while more critical supervisors produced counter-productive defensiveness in subordinates. Likert (1967) found that supportive sales managers got better sales results and higher satisfaction from sales personnel than the totally task-oriented managers.

Larson, Knapp, and Zuckerman (1969) found that patients in nursing homes responded better to treatment from nurses who were perceived as more supportive, " . . . more benevolent, less restrictive, less authoritarian, and more positive mental-hygiene oriented in their attitudes". They summarize some prior literature by concluding that " . . . studies support the notion that a systematic relationship exists between staff attitudes and institutional outcomes" These attitudes are subsequently reflected in the types of communication behaviors exhibited.

Jain (1973) found that the quality of supervisory communication (as perceived by subordinates) was highly correlated with the quality and amounts of subordinates' performance in urban hospitals. Hain and Widgery (1973), Hain and Tubbs (1974), and Widgery and Tubbs (1975) found that quality of communication (as perceived by subordinates) was highly correlated with high performance, high product quality, low grievances, low absenteeism, and low job turnover in automotive manufacturing plants.

Similar results have been found in totally different contexts. Hoyt and Mushinsky (1973) and Mushinsky (1974) found that engineering supervisors rated engineers more heavily on their communication abilities than their technical abilities in evaluating job performance. In other words, communication skills were better predictors of job success for engineers than *engineering abilities!*

Tubbs and Hain (1975) found in another factor analytic study, that successful college professors' teaching evaluations were more a function of their supportive interpersonal communication style, both in and out of the classroom, than their technical subject knowledge. This supports a theoretical formulation set forth by Tubbs (1972, 1974).

By now you may be wondering how do I learn to be a supportive leader/communicator? First, the change does not occur overnight. Second, the change in supervisory behavior is only one of several methods available for improving organizational performance (see Tubbs and Baird, 1976 for further material on this topic). But if you want to make a good start next Monday on the job, try this approach. *Pretend* that you work for a company like IBM which has a policy that *any* employee who is not satisfied with any encounter he or she has with their boss is encouraged to call the president of the company to report this complaint. IBM very seriously enforces this policy. With over 200,-000 employees you may wonder how this can work. It works because every supervisor knows about the policy and works especially hard to communicate in a way that he or she thinks will be seen as fair *in the eyes of the subordinate.* Out of all the material I have studied in over ten years in the communication field, this one pretending technique helps me improve my on-the-job communication more than any other one theory or technique.

The reason it works is because it forces us to be receiver-centered, and it motivates us to try much harder than we would otherwise. If you are suspicious, try it out for a week and judge the results for yourself. I think after you have tried it, you may want to stay with it.

In addition, observe your supervisor's communication behavior. Try to answer the question, "Does he or she seem basically to be for me or out to hurt me?" The supervisors who get better results are those whom we see as basically supportive.

The question of how to be a more effective leader is one which will always be with us. I have not attempted to offer a panacea as an ultimate answer. However, increasingly we are learning that our communication effectiveness in organizations can make a difference in our leadership effectiveness.

REFERENCES

Jack R. Gibb. "Defensive Communication," *Journal of Communication, 11,* 1961, 141-148.

Tony Hain and Stewart L. Tubbs. "Organizational Development: The Role of Communication in Diagnosis, Change, and Evaluation," a paper presented at the annual convention of the International Communication Association, New Orleans, April, 1974.

Tony Hain and Robin N. Widgery. "Organizational Diagnosis: The Significant Role of Communication," a paper presented at the annual convention of the International Communication Association, Montreal, April, 1973.

D. P. Hoyt and Paul Mushinsky. "Occupational Success and College Experiences of Engineering Graduates," *Engineering Education* (May, 1973), 622-623.

Harish Jain. "Supervisory Communication and Performance in Urban Hospitals," *Journal of Communication, 23,* 1973, 103-117.

Carl E. Larson, Mark L. Knapp, and Isadore Zuckerman. "Staff-Resident Communication in Nursing Homes: A Factor Analysis of Staff Attitudes and Resident Evaluations of Staff," *Journal of Communication, 19,* 1969, 308-316.

Rensis Likert. *The Human Organization* (New York: McGraw-Hill, 1967).

H. H. Meyer, E. Kay, and J. R. P. French. "Split Roles in Performance Appraisal," *Harvard Business Review, 43,* 1965, 123-129.

Paul Mushinsky. "Performance Ratings of Engineers: Do Graduates Fit the Bill?" *Engineering Education* (November, 1974), 187-188.

Stewart L. Tubbs. "New Directions in Communication: Getting It Together," in Stewart L. Tubbs (ed.), *New Directions in Communication* (Flint, Michigan: International Communication Association, 1972), 1-7.

Stewart L. Tubbs. "The Importance of Watzlawick's Content and Relationship Aspects of Communication in the Classroom," a paper presented at the annual convention of the Central States Speech Association, Milawaukee, April, 1974.

Stewart L. Tubbs and John W. Baird. *The Open Person . . . Self-Disclosure and Personal Growth* (Columbus: Charles E. Merrill, 1976).

Stewart L. Tubbs and Tony Hain. "A Factor Analysis of Teacher Evaluations in Communication Courses," a paper presented at the annual convention of the Central States Speech Association, Kansas City, April, 1975.

Robin N. Widgery and Stewart L. Tubbs. "Using Feedback of Diagnostic Information as an Organizational Development Strategy," a paper presented at the annual convention of the International Communication Association, Chicago, April, 1975.

Betsy D. Gelb and Gabriel M. Gelb
STRATEGIES TO OVERCOME PHONY FEEDBACK

You are sitting in a restaurant muttering about the slow service when finally the food comes—cold. You eat reluctantly, get up to pay the check, and hear the cashier ask, "Was everything all right?"

Somewhere up the organizational pyramid from that cashier is a manager who thinks he is going to find out something useful from your answer to the cashier's question. He supposes that forcing customers to offer answers because they are in a social situation provides *feedback,* as he calls it.

Likewise, somewhere high up on a number of organizational charts sit managers who once believed that suppliers would warn them about impending shortages. Or they thought their own purchasing people would sound the alarm. And everywhere are managers reviewing computer printouts and narrative summaries hoping to discover what threatens their organizations or where their opportunities lie.

Unfortunately, all these managers may find themselves the victims of feedback that is forced, fuzzy, or filtered—in sum, *phony* feedback. They—and all of us—need to look carefully to distinguish the useful from the deceptive; only then can we understand how to obtain dependable news about the results of our organization's efforts.

The whole feedback concept entered organizational thinking from the world of thermostats; therefore, it is hardly surprising that its usefulness in a world of human beings was overestimated. Seeing an organization as a system, various writers on organizational theory seized on the analogy to a heating system, in which the temperature in the room provides the feedback to direct the furnace to begin. Charmed by the efficiency of such a system, they envisioned a world where, for example, rising profit margins of a firm's Product *A* as contrasted to its Product *B* would automatically shift advertising dollars to *A,* until such time as *A*'s margin dropped due to high advertising expenses, at which time *B*'s margin would be higher and the advertising dollars would shift over to *B.*

Even in this kind of application, problems arose. A business differs dramatically from a situation where the cause of a cold room may be of interest in the long run, but in the short run the occupant wants heat. In a business, by contrast, more advertising may not always be desirable for a hot product; the Federal Trade Commission may be ready to swoop in if market share reaches 50 percent. Furthermore, the spurt in umbrella sales in Kansas City

Betsy D. Gelb and Gabriel M. Gelb, "Strategies to Overcome Phony Feedback," MSU *Business Topics,* Vol. 22, No. 4 (Autumn 1974), pp. 5-7. Reprinted by permission of the publisher, Division of Research, Graduate School of Business Administration, Michigan State University.

that diverts advertising funds to umbrellas can hardly prove a useful guide for allocation of advertising expenditures during a Midwestern drought.

Therefore, more sophisticated writers shifted to defining organizations as *open system*, affected by the outside world as well as by the results of their own output.[1] They began to take into account the human element that influences the reporting of results, understanding that this human element distorts reality as part of the process of supplying a manager with feedback. The cashier's question to the restaurant patron, for example, is a device conspicuously different from the thermostat: for the restaurant manager, the measurement of results involves people. And the presence of people offers the hazard of forced, filtered, or fuzzy feedback.

FORCING AN ANSWER

Forced feedback results from social pressure: it is rude to ignore a face-to-face question. So a restaurant patron mumbles that "everything was fine" to the cashier, knowing perfectly well that he's lying. Then, of course, he dislikes the restaurant on two counts: it served him a cold meal and forced him to lie. Similar results await the salesman who asks a buyer of his company's valves, textiles, or real estate what the buyer thinks about the company's products or service. Fudging the truth seems preferable to giving an honest answer that will provoke an argument or at least provoke more questions.

THE FUZZY ANSWER

Fuzzy feedback provides another substitute for either of the two honest answers of "I don't know" or "It wouldn't be smart strategy for me to give the facts." It arises, for example, when a purchasing agent, in times of scarcity, asks a supplier how prospects look. If things look grim, the supplier reports them as "so-so" rather than admit how scarce the product is, which will send a buyer shopping elsewhere. Hedging represents a common kind of fuzzy feedback—and it's just as fuzzy when dignified by a formal report format. Not much can be gleaned from the organizational equivalent of a weather report that reads: *Fair today, unless it rains.*

ORGANIZATIONAL FILTERS

Filtered feedback results when a manager asks a subordinate what's happening in the organization. Inevitably, as noted by Robert Heilbroner, "Armies and corporations alike have ways of sweetening the news as it ascends the hierarchy of command."[2] As one example, a clerk reports "No more orders from Widget, Inc.—they're mad at us." The supervisor's interpretation reads, "Widget, Inc. will not be placing further orders." The manager notes, "We do not expect further orders from Widget, Inc. at this time." The vice president

---

[1] Among many examples of authors advocating the systems approach are Daniel Katz and Robert L. Kahn, *The Social Psychology of Organizations* (New York: John Wiley & Sons, 1966) and John A. Seiler, *Systems Analysis in Organizational Behavior* (Homewood, Ill.: Richard D. Irwin, 1967).
[2] Robert Heilbroner and others, *In the Name of Profit* (Garden City, N.Y.: Doubleday & Company, 1972), p. 226.

reports "Widget, Inc. is not ordering this month," and the executive vice president passes along, "It will be next month before we receive an order from Widget, Inc."

WHAT CAN MANAGERS DO?

If forced feedback, fuzzy feedback, and filtered feedback are dangerous to an organization's health, what does a manager do to find out what's happening? "Phony" data is obviously no use in decision making, but how do you avoid it? Four suggestions may help:

1. cultivating feedback rather than forcing it
2. rewarding and acting on useful feedback
3. avoiding unnecessary dependence on feedback
4. reporting on feedback results.
    (a) You don't force feedback—you cultivate it. In the restaurant, the cashier might simply smile and offer the conventional "We hope you enjoyed your meal." Then a week later, a sample of customers get a phone call or post card from a consultant asking for comments (he got the names from credit card slips). He doesn't hit 100 percent response, but because he is independent of the firm and promises anonymity, the people who do answer have no reason to lie.
    (b) You reward useful feedback and you act on it. In a tight supply situation, a supplier who tells you forthrightly that deliveries will be a month behind is still supplying something timely: information. But that is a commodity that brings him no commission or profit—unless you provide the payoff, like a promise to give his firm priority if all delivery times turn out to be equal. Accurate reports from employees merit rewards, too—from the conventional "suggestion box" bonus to the obvious reward for a middle-manager: an offer to put him in charge of correcting the problem he's found, or an offer not to put him in charge of that particular can of worms if he prefers to avoid it. That last reward is important: many subordinates hesitate to bring in news of something wrong for fear they'll automatically be told to make it right.
    (c) You circumvent the need for feedback—you go and take a first-hand look. Peter Drucker offers a rationale for top managers to become the "sensing organ" for the organization; he notes that "if they remove themselves from market and customer and come to rely on reports and inside information, they will soon lose their ability to sense and anticipate changes in the market and to perceive, let alone to appreciate, the unexpected."[3]

Specifically, a department store executive can shop at his own store and the stores of competitors. Any company president can, as Robert Townsend suggests, personally use every new form proposed for adoption in his company.[4] What discourages first-hand investigation is usually fear of being caught:

---

[3] Peter F. Drucker, *Management: Tasks, Responsibilities, Practices* (New York: Harper & Row, 1973), p. 662.

[4] Robert Townsend, *Up the Organization* (New York: Alfred A. Knopf, 1970), p. 84.

"How would my people feel if they thought I were spying?" But of course the way they would feel depends largely on how many compliments, not just complaints, flow from your office as a result of direct observations.

(d) You report on feedback results—in other words, feed back the feedback. Employees and customers are naturally delighted when you tell them how their ideas have led to improvements in products or services. This can be done in employee publications, mass mailings to customers, mentions in the annual report, or even in media advertising. Almost nothing affects people in a more positive sense than to let them know that "We hear you," in Bell Telephone's excellent phrase.

One final roadmap to a disaster area: some managerial actions result in feedback that is forced, fuzzy, *and* filtered. Suppose, for instance, that a manager sets a pet project in motion, then asks a subordinate how the project is doing. Forced to answer, the unlucky underling fuzzes and filters wildly: a favorite example is the "assistant to" who scanned the red ink on a project he had secretly opposed, then announced to his beaming boss: "Sir, that idea of yours has met my every expectation."

Barry Sullivan

TEARING DOWN THE BARRIERS

Winning the respect of the employee, developing mutual feelings of trust between management and the workforce, and opening the clogged lines of communication in the plant are the kinds of accomplishments most managers hope for but few are able to achieve.

Instead, management must deal with the reality of an alienated workforce, a group which the whitecollar faction neither trusts nor, in most cases, even likes.

In our company, which manufactures lighting fixtures, parachute ripcords, and precision-molded rubber products, we decided to trust our 200-plus employees. And these are some of the changes that our "broken barriers" plan has brought about since 1969:

1. Abolition of the time clock and the timecard.
2. Development of an employee assistance program.
3. Creation of an employee self-rating system.
4. Monthly management-employee meetings to permit extensive one-to-one questioning by our workers.
5. Elimination of such whitecollar "privileges" as reserved parking spaces, separate restroom facilities, and separate plant entrances.

IN THE BEGINNING

The assault on the barriers between whitecollar and bluecollar workers in our company began in earnest in 1969. Inspired by Japanese businessman Shigeru Kobayshi's book, *Creative Management,* which urged trust and open lines of communication between employer and employee, we surveyed our workers to find out how they felt about conditions at Wasley.

Basically, the survey showed we weren't communicating well enough with our people. It also indicated that our employees' understanding of company policy could be improved.

Based on the survey results, we embarked on a determined campaign to establish the mutual trust and credibility which Mr. Kobayshi had achieved in Japan.

Our goals were to:

1. Improve productivity.
2. Compete more effectively for the best employees with national, unionized industries in our area.
3. Lessen employee turnover.
4. Obtain greater believability of management's messages on safety, scrap reduction, product defects, and company benefits.

Barry Sullivan, "Tearing Down the Barriers," *Industry Week,* Vol. 188, No. 9 (March 1, 1976), pp. 38-40. Copyright © by Penton Publishing. Permission granted for reprint.

NEW POLICIES, NEW PROGRAMS

To reach these goals, we took a long, hard look at our company policies. We knew we had to convince our people that we were giving them all the facts about the operation. We wanted to make it easier for them to have input into the system, to air their grievances.

To implement the overall policy of smoother employee-management dialog, such projects as the self-rating system, the employee assistance program, biannual employee surveys, the monthly employer-employee meetings, a direct line system for complaints and survey responses, and a foreman-building program were initiated.

And we resolved to continue this program until the expected results were achieved. Obviously, trust and liking have to be demonstrated over and over again for a long period of time before attitudes change.

We began by tearing down the most obvious of the barriers: the time clock and the timecard. Employees learned of the new policy via another of our communications tools, the "news center" board, which draws employee traffic by strategic placement, illumination, frequent message changes, and "stopper" news photos and captions from national wire services.

We haven't regretted the change. Instead of dealing with hundreds of timecards, the payroll department now gets all its information from a form kept by each foreman, who in turn gets his data from employees who are trusted to report their hours accurately.

NO HOLDS BARRED

Crucial to our full-disclosure policy are monthly meetings attended by employees and members of top management.

To permit employees from all three shifts to attend, meetings are scheduled for 7:30 a.m. and 3 p.m. The names of those who will be attending the meetings are posted on the "news center" board about a week before each meeting, so that co-workers can bring questions to them to be presented to management.

No holds are barred, and all questions, except those which should be more properly discussed by an employee and his supervisor, are answered fully.

Some 15% of the Wasley workforce has already benefited from our unique "employee assistance program", established in 1974 as a counseling and referral program designed to deal with such employee problems as alcoholism, drugs, disturbed children, and marital difficulties.

Operated in conjunction with Wheeler Affiliates, an informal confederation of hospitals and other helping associations, the program has effectively reduced the number of quits and firings which serious personal problems can cause.

The employee self-rating occurs on each employee's anniversary with the company.

He and his foreman each fill out a rating form—and meet within a week to discuss the two ratings. With one exception in the three years we have used this system, employees either rated themselves lower than or about the same as the foreman did.

Not only does the self-rating system give the employee a chance to evaluate his performance each year, it also allows the foreman to recheck his records and take stock of each employee. The discussion session between foreman and employee is an opportunity for the foreman to comment directly to the worker on his work habits and to inform him of any new benefits he may become eligible for in the next year.

The rating form will also tell a foreman if a worker has been upgrading himself on the job. One foreman recently found that a woman had learned and was doing her own setup and inspection of her work—thus upgrading herself three pay grades.

FOREMEN IN A KEY ROLE

Obviously, none of our improvement measures could have worked if we didn't have competent foremen.

Foremen play a vital role throughout the program and thus they are encouraged to take as many management courses as they wish to. They donate the time; we pay their tuition.

Without the cooperation of the foremen, the elimination of timecards could not have succeeded, because all the burden of timekeeping and making the new system work fell on them.

A case involving a 50-year-old employee and a 28-year-old foreman demonstrates the blossoming relationship that's possible between employee and foreman—and foreman and management.

The employee, who previously had a good record but had begun to show signs of a drinking problem, came to the plant one day to announce to the foreman he had found another job and was quitting.

However, the next day he went to the foreman's home, admitted he did not have another job, and said he was undergoing treatment for alcoholism.

Based on the man's past performance and the fact that one of his children had recently been killed in an auto accident, the foreman recommended to management that the man's quit request be denied. We agreed and placed the man on medical disability until he returned to his job.

We have also tried to make every piece of paper connected with the hiring and processing of an employee advance our communication goals.

Our classified ads emphasize our "people" orientation. Our job application form has been designed to save time for ourselves and for the prospective employee. For instance, there is a question about what the applicant liked and disliked most about his last job. If the person did not like the high temperatures involved in his previous position, we wouldn't assign him to a high-heat situation.

We have an information sheet for each applicant that describes Wasley and answers the most common questions asked by applicants. Once hired, the new employee receives a personalized handbook, with his supervisors' names written on it, along with such pertinent information as his pay grade, working hours, and so on.

EVALUATING AGAIN

To evaluate the entire program, we had outside consultants conduct follow-up surveys of our employees in 1972 and 1974.

The surveys showed that company credibility is definitely improving and continues to improve each year. They also revealed that we had taken

major strides toward driving home company policy to the bulk of our employees, getting other messages across, and making our foremen productive
and respected members of the management team.

As an example, in 1969 only 27% of our employees thought the letters
we sent to their homes were a credible source of information about the company. In the 1972 study, 60% found them believeable. The news centers were
believed by 57% in 1969 and by 63% in 1972.

In the 1972 survey, nearly 80% of our employees said they understood
the company's policies compared with 22% in 1969. Although not directly
comparable because we changed rating companies in 1974, the 1974 figures
show corporate credibility is continuing to improve.

The surveys are one medium for identifying employee complaints. Our
"direct line" box and a form we send to former employees' homes after their
departures have also proved to be effective ways of isolating complaints—each
of which is investigated.

For the company, a policy of openness, honesty, trust, and continual
communication has paid off in lower turnover, a greater number of applicants
who say they want to work for Wasley because of the recommendation of a
current employee, and increased credibility of management and its channels
of communication.

Our efforts to improve credibility and communications are based on
the premise that we never have been perfect, never will be perfect, but we're
going to keep on trying for perfection.

As one visitor to our shop, who had heard of our program and wanted
to see it in action, remarked recently: "I had expected to see a bunch of spoiled,
contented, and very slow-moving people. But, by God, your people hustle!"

MASS
COMMUNICATION _____ 8

     This section begins with Greenberg's selection which reminds us of the pervasive influence that mass communication has upon us. In the second selection, Cox reviews some research findings which indicate that audiences do not consume all that is offered by the mass media.

     Stauffer and Frost show empirical evidence of reader reaction to "pulp" magazines in the third selection. It confirms what we may not have suspected—that men enjoy viewing nude women in such magazines significantly more than women enjoy viewing nude men.

     In the fourth selection, Gumpert explores the provocative concept of uni-communication, or individual messages designed for mass audiences. Bumper stickers, tatoos, and graffiti are perhaps the most easily identifiable examples.

     The final selection by Goldsen and Bibliowicz describes a subject near and dear to many of us, namely, *Sesame Street.*

Bradley S. Greenberg

MASS COMMUNICATION AND SOCIAL BEHAVIOR

Try to imagine a home in the United States without a radio, television, newspapers, books, magazines, or stereo. Try to imagine a car without a radio. Try to imagine a school without television monitors, a library, or a school newspaper. Try to imagine a community without at least one newspaper, one radio station, perhaps a cable television facility, several network channels, and an educational station that few people watch or listen to. It boggles the mind; what could we possibly find to do with ourselves without such mass-media diversions? No other social institution so pervades our lives, wherever we go or whatever we happen to do. We might escape physically from our family, our church, or our school, but one of the strictures of contemporary life in the United States is a virtual inability to find a hermitage free from the mass media.

The question is not whether the mass communication system has any effects on social behavior. Let us take this as a given. Rather, the intriguing quest for social researchers is to identify which social behaviors are most likely to be altered, and then to isolate just what effects on these social behaviors the mass media may be having.

Perhaps it would be useful to verify our assumption that the mass media overlap a major portion of our lives. This argument is occasionally difficult for college students to accept. Coming to college is a temporary dislocation of mass-media activities; TV is somewhat more inaccessible, newspapers may be irrelevant (save for some college news) and the radio and record-player become the most used media. This serves to distort perceptions of what is going on elsewhere. Out there, over the past 10 years, there has been a persistent, increasing trend toward allocating more and more non-work time to mass media activities.

The daily activity of the typical American man between 35 and 45 years of age looks quite a bit like this: Given that he is confined to a 24-hour day (despite his chauvinism), he sleeps one-third of that total, and works another one-third. This leaves him about 8 hours, not all of which is leisure time. About 3 more hours go to eating, dressing, bathing, resting, necessary errands, and child-caring. Now, we are down to some 5 hours of what might be termed "free time," in the sense that the individual may now make some decisions as to where this segment of time goes. By 1974 over 3 hours—on the average—were going to television-watching each and every weekday, with an extra 1½ hours on weekends. On top of that, radio listening averages some two hours a day, although a good portion of that may be while commuting; a newspaper is delivered to 90 percent of all homes, and some 15 to 30 minutes is spent with the paper. Our typical American also probably looked at some magazine in the last week, but does not often go out to movies. Why should he? There is an adequate supply on television, save for "blue flicks." And if we shifted sexes and talked about his wife or girl-friend, her allocation of free time is not particularly different. Despite male protestations, the typical woman has only the same total amount of free time to divide. One point not to be lost in all this is that television-watching has increased by an hour a day per adult during the last decade; although there has been an increase in set ownership during that period—today well over 95 percent of all homes in the U.S. have at least one TV set, and nearly 60 percent now have color—this cannot account for the daily increase in overall viewing habits.

Of more interest to this writer is the manner in which young people spend their time. If the school year is the focal point, then children typically sleep about 10 hours, and spend 6 to 7 hours going to, in, or coming from school. Knocking off another 2 to 3 hours for chores, homework, and eating, there remains a similar critical mass of 5 to 6 hours of free time for the youngster.

In recent studies in urban sites, nine- to ten-year-old children averaged more than four hours a day watching television, another hour of radio-listening, and about a half-hour of record-playing. Their adolescent counterparts, however, may set the pace for media diversity and saturation. Teenagers, in a Philadelphia study, according to self-reports from a cross section of social classes and races, managed to:

1. Average almost four hours of television a day,
2. Listen to the radio two hours a day,
3. Look at a daily newspaper,
4. Look at three magazines a week,
5. Go to two movies in the last month,
6. Listen to records an hour each day.

Perhaps we have overstated the case. Obviously the figures now add up to more than 24 hours a day. Some of these activities are primary ones (i.e., they are the major activities of the moment), and others are secondary (i.e., other things are going on at the same time, making for simultaneous multiple uses of leisure time). But only two of these media efforts may be classified as secondary; radio and record-listening. Much, if not most, television watching is a primary activity, absorbing effort and attention at a given time.

From such a log of media-time expenditures, it is apparent that a principal social behavior related to the availability of mass communication is the activity-choosing behavior done within that system. The decision as to what to do with free time is a major social act. A predominant number of individual decisions lead to mass-media choices, and television in particular.

From that beginning, it is mandatory to choose a focus for our discussion. We will deal primarily with the most ubiquitous of media—television—and with that audience segment most susceptible to its influence—young people. (We do not suggest that other media do not have social impact, nor that adults are unaffected in their social behaviors. We would indeed argue just the opposite, given time and space to do so.)

A basic premise in our thinking and research, and one accepted and supported by others, is that what a viewer will derive from a given mass-media message depends in great measure on what he brings to the message. His background, his experiences, his knowledge, his personality, all may affect the manner in which any given message affects him. One advantage of working with young people is that they may have fewer or less intense sets of experiences that can interfere with direct message impact. That is, to the extent that the message travels through fewer individual "filters," its impact may be more impressive. For example, a young person watching a public television program on venereal disease would likely have undergone large-scale knowledge and attitude change. His own experiences would have been limited, few messages on that topic would have been received previously from parents, school, church, etc. In contrast, that same viewer, watching a western for the umpteenth time, would be unlikely to go away with many new thoughts about sheriffs, Indians, or horses. Many prior messages would have preconditioned the viewing of such material.

Another set that the viewer brings to the media situation may affect the nature of his subsequent social (or antisocial) behavior. These are his *motivations* for spending this particular time period with a given mass medium and the content it happens to be making available then. What are the gratifications he is seeking from the time allocation he is making? Or, as others have labeled it, what are the functions that television provides for the viewer?

This question can be approached with two kinds of theoretical notions in mind. One is more *content*-oriented. Here, the viewer's behavior is conceived of as selecting certain specific programs because of the content they offer; whatever motivation he has for turning to television is directed at a particular kind of content (e.g., he wants some information, so he turns on the news). An alternate approach, and the one we shall develop in detail here, is to conceive of his behavior more as *medium*-oriented. The viewer, whatever his specific motivation, turns to an accessible medium to satisfy that motivation, perhaps regardless of the specific content offering at a particular time. His prior experiences with the medium precondition him to expect the medium, through some offering, to partly satisfy his momentary needs. These are not contradictory notions. Perhaps the best explanation may encompass partly a content-and partly a medium-orientation. The rationale would be that some kinds of content, within some kinds of media, are better able to satisfy different motivations sought by audience members. But let us turn directly to recent evidence on basic motivations for the amount of viewing which occurs regularly.

Studies we have done with young people between 9 and 15 years of age in both the United States and England have isolated seven basic motivations for watching television. These reasons are largely independent of each other; that is, a child who expresses one of these motivations for watching television may or may not express any of the others. These are the main reasons that young people (and probably older ones as well) turn to television:

To pass time. This was one of the two most ardently and frequently expressed motivations for watching TV. Its position of prominence does not change from the youngest child to the oldest teen-ager. Here are some sample responses which express this motive:

> "It gives you something to do when you haven't got anything to do."
> "It fills up time."
> "Sometimes I get bored with everything, so I turn on the TV."

For enjoyment. This is a less specific motivation, but it occurs with great frequency. That it is least frequent among older teenagers may reflect more specific articulation of reasons with increasing age. They said:

"I just like to watch."
"It's so interesting."
"It's a habit."

For companionship. This motivation and the two that follow have occurred with a lower level of frequency and intensity than the preceding ones, but are still expressed by a majority of youngsters. For many children, television provides a means of obtaining vicarious companionship, expressed in these ways:

"It's almost like a human friend."
"It's very comforting if you're alone."
"When there's no one to talk to."

For arousal. Many children respond that they seek out television in order to be stimulated. The stimulation sought encompasses a variety of emotional arousal types:

"It gives me a thrill."
"It excites me."
"It makes me laugh (. . . or cry)."

To learn. Our original conception of a possible motivation base in terms of learning was that there would be two separate types of learning sought from television. One of these would be *"hard"* learning, or the seeking of content full of information and news to supplement school-type learning. The other would be informal or *social* learning, i.e., seeking content which would be of use to the viewer in his social interactions with other people. However, these two appear to merge undifferentiated in the responses of young viewers. Here are examples of both kinds of learning, which appear to be a single type of television gratification:

"It teaches me things I don't learn at school."
"I want to know what's going on in the world, in other places."
"I can learn how to do things Ive never done before."

"It helps me learn things about myself."
"So I can learn how I'm supposed to act."

For relaxation. This was one of the two final motivations identified, and was reflected by about half of the youngsters studied. Its seeming contrast, perhaps even contradiction, with the arousal motivation is worth noting. The children said:

"It relaxes me."
"It's a pleasant rest."
"You don't have to do anything."
"It's easy to watch."

As a source of refuge. Many young people sought out television in order to divert their attention from specific kinds of problems. This appears to be a more goal-directed motivation than the one we labeled "to pass time," although both have escapist attributes. For example:

"It helps me forget my problems."
"It keeps me out of trouble."

"I want to get away from the rest of my family."
"I can just shut everything else away from me."

Thus, if you try to extract from young viewers their own bases (or rationalization) for activity-time allotments to television, you arrive at such factors. These isolate the major parameters perceived by the viewer for his television behavior. However, at least one large *caveat* is needed. We have been implying that these major sets of responses are reasons or motivations for going to the medium. It would be almost as easy to argue that they are gratifications obtained from having gone to the medium. The research is not yet clear on this point. And the answer probably lies somewhere between. As we suggested earlier, what the viewer brings to the medium affects what he goes away with. So, if a child seeks arousal, he probably will be aroused somewhat; if he seeks companionship, he probably will feel he has obtained it somewhat. Therefore, some segment of the social behaviors which arise from exposure to the mass media may be deliberately sought. Those areas in which primary seeking occurs have been elaborated in this discussion. How well the mass media may satisfy certain needs or motivations for exposure remains an open question. However, if a viewer were not at least partly satisfied or reinforced in terms of what was sought, it is likely that alternative activities would be undertaken. Given the evident persistency of exposure, many needs are being met frequently enough to continue the particular media behavior involved.

Donald F. Cox

CLUES FOR ADVERTISING STRATEGISTS

Basically there are two ways of viewing the audience—what I call the "egotistical" and the "realistic" views. Of these two, the most satisfying to the mass communicator is the first, which enables him to think of the audience as a relatively inert and undifferentiated mass that he can often persuade or influence. It is "egotistical" because it attributes great powers to the communicator and regards the audience as a swayable mass. Proponents of this view would probably hold that if you "hit them hard enough" (or "loud enough, long enough, and often enough"), sooner or later they will buy your product.

Perhaps the "realistic" view is more valid. With it, the audience is regarded as a body of individuals who may respond to a communication or commercial in a variety of ways, depending on their individual predispositions. This view also holds that while the communicator, the communication, and the medium play important roles in the communications process, in the final analysis it is the audience which decides whether (and to what extent) it will be influenced. Further, this view acknowledges the importance of the audience in its own right, through the process of social and personal influence.

Let us examine some evidence which should demonstrate that the "realistic" view *is* realistic, and the "egotistical" view *is* egotistical.

In order for an audience to be influenced in the desired manner by a communication, several conditions must be met:

1. The audience must, somehow, be *exposed* to the communication.
2. Members of the audience must interpret or *perceive* correctly what action or attitude is desired of them by the communicator.
3. The audience must remember or *retain* the gist of the message that the communicator is trying to get across.
4. Members of the audience must *decide* whether or not they will be influenced by the communication.

We might consider these four conditions—exposure, perception, retention, and decision—as the gateways to effective communication and persuasion.

Communications research has established beyond much doubt that the processes of exposure, perception, retention, and decision do not often occur in a random fashion among the population. To varying degrees, people are predisposed to expose themselves to certain kinds of communications and media and not to others. Different people tend to get different meanings from the same communication and to remember or forget different aspects of a communication. Finally, different people make different decisions as to whether or not they will be influenced.

Donald F. Cox, "Clues for Advertising Strategists," *Harvard Business Review*, Vol. 39, No. 6 (November-December 1961), pp. 160-164. Permission granted for reprinting by the *Harvard Business Review*.

Since each of these processes involves a selection or choice by individual members of the audience, we may refer to them as *selective exposure, selective perception, selective retention, and selective decision*. Let us first examine some studies which illustrate the operation of the selective processes, and later discuss the implications of these studies in the area of advertising strategy.

Selective Exposure. The conditions under which people engage in selective exposure and the extent to which this process is operative have not been fully specified or documented by communications research. However, the general conclusion seems to be that most people tend to expose themselves to communications in which they are interested or which they find congenial to their existing attitudes and to avoid communications that might be irritating, or uninteresting, or incompatible with their own opinions. The following studies are illustrative:

> Danuta Ehrlich, Isaiah Guttman, Peter Schönbach, and Judson Mills found that new car owners were much more likely to read advertisements for the car they had just purchased than were owners of the same make but an earlier model.[1] The new car owners were also much more likely to read ads about their own car than they were to read about other makes. The hypothesis is that the new car owners were seeking reassurance by exposing themselves to what were, no doubt, very "congenial" communications.
>
> Charles F. Cannell and James C. MacDonald found that only 32% of a sample of male smokers were consistent readers of articles on health (including articles dealing with the relationship between smoking and lung cancer), whereas 60% of non-smoking males read such articles.[2]

Selective Perception. Even when people are accidentally or involuntarily exposed to a communication, they sometimes misinterpret or distort the intended meaning of the communication. For example, Patricia L. Kendall and Katherine M. Wolf report a study in which cartoons which were intended to ridicule prejudice were misinterpreted in some way by 64% of the people who saw them.[3] Misinterpretation was most frequent among prejudiced respondents who either saw no satire in the cartoons or interpreted them as supporting their own attitudes. One respondent felt that the purpose of a cartoon intended to ridicule anti-Semitism was "to show that there are some people against the Jews and to let other people feel freer to say they're against 'em too, I guess."

Carl I. Hovland, O. J. Harvey, and Muzafer Sherif presented communications arguing the desirability of prohibition to three types of people—"Drys," "Wets," and those "Moderately Wet."[4] They found that the greater

---

[1]"Postdecision Exposure to Relevant Information," *Journal of Abnormal and Social Psychology*, Volume 54, 1957, pp. 98-102.

[2]"The Impact of Health News on Attitudes and Behavior," *Journalism Quarterly*. Volume 33, 1956. pp. 315-323

[3]"The Analysis of Deviant Cases in Communications Research," in *Communications Research*, edited by Paul F. Lazarsfeld and Frank N. Stanton (New York, Harper & Brothers, 1949), pp. 152-179.

[4]"Assimilation and Contrast Effects in Reactions and Attitude Change," *Journal of Abnormal and Social Psychology*, Volume 55, 1957, pp. 244-252.

the difference between the attitude of the recipient and the position advocated by the communication, the more likely the recipient was to regard the communication as propagandistic and unfair, and even to perceive the stand advocated by the communication as further removed from his own position than it actually was. Conversely, when the distance was small between the recipient's own stand and the position advocated by the communication, the recipient was likely to view the communication as being fair and factual and to perceive it as being even closer to his own stand than it actually was.

Habits also can cause distortion of a communication because people often see or hear that which, on the basis of past experience, they expect to see or hear. Gordon Allport and Leo Postman report that a picture in which a Red Cross truck was shown loaded with explosives was ordinarily perceived by subjects as a Red Cross truck carrying medical supplies (because that is the way it "ought" to be).[5]

In summary, the research cited indicates that under certain conditions people misinterpret or distort a communication so that it will be more compatible with their own attitudes, habits, or opinions.

Selective Retention. There is another way a person can reduce the dissonance or lack of internal harmony resulting when there is a discrepancy between his attitudes and those expressed by a communication with which he is faced. He can simply forget rather quickly the content of the communication! If this process is operative, we should also expect that a person would learn more quickly, and remember for a longer period, communications which *are* compatible with his own attitudes.

A study by Jerome M. Levine and Gardner Murphy supports these contentions.[6] Here it was found that procommunist material was better learned and better remembered by procommunists than by anticommunists; and the reverse was true for anticommunist material. Another example of selective retention occurred in an experiment by Claire Zimmerman and Raymond A. Bauer.[7] Given some material which was to be used in preparing a speech, subjects remembered fewer of the arguments which might have been received unfavorably by the audience they were slated to address.

Selective Decision. Even when a person has been exposed to a message, correctly perceives its intent, and remembers the main content, he still must decide whether or not to be influenced in the manner intended by the communicator. Because of individual predispositions, different people make different decisions as to whether or not (and to what extent) they will be influenced.

For example, in not one of the studies which I have reported has there been an instance in which every member of the audience made the same decision. In every case, some people decided to be persuaded; others did not. We can only assume that just as certain people are predisposed to expose themselves selectively to certain kinds of communications and to avoid others, they

[5]"The Basic Psychology of Rumor," *Transactions of the New York Academy of Sciences,* Series II, Volume 8, 1945, pp. 61-68. Reprinted in *Readings in Social Psychology,* edited by E. E. Maccoby, T. M. Newcombe, and E. L. Hartley (New York, Henry Holt & Company, Inc., 1958), pp. 54-64.

[6]"The Learning and Forgetting of Controversial Material," *Journal of Abnormal and Social Psychology,* Volume 38, 1943, pp. 507-517.

[7]"The Influence of an Audience on What is Remembered," *Public Opinion Quarterly,* Volume 20, 1956, pp. 238-248.

268 *Shared Experiences in Human Communication*

are also predisposed (i.e., more susceptible) to being influenced by some types of communications and appeals and not by others. In the Hovland, Harvey, and Sherif experiment, those whose attitudes strongly favored prohibition were predisposed *not* to be influenced by arguments against prohibition, and vice versa. Persuasion occurred most often when the individuals' attitudes toward prohibition were only slightly different from those advocated by the communication.

The evidence which I have thus far introduced seems to indicate quite clearly that people are very capable of resisting attempts to *change* their attitudes and behavior. If a persuasive communication seems incompatible with their own attitudes, they may avoid it, distort its meaning, forget it, or otherwise decide not to be influenced.

John Stauffer and Richard Frost

MALE AND FEMALE INTEREST IN SEXUALLY ORIENTED MAGAZINES

Until recently, sexually oriented magazines and pornography have been produced exclusively for men. The purveyors of this material simply assumed that women were not in the market for their products.

This presumption runs through much of the early literature on female sexuality. For instance, in the Kinsey studies published in 1949 and 1953, 88 percent of the females compared to 46 percent of the males reported that they were *never* aroused by observing portrayals of nude figures. More recent research, however, casts doubt on these conclusions (1,3,5,6). These findings suggest that sexually oriented magazines and pornography may have an appeal to women.

The stated aims of these publications are to explore human sexuality, to liberate women from traditional sex-role stereotypes by encouraging women to recognize that they, like men, have legitimate sexual urges, and to help both men and women gain a new awareness of their bodies and sexual expression. Articles deal with problems and concerns of women such as venereal disease, rape, and natural child birth. There are also the usual features found in other consumer magazines such as book, movies, and music reviews, fiction articles, a fashion section, and a reader's column.

One such magazine, *Playgirl,* began publishing in June, 1973, and quickly established itself as the most explicit of this new generation of women's magazines. The magazine reports a paid monthly circulation of 1.5 million and is growing. It is described in its sales brochure as "an original that stands alone among magazines for women."

In point of fact, *Playgirl* isn't original at all. From its title to its format and content, it is almost a mirror image of *Playboy*. Many features such as the photo essays, centerfolds, cartoons, interviews, and articles have their counterparts in *Playboy.* Where *Playboy* has a centerfold of a female nude, *Playgirl* has one of a male nude, where *Playboy* has a sexually oriented cartoon for men, *Playgirl* has one for women, and so on. Features often appear in the same order. The creators of *Playgirl* must have assumed that, freed from cultural influences, a woman's sexual interest is like that of a man's and that a successful women's magazine can be created by imitating a successful male one.

The existence of two such magazines, available at the newsstand at the same time, gave us an opportunity to investigate how men and women would react to viewing nudity of the opposite sex.

Reprinted from "Male and Female Interest in Sexually-Oriented Magazines" by John Stauffer and Richard Frost in the *Journal of Communication,* Vol. 26, No. 1 (Winter 1976), pp. 25-30. Copyright © 1976 by the Annenberg School of Communications.

One hundred persons participated in a survey designed to determine if men and women would indicate similar interest in parallel features of sexually-oriented magazines. Our sample was evenly distributed by sex, between the ages of 16 and 23 (the average age was 19), and was composed of students drawn from two small colleges in the suburban Boston area. Participants were predominantly white with upper middle-class backgrounds and were born in the United States.

The participants were asked to rate their interest in eleven parallel features in *Playboy* and *Playgirl,* with men rating *Playboy* and women rating *Playgirl.* The features included letters to the editor, film review, personality interview, photo essay, cartoon, fictional article, non-fictional article, an advertisement for sexually oriented products such as satin sheets and revealing nightgowns, a non-sexually oriented advertisement, a fashion section, and centerfold. Since the magazines often contain multiple numbers of each type of feature, specific items were selected at random.

Students were asked to rate two different issues of *Playboy* and *Playgirl* as a check on interest consistency. Also, two issues of the recently revived *Saturday Evening Post* were judged on eight parallel features (the *Post* does not contain a fashion feature, sexually oriented advertising, or a centerfold) for purposes of comparison. We wanted to see if there were differences between males and females when they rated features in a nonsexual magazine.

The respondents were told they were participating in a magazine interest survey and that all responses would be anonymous. The survey was administered to men and women separately and by a member of their own sex. The respondents were asked to rate their degree of interest in reading or viewing a feature using an adaption of Jack Haskins' thermometer interest scale. A response of zero degrees indicated they were extremely sure they did not want to read or view the feature. A response of 80 degrees indicated they were extremely sure they wanted to read or view the feature. The respondents could indicate interest levels between these extremes by intervals of ten. For analysis of the data, interest ratings were grouped into three equal categories designating low (0°-20°), medium (30°-50°), and high (60°-80°) interest. After the respondents completed the rating of the 38 features in all four magazines, they were asked to respond to a questionnaire.

Men gave higher interest ratings than women on the sexually-oriented products and cartoons, photo essays and centerfolds, which accounted for differences that were highly ($p < .01$) and very highly ($p < .001$) significant. At lower levels of significance men rated the interviews higher and women displayed greater interest in the letters to the editor (see Figure 8-1).

The greatest difference between men and women was found when ratings for the centerfold and photo essay were combined. Almost twice as many men (88 percent) as women (46 percent) gave these features high ratings. None of the men rated them low, while 14 percent of the women did. Both features consisted of color photographs of frontal nudity of the opposite sex.

We explored why there might have been such a difference. One possible explanation was that all this was something new for many women. While the entire male sample had seen *Playboy* before, only 52 percent of the women had read *Playgirl.*

Men and women also differed significantly in owning at least one sexually-oriented magazine, with 64 percent of men having at least one at the

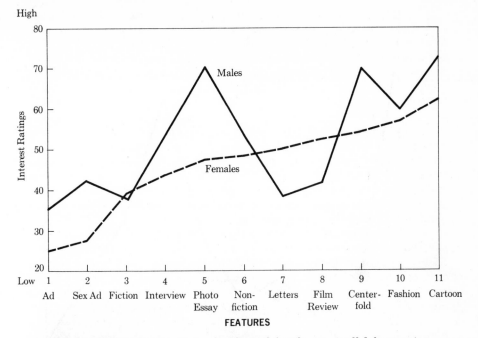

FIG. 8-1. *Mean interest ratings of males and females on parallel features in* Playboy *and* Playgirl

time of the study as compared to only 28 percent of the women. Owners of these magazines rated the centerfold and photo essay significantly higher than non-owners. When asked if they might buy future issues of *Playboy/Playgirl,* 84 percent of the men said they would, while 80 percent of the women said they would not.

Women's lack of ownership of sexually-oriented magazines may be due to fears of social disapproval. Fully 80 percent of the men believed that people in general would approve of their reading *Playboy,* while only 34 percent of the women were as confident. Men's perception of approval also exceeded women's when asked more specifically about the opinions of parents, men they respected, and women they respected.

When asked to rate the nudity as either "much too conservative," "too conservative," "appropriate," "too explicit," or "much too explicit," a total of 90 percent of the men responded "appropriate." This was true for only 60 percent of the women, 22 percent of whom judged the nudity as "too" or "much too" explicit.

We asked the subjects to list five adjectives to describe how they felt after having read *Playboy* or *Playgirl.* Most of the adjectives listed by men were favorable to the sexual content of *Playboy.* The female reaction was much more varied. About a third of the women reported that they felt relaxed, sophisticated, sexy, interested, and feminine, adjectives that we interpreted as favorable. Another third said they felt dirty, cheap, guilty, rotten, and bad, adjectives which were obviously unfavorable. The remaining third reported both favorable and unfavorable adjectives; for these women, the viewing of male nudity seemed to produce an ambivalent response.

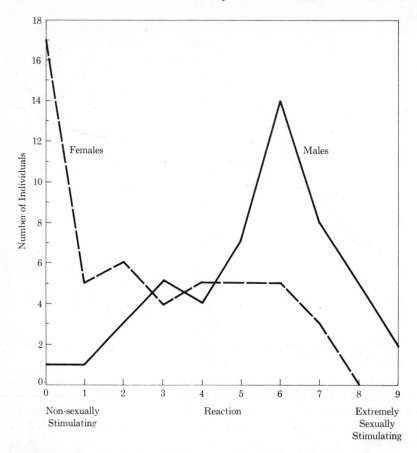

FIG. 8-2 *Reported reaction of males and females to nudity in* Playboy *and* Playgirl

Responses were recorded on a ten-point scale from 0 to 9 which, at the zero point, indicated that the respective nudity was "not sexually stimulating" and at nine indicated it was "extremely stimulating." Seventy-four percent of the female respondents were on the lower half of the scale, with fully one-third stating that the male nudity was not stimulating at all. On the other hand, 75 percent of the men were on the upper half of the scale with 58 percent indicating it was definitely sexually stimulating (see Figure 8-2). Some women however, rated the nudity more sexually stimulating than men did. Being a man or woman was not, then, the only determinant of sexual stimulating ratings.

In a written summary of their feelings toward the nudity presented in these magazines male/female differences were clear, with 70 percent of male responses coded as "positive" as compared to 26 percent for females. Female negative comments tended to fall into three broad areas;
Those who denied physical stimulation as an effect of viewing male nudity:

> *I don't think looking at male nudes is sexually stimulating to women. I'm not at all turned on. I'd rather see and feel my own than a picture which has been published throughout the country.*

Those who expressed or feared social disapproval:

> *I do not care to read women's magazines which play on nude males for attracting its readership. Although the fiction appears interesting as well as the film reviews, I would feel uncomfortable reading it because the manufacturers would believe I read it for the nude males.*

Those who were openly hostile with no particular rationale:

> *I found nothing substantially worth publishing—a waste of good paper. It seems to be for the woman who is frustrated or in desperate need of a friend. Definitely would not waste money to buy it.*

We then asked our respondents, "Is there anything about yourself that you can think of that makes you react to *Playboy/Playgirl* the way you do?" About a third of the men (36 percent) offered a physiological explanation for their mostly favorable reaction to *Playboy* such as "I'm just a normal male who likes to see naked women." Only two women (4 percent) explained their response to *Playgirl* in these terms. Most (68 percent) explained their reactions in terms of their family background and personal value system. The following reactions were typical:

> *I believe it was the way I was brought up. My parents know that I know what is right and wrong.* Playgirl *comes under the category "wrong." There are better things to do than read* Playgirl.

> *I guess my personal pride makes me feel the way I do. I respect myself and feel that what I look like under my garb is not for public viewing. I feel one's self is private.*

We completed the survey by asking women what kinds of things they might find more sexually stimulating than viewing male nudity. Most women expressed a desire for a more realistic, contextual representation of sexuality —one in which a relationship was clearly defined between the participants and could reasonably lead to nudity and sexual activity. This desire may account for the large portion of women (33 percent) who expressed ambivalent feelings about the isolated male nudes in *Playgirl.*

In the two issues of *Playboy* and *Playgirl* respondents were asked to rate two essays. For men, one *Playboy* offered a number of nude and partially nude females in a ski motif and in the other, several photographs of one model partially adorned with nightgown, top hat, and costume jewelry. Women were shown photos of a man in the woods who disrobed to go for a swim and another of a man who, after engaging in calisthenics, bared all to take a shower. Men gave their photo essays an average rating of 70, which placed it in second position, after cartoons. Women were much less enthusiastic and gave the essays a rating of 47, which was 23 points lower than their male counterparts. For women, the photo essays stood a poor seventh, after cartoon, fashion, centerfold, film review, letters to the editor, and non-fiction.

In light of recent research showing that men and women are equally able to respond to erotic materials, the women's ambivalence about male nudity in *Playgirl* may reflect their reaction to social meanings, rather than only to sexual content, and to still powerful traditional social pressures.

REFERENCES

1. Commission on Obscenity and Pornography. *Report of the Commission on Obscenity and Pornography.* New York: Bantam Books, 1970.
2. Haskins, Jack, B. "Pretesting Editorial Items and Ideas for Reader Interest." *Journalism Quarterly* 37, 1960, pp. 224-30.
3. Hunt, Morton. *Sexual Behavior in the 1970s.* Chicago: Playboy Press, 1974.
4. Kinsey, Alfred C., *et al. Sexual Behavior in the Human Female.* New York: Simon and Schuster, 1953.
5. Lehrman, Nat. *Masters and Johnson Explained.* Chicago: Playboy Press, 1970.
6. Masters, William H., and Virginia E. Johnson. *Human Sexual Response.* Boston: Little, Brown, 1966.

Gary Gumpert

THE RISE OF UNI-COMM

"Uni-comm" is defined as communication from one to
many of values prescribed by associations in the
environment through non-electronic media. "Uni-comm"
refers to mediated interpersonal behavior.

Individuals live in a world which bombards, surrounds, and besieges them with countless media stimuli. Some can be controlled by the individual. The television set is turned to a particular channel. One of many radio stations is selected. A journey and a ticket are required for admission to the motion picture theatre. The choice of a newspaper, magazine, book, or recording involves decision and selection. In a journey of several city blocks countless impressions impinge upon one's awareness. Many of these impressions are forms of advertising seeking to reach potential customers and clients. Billboards, posters, illuminated signs, vehicles with advertising and transit ads flit about the sensory awareness of every person, and these stimuli are less controllable.

The spectrum of mediated communication includes radio, television, film, and newspapers. These have received the attention of scholastic investigation because of their artistic and social consequences. But there are examples of mediated communication which have not been examined thoroughly and which are curiously ambiguous in their function: a bumper sticker proclaims "Make Love, Not War"; a button shows a large beetle and the words "Nixon Bugs Me;" a series of college decals displayed on the rear window of the car says something.

A MATRIX FOR ANALYSIS

Within the framework of "Communication," subdivisions have been established for the purpose of scholarship and definition. They are based on both the number of individuals involved in the communication process and/or the nature of the medium utilized in the process. Intrapersonal Communication, Interpersonal Communication, and Mass Communication constitute the divisions of a communication matrix most frequently mentioned by communication scholars. Of course, each of these divisions is further broken down into more specific areas. The matrix is extremely important because often it signifies and determines scholastic organization, academic territory, and research orientations. I argue that the present communication matrix is incomplete and that at least two other divisions should be added: "Mini-Communication"[1] and "Uni-Communication."

"The Rise of Uni-Comm," by Gary Gumpert in Today's Speech, Vol. 23, No. 4 (Fall 1975), pp. 34-38. Copyright © 1975. Reprinted by permission of Eastern Communication Association.

[1] Gary Gumpert, "The Rise of Mini-Comm," *Journal of Communication,* 20, (September, 1970), 280-290.

It is necessary to briefly define the matrix to clarify the interrelation-ships of the divisions and to establish the argument for the suggested additions.

"Intrapersonal Communication" refers to the encoding-decoding proc-ess which occurs within the individual. It is communication with the self, or of the self, but is always affected by external influences.

"Interpersonal Communication" refers to the non-mediated relation-ships between two or more individuals involving both verbal and non-verbal communication. This division includes a wide spectrum of situations based upon form and number, from diadic and small group to larger audience situa-tions.

The term "Mass Communication" connotes a separation in time and/ or space between encoder and decoder which is overcome through electronic and/or typographical means of replication. The following basic characteristics, described elsewhere in depth,[2] define the mass communication event:

1. Mass communication is public communication.
2. The content of the mass media is transient.
3. The direct cost of mass communication to the public is minimal.
4. The mass communication audience is large, heterogeneous, and anonymous.
5. The dissemination of mass communication content is rapid.
6. The nature of the mass communication institution is complex. It should be noted that the concept of "Mass Communication" is inexora-bly tied to communication between relatively monolithic media and extremely large audiences.

Because of changes in the technology of media in relation to societal needs, I postulated another communication subdivision in 1970 labeled "Mini-Comm." The original description stated:

> There is a psycho-sociological want for media which are addressed to us, our own group—as we see ourselves as members of a society. As isolated entities in a mass society individuals wish to be heard, to be linked with others like themselves. This coupling is manifested in geographical or avocational binding. At times, the focus is on the immediate community. At other times, the forcus is upon a belief system which transcends geographical lines. This focusing is accom-plished through media of communication which reach specific select audiences, and yet these audiences consist of enough people to fit the criteria of a mass audience. In addition, this audience is motivated to non-standardized content . . . . Mass-comm still exists and serves im-portant functions, but it is coexistence and not sole-existence.[3]

The trend away from "mono-media" and toward fragmented media has continued. The miniaturization of technology, exemplified by portable video equipment, 8mm and super-8 motion picture cameras, and the offset press, makes every individual a potential publisher. The media giants have had to diversify in order to compete with those which more directly serve the social needs of their audiences. *Life, Look,* and the *Saturday Evening Post* became

---

[2]*Ibid.*
[3]*Ibid.,* pp. 285-286.

expendable. The advertisers were being presented to the wrong audience, economically speaking, and because their homogenized audience began to fractionalize into smaller socio-economic groupings, the media giants became relics of the past. To some extent, the relationship between "Mass-comm" and "Mini-comm" is a symbiotic one. Mass communication is to society as Mini-communication is to subgroup. Both exist, but the former parental relationship has changed. One is not more generic or more important than the other.

Whereas "Mass-comm" refers to communication from a large organization to an audience of many and "mini-comm" to communication from a number of sources to smaller portions of an available population, "uni-comm" represents a reversal of these processes. In a way, it is a form of feedback, because people find themselves responding individually through a variety of media. "Uni-comm" is defined as communication from one to many of values prescribed by associations in the environment (subgroup affiliations) through various non-electronic media. While the term "uni-comm" lacks the precision and grace of legendary rubrics, it is fairly obvious that I am attempting to parallel two other areas found within the communication matrix. Therefore, the term is offered on a provisional basis.

"Uni-comm" is a type of mediated interpersonal behavior. What is to be included in this category? The following is a non-inclusive list of types of "uni-communication": Graffiti, postage stamps, buttons, bumper stickers, clothing (costume), hair and beard styles, medallions and ornamentation, tattoos, shopping bags, and decals. "Uni-comm" utilizes a variety of available media from a variety of sources which are worn or displayed by an individual. The individual (communicator) does not reproduce or duplicate the object, although the original source has produced the object in relatively large quantities. The recipients of "uni-comm" do not control the message. Those who come in contact with an individual bearer of a "uni-comm" message can turn away. They can avoid contact, but they cannot turn the message on or off. Several examples will clarify the concept.

Postage stamps are generally produced in large quantities and in great variety by governments. They serve the utilitarian function of producing revenue. At the same time stamps serve the cause of correlation or propaganda. The public which is required to use postage has a choice of stamps and that choice may indeed have a communicative motive. Not all individuals using postage stamps are making statements, but certainly some people are quite aware that they are using a stamp which commemorates the space program or which celebrates a religious holiday. Opponents of the Vietnam war pasted a particular stamp upsidedown as a signal of individual policy. The decision not to use a particular stamp also implies a statement.

Bumper stickers are produced in large quantities at the request of an individual or group and are distributed to others interested in the case being proclaimed. "Better Red Than Dead," "Jesus Saves," "Warning! I Brake For Animals," represent the public display of deeply felt beliefs. The humorous slogan often masks a grievance. It is clear that the automobile is more than a means of transportation. It obviously reflects status and personality, but it also has become a vehicle of communication with the addition of bumper stickers, specially requested license plates, decals indicating educational institutions and vacation resorts visited, and ethnic affiliation. Each display is expressively important to the individual.

The media of "uni-comm" divide into two categories. One category contains messages having symbolic value. The primary function of a religious medallion or a wedding ring is clearly symbolic. The second category requires the addition of symbolic value to conventionally utilitarian objects. For example, a number of international airlines provide tourist bags to their passengers as a form of advertising. Obviously the tourist bag serves a communicative function for the airline, but for the tourist the bag functions to carry and store material. However, for many people the bag also assumes a symbolic value. It is an advertisement of the self; it is a status symbol; it communicates the sophistication of travel. A host of similar examples exist, since numerous groups such as collegiate and professional athletic clubs produce items such as bags, caps, jackets, and shirts. The author nostalgically remembers his fondest pubescent possession—a Philadelphia Phillies baseball club jacket. That jacket provided to the wearer both a sense of identity and magical athletic ability. In a similar vein, most well known hotels are aware of the souvenir value of their ashtrays. I returned from my sabbatical year abroad on one of the last voyages of "The France" and toward the end of the voyage delicately purloined an ash tray from that famous ship. On the last day of the trip the passengers were given a present courtesy of the crew—an original "France" ashtray. Both the chagrined thief and the company recognized the non-utilitarian, but communicative function of the innocuous object: status.

Clothing illustrates an interesting aspect of "uni-comm." In *The Psychology of Clothes,* Flugel discusses the three functions of clothing, arranged from the most to the least important: decoration, modesty, and protection.[4] Both decoration and modesty manifest revelation of the self, but aesthetic functions can be contrasted with the direct type of communicative statement that is superimposed with the introduction of "style" and "fashion." (For the sake of simplification, the aesthetic facets of "uni-comm" are excluded as communicative statements, although there are strong arguments against this exclusion.) When style is ignored, the selection of clothing can be rather eclectic. But when style determines choice, clothing is transformed into costume or uniform and communication is stressed. At the same time clothing is transformed into a medium of "uni-comm." The degree to which clothing serves the function of communication is demonstrated on any college campus or by a visit to your friendly stock-broker. "Hippy," "Hard-hat," "Super-straight," "Freak," and "Pimp" are all concepts characterized by either stereotypical-symbolic dress apparel and/or hair style. Ask the typical college student why he or she is wearing a particular outfit and the student says, "it's the first thing I found in the closet," or "it's comfortable." The student is, at first, not willing to admit that the choice of apparel is quite limited to styles which comply with the self-image of the student operating within guidelines dictated by his compatriots. Opposition to the norm can result in rejection or ridicule. "It is not who you are, but what you wear!" George Melly discusses fashion in his analysis of the Pop Arts in Britain and particularly points out the Teddy-boy style of the middle fifties: " . . . what made it significant style was that it represented one of the first successful attempts to establish a male working-class fashion with

---

[4]J. C. Flugel, *The Psychology of Clothes* (New York, 1969), pp. 16-17.

a symbolic rather than a functional raison d'etre."[5] Important here is the relationship between the symbolic and functional motives which result in often surprisingly hostile reactions to the "outsider."

Certainly hair styles of young people have received an unusual amount of attention during the past few years. Perhaps intuitively, the more conservative members of society saw that the change represented not only a frivolous temperament, but also a breach in social values expressed through the medium of hair styles. "Hair as public symbol" is discussed by Raymond Firth in his analysis of *Symbols: Public and Private:* "In the wearing of the hair one may recognize custom, or standard modes of behavior, and fashion, or an oscillation of focus on particular Styles. But in addition to these norms, the manner of wearing the hair has sometimes been used to make a more personal statement." [6] The concept of hair as a form of expression is not new, but the consideration of hair (as well as many other examples of "uni-comm") as a communicative statement, related to other divisions of a communication matrix, represents a fresh point of view:

> Upwards of twenty years ago a teenager 'going steady' with a young man could let this be known by various signs—such as a single earring 'for one man. One such sign was braids or none at all if she was free. A more recent kind of statement, indicating not a personal relationship so much as a personal commitment, has been the wearing of 'Afro' hair styles by black American women.[7]

MOTIVATION AND "UNI-COMM"

It is the communicator's intent which converts the function of an object into a symbolic mode, like books which are never read, but are essential to the living room because of their impression upon visitors. A conscious decision is involved in wearing a protest button or in selecting a rose-patterned checkbook. These motives are complex, but academic simplification suggests four, not mutually exclusive, basic motives for the adoption or rejection of a medium of "uni-comm":

1) as an expression of protest
2) for the revelation of affiliation
3) for the revelation of identity
4) as an expression of social and cultural status.

The decal on the rear window of automobiles with the tricolors of either Italian, Irish, or Black power expresses a sense of fellowship to members of those groups who follow or pass by. A motive might be to point out a grievance on the part of the driver against treatment by society or merely to label oneself and thereby identify the self. The engagement ring can be more than a simple announcement of future property rights of one individual over another, since size and carats can suggest a position on the economic-social pecking order. Note the importance of the wedding ring as a symbol to the

[5]George Melly, *Revolt Into Style: The Pop Arts in Britain.* (Middlesex: England, 1972), p. 148.
[6]Raymond Firth, *Symbols: Public and Private,* (New York, 1973), p. 272.
[7]*Ibid.,* p. 273.

Women's Liberation movement, to the traditional proponents of marriage, or even to nuns. Graffiti is more than the malicious act of a prankster. It is a rhetorical act which exists, and has existed for centuries, because other means of public self-expression are barred or limited to the individual. Why do so many people wear religious medallions? There are a number of possible explanations. It is an assurance that one's faith is not forgotten. The star or cross can be a means of social control, an attempt to proselytize, or a way to avoid social interaction with nonbelievers. Clearly, each example is a rhetorical act recognized by other members of society through means approved by a series of subgroups to which every individual relates. It is assumed that each person relates to more than one subgroup or displays association with more than one subgroup. Therefore, the individual submits to the pressures and accouterments of each group. Membership, not necessarily commitment, to the group is through the public display of "uni-comm." There is a distinction between commitment and facade. No matter how hard those above the age of forty seek to assume the identity of the emancipated "now" generation through the adoption of accouterments and language, through the media of "uni-comm," that person remains above forty and probably never escapes from his generational trap. Is such a person aware of his actions? A problem exists when the question of motivation is examined. Must a conscious decision always be part of a "uni-comm" statement? Must the individual be aware of the communicative nature of his actions? Group pressure, integral to the "uni-comm" concept, might result in individual decisions, but the recognition of function might never be realized by the person. The pervasive influence of the unconscious upon behavior is quite evident. The degree of awareness is more difficult to establish. For the decoder of a "uni-comm" statement the question of awareness on the part of the encoder is almost irrelevant since the perception of motive is the important factor. If, however, the goal of self-awareness of the encoder in the communication process is the focus, then clearly the concept of motive requires much more attention and analysis.

THE ACADEMIC TERRITORY

Historically, the study of "Mass Communication" has emphasized the artistic and social development of radio, television, film, and print. Typically the academic label defines the territory. As a result certain areas of investigation are defined out and examined elsewhere. There is a relationship between a departmental structure and portions of the communication matrix. Within a school or department of Communication is found a variety of areas of specialization: Public Address, Interpersonal Communication, Rhetoric, Radio and Television, Film, Psycholinguistics, Communication Theory, etc. The purpose of the communication matrix suggested in this essay is not to stress division, rather its raison d'etre should be to demonstrate relationships within the broad scholastic rubric of "Communication." Therefore the matter of exclusion by definition of academic labels becomes quite important since those areas of human interaction represented by the "uni-comm" concept are, with some exceptions,[8] generally not found within the territory of either "Communica-

---

[8]One exception is found in the recent publication of the following volume: David R. Olson (ed.) *Media and Symbols: The Forms of Expression, Communication, and Education: The Seventy-Third Yearbook of the National Society for the Study of Education.* (Chicago, 1974).

tion" or "Mass Communication." Ironically, the recognition of that area of knowledge which is suggested by "uni-comm" is found outside the aegis of "Communication." In particular Semiology and Anthropology provide insights that have been absent in the study of the environment by communication scholars. The mutual interests of the disciplines of communication and anthropology is expressed by Raymond Firth:

> Popular, unanalysed expressions of symbolism are of interest to anthropologists because they are part of the raw material for comparative study of processes of human thought and action. They reveal the direction and extent of peoples' involvement in social processes of various kinds, and the quality of abstraction applied to these processes.[9]

"Uni-comm" completes a communication matrix whose application will result in a more systematic and comprehensive examination of communication phenomena. The analysis of specific rhetorical events or the examination of social movements through the matrix of "intrapersonal communication," "interpersonal communication," "mass communication," "mini-communication," and "uni-communication" will yield a fuller understanding of the dynamics and forces involved in a turbulent environment.

---

[9]Firth, p. 29.

Rose K. Goldsen and Azriel Bibliowicz

PLAZA SÉSAMO: "NEUTRAL" LANGUAGE OR "CULTURAL ASSAULT?"

Planning for the Spanish language version of *Sesame Street* was aided by a group of Latin American consultants who met with production personnel in Caracas, Venezuela, in 1971 and 1972. One problem was specified early in the Caracas seminars: how could a single production from one centralized source do justice to the many cultures and subcultures of 22 million Latin American preschool children?

Eight of the 40 segments that make up each 54-minute program of the first series of *Plaza Sésamo* are videotaped action in "the Plaza." These are made in Mexico with Latin American actors. The action on the Plaza usually accounts for only about 20 percent of a program. Another two-thirds is material drawn from CTW's International Library. These segments were said to be culturally neutral. "They are universal in their appeal to children. . . . They carry no cultural identification and the local language can easily be dubbed"

The same casual treatment was accorded the problem of language: "A neutral Spanish should be used, which would take into account the diverse pronunciations and diverse vocabularies of the continent"

But there is no such thing as an acultural language. Language doesn't deliver culture. Language is culture. There are many regional variations in the Spanish used throughout the hemisphere: accents, intonations, idioms, proverbs, characteristic sentence construction, even dialects.

Decisions about language also carry sociological clout. For example, an original English version of a film clip or animation will have only one form for the second person: *you*. But in Spanish, a decision must be made whether to say *Usted*, the formal mode of address, or *tu*, the informal mode. The decision makes cultural distinctions of social distance and familiarity. These distinctions have not been standardized throughout the hemisphere.

And what about *vos* and *che?* These forms of the second person are used in Argentina and Uruguay and parts of Chile and Colombia. What is neutral about a decision to model for all these nations' children a language that blacks out their own culture's forms of address?

Plaza Sésamo also shows scenes of family structure and family relations, food and table habits, household arrangements, occupational roles, and age and sex roles, rural and urban behavior patterns, economic pursuits such as buying and selling and going to work, vehicles and dress fashions, body language, rhythming, timing and . . . well, just about everything. The notion that these elementary units of culture and social interaction can be emptied

Reprinted from "Plaza Sésamo: 'Neutral' Language or 'Cultural Assault?' " by Rose K. Goldsen and Azriel Bibliowicz in the *Journal of Communication,* Vol. 26, No. 2 (Spring 1976), pp. 124-125. Copyright © 1976 by the Annenberg School of Communications.

of their cultural content—can be presented "neutrally"—is a contradiction in terms.

One issue was raised whose solution was *not* to find a "neutral" mode of presentation. That was the matter of music. At the first Caracas seminar, the consultants decided that *Plaza Sésamo* should utilize the rich folk music so easily available in every Latin American country.

But alas! When the first *Plaza Sésamo* series came out, in each 54-minute program there was at best one selection of Latin American music. The rest was rock.

For the first time in human history, a whole continent's preschool children—22 million—are the targets of largely standardized cultural material. The *Plaza Sésamo* programs amuse and attract children. But these programs also lay down an important part of the cultural scaffolding that Latin American children will build on. They expose the continent's children to a massive cultural assault whose consequences are incalculable.

REFERENCES

1. "A Special Report from the Children's Television Workshop." Mimeographed, 1972.
2. "Summary of the first Preparatory Seminar for the Spanish Television Series *Plaza Sésamo*," Mimeographed, 1971.

APPENDICES

RELATED TEXTBOOKS

Applbaum, Ronald, Karl Anatol, Ellis Hays, Owen Jenson, Richard Porter, and Jerry Mandel. *Fundamental Concepts in Human Communication* (San Francisco: Canfield Press, 1973).

Brooks, William. *Speech Communication*, 2nd ed. (Dubuque, Iowa: Wm. C. Brown, 1974).

Hybels, Saundra and Richard L. Weaver, II. *Speech/Communication* (New York: D. Van Nostrand, 1974).

Keltner, John W. *Interpersonal Speech Communication: Elements and Structures* (Belmont, Cal.: Wadsworth, 1970).

McCroskey, James, Carl Larson, and Mark Knapp. *An Introduction to Interpersonal Communication* (Englewood Cliffs, N.J.: Prentice-Hall, 1971).

McCroskey, James and Lawrence Wheeless. *Introduction to Human Communication* (Boston: Allyn and Bacon, 1976).

Pace, R. Wayne and Robert Boren. *The Human Transaction* (Glenview, Ill.: Scott, Foresman, 1973).

Sereno, Kenneth and Edward Bodaken. *Trans-Per: Understanding Human Communication* (Boston: Houghton-Mifflin, 1975).

Tubbs, Stewart L. and John W. Baird. *The Open Person: Self-Disclosure and Personal Growth* (Columbus, Ohio: Charles Merrill, 1976).

Tubbs, Stewart L. and Sylvia Moss. *Human Communication*, 2nd Ed. (New York: Random House, 1977).

Wenburg, John and William Wilmot. *The Personal Communication Process* (New York: Wiley, 1973).

CROSS REFERENCE GUIDE TO RELATED TEXTS

	Intro.	Fundamental Concepts	Verbal Messages	Nonverbal Messages	Two-person Communication	Small Group Communication	Public Communication	Organizational Communication	Mass Communication
Applbaum, et. al. 1973	/	/		6	3	4	7,8,9		
Brooks, 1974	/	/	3	6	7	8	9,10,11		12
Burgoon, 1974	/		3	4	6	7	1,2,3,8,		5,9
Hybels & Weaver 1974	/	/	4	3	2	7	5		6,8
Keltner, 1970	/	2,3	4	6	12	13	10,14		
McCroskey, Larson, Knapp, 1971	/	2	8	6	9	11	5,8	10	11
McCroskey & Wheeless, 1976	1,20	2	9	10	11,13				4,16 17,18
Pace & Boren, 1973	1,8,9		3		10				11
Sereno & Bodaken, 1975	1,2,4	3	5	5	8	9	7	10	
Tubbs & Baird, 1976	4,5	1,2,3	4	2	5,7	4		6	
Tubbs & Moss, 1977	1,7	1,2	7	8	9	10	11	12	13
Wenburg & Wilmot, 1973	/	8	5	6	2	2	9,10 11		7

The table above can be used to relate the topic areas in this book to similar concepts which are described in the leading textbooks listed in the left hand column. The numbers in the boxes above indicate the chapter numbers in the other books.

INDEX